# What We Know about Suicidal Behavior and How to Treat It

*Edited by*
Stanley Lesse, M.D., Med.Sc.D.

Jason Aronson Inc.
Northvale, New Jersey
London

10 9 8 7 6 5 4 3 2 1

**Library of Congress Cataloging-in-Publication Data**

What we know about suicidal behavior and how to
    treat it.

    Reprints of articles from various issues of the
American journal of psychotherapy.
    Includes bibliographies and index.
    1. Suicide—Psychological aspects.  2. Children
—Suicidal behavior.  3. Psychotherapy.    I. Lesse,
Stanley, 1922-    . II. American journal of
psychotherapy.  [DNLM: 1. Psychotherapy—collected
works.  2. Suicide—prevention & control—collected
works.  3. Suicide—psychology—collected works.
HV 6546 W555]
RC569.W477  1988     616.85′8445          88-19324
ISBN 0-87668-878-4

Manufactured in the United States of America.
Jason Aronson Inc. offers books and cassettes.
For information and catalog write to
Jason Aronson Inc., 230 Livingston Street,
Northvale, N.J. 07647

To the past and present members
of the Editorial Board
of the *American Journal of Psychotherapy*

# Contents

## PART II: TREATMENT

# Preface

Suicide is one of the more common causes of death in the United States. The recent literature has been bombarded by a seemingly unlimited number of papers and books on suicide that deal with the subject from many perspectives – sociologic, psychopathologic, psychodynamic, and biodynamic. Despite this fact, patients with suicidal tendencies are often inadequately managed, in that psychiatrists and psychotherapists are frequently unable to accurately differentiate between the presence of *suicidal ideas* and *suicidal drives*.

Many times, patients with suicidal ideas are not treated with a proper sense of urgency. It is most imperative that patients with suicidal drives be monitored continuously and treated as if they were emergencies.

Almost all suicides are avoidable if patients are properly diagnosed, monitored, and treated in an appropriate, timely manner. Dependency on rating scales and biologic testing is inadequate to judge the depth, intensity, and momentum of a patient's suicidal ideas or drives. Effective patient management requires frequent, epicritic, clinical evaluations. It also necessitates close contact and intervention with persons who are important in the patients' lives.

Not all psychiatrists and psychotherapists are emotionally

equipped to manage suicidal patients. Some lack the broad spectrum, therapeutic armamentarium that is necessary to protect and treat suicidal patients. Others do not have ready access to adequate hospital facilities for emergency admissions.

This book is divided into three sections. Part I, "Understanding Suicide," introduces a generous range of background material concerning genetic, epidemiologic, philosophic, and sociologic factors that contribute to the development of suicidal propensities. The taxing problem of suicide prediction is thoughtfully presented, along with a general overview of problems such as suicide in the hospital, double suicide, suicide in manic-depressive disorders, and erotized repetitive hangings. This section also deals with the pertinent subject of rational suicide.

Part II, "Treatment," includes a pragmatic method for the quantification of suicidal ideas and suicidal drives, and illustrates how these ideas can evolve into drives. There is a broad spectrum discussion of electroshock, antidepressant drug treatment, and antidepressant drug therapy in combination with psychotherapy. Many psychotherapeutic procedures are discussed in detail.

Part III is devoted to the diagnosis, management, and treatment of depressed, suicidal children and adolescents, and it discusses suicidal patterns as they occur in these age groups. It also deals with treatment modalities in both outpatient and inpatient facilities and the growing problem of suicide among college students.

Those of us who treat large numbers of suicidal patients become highly sensitized to the dangers inherent in their management. The readers of this book will find that their diagnostic sensitivities, therapeutic acumen, and overall management skills will be enhanced.

All of these authors have expertise in the field of suicidology. Their chapters in this book represent some of their outstanding contributions. Many were presented initially at conferences sponsored by the *Association for the Advancement of Psychotherapy*, the parent organization of the *American Journal of Psychotherapy*, in which these chapters were originally published.

They reflect the interest I have had in depression and suicide over a long period of time, both as Editor-in-Chief of this journal and as a clinical neuropsychiatrist.

I would like to thank Edith Friedlander for her patient assistance in the preparation of this publication.

Stanley Lesse, M.D., Med.Sc.D.

# Contributors

*Aaron T. Beck, M.D.* Professor, Department of Psychiatry, University of Pennsylvania, Philadelphia, PA.

*Howard S. Benensohn, M.D.* Clinical Director, Suicide Studies Unit, St. Elizabeth's Hospital, Washington, DC.

*Mairin B. Doherty, M.D.* Assistant Professor of Psychiatry, Brown University Program in Medicine, Emma Pendleton Bradley Hospital, East Providence, RI.

*Ronald R. Fieve, M.D.* Chief of Psychiatric Research, New York State Psychiatric Institute; Medical Director, The Foundation for Depression and Manic Depression, New York, NY.

*Amasa B. Ford, M.D.* Associate Dean for Geriatric Medicine; Professor of Epidemiology and Community Health; Professor of Family Medicine; Associate Professor of Medicine, Case Western Reserve University School of Medicine, Cleveland, OH.

*Fred H. Frankel, M.B.Ch.B, D.P.M.* Director of Clinical Psychiatry, Beth Israel Hospital, Boston, MA; Professor of Psychiatry, Harvard Medical School, Cambridge, MA.

*Calvin J. Frederick, Ph.D.* Assistant Chief, Center for Studies of Suicide Prevention, Division of Special Mental Health Programs, National Institute of Mental Health, Chevy Chase, MD.

*Ngaere Goldring, Ph.D.* Clinical Service Director, The Foundation for Depression and Manic Depression, New York, NY.

*Herbert Hendin, M.D.* Professor of Psychiatry, New York Medical College, Valhalla, NY.

Stanley Lesse, M.D., Med.Sc.D. Editor-in-Chief, *American Journal of Psychotherapy*, New York, NY.

*Ronald S. Mintz, M.D.* Associate Professor, Department of Psychiatry, UCLA Center for the Health Sciences, Los Angeles, CA.

*George E. Murphy, M.D.* Director, Outpatient Psychiatric Services, Department of Psychiatry, Washington University School of Medicine, St. Louis, MO.

*Harry S. Olin, M.D.* Chief of Psychiatry, Brockton Veterans Administration Hospital, Brockton, MA.

*Israel Orbach, Ph.D.* Department of Psychology, Bar-Ilan University, Ramat Gan, Israel.

*Cynthia R. Pfeffer, M.D.* Associate Professor of Clinical Psychiatry, Cornell University Medical College; Chief, Child Psychiatry Inpatient Unit, New York Hospital-Westchester Division, White Plains, NY.

*John D. Rainer, M.D.* Professor of Clinical Psychiatry, College of Physicians & Surgeons, Columbia University; Chief of Psychiatry Research (Genetics), New York State Psychiatric Institute, New York, NY.

*H. L. P. Resnik, M.D.* Former Chief, Center for Studies of Suicide Prevention, Division of Special Mental Health Programs, National Institute of Mental Health; Clinical Professor of Psychiatry, George Washington School of Medicine, Washington, DC.

*Lillian H. Robinson, M.D.* Professor of Psychiatry and Pediatrics; Director of Child Psychiatry; Training and Supervising Analyst, Psychoanalytic Medicine Program, Department of Psychiatry and Neurology, Tulane University School of Medicine, New Orleans, LA.

*Perihan A. Rosenthal, M.D.* Director, Division of Child/Adolescent Psychiatry, Department of Psychiatry, Newark Beth Israel Medical Center; Clinical Associate Professor of Psychiatry, University of Medicine and Dentistry of New Jersey, Newark, NJ.

*Stuart Rosenthal, M.D.* Director, Department of Psychiatry and the Community Mental Health Center, Newark Beth Israel Medical Center; Clinical Professor of Psychiatry, Boston University School of Medicine, Boston, MA.

*Michail Rotov, M.D.* Deputy Medical Director, Trenton State Hospital, Trenton, NJ.

*A. John Rush, M.D.* Associate Professor, Department of Psychiatry, University of Texas, Health Science Center, Dallas, TX.

*Norman B. Rushforth, Ph.D.* Professor and Chairman, Department of Biology; Associate Professor of Biometry, Case Western Reserve University School of Medicine, Cleveland, OH.

*Donna Santora, M.A.* Child Mental Health Unit, University of Massachusetts Medical Center, Worcester, MA.

*Patricia A. Santy, M.D.* Assistant Clinical Professor of Psychiatry, Department of Psychiatry and Biobehavioral Sciences, University of California, Los Angeles, Los Angeles, CA.

*Kenneth Seeman, M.D.* Clinical Associate Professor of Psychiatry and Behavioral Sciences, Stanford University School of Medicine; Veterans Administration Medical Center, Palo Alto, CA.

*Edwin S. Shneidman, Ph.D.* Professor of Medical Psychology, Neuropsychiatric Institute, University of California, Los Angeles, CA.

*Karolynn Siegel, Ph.D.* Director of Research, Department of Social Work, Memorial Sloan-Kettering Cancer Center; Assistant Professor of Sociology in Public Health, Cornell University Medical College, New York, NY.

*Alan A. Stone, M.D.* Professor of Psychiatry, Harvard Medical School; Professor, Harvard Law School, Cambridge, MA.

*Howard S. Sudak, M.D.* Professor of Psychiatry, Case Western Reserve University School of Medicine; Chief, Psychiatry Service, Cleveland Veterans Administration Medical Center, Cleveland, OH.

*James M. Toolan, M.D.* Assistant Professor of Psychiatry, Department of Psychiatry, University of Vermont Medical School, Burlington, VT.

*Leslie Widrow, A.B.* Research Associate, Veterans Administration Medical Center, Palo Alto, CA.

*Jerome Yesavage, M.D.* Assistant Professor of Psychiatry and Behavioral Sciences, Stanford University School of Medicine; Veterans Administration Medical Center; Psychiatric Intensive Care Unit, Palo Alto, CA.

The material in these chapters first appeared or was presented as a paper* on the following dates:

Chapter  1.  November, 1983*
Chapter  2.  May, 1970*
Chapter  3.  November, 1983*
Chapter  4.  May, 1970*
Chapter  5.  April-May, 1977*
Chapter  6.  July, 1986
Chapter  7.  November, 1983*
Chapter  8.  April, 1970
Chapter  9.  October, 1984
Chapter 10.  January, 1982
Chapter 11.  December, 1969*
Chapter 12.  November, 1974*
Chapter 13.  November, 1983*
Chapter 14.  May, 1972*
Chapter 15.  May, 1970*
Chapter 15.  October, 1981
Chapter 17.  May, 1977*
Chapter 18.  May, 1970*
Chapter 19.  October, 1980*
Chapter 20.  November, 1983*
Chapter 21.  November, 1983*
Chapter 22.  April, 1986
Chapter 23.  July, 1984
Chapter 24.  October, 1980*
Chapter 25.  October, 1986
Chapter 26.  November, 1974*

# PART I

# Understanding Suicide

# 1 Genetic Factors in Depression and Suicide

### John D. Rainer, M.D.

*Not all depressed patients attempt suicide, and not all suicidal persons are depressed. Genetic investigations have tried to determine whether suicide has a biological basis independent of depression. Such an approach illustrates some of the important theoretical and practical complexities in the area of psychiatric genetics.*

An ever-increasing body of evidence points to a genetic component in major affective illness. There are also data implicating suicide in the family as a significant risk factor for suicide. However, genetic factors account directly for biological vulnerability to disorder. In some disorders, such as Huntington disease or phenylketonuria, all individuals whose genetic constitution provides them with this vulnerability show some form of the disease, although even here the expression of the genetic potential may vary in terms of severity or symptomatology. When it comes to the determinants of overt behavior, we tend to believe that genetic vulnerability interacts with other predisposing or precipitating factors, such as stressful life events, developmental traumata, physiological, metabolic, neurological triggers, and sociological factors. Genetic studies are complete only if the complete interactions are described, and the relation between depression and attempted suicide is a complex one of partial overlap. On the one hand, many depressives report suicidal feelings but few make suicide attempts; on the other, many suicide attempters do not experience a full and persistent depressive syndrome but show evidence of personality disorder.

This review will present first the evidence for a genetic factor in affective disorder, with the understanding that such data alone cannot explain the incidence of suicide from a genetic point of view. After that, data bearing on hereditary risk and family incidence of suicide itself will be presented historically, followed by some recent reported attempts to distinguish by biological means suicidal patients from other patients who are depressed.

### Evidence for Genetic Factors in Depression

Genetic aspects of depression have been considered as far back as Kraepelin. In the early studies, the rate of affective disorder in siblings of patients was of the order of 10 percent, about 10 times that of the general population. If one parent was affected, the risk increased to almost 25 percent and if both parents were affected, to over 40 percent.

After 1966, studies in the genetics of affective disorder separated bipolar and unipolar disease. In more recent studies of bipolar disorder the risk for affective disorder of the bipolar or unipolar type in first-degree relatives was over 20 percent, about half of these relatives themselves having bipolar disorder, the others having unipolar disorder. The risk for female relatives was about 1½ times the risk for male relatives, similar to the male-female ratio for bipolar illness in the general population. It may be concluded from the many studies done in the past two decades that bipolar disorder has a genetic component which can be expressed in relatives as either bipolar or unipolar disease.

Among the relatives of unipolar affective-disorder patients, the risk for bipolar disorder was no greater than that in the general population, while the risk for unipolar disorder was 10 to 15 times as high. Again females had a greater risk than males.

As in all psychiatric genetic studies, family-risk studies

themselves do little to separate genetic from intrafamilial environmental components, and therefore data derived from twin and adoption studies have been used in the attempt to separate the genetic risk from that due to family rearing. In affective disorder, major twin studies strongly support an important genetic factor. From a recent survey of a large group of studies of twins over many decades, Schlesser and Altshuler (1) concluded that the concordance in monozygotic pairs was almost 75 percent, in dizygotic pairs under 20 percent. Every study quoted showed a large and significant differential. Moreover, the morbidity risk in dizygotic twins of affected twin index cases approximated that among siblings as noted in the family studies.

Reviewing the early twin studies, Zerbin-Rüdin (2) noted that in most cases both twins in the concordant pairs were either bipolar or unipolar, although there were a few in which one twin was bipolar while the other, at least at the time of the report, showed only unipolar depressive symptoms. In a twin study of manic-depressive disorders done in Denmark by Bertelsen (3), concordance for unipolar disease was 54 percent in monozygotic twins, and 24 percent in dizygotic twins, using strict diagnostic criteria. If uncertain cases (including, by the way, undiagnosed suicide) were included, the concordance rates in unipolar disease were 77 percent for monozygotic pairs and 35 percent for dizygotic pairs. In the unipolar pairs all concordant cotwins were diagnosed as having unipolar disorder. With bipolar disease in the index twins, using strict diagnoses, 79 percent of monozygotic cotwins were affected as opposed to 19 percent of dizygotic cotwins. Using a wider diagnostic classification, the concordance rates were 97 percent for monozygotic pairs and 38 percent for dizygotic pairs. In those cases where the index twins had bipolar disease, the affected cotwins in the concordant pairs had either bipolar or unipolar disorder.

The second major tool for separating familial environmental factors that are not genetic from genetic factors is the strategy that involves comparing the families of normal and disordered adoptees, or the adopted-away offspring of normal or disordered parents. This strategy has been used extensively in studying the generic factors in schizophrenia, less so in affective disorders. Mendlewicz and Rainer (4) studied the biological and adoptive parents of 29 adopted children who grew up to have bipolar disorder, together with three sets of controls: (a) biological parents of nonadoptees who later developed bipolar disorder, (b) biological and adoptive parents of a group of normal adopted children, and (c) biological parents who raised children who developed poliomyelitis. In this study the only groups of parents who showed a significantly increased morbidity risk for affective disorder and related syndromes were the biological parents of individuals who had developed bipolar illness, and this increased risk held equally whether the individual had been raised by these biological parents or had been raised in an adoptive home. The adoptive parents of the children who grew up to have bipolar illness showed no increase, nor did the parents who had the difficult task of raising a child with a severe neurological illness. Recently von Knorring et al. (5) reported a study of the biological and adoptive parents of 115 adoptees with affective disorders or histories of substance abuse. They were matched with 115 nonpsychiatric adoptees for a family study. This study did not show overall difference between index and control biological families, and actually showed an excess of psychiatric illness in the adoptive parents of the index cases. However all but 5 of 56 subjects with affective disorders had nonbipolar, often non-psychotic, depression.

In another adoption design, Cadoret (6) studied the offspring of normal and affective-disordered biological parents who were adopted at birth by normal adoptive parents. In the children of the affective-disordered biological parents, 38 percent had unipolar or bipolar affective disorder compared with only 7 percent of the adoptees who had normal parents.

Regarding the mode of transmission for bipolar disorder, a dominant mode is possible but one would have to include a reduced penetrance to account for the fact that less than 25 percent of first-degree relatives are affected rather than the 50 percent that would be called for by a dominant pattern. Nevertheless, it is the clinical impression that many manic-depressive patients do have parents with a similar disorder. In unipolar affective disorder the possible patterns of inheritance are less clear. There has been some discussion in recent literature that some pedigrees of bipolar affective disorder may suggest linkage with color-blindness loci on the X-chromosome. This would account for the preponderance of females; it would also require that there be no father-to-son transmission. Not all pedigrees when analyzed show evidence for such linkage, but a recent analysis indicates that a subclass may fall into this category.

## Genetic Studies of Suicide—Twin-study Method

When it comes to suicide, the same strategies of genetic investigation have been applied, but the results are tentative or equivocal. One of the earliest studies was reported in 1946 by Kallmann and Anastasio (7). This study not only is of historical interest as one of Kallmann's earliest applications of the twin-study method, but also illustrates how this investigator, usually characterized as strongly hereditarian, thought about the role of genetics in specific behavior, and how he allowed negative results in a twin investigation to influence his conclusions.

Kallmann began his paper (7) by discussing the social significance of suicide as the 11th cause of death in our culture at that time, indicating the increase in male over female and the increase in whites over blacks even under comparable socioeconomic conditions, and the role of social and cultural factors in modifications of the general suicide rate. He noted that outside of religious or political compulsion, mental disorders were most frequently associated with suicide, including depressive and delusional syndromes, hypochondriacal states and severe neurotic reactions to loss of a love object. He mentioned that in psychological terms suicide had been described as an aggressive act, with the inference that no one commits suicide who does not want another person to die. Kallmann recalled Kraepelin's estimate that over 30 percent of all suicidal cases had a known history of mental disease, with about 70 percent of such psychotic cases classified by early psychiatrists as manic-depressive. Nolan Lewis was quoted as saying that many apparently "philosophical" suicides were misinterpreted as the result of overwork, sex problems, alcoholic conversions, or physical disabilities, rather than as a symptom of disguised endogenous depression.

Turning to the effect of heredity, Kallmann noted anecdotal reports of accumulation of suicide in certain families, including a story, recent at that time, about a Spanish family in which a direct male descendant had committed suicide at the age of 45 in five consecutive generations. In his own Berlin family study of schizophrenia, Kallmann recalled that the suicide rates of various groups of relatives of schizophrenic patients were higher than that of a comparable general population group. But he then went on to say:

> for obvious reasons one cannot expect that there would be a specific combination of genetic factors determining the occurrence of suicide as such. There is no inheritance of any finished human traits, but only a transmission of potential capacity for the development of these traits under certain life conditions. It is conceivable however, that genetic elements may play a significant part either in the formation of some personality types with particular vulnerability to suicide under stress or in the development of special forms of mental disease which favor the tendency to self-destruction (7) (p. 42).

Turning to the twin study method, Kallmann pointed out:

> if hereditary factors play a decisive role we should find a concordant tendency to suicide more frequently in one-egg than in two-egg pairs regardless of ordinary differences in environment. If the main emphasis is placed on certain constellations of non-genetic factors, concordance should be expected in some twin pairs of either type, who shared the same environment and responded to a similar degree of distress with the same type of psychosis (7) (p. 43).

At that time there were only 6 references to twin suicide cases in the literature. In 2 cases the pairs were discordant; both members of each pair were females with apparently manic-depressive psychosis, but only one member of each pair committed suicide. The other 4 cases, much earlier in time, involved a suicide pact in 2 twin brothers, and 1 case soon after the American Revolution, in which 2 probably identical twin brothers took their lives in the same manner about 2 years and 200 miles apart.

In his own material drawn from 2500 twin index cases collected from mental institutions, TB hospitals, old age homes, and other sections of the New York State population, Kallmann found only 11 twin pairs with suicide of 1 member, none with suicide in both. Three pairs were monozygotic, 8 were dizygotic, 5 had no history of psychotic manifestations, the other 6 had been admitted to mental hospitals. Of these 6, 3 were classified as manic-depressive psychosis, 2 involutional melancholia and 1 schizophrenia. The suicidal methods used consisted of 4 poisoning, 2 drowning, 2 gas, 2 hanging, and 1 jumping from a high place. The paper describes the life histories of these 11 pairs, particularly the comparative life histories of the 3 monozygotic pairs, which are full of fascinating detail. Kallmann concluded that the life events in each twin who ended by suicide were more adverse, and his general conclusion was that

> except for rare suicide pacts, the committment (sic) of suicide does not seem to occur in both members of twin pairs, even if the twins are alike in type of personality, cultural setting, social frustrations and depressive features of a psychosis (8) (p. 53).

The rather remarkable finding of apparently consistent discordance of twin pairs thus led Kallmann to state (8) that

> there is no statistical evidence for the popular notion that the tendency to commit suicide recurs in certain families as the result of a special hereditary trait or of a particular type of genetically determined personality deviation (p. 126) [and that] suicide seems to be the result of such a complex combination of motivational factors as to render a duplication of this unusual constellation very unlikely even in identical twin partners who show the same type of psychosis and a very similar degree of social privation (7) (p. 54).

A few subsequent twin studies did show an increased concordance in monozygotic twins; they drew from small series or cases scattered in the literature and were not felt to be conclusive regarding a genetic risk for suicide. Haberlandt (9) in 1967 reported on 149 pairs of twins in the literature in which 1 twin had committed suicide. In 9 of these sets, the other twin had also suicided, and these were all found among the 51 monozygotic pairs. No dizygotic twin pairs were found in Haberlandt's material in which both twins had committed suicide.

Another twin study by Juel-Nielsen and Videbech (10) in Denmark reported in 1970, drew upon the psychiatric register which had been established by Harvald and Hauge and comprised all twins born in Denmark from 1870 to 1920. These authors found a total number of 77 same-sex pairs—19 monozygotic and 58 dizygotic—with one member of each pair a suicide. The preponderance of males over females was borne out in these twins. The authors found 4 concordant pairs among their 19 monozygotic pairs and none among their 58 dizygotic pairs. In 1 of the concordant pairs, both had been diagnosed as manic-depressive, in another, there were 5 suicides among close relatives, in the third, both suffered from endogenous depression and in the fourth, both had been depressed or melancholic although their suicides occurred 25 years apart. No less than 1/5 of the monozygotic pairs, therefore showed concordance. The authors also pointed out the high frequency of affective disorders among both concordant and discordant pairs.

In 1977 Bertelsen, Harvald, and Hauge (11) reported on 10 pairs of twins, 9 monozygotic and 1 probably monozygotic. All were concordant for affective disorder, but only 3 pairs were concordant for suicide. Their conclusion was that concordant findings reflected the severity of affective disorder but only indirectly a genetic predisposition to suicide. Juel-Nielsen (12) reviewing these data advanced the intriguing (though difficult to verify) suggestion that the occurrence of concordance or discordance might be related to psychological aspects of being a twin; that is, in some of these cases the suicide of one twin might have influenced the other monozygotic partner either in the same or the opposite direction. He noted that the risk of suicide in manic-depressive patients is high; one of ten suicides is committed by a manic-depressive patient, and one of seven manic-depressive patients ends his life by suicide. But he concluded, as Kallmann did:

as regards factors that precipitate or prevent suicide risk in manic-depressive disorders, it can be stated that if genetic factors are of importance they probably work only indirectly, whereas environmental factors, of a very complex nature, probably play the major role for the risk of suicide in manic-depressive patients (pp. 274–75).

## Adoption Studies of Suicide

A family study of suicide using the adoption strategy and Danish hospital records was reported in 1979 by Schulsinger et al (13). These authors described the distribution of suicides among the biological and adoptive relatives of index adoptees with schizophrenia, psychopathy, or affective disorder as well as among the relatives of healthy control adoptees. They found a significant increase in suicide in the biological relatives of the index probands as compared with the biological relatives of control probands and the adoptive relatives of both the index and control probands. To be sure, the incidence of suicide in the relatives of adoptees with affective disorders was greater than in the psychopathy and schizophrenia groups.

The Schulsinger group then went on to screen the causes of death in their total sample of adoptees as well as in a nonadopted comparison group, consisting of persons of the same sex, age, and social class usually living in the same neighborhood as the adoptee. They found that 57 of the adoptees and 34 of the nonadopted comparison group had committed suicide, a significant difference between adoptees and nonadoptees. Control probands were then matched with these 57 adopted and 34 nonadopted probands. Among the relatives of the adopted probands who had committed suicide, there were 12 out of 269 biological relatives who themselves committed suicide; among the relatives of the control nonsuicidal group of adoptees there were only 2 out of a group of 269 biological relatives who had committed suicide. This difference was statistically significant below the 1 percent level.

There were no suicides among the adoptive relatives. The 34 nonadopted suicidal probands had 128 relatives, 3 of whom had committed suicide, whereas in the control group there were no suicides out of 125 biological relatives.

Further preliminary analysis of their data indicated that there was a correlation between suicidal probands who had no psychiatric history and relatives who were nonpsychiatric and nonsuicidal. In considering this finding, they suggested the possibility of a genetic factor independent of the common psychiatric conditions so frequently associated with suicide, particularly affective disorder and alcoholism. They realized that these findings were in contradiction to results from earlier studies and speculated that they might have something to do with the nature of the sample, mainly the phenomenon of adoption, so that in stable adoptive homes only those with specific inherited biological deviations might commit suicide.

**Family Studies of Suicide**

Tsuang (14) studied the risk of suicide among first-degree relatives of 195 schizophrenic and 315 manic-depressive patients. In a long-term follow-up, he found that the relatives of the psychiatric patients had a higher rate of suicide than relatives of a matched group of nonpsychiatric control patients, and that male relatives had a higher risk of suicide than female relatives. Moreover he found a higher suicide rate in relatives of patients who committed suicide than in relatives of patients who did not commit suicide. The suicide rate in relatives of depressives was higher than that in relatives of schizophrenics or of manics, although the rate in relatives of manics who committed suicide was not significantly different from that in relatives of depressives who committed suicide.

Another family study of suicide, this one of attempted as well as completed suicide, was reported from the Clark Institute of Psychiatry in Toronto by Roy (15). A record was kept for 5 years of all psychiatric inpatients at that institute known to have a family history of suicide. The aim of the study was to compare the rates of attempted suicide and of depressive disorder in those patients with a family history of suicide with the rates in those psychiatric patients at the same institute who did not have such a family history. The data base consisted of a consecutive series of 243 patients with a definite history of suicide in a first- or second-degree relative. The control group was composed of the remaining 5,602 psychiatric inpatients admitted during the same period who had no family history of suicide.

Among the conclusions of this survey were the following: Of the 243 patients with a family history of suicide almost half (48.6 percent) had attempted suicide, more than half (56.4 percent) had a depressive disorder and more than a third (34.6 percent) had a recurrent affective disorder. Regardless of the primary diagnosis, the great majority (84 percent) of all the patients with a family history of suicide had a depressive episode meeting *DSM III* criteria at some time. During the 7½ years of the study, 7 of these 243 patients actually committed suicide. Of these 7, 2 were women and 5 were men, 5 of the 7 had bipolar disorder and 2 had schizophrenia. Of the patients with no family history of suicide only 21.8 percent had attempted suicide, significantly less than the 48.6 percent of those with a family history. Significant differences between the family-history and nonfamily-history patients held for the total group as well as for schizophrenic, bipolar, unipolar, depressive neurosis, and personality disorder subgroups. (It is interesting to note, however, that there was no significant difference in the rate of suicide attempts between patients with a first-degree relative and those with a second-degree relative committing suicide. This pattern would be unlikely with any known pattern of genetic transmission.) Conversely, of all patients who attempted suicide 8.8 percent had a family history of suicide.

This family study reported, therefore, that among patients who have relatives with a family history of suicide there is a preponderance of depressive disorder both among the patients themselves and among their families, and that a sizeable percentage of those who attempt suicide have a family history of suicide. An additional finding was a significant difference in the rate of suicide attempts between patients who had a parent who suicided when they were under 11 years old and those who had a parent who had done so later. Twelve of the 16 patients who were less than 11 years old when a parent committed suicide later attempted suicide; of the 47 who were more than 20 years old when the parents suicided, 22 later attempted suicide.

## Evaluation of Genetic Evidence in Suicide

On the basis of this survey of the literature on genetic and family transmission of suicide, it does not appear that the case for a purely genetic transmission of suicidal behavior is made. The twin studies are relatively small, equivocal, and often overlap—the Scandinavian studies reporting on the same few pairs of twins. The NIMH-Denmark adoption study does not establish whether suicide is transmitted independently of depression or other psychiatric diagnosis. The family studies indicate a familial risk, the genetic component of which is unknown. In particular, the Toronto family study found an increase in suicide attempts among patients whose relatives had committed suicide but found no difference between the rate among those with first-degree relatives and those with second-degree relatives who have committed suicide. The study deliberately omitted patients with suicide in a third- or fourth-degree relative, a spouse, other nonblood relatives, or friends, groups which might have shed further light on nongenetic components in family transmission.

It may be concluded from these studies, therefore, that the relation between suicide and depression and to a lesser extent schizophrenia is well established, that the genetic transmission and expression of these conditions is substantiated, but that the expression of overt suicidal behavior in predisposed individuals may be largely conditioned by nongenetic factors. Among these factors a strong one is the suicide of a relative, perhaps even more significantly the suicide of a parent when the individual was young. The role of identification in this phenomenon has been explored in the psychoanalytic literature and may play a part.

## Biological Factors in Suicide

Another approach to the problem of suicide is to explore the possibility that there are some biological findings specific to suicidal patients that are distinct from those of the associated psychiatric and particularly depressive conditions (16, 17). There have been a number of tentative and sometimes controversial observations. One of these refers to serotonin metabolism. Asberg et al. (18) reported that the serotonin metabolite 5-hydroxyindoleacetic acid (5-HIAA) level has a bimodal distribution in the cerebrospinal fluid of depressed patients, and that among the low 5-HIAA level group a significantly increased propensity for suicidal behavior was found. A low level was found, particularly if violent methods were used in a suicide attempt. These findings were questioned, since even though nonpsychotic, the suicide attempters may have been depressed. Van Praag (19) therefore studied CSF 5-HIAA levels in a group of nondepressed schizophrenic patients who attempted suicide, usually by violent means, as a response to hallucinatory commands. They were compared to a nonpsychotic control group, and to a matched group of nondepressed, nonsuicidal schizophrenic patients. The experimental group had a significantly lower mean CSF 5-HIAA level, although with considerable overlap with the other two groups. Van Praag suggested that the data supported the hypothesis that low CSF 5-HIAA was correlated with dysregulation of aggression, and was lowest when aggression was accompanied by depression. Similar findings of low CSF 5-HIAA in aggressive, suicidal, nondepressed patients, were reported by Brown et al. (20)

Stanley and Mann (21) reported an increase in presynaptic and postsynaptic serotonin receptors and decreased imipramine binding in the frontal cortex of suicide victims, but these studies did not distinguish between depression and suicidal behavior as the controlling factor. The receptor findings were not replicated by Owen et al. (22) and their relation to previous antidepressant treatment was suggested. Equally nonspecific as to depression were findings by Stanley et al. (23) of decreased tritiated imipramine binding in the frontal cortex of suicides. Another observation of note has been the finding of elevated urinary 17 hydroxycorticosteroids, a secretion of the adrenal cortex, in suicidal as opposed to nonsuicidal depressed patients. This finding has been disputed in replicated studies.

### EEG Findings and Suicidal Risk

There have been a good number of studies attempting to relate EEG findings to suicidal behavior. The results are scattered and equivocal even though there are a number of studies that seem to suggest a possible correlation between impulsively suicidal patients and paroxysmal EEG dysrhythmia. In particular, Struve (24) in a careful study at Hillside Hospital, found that among adult psychiatric patients, paroxysmal EEGs were significantly related to suicidal ideation and suicide attempts. However, he pointed out that although such patterns were elevated among suicidal as contrasted with nonsuicidal patients, the absolute incidence of such dysrhythmia was not unusually high and that the majority of suicidal patients had normal EEGs. He discounted the possibility that such brain-wave abnormality in and of itself led to suicidal urges, but rather considered the possibility that cerebral dysrhythmia interacts with psychiatric disability, rendering suicidal behavior more likely by adding a neurophysiologic handicap to the already greater vulnerability of the psychiatric patient to the effect of stress. There have been many attempts to link impulsive and aggressive behavior to cerebral dysrhythmia, and it is possible that some aspects of suicide could fall within this concept of episodic discontrol, so that such brain dysfunction may lead to impulsive suicide in a reaction to stress. As Struve was careful to point out, the EEG findings do not at present allow individual prediction of the degree of suicide risk nor do they allow identification of those patients most likely to make successful attempts.

### CONCLUSION

Against the background of major psychotic disorders which certainly have a genetic component, there is, then, the fair amount of data, not entirely consistent, regarding patterns of suicide in families, including twins and adoptees. None of these patterns seem to indicate a specific or strong genetic component to suicide as such, but they suggest that superimposed upon a psychotic or personality disordered anlage, biological, neurophysiological, biochemical, or psychological factors may precipitate actual suicidal behavior in a portion of these vulnerable individuals. Undoubtedly other approaches dealing with psychotherapy in suicidal patients, with antidepressants in depressed suicidal patients, and with statistical predictions of suicide, may suggest other interacting factors to better clarify the etiology of this most serious behavioral phenomenon.

## SUMMARY

There is a large body of evidence implicating a genetic factor in major affective disorder, particularly bipolar type. Studies of family risk, of twin concordance, and of adoptees and their families have contributed to this consensus. In the case of suicide, completed or attempted, the evidence is less clear. Twin studies have been based on a small number of pairs and have been inconclusive, and family and adoption studies have not yet satisfactorily separated suicide risk from risk for depression. Biological studies involving neurotransmitter levels suggest that suicide even without depression may be uniquely characterized, and there have been reports of associated brainwave dysfunction. The interacting role of psychological or biological precipitating factors with the genetic component of psychosis or personality disorder still needs further clarification.

## REFERENCES

1. Schlesser, M. A., and Altshuler, K. Z. The Genetics of Affective Disorder: Data, Theory, and Clinical Applications. *Hosp. Community Psychiatry* 34:415–422, 1983.

2. Zerbin-Rüdin, E. Zur Genetik der depressiven Erkrankungen. In *Das Depressive Syndrom;* Hippius, H., and Selbach, H., Eds. Urban & Schwarzenberg, Berlin, 1969, pp. 35–36.

3. Bertelsen, A. Danish Twin Study of Manic-depressive Disorders. In *Origin, Prevention and Treatment of Affective Disorders,* Schou, M., and Strömgren, E., Eds. Academic Press, New York, 1979, pp. 227–239.

4. Mendlewicz, J., Rainer, J. D. Adoption Study Supporting Genetic Transmission in Manic-depressive Illness. *Nature* 268:327–329, 1977.

5. von Knorring, A-L., Cloninger, C. R., Bohman, M., and Sigvardsson, S. An Adoption Study of Depressive Disorders and Substance Abuse. *Arch. Gen. Psychiatry* 49:943–950, 1983.

6. Cadoret, R. J. Evidence for Genetic Inheritance of Primary Affective Disorder in Adoptees. *Am. J. Psychiatry* 135:463–466, 1978.

7. Kallmann, F. J., and Anastasio, M. M. Twin Studies on the Psychopathology of Suicide. *J. Nerv. Ment. Dis.* 105:40–55, 1947.

8. Kallmann, F. J., DePorte, J., DePorte, E., and Feingold, L. Suicide in Twins and Only Children. *Am. J. Hum. Genet.* 1:113–126, 1949.

9. Haberlandt, W. Der Suizid als Genetisches Problem. *Anthrop. Anz.,* 29:65–89, 1965.

10. Juel-Nielsen, N., and Videbech, T. A Twin Study of Suicide. *Acta Genet. Med. Gemellol.* 19:307–310, 1970.

11. Bertelsen, A., Harvald, B., and Hauge, M. A Danish Twin Study of Manic-depressive Disorders. *Br. J. Psychiatry* 130:330, 1977.

12. Juel-Nielsen, N. Suicide Risk in Manic-depressive Disorders. In *Origin, Prevention and Treatment of Affective Disorders,* pp. 269–276.

13. Schulsinger, F., Kety, S. S., Rosenthal, D., and Wender, P. H. A family history of suicide. In *Origin, Prevention and Treatment of Affective Disorders,* pp. 277–87.

14. Tsuang, M. T. Risk of Suicide in the Relatives of Schizophrenics, Manics, Depressives, and Controls. *J. Clin. Psychiatry* 44:396–400, 1983.

15. Roy, A. Family History of Suicide. *Arch. Gen. Psychiatry* 40:971–974, 1983.

16. Åsberg, M., Schalling, D., Rydin, E., and Träskman-Bendz, L. Suicide and Serotonin. In *Depression and Suicide,* Soubrier, J. P., and Vedrinne, J., Eds. Pergamon Press, Paris, 1983, pp. 367–404.

17. Linkowski, P., and Mendlewicz, J. Biological Correlates of Suicide. In *Depression and Suicide,* pp. 411–415.

18. Åsberg, M., Träskman, L., and Thoren, P. 5-HIAA in the Cerebrospinal Fluid: A Biochemical Suicide Predictor? *Arch. Gen. Psychiatry* 33:1193–1197, 1976.

19. van Praag, H. M. CSF 5-HIAA and Suicide in Non-depressed Schizophrenics. *Lancet* ii:977–978, 1983.

20. Brown, G. L., Ebert, M. H., Goyer, P. F., et al. Aggression, Suicide, and Serotonin: Relationship to CSF Amine Metabolites. *Am. J. Psychiatry* 139:741–746, 1982.

21. Stanley, M., and Mann, J. J. Increased Serotonin-2 Binding Sites in Frontal Cortex of Suicide Victims. *Lancet* ii:214–216, 1983.

22. Owen, F., Cross, A. J., Crow, T. J., et al. Brain 5-HT$_2$ Receptors and Suicide. *Lancet* ii:1256, 1983.

23. Stanley, M., Virgilio, J., and Gershon, S. Tritiated Imipramine Binding Sites Are Decreased in the Frontal Cortex of Suicides. *Science* 216:1337–1338, 1982.

24. Struve, F. A. Clinical Electroencephalography. In *Suicide: Theory and Clinical Aspects*, Hankoff, L. O., Einsidler, B., Eds. PSG Publishing Co., Littleton, Mass. 1979, pp. 111–130.

# 2. How Suicidal Behaviors are Learned

Calvin J. Frederick, Ph.D.
H. L. P. Resnik, M.D.

Suicidal behaviors like many other patterns of behavior can be learned. Such an hypothesis, if true, should stimulate the development of treatment techniques founded upon learning principles. To date, there has not been a single article dealing specifically with suicidal behaviors as learned behaviors nor any reference to treatment techniques based on learning theory. "Suicidal behaviors" utilize the plural to suggest the variety of behaviors observed, ranging from threats and attempts to completions, all of which can be suicidal and any of which can be learned.

It would be difficult to support any notion that self-destructive behavior could be fully explained without employing learning principles. There is no evidence that such complex behavior as one's own self-destruction resides in the genes. Behavior is motivated and it is learned, although structure, unconscious conflicts, and neurobiochemistry do affect the way in which it is learned, felt, and expressed.

Clinical terms related to suicide such as anxiety and depression have been difficult to define, but they have great impor-

The authors would like to acknowledge the helpful suggestions of Michael Serber, M.D. who critically read the initial manuscript.

tance physiologically, clinically, and experimentally. With the advent of behavior therapy procedures, experimental psychologists and psychiatrists have been attracted to the perplexing problems found in the world of the clinician. It matters little to behavior scientists what something is called as long as one is able to measure it. For example, the physiologic psychologist could define anxiety as a mild and chronic form of fear, using autonomic nervous system indices to measure it. A psychologist oriented toward reinforcement learning theory might define it as a variable measured by a score on an anxiety scale. An operant conditioning advocate could view anxiety as a response to the presence of threatening stimuli with emphasis upon the frequency of responses.

On the other hand, to the behavior modification proponent, depression might be seen as the absence or diminution of the number of emitted responses even in the presence of customary reinforcers. To a clinically oriented experimentalist it might be assessed as a score on a depression scale. By a learning theorist it has been defined simply as a function of insufficient reinforcers (1).

Now, many clinical entities are not unitary phenomena; they cut across a variety of diagnostic categories and behavioral patterns. For this reason, a unitary treatment method is unlikely to be broadly effective. This problem has been encountered in several forms of clinical problems. Farrar, Powell, and Martin (2) raise this question with regard to the conflicting results found in various conditioning approaches to the treatment of alcoholics, while Frederick (3) and Martyn and Sheehan (4) have made similar points with regard to the treatment of stutterers. In addition, Lazarus (5) notes the elusiveness encountered in measuring different clinical presentations of depression.

Suicidal behavior presents the same problem since it is not a unitary disorder but spans a broad spectrum of nosologic categories, in some instances even falling within the normal range. While many suicidal persons are depressed, some are not. Behavior signs are not always present and it would be unduly presumptuous to force such a label on them. Although many suicidal behaviors do have the advantage of being reasonably definitive, clinicians regard some of them as equivocal and sub-intentioned. Suicidal behaviors may or may not be symptomatic of an underlying mental illness. In evaluating any behavior one has to determine whether it represents a unique symptom or a syndrome pointing to a broader entity. Actually, the classification of most mental disorders suffers from a lack of precision, in contrast to physical illnesses where definitive etiologic agents can be identified. For this reason, the operational approach of behavior scientists may have much appeal.

An operational definition of suicidal behavior might be that willful act designed to effect the cessation of life. This avoids dealing with mental or emotional states and simply notes the behavior. Although the term "willful" is subject to equivocation, at least an effort is made to describe the measurable conditions (the essence of operationalism) under which the behavior occurs.

The concepts elaborated in this paper are primarily theoretical, with much of our thinking predicated upon established learning theory principles synthesized with our clinical data. While various procedures in learning and behavior therapy are mentioned, our orientation will be relatively generic in an attempt to place suicidal behaviors in the context of learning theory as a whole rather than with a particular school of thought.

## REACTION PATTERNS AND MOTIVATIONS FROM EARLY LIFE

### Self-destructive Behaviors with the Clinical Depressive Syndrome

Self-destructive acts as part of a depressive syndrome may be formulated quite definitively through concepts related to learning theory. Although it has been difficult to objectify satisfactorily, depression may be defined and studied together with its behavioral consequences. The classical depression symptoms such as anorexia, insomnia, weight loss, psychomotor retardation, loss of sexual drive, and the like, form a reasonably consistent agreed upon syndrome of behavior.

Since disturbances in oral drive are frequently related to the appearance of depressive phenomena, some comment is required on the topic. Changes in oral drive can depend upon learning for their expression (6–9). Both behavioral and verbal acts become instrumental in establishing environmental events which are necessary for a goal response to follow. The child cries in association with hunger and the mother appears with food, which reduces the state of hunger. Thus, an environmental situation is established in which the crying becomes associated with the mother and the reduction of the unlearned drive. When the oral behaviors of crying and feeding become associated with the hunger drive and its need for reduction in intensity, the mother or mother surrogate becomes associated or paired with the environmental events leading to the reduction of the hunger drive. If relief does not occur, anxiety continues unabated (10). Moreover, Ferster (1) describes how a shift in reinforcement contingencies or their absence can give rise to depression. Lazarus (5) believes that a depressed person is "on an extinction trial," noting that some significant reinforcer has been withdrawn such as the loss of money, a loved one, or prestige.

The direction of aggression and frustration as various aspects of social learning in stimulus-response terms has been discussed by Miller and Dollard (11). Hall and Lindzey (12) cite Freud's postulate that the aggressive drive is self-destruction externalized against substitute objects. The death wish is blocked by life forces and other obstacles in the personality which counteract the death instincts. One may generalize further that depression can result directly from prolonged frustration of an aggressive drive or be secondary to anxiety as a relief from its continuous stress.

When depression becomes reinforced by both physical and psychologic attention, it can move forward in the sequence of behavioral reactions and may be triggered much more quickly without the prior appearance of prolonged anxiety. As the child grows older and more verbal, the earlier crying and accompanying physical demonstrations of anxiety and depression are put into words: "I don't feel good." If verbalizations of this type obtain gratification to reduce the intensity of the feeling, they become cues to evoke future reactions from the listener when the subject feels depressed, angry, frustrated, or unhappy. The relationship between verbalization and reinforcement can be readily demonstrated and should be, especially with regard to depression and self-destructive acts. The child returns to what worked before expecting it to do so again, particularly where recurrences of such behavior have occurred.

It makes little difference whether the origin of the depressive behavior has arisen from within the organism as suggested by the catecholamine hypothesis of depression or from outside the organism by virtue of a personal loss. Early behavior patterns become reinforced and their likelihood of recurrence is strengthened very quickly, whether in responding to a loss one has experienced or to an internally perceived affect. If depression is a blocking or turning inward of anger, as psychoanalytically postulated, then a child's mode of angry expression can become learned as a depressive reaction. In effect, the depression may be a more acceptable response to those around him than anger, thereby allowing him to receive more positive reinforcement. Even in an infant, expressions of aggression and anger soon receive negative reinforcement. When blockage to a goal occurs repeatedly, the ensuing frustration may eventuate in turning aggression on the self, at first accidentally, and later to increase sensory input and decrease feelings of helplessness (13).

## Self-destructive Behaviors
## without the Clinical Depressive Syndrome

These behaviors are overt, direct, and observable but are not necessarily congruent with the signs usually accepted in the depressive syndrome. Most workers in crisis intervention would list such acts as verbalizing one's intent, loss of interest, job inefficiency, obtaining a lethal weapon, dwelling upon disappointments with a significant other, giving away a prized possession, and suddenly putting one's affairs in order. The learning of such acts begins either in early or later life. In applying the concepts of Mowrer (14, 15) it may be seen that anxiety, even when not associated with depression, may constitute a secondary drive mechanism, and reinforce responses in the same manner as primary drives. Certainly one way of reinforcing suicidal behavior in adults is by rewarding it. Theoretically, any response from the environment might be construed to be a positive response. Does the existence of suicide prevention services select out and reinforce suicidal behavior as "tickets" to this care-giving system? Such behavior is dramatic and invariably evokes a response from other individuals when nothing else will.

Physicians will frequently write prescriptions for depressed or anxious suicidal patients when they might be reluctant to do so for others who are more covert in their behavior. Reaction patterns which are both attention-getting and tension-reducing will become doubly reinforced. In addition to the drive- or tension-reduction experienced by the patient, secondary gain also evolves in the form of receiving sympathy, which adds further strength to the reinforcing qualities of the self-destructive response. The physician sometimes reinforces his personal reaction patterns by reducing his own anxiety about the patient through writing a prescription because the patient often improves temporarily. His tension abates and the possibility increases that he will readily write the prescription again when the patient's suicidal behavior recurs. This is especially so when drugs are given without accompanying treatment, since little else is done to abate the feelings. If the physician is unable to provide the psychologic support needed, he should arrange for the patient to obtain it elsewhere. Of course, nonmedical therapists can reinforce aberrant responses by methods other than through the administration of drugs.

An infrequently recognized determinant of suicidal behavior may be severe punishment in childhood. The child learns to treat himself as others have and to reduce his tension as well as his parents' anger through whippings. As the youngster grows older, self-punishment (as mediated by the superego) may precede punishment from others and gain reinforcement, especially if the youngster is in conflict with himself at the time. This phenomenon may be unrelated to depression.

An individual resolves his suicidal conflict by making a decision to act, which immediately reduces the tension being experienced so that he may be in a remarkably calm state just prior to the suicide attempt. This state of calm then becomes a part of the suicidal act; it is often misleading to inexperienced clinicians who are looking for more obvious signs of disturbed behavior.

Moreover, the associative learning principle of preservation of the postrem response as elaborated by Voeks (16) would appear relevant here. This concept is that the response last made in a situation is fixed and no unlearning is possible after the subject is removed from it. When placed again in the situation, the subject will do what was done last under that condition, irrespective of whether it is "right" or "wrong." Such a concept would help explain the many clinical situations in which patients remain or are returned to the very same conditions present at the time of a suicide attempt.

We would like to introduce the idea here, as it is not mentioned elsewhere in the literature on suicide prevention programs, that various behaviors by physicians and mental health professionals, as well as by suicide prevention centers, may, paradoxically, reinforce suicidal behaviors. That is, by responding immediately (whether appropriately or not is another issue), the suicide attemptor's or caller's behavior is reinforced and learning occurs. The sequence (attempt and/or phone call/environmental response) is set up. When the "cry for help" has been successful in achieving a real or fantasied change in interpersonal relationships and/or environmental surroundings, suicidal behavior may then have been learned as a successful method of coping. (Let us, for the moment, not consider the value judgment of whether this is a good or bad result, that is, whether it is better to invite callers all the while recognizing some risk in reinforcing the very behavior we wish to eliminate.) Suffice it to say that such learning can be imitated (as we have indicated earlier), can become a *preferred* response to a difficult situation, and, paradoxically, can become so repetitious that it no longer receives the earlier desired response(s) (as with the shepherd who cried "wolf" once too often). By answering "emergency" cries or urging people to come for assistance, we must be careful *not* to imply or state that we have treatment and intervention modalities that will always, or even usually, be of assistance.

## LEARNING ASPECTS IN THEORIES OF SUICIDE

All theories of suicidal behavior can be complemented by including some aspects of learned behaviors, though they have not been formulated to date. Since we are merely seeking to illustrate our thesis, we will cite only some representative theoretical examples.

### Psychodynamic Theories

Psychodynamic theories explaining self-destructive behavior such as those of Freud (17), Fenichel (18), and Abraham (19), incorporate beliefs which include disturbances in the expression of oral libido, the clinical depressive syndrome, and conflicts associated with hostility and aggression. Horney's variations (20) point to self-hate, despair, defiance, and vindictiveness as the elements in self-destruction. Although not thinking in learning terms, she suggested that therapists attend to the less dramatic behavioral signs and discuss them sooner with the patient so the latter could learn to avert suicidal behavior. The idea would be to drain off anxiety before it mounted to unbearable heights. This might constitute one aspect of the application of learning theory to a clinical situation.

Litman more recently has presented a cogent argument for the importance of "separation anxiety" as a precursor to suicidal behavior (21). Here, as elsewhere, individual differences underscore the importance of a learning component. Actually, what is common to psychoanalytic therapy is the learning or unlearning that takes place in the treatment situation. New and more appropriate responses are introduced and reinforced so as to increase the ego's problem solving and coping abilities with rewards coming from self-realization reinforcement from the therapist. The achievement of insight, a goal so valued in psychoanalytic psychotherapy, has many elements of newly learned more adaptive behavior in it.

## Sociological Theories

Durkheim's historic work (22) will serve to exemplify an important theoretical position from the discipline of sociology. He described four types of suicide: egoistic, altruistic, anomic, and fatalistic. These types were characterized by feelings and attitudes surrounding lack of societal integration, heavy societal integration, loss of cultural guideposts, and foreordained suicidal behavior, respectively. One difficulty with Durkheim's formulations is the lack of consideration of personal motivation under stressful conditions. Beall (23) comments that Durkheim made a major error in using statistical data to be explanatory rather than merely descriptive.

One may approach the behavior of entire cultures or societies in learning theory terms although it would be difficult to carry out experimentally. However, individual motives and personality differences are controllable and necessary to complete an explanation of why some do and others do not commit the act. The use of external controls is learned. When a breakdown in environmental supports occurs in the face of stress, behaviors from early life may come to the fore. Two instances of culturally learned self-destruction are suttee, the custom in certain Indian regions where a wife commits a ritualized suicide on her husband's funeral pyre and the practice of hari-kari among the Japanese. Yet, even then some individuals do not always go through with these rituals.

## Psychologic Theories

Psychologic views may encompass cognitive approaches, developmental data, and sociopsychologic explanations. Surprisingly, learning concepts, per se, have not been delineated as an important factor.

Shneidman and Farberow's categorization of suicidal thinking into logic types (24) might be more nearly complete by exploring the manner in which specific suicidal thinking patterns have been learned. Farber's (25) sociopsychologic formula for suicidal behavior describes personal and environmental factors. He deduces the value of preventive measures such as the need to develop a strong resilience in children and a sense of confidence to meet the pressures of adult life. Lack of hope and feelings of personal competence are the key ingredients of this position. The learning aspects inherent in this view of suicide prevention are not developed.

Hendin (26) attributes both personality difference and suicide potential among the Scandinavians to child-rearing practices. He holds that the low rate in Norway is largely associated with the cultural aspects of personality. Just as a child learns the language of his country, he can also learn character traits of a cultural nature which may predispose him to specific behaviors under stressful conditions. Hendin found Swedish competitiveness and Danish passivity to be character traits associated with high suicide rates.

What is of more concern is the influence upon the family of suicidal behaviors among its members. We are aware of situations where children view the circumstances leading to a suicide attempt. They see the individual responses to such behavior and incorporate them within their own personalities. They may observe the success of a manipulative attempt, the guilt following a hostile act, or the pleasure of being cared for solicitously. Any of these suicidal conditions can become reinforced behavior when the individual experiences tension and behaves in a similar way himself. This may be related to the controversy about watching violence on television.

### Theoretical Aspects of Learning and Suicide Prevention

Rewarding or punishing states of affairs or satisfiers and annoyers have traditionally been regarded as sufficient to account for learned behavior. Although the words reward and punishment are still used, there is an attempt today to employ terms which seem less judgmental and more objective. Phrases such as "positive reinforcers" are likely to be used to describe rewarding conditions while "negative reinforcers" and noxious or aversive stimuli are preferred to the word "punishment." Learning theories have been accustomed to saying that in order to mold behavior one simply rewards desirable responses and does not reward or punishes undesirable ones. However, such a basic procedure fails to suffice for abnormal behavior because it is particularly complex and often does not extinguish with negative reinforcement. This difficulty has been found in the experimental investigation of alcoholism, by Farrar, Powell, and Martin (2) and Madill *et al.* (27); in stuttering by Frederick (3), Frick (28), Sheehan (29), and Van Riper (30); and even in smoking by Grimaldi and Lichtenstein (31).

The learning of suicidal behavior patterns is a function of a number of complex variables, among them personality, motivating conditions, reinforcements, environment or setting, and the strength of past responses made under similar situations. Any theory ultimately should be capable of being translated into measurable terms, even though broadly conceived. The development of the concepts which follow are intended to clarify learning theory in explicit symbolic terms.

**Relevance of Stimulus-Response Concepts**

Extending Lazarus's point that "a careful S-R analysis is considered indispensable for adequate diagnosis and therapy" (5), let us first exposit how this may occur with self-destruction. Like any other behavior suicide can be considered a direct multiplicative function of drive or motivation multiplied by those past learned associations or habits connected with such behavior. Traditional stimulus-response learning theory advanced by Hull (32) and Spence (33) employs this approach. While the simplicity of this concept has merit, it neglects the highly important dual forces within the individual at the time of the suicidal act, namely the ambivalence which the person feels, or the strong and the weak forces which are operating concomitantly.

$sBr = f (H \times M)$ is a more suitable delineation of the traditional S-R learning concept, sBr meaning the stimulus and response components likely to evoke behavior, which, in this instance, relates to the suicidal potential. H equals the strength of past habits and M equals the drive strength or motivation toward behavior.

It is important to note that learning affects the development of each factor. It is indeed the sine qua non for predicting, explaining, and treating suicidal behavior in a planned fashion. A ratio of weak to strong behavioral impulses seems more appropriate to account for this behavior in learning theory terms.

It will be helpful to illustrate how both reward and punishment of a suicide attempt can increase the response growth initially, as a function of the unrealized sBr. Under high anxiety or tension states in which the patient frequently finds himself, a suicidal response may serve to reduce the anxiety or drive.

To enunciate this principle theoretically, let the rate of growth for evoking the suicidal response equal one-tenth of the unrealized H and arbitrarily assign theoretical initial values of 100 to H and 3 to M or drive strength. Under the reward condition, even as the anxiety (M) goes down, the strength of the response or the habit (H) of engaging in suicidal acts is increased, and so is the behavioral potential. Under the punishing condition the drive state as an expression of anxiety and tension is not reduced, but will continue at the same intensity. When this occurs, the rate of growth for the suicide response is even greater.

Traditional learning theory holds that drive states remain constant in their effect upon response-evocation. The drive-reduction which accompanies reinforcement contributes to the strength of the response so that its frequency of occurrence is likely to increase as a result. The drive state, however, is only temporarily reduced and returns to its original intensity for the next reinforcement or series of reinforcements. In other words, when an individual is hungry and eats, he is reinforced for the behavior which was occurring at the time. Even though the food temporarily reduces his hunger, it is reactivated again. For illustrative purpose, this constant drive state has been assumed in the punishment condition but not in the reward condition listed in Table 2-1.

It is questionable that a drive state will continue to remain at the same level of intensity ad infinitum following all positive and negative reinforcing states of affairs. While this may be

TABLE 2-1

Hypothetical Values Showing Development of Differing Amounts of sBr = (H × M), or the Behavior Potential of Suicidal Behaviors

| Reward | | | H Unrealized | Punishment | | |
|---|---|---|---|---|---|---|
| 0 | = 0 | × 3.0 | 100 | 0 | = 0 | × 3 |
| 25 | = 10 | × 2.5 | 90 | 30 | = 10 | × 3 |
| 38 | = 19 | × 2.0 | 81 | 57 | = 19 | × 3 |
| 40.65 | = 27.1 | × 1.5 | 72.9 | 81.3 | = 27.1 | × 3 |

Rate of growth equals 1/10 of the unrealized H.
sBr = Behavior potential of response.
H = Strength of habitual behavior as a function of the number of reinforcements.
M = Motivation or drive strength.

more likely to hold for primary drives, it is less apt to obtain for secondary drives such as anxiety.

Clearly, one would want to neither positively nor negatively reinforce suicidal responses. Rather, a principle of nonreinforcement could be better employed to extinguish the behavior. The value of nonreinforcement has been cited by Sheehan (29) in modifying stuttering behavior and by Stampfl (34) as a current Implosive Behavior Therapy procedure.

### Extension of Stimulus-Response Factors to Suicide Potential

Let us consider the weak and strong (ambivalent) factors within the individual at the time of the self-destructive act. In general terms, this concept may be expressed as the ratio:

$$Bsu = f \frac{\text{Weak factors}}{\text{Strong factors}}$$

where the inclination toward suicidal behavior (Bsu) is a function of such factors. Weak factors may include prior experiences within the individual to make him suicidal, such as early separation from or death of a parent, loss of job, or love object, alcoholism, or a bad experience with a therapist. Strong factors may include anything which is health-promoting and anti-suicidal such as a good job, good health, happy family, and freedom from debilitating neurotic conflicts. Of course, the assignment of values to each variable must be worked out.

It is clear that, as the weak forces increase, the likelihood of an aberrant behavioral response also increases. When the ratio of weak to strong factors is equal, the likelihood of suicide would be 1; if the strong factors in the individual's life outweigh the weak ones, the probability would be less than 1. Hence, anything less than 1 might be considered reasonably normal and anything greater than 1 would be suspect of abnormal functioning. In further delineating the components which could operate in the individual's life at the time of the suicidal act, the specific factors are shown by the following formula:

$$Bsu - f \ \frac{Pw \times Ew \times (Hw \times Mw)}{Ps \times Es \times (Hs \times Ms)} \ \text{or} \ Bsu = f \ \frac{Pw \times Ew \times sBrw}{Ps \times Es \times Sbrs}$$

namely,

Bsu  = suicidal behavior.
Pw   = weak aspects of the personality such as an oral depressive character structure.
Ew   = an environment with weak and debilitating resources.
Hw   = habits or responses which have been associated with suicidal behavior and have been reinforced.
Mw   = motivation to weak or undesirable behavior.
Ps   = good ego strength and strong personality character-istics, capable of withstanding stress and the presence of hope and competence.
Es   = availability of positive environmental resources.
Hs   = habits and past associations where stress has been met favorably.
Ms   = motivation to strong or desirable behavior.

The therapist must reinforce the means to tension-reduction provided by *other factors* which are more desirable and available to the patient than undesirable ones. The patient should be commended and rewarded for nonsuicidal behavior such as engaging in productive physical activity, making it a point not to be alone during a crisis or telephoning the therapist or a suicide prevention-crisis intervention service. Hopefully, such positive responses will be more likely to recur, gain increasing importance in the patient's response pattern, and self-destructive behaviors will weaken and ultimately drop out. Associative learning principles state that the only way to eliminate a previously fixed response is to place the person back in the situation while he makes other responses to the same stimuli. Thus, new reactions are established to the previous situation. Upon removal from the situation, the last response made to it becomes preserved. Moreover, the patient can be shown that his anxiety and/or depression are bearable and that they will pass. With reinforcement added each time this happens, the likelihood of an undesirable response occurring will be lessened.

Operant conditioning utilizes the actions which the subject undertakes himself. Operants are responses emitted by the subject since he operates upon the environment about him. Voluntary acts of human beings are clear examples. The importance of behavior therapy in this context is that its two most distinguishing aspects are: (a) treating the behavior itself rather than searching out time-consuming psychodynamic causes; and (b) making capital of real life situations, so as to establish new reactions to old stimuli.

## Integration of Personality, Environmental, and Learning Variables into General Theory

The addition of personality (P) and environmental (E) variables is necessary to complete a logical formula. However, by holding P and E values constant, the theory is easier to demonstrate at this point. Substituting into our formula, then, the arbitrary values of 3 for Personality, 1 for Environment and from Table 2-1, 25 for the initial strength of sBr or H $\times$ M into the numerator, the result is 75. If no additional reinforcement for it occurs, the denominator will remain constant even after having some initial value where the strong behavior is greater than the weak. The next time the reinforcement occurs the value increases to 114. It continues to rise so that the third reinforcement will show sBrw reaching a value of 121.95. Although anxiety is reduced, by the administration of tranquilizers or antidepressant drugs, for example, Bsu continues to increase. Then, growth in suicidal behavior will overtake the nonsuicidal behavior with subsequent reinforcement of the former.

This can be shown by introducing 30 as the value of the first reinforcement from Table 2-1 into the denominator, thus yielding a suicidal potential of .80, which is less than 1. Hence, while it might appear initially that we have helped the individual and reduced his suicide potential, the situation may not continue to remain so. If punishment is added, the Bsu develops all the more rapidly. This will occur even though it is interspersed with the administration of anxiety-reducing medication. This is readily observable by merely noting the growth rate of punishment in Table 2-1.

Mathematically illustrated in the expanded formula to follow, it can be demonstrated that behavior which was thought to be nonsuicidal can quickly become suicidal, merely by reinforcing suicidal behavior patterns. A single reinforcement can move the patient from a nonsuicidal state immediately into a suicidal one. The suicidal behavior potential then presents a value beyond the dividing point of 1, with a ratio of 1.26, instead of the previous 0.80.

$$\text{Bsu} = \frac{\text{Pw} \times \text{Ew} \times (\text{Hw} \times \text{Mw})}{\text{Ps} \times \text{Es} \times (\text{Hs} \times \text{Ms})} \quad \text{or} \quad \frac{\text{Pw} \times \text{Ew} \times \text{sBrw}}{\text{Ps} \times \text{Es} \times \text{sBrs}}$$

$$= \frac{3 \times 1 \times 25}{3 \times 1 \times 30} = \frac{75}{90} = 0.80$$

$$= \frac{3 \times 1 \times 38}{3 \times 1 \times 30} \quad 114 = 1.26$$

Any number of occurrences in the response hierarchy of the individual's repertoire can be prearranged as a result of past associations so that suicidal behavior might be evoked with one additional reinforcement. If the balance is delicate and then the patient loses his job, or his wife goes off with another man, or the therapist mishandles the situation, self-destructive behavior can become a consequence. Penetrating confrontations of behavior or interpretations of rage and hostility early in the acute phase may trigger the suicidal act by heightening the drive state. It is necessary to be realistic with the patient and keep him task-oriented once the acute phase has passed, as we have noted elsewhere (35).

## THE BEHAVIOR THERAPIES AND
## SELF-DESTRUCTIVE BEHAVIOR

### Systematic Desensitization Therapy

The procedures of desensitization and relaxation originally advanced by Wolpe (36) aim at the diminution of anxiety-laden reactions to previously upsetting stimuli. If the person is depressed and no longer anxious, other methods need to be invoked. Wolpe's techniques are based upon the notion of relaxation followed by systematically bringing anxiety-provoking stimuli into one's thoughts. The assumption is that a patient cannot be both anxious and relaxed simultaneously. Salient information is obtained using behavior analysis and case history data. Gradually, by establishing a hierarchy of severely anxiety-provoking to slightly anxiety-provoking pictures in the patient's thoughts, the therapist can move up the hierarchy and gradually eliminate the old feared or undesirable responses through relearning and desensitization.

In a period of acute crisis, the aim is to ameliorate the patient's severe anxiety before depression sets in, if it is still operating at the time suicide is threatened, without rewarding such behavior. One means of accomplishing this is to provide other avenues which are more acceptable to the patient.

Tension-reducing or drive-reducing responses constitute the essence of how most behavior is learned. The clinician should be careful not to permit the patient to associate him with undesirable behavior. The trouble with the use of punishment in managing adults as well as children is that it is associated all too often with the punisher in the mind of the recipient rather than with the undesirable act. The individual begins to hate the person administering the behavior. Subsequently, he may turn to suicide rather than to the punisher for help. One reason for this is temporal delay since reinforcement should occur near the time of the act while kinesthetic cues and actions are at their height. It is frequently impossible to administer the punishment at the exact time the undesirable act occurs. The patient should learn that the therapist will neither reward nor punish his suicidal behavior but rather will be available to assist him toward constructive avenues to action. The value of selective nonreinforcement has been well described (19, 34).

When the number of action choices is small, the likelihood of suicide increases statistically as well as in terms of response strength. Few response choices lead to the development of strongly reinforced responses. The greater the number of responses available, the less likely the suicidal response will be chosen on the basis of chance alone. Added to this is the probability that other responses will receive their share of reinforcement, which lessens the chance that the suicidal one will occur. It is the task of the therapist to widen the available choices in the patient's life-space no matter what kind of therapy he employs, although desensitization stresses intensity diminution.

## ILLUSTRATION 1

An acutely anxious young man is in crisis due to a brief homosexual contact and fears that a repetition will occur because the previous stimulus (other male) continues to be present in his life. The patient whose father had died while the boy was a child, sees suicide as a preventive measure against future homosexual acts and as a means of alleviating shame.

A series of anxiety-provoking scenes surrounding males, including the offending partner, are pictured and arranged in a hierarchy. Relaxation and desensitization are employed to reduce the fear while building in other satisfying associations to sexual stimuli. A suicide response is never included as one of the alternate possibilities.

### Assertive Training

This technique teaches the patient to act in positive, assertive ways and is likely to be more useful in an outpatient or office situation, particularly when family members can become involved.

The authors have found it of particular value with depressive patients to utilize a family therapy approach in conjunction with assertive training. The family members' attitudes toward one another are explored together. The nonsuicidal members are instructed in selective reinforcement procedures. The other members of a person's environment tend to reinforce depressive types of behavior without realizing it.

## ILLUSTRATION 2

A forty-two-year-old wife and mother approaching menopause has experienced a depressive reaction following the death of her mother. After rescue following an overdose of medication she has returned home. Rehospitalization is not felt to be necessary. The doctor now wisely becomes more cautious regarding medication and declines to provide sleeping pills. The patient objects and begins her pattern of becoming morose, moody, and lacking in any overt expression of energy. In most instances, it would be advisable for the patient to remain hospitalized for several days. During that time a ward program using behavior therapy procedures can be instituted, and followed up at home.

In keeping with instructions, the family discourages lying in bed and other regressive forms of behavior and the patient improves because of lack of reinforcement for her psychopathology. Motor activity is important in combating depression, particularly if some tangible constructive act is tied to it, such as making one's bed, cleaning the house, and so on. Acceptable behavior is reinforced by positive responses from the family while antithetical responses are ignored, nonreinforced, and thereby weakened. The therapist exerts his influence by verbalizing his positive expectations to the patient. He must isolate various stimuli which are important in the patient's life in order to evaluate their effectiveness appropriately. It is virtually impossible to work alone on a one-hour-a-week or even one-hour-a-day schedule and hope for results except for cases of straight desensitization. In fact, a combination of any behavior therapy and psychotherapy is probably most useful (37).

## Aversion Therapy

As Keller and Schoenfeld (38) point out, aversions like appe-
tites form a major class of drives. They cite two criteria for
determining whether a stimulus is aversive or not: (a) a
response made in its presence ought to be strengthened by its
removal, and (b) a response made in the absence of the
stimulus should be decreased if it is followed by the administration of the stimulus. These are also criteria for negative
reinforcers. Hilgard and Marquis (39) commented in their
pioneering work three decades ago that there was a difference
between escape training and avoidance training. Some of the
current aversion therapy situations might be more accurately
called avoidance training. In escape training, responses are
strengthened through the termination or reduction of noxious
(negatively reinforcing) stimuli while avoidance training is
accomplished when the learned reaction prevents the appearance of a noxious stimulus. Generically, both are aversive in
the sense that there is a turning away from or a repugnance to
noxious stimuli. If aversions can be developed without being
punishing, this should be done when suicidal persons are
treated. Both may be considered as operant procedures although differences exist. In aversion therapy a strong approach
drive needs to be altered or eliminated; in nonaversion operant
therapy a strong avoidance drive is present which needs to be
altered or eliminated. Thus, customary operant procedures are
valuable with fearful or anxiety-laden behavior while aversion
techniques can be valuable for conditions without anxiety as a
primary factor. As previously mentioned, punishing situations
are apt to create or add to anxiety.

Certainly, most present-day aversion is used to break up an
existing association between a conditioned stimulus which is
considered undesirable and a pleasant response. This occurs by
linking the conditioned stimulus to an unpleasant response
and thereby interfering with the old association. To the extent
that smoking or drinking may be self-destructive, aversion
techniques apply. Smoking is an undesirable habit that evokes
pleasure which should respond to avoidance training techniques. The unpleasant tasting reactions which some medica-

tion can produce when a subject is smoking could be helpful. If programmed under controlled conditions many hours each day and related to the symptom so as to avoid anxiety, which could create other symptoms, then effective results might be expected (31). Follow-up is necessary with this approach and should be a standard practice with self-destructive persons.

While aversive conditioning techniques have been described with some success (40–44), they may not be especially suited to suicidal behavior for several reasons: first, self-destruction cannot be viewed as pleasure-seeking approach behavior for the subject, although it may meet an overriding psychologic need. Secondly, since negative reinforcers can increase anxiety, deliberately punishing a suicidal response could evoke a heightened drive to complete the act coupled with the thought the individual might feel he had nothing more to lose. Thirdly, there has to be an available substitute response or class of responses which have the same value for the subject as the one in existence. Punishing a response does not always create an aversion or decrease the stimulus, particularly in a conflict situation.

Keller and Schoenfeld (38), citing the work of Tolcott, comment how simultaneous drives bring about conflict with alternate flurries of responses which are made at the same rate as those made in the presence of one stimulus alone. This increase in rate develops because spurts of responses occur during the alternation process. They note that this is in line with findings that punishment is not necessarily sufficient to reduce strength. In fact, it appears as if "it is this very inefficacy of punishment that allows the conflict to continue unabated." Merely punishing abnormal behavior can serve to increase it under some conditions (2, 28, 44). Conversely, electro-convulsive therapy (ECT) given for some severe cases of depression is not aversive conditioning.

## A Ward Behavior Therapy Program

A ward program for inpatients might prove highly successful for severely depressed and suicidal patients. The authors are in the process of formulating such an effort. The procedures to be included are outlined as follows:

1. Chart behaviors which occur in connection with depressive or suicidal acts.
2. Ask ward personnel to observe the kinds of behaviors the patient shows which are tied to suicide or depression.
3. Count the frequency of occurrence of these behaviors within a specific time period.
4. Find out what is important to the patient other than the current behaviors, then use these as positive reinforcers for not engaging in depressive or suicidal acts.
5. Relate the frequency of occurrences of these depressive or suicidal behavior indicators to specific time periods during and after treatment.
   a. *Verbal Examples*
      suicide: Any direct or indirect comment about feeling depressed or suicidal.
         Direct: "I plan to kill myself."
         Indirect: "I probably will not be here next week, you may have my fountain pen."
      depression: "I feel bad today."
         "I think I'll go back to bed."
         "I don't want to eat."
   b. *Behavioral Examples*
      suicide: Effort to hoard pills; possessing a lethal weapon; self-assault.
      depression: Increased time in bed; early morning rising time; psychomotor retardation; continued loss of appetite; continued loss of sleep, despite increased time in bed; less talk; withdrawal; reduction in interpersonal contacts.

If a diminution in the frequency of these behaviors occurs, which continues to maintain itself, a relearning can be said to have taken place and treatment can be tentatively assumed to have been successful.

Clinical procedures ought to be congruent with principles of basic learning. For example, in employing reinforcement, one should support the person in crisis, *not the act*. These principles of selective reinforcement and selective nonreinforcement constitute an essential aspect of what the authors believe occurs in suicidal crisis intervention.

While it is possible at some future time that certain weights or values may be inserted into the formulae presented in this article, when more data from research are available, no recommendation to do so is intended at this point. The need for the development of explicit theoretical concepts utilizing psychodynamic, social, and learning information is apparent. We trust that our preliminary attempt to incorporate concepts from learning theory into the treatment of suicidal behaviors will encourage other workers to add their own efforts to the task of developing a comprehensive theory of suicide prevention.

## SUMMARY

Many aspects of suicidal behaviors can be learned and treatment techniques based upon general learning theory have been discussed. Examples from clinical, social, and experimental information have been condensed with an attempt to integrate them with theoretical concepts. The use of various learning theory approaches toward understanding and managing self-destructive behaviors was advanced.

## REFERENCES

1. Ferster, C. Classification of Behavior Pathology. In *Research in Behavior Modification*. Krasner, L. and Ullman, L., Eds. Holt, Rinehart & Winston, New York, 1965.

2. Farrar, C., Powell, B., and Martin, L. Punishment of Alcohol Consumption by Apneic Paralysis. *Behav. Res. Ther.* 6:13, 1968.

3. Frederick, C. An Investigation of Learning Theory and Reinforcement as related to Stuttering Behavior. Paper presented to the American Speech and Hearing Ass. Convention, Los Angeles, November, 1955.

4. Martyn, M. and Sheehan, J. Onset of Stuttering and Recovery. *Behav. Res. Ther.* 6:295, 1968.

5. Lazarus, A. Learning Theory and the Treatment of Depression. *Behav. Res. Ther.* 6:83, 1968.

6. Levy, D. M. Finger-Sucking and Accessory Movements in Early Infancy. *Am. J. Psychiat.* 7:881, 1928.

7. _____ . Experiments on the Sucking Reflex and Social Behavior of Dogs. *Am. J. Orthopsychiat.* 4:203, 1934.

8. Sears, R. R. and Wise, G. W. Relation of Cup-Feeding in Infancy to Thumb-Sucking and the Oral Drive. *Am. J. Orthopsychiat.* 20:123, 1950.

9. Davis, H. V., Sears, R. R., Miller, H. C., and Broadbeck, J. J. Effects of Cup, Bottle and Breast Feeding on Oral Activities of Newborn Infants. *Pediatrics* 3:549, 1948.

10. Wolpe, J. and Lazarus, A. *Behavior Therapy Techniques.* Pergamon Press, Oxford, 1966.

11. Miller, N. and Dollard J. *Social Learning and Imitation.* Yale University Press, New Haven, Conn., 1941.

12. Hall, C. and Lindzey, G. *Theories of Personality.* Wiley, New York, 1957.

13. Dizmang, L. Loss, Bereavement and Depression in Childhood. *Int. Psychiat. Clin.* 6:175, 1969.

14. Mowrer, O. H. A Stimulus-Response Analysis of Anxiety and its Role as a Reinforcing Agent. *Psychol. Rev.* 46:553, 1939.

15. _____ . Anxiety Reduction and Learning. *J. Exp. Psychol.* 27:497, 1940.

16. Voeks, V. What Fixes the Correct Response? *Psychol. Rev.* 52:49, 1945.

17. Freud, S. Mourning and Melancholia. In *Collected Papers,* Vol. IV. Hogarth Press, London, 1948.

18. Fenichel, O. *The Psychoanalytic Theory of Neurosis.* Norton, New York, 1945.

19. Abraham, K. Notes on the Psychoanalytic Investigation and Treatment of Manic-Depressive Insanity and Allied Conditions. In *Selected Papers on Psychoanalysis.* Hogarth Press, London, 1927.

20. Horney, K. *Neurosis and Human Growth.* Norton, New York, 1950.

21. Litman, R. Sigmund Freud on Suicide. In *Essays in Self Destruction,* Schneidman, E., Ed. Science House, New York, 1967.

22. Durkheim, E. *Suicide: A Study in Sociology.* Free Press, Glencoe, Ill. 1951.

23. Beall, L. The Dynamics of Suicide: A Review of the Literature, 1897–1965. *Bulletin of Suicidology,* National Clearinghouse for Mental Health Information, Washington, D.C., March 1969.

24. Shneidman, E. and Farberow, N. The Logic of Suicide. In *Clues to Suicide,* Shneidman, E. and Farberow, N., Eds. McGraw-Hill, New York, 1957.

25. Farber, M. L. *Theory of Suicide.* Funk & Wagnalls, New York, 1968.

26. Hendin, H. *Suicide in Scandinavia.* Grune & Stratton, New York, 1964.

27. Madill, M., Campbell, D., Laverty, S., Sanderson, R., and Vanderwater, S. Aversion Treatment of Alcoholics by Succinylcholine Induced Apneic Paralysis. *Quart. J. Stud. Alcohol.* 27:483, 1966.

28. Frick, J. An Exploratory Study of the Effect of Punishment upon Stuttering Behavior. Doctoral Dissertation, University of Iowa, 1951.

29. Sheehan, J. The Experimental Modification of Stuttering Through Non-Reinforcement. *J. Abnorm. Soc. Psychol.* 46:51, 1951.

30. Van Riper, C. *Speech Correction: Principles and Methods.* Prentice-Hall, New York, 1947.

31. Grimaldi, K. and Lichtenstein, E. Hot Smoky Air as an Aversion Stimulus in the Treatment of Smoking. *Behav. Res. Ther.* 7:275, 1969.

32. Hull, C. *Principles of Behavior.* Appleton-Century, New York, 1943.

33. Spence, K. W. Theoretical Interpretations of Learning. In *Comparative Psychology,* Stone, C. P., Ed. Prentice-Hall, New York, 1951.

34. Stampfl, T. and Levis, D. Implosive Therapy—A Behavioral Therapy? *Behav. Res. Ther.* 6:31, 1968.

35. Frederick, C. and Resnick, H. L. P. Interventions with Suicidal Patients. *J. Contemp. Psychother.* 2:103, 1970.

36. Wolpe, J. *Psychotherapy by Reciprocal Inhibition.* Stanford University Press, Stanford, 1958.

37. D'Alessio, G. The Concurrent use of Behavior Modification and Psychotherapy. *Psychotherapy* 5:154, 1968.

38. Keller, F. and Schoenfeld, W. *Principles of Psychology.* Appleton-Century-Crofts, New York, 1950.

39. Hilgard, E. and Marquis, D. *Conditioning and Learning.* Appleton-Century, 1940.

40. Bandura, A. *Principles of Behavior Modification.* Holt, Rinehart & Winston, New York, 1969.

41. Krasner, L. and Ullman, L. P. *Research in Behavior Modification.* Holt, Rinehart & Winston, New York, 1965.

42. Lovaas, C. I., Freitag, G. Gold, V. G., and Kassorla, I. C. Experimental Studies in Childhood Schizophrenia: I. Analysis of Self-Destructive Behavior. *J. Exp. Child Psychol.* 2:67, 1965.

43. Bandura, A. and Walters, R. *Social Learning and Personality Development.* Holt, Rinehart & Winston, New York, 1963.

44. Skinner, B. F. *Science and Human Behavior.* Macmillan, New York, 1953.

# 3 The Prediction of Suicide

## George E. Murphy, M.D.

*Efforts to develop patient profiles predicting future suicide fall prey to an inexorable constraint in the statistical properties of rare events: they identify unacceptably large numbers of false positives. Clinical recognition of persons at increased risk of suicide is nevertheless feasible. Through appropriate diagnosis and treatment, suicide prevention is possible.*

If, by prediction, we mean the identification of persons who at some time in the future will commit suicide, the problem is largely a statistical one and its difficulties are immense. But if, by prediction, we mean the identification of persons who are at immediate or near-term risk of suicide, the focus is clinical, and the problems are different. In order to understand these problems, it will be necessary first to review certain general aspects of case identification or clinical prediction.

## THE RARE EVENT

For purposes of treatment, clinicians are interested in identifying a particular kind of case amidst a background of many other kinds of cases as well as non-cases. Ideally, they would identify all cases of a certain kind without misidentifying others at the same time. The ideal is rarely approached for a variety of reasons, not alone the discriminating ability of the test employed. The accuracy of a test used in the identification of persons at risk has two components: sensitivity and specificity. The proportion of all cases of a condition that is detected by a test is the *sensitivity* of the test. If it is positive 9 times out of 10 in the presence of the condition, it is 90 percent sensitive. A sensitive test is positive in the presence of the condition tested for (1). It is also desirable that a test be negative in the absence of the condition. The proportion of cases correctly identified as negative is the test's *specificity*. If it misidentifies only one true negative in 100 unaffected cases it is 99 percent specific. But the satisfactoriness of a test is not solely dependent on the levels of sensitivity and specificity. The relative frequency of the condition under investigation is also important.

As case frequency diminishes, prediction suffers because of the decreasing statistical probability of any case being positive. Since there are no perfect tests, there will always be false positives as well as false negatives. If the base rate—the frequency of cases in the population—is quite low, a test that is better than 99 percent specific (false positive rate < 1 percent) will identify formidable *numbers* of patients falsely.

**Impact on Case Identification**

Galen and Gambino (1) have discussed lucidly the problem of clinical prediction of a diagnosis or an event in the face of a very low base rate. They cite in illustration of this problem the case of phenylketonuria (PKU). This disease has an incidence of between 5 and 10/100,000 live births, not far from the annual incidence of suicide in the U.S. By setting the acceptance level of urine phenylalinine at 6 mg/dl, 100 percent sensitivity can be achieved. At that point the specificity of the test is 99.95 percent. But at that level, 83 percent of the babies identified as positive will *not* have PKU! Setting the cutting point at 20 mg/dl gives a specificity of 99.99 percent, nearly eliminating false positives. This setting, however, would actually miss more than 20 percent of PKU babies, an undesirable false negative rate. This extreme result of 83 percent of cases being false positives when sensitivity is set at 100 percent is owed in part to the fact that every newborn is required to be screened for PKU. Thus, the number of babies screened is huge, while the number of cases of PKU is very small. Even though only one baby in 20,000 was misclassified, this amounted to 83 false positives for every 17 cases of PKU actually found!

## Enriching the Base Rate

In the case of a problem such as suicide, there is no thought of screening the entire population. Only those patients coming to medical attention will be screened. For that population the base rate for suicide should be substantially higher than the current general population rate of 12/100,000 live population/year. In the hope of improving risk assessment for clinical intervention, two large-scale prospective studies of suicide have been carried out. Both took advantage of the already known fact that most suicides are psychiatrically ill by starting with persons admitted to psychiatric inpatient units. This was a logical strategy to enrich the base rate for suicide by studying populations of persons at greater than normal suicide risk. By using a prospective model it was possible to gather psychosocial and clinical data first hand rather than having to rely on outside observers as retrospective studies of suicide are forced to do. Clues were sought among clinical, historical and descriptive variables that were later examined for possible correlation with and ability to predict subsequent suicide. It was hoped that knowledge of outcome could guide the selection of predictors.

Pokorny (2) studied 4,800 patients consecutively admitted to the psychiatric inpatient services of the Houston, Texas Veterans' Administration Hospital. He employed a set of rating instruments that included most of the items shown in earlier studies to have a greater than chance correlation with suicide. An *a priori* prediction of high risk was made on the basis of conventional risk-related items such as suicide attempt or threat. Patients so characterized (about 15 percent of the sample) were studied more intensively. All patients were followed up four to six years later (mean, five years) to determine outcome. Sixty-seven of the probands were found to have committed suicide.

Calculations of suicide rates for the sample yielded the following: for the hospitalized group as a whole, 279/100,000 persons per year, about 12 times the expected rate for veterans and 23 times the general population rate; for the *a priori* high-risk group, 747/100,000 persons per year, about 32 times the rate for veterans; for affective disorder, 695/100,000; for schizophrenia, 456/100,000; and for alcoholism 187/100,000. The figures are approximations, since the size of the various groups ranged from slightly over 500 with affective disorder to 1600 diagnosed as suffering from alcoholism. Large as the sample is, the basis for calculation is far from 100,000 persons. Patients with the *a priori* characterization of high risk had nearly triple the rate of suicide found in the entire series of hospital admissions.

## Clinical Dimensions as Predictors

Predictably, no feature of the patients studied distinguished suicides from nonsuicides. Computer-assisted search generated several factors correlating more highly with suicide than with nonsuicide. Almost a third of 281 individual items and factors or summary scores correlated significantly with subsequent suicide or suicide attempt. A stepwise discriminant analysis was used to select weighted combinations of variables that it was hoped would predict suicide. The computer was then given the patient-by-patient raw data and asked to use the discriminant functions to make that prediction.

First, the computer was allowed to assume that the frequencies of suicide and nonsuicide were equal in the population sample. Under these circumstances, sensitivity of the test was 55 percent and specificity was 26 percent; seventy-four percent of patients were classified correctly. Slightly more than half of the suicides were identified correctly, but there were 1200 false positive predictions. When the computer was instructed as to the actual probabilities, the known base rate of each outcome, it classified 98.6 percent of cases correctly (specificity was now 99.99 percent). Yet it was unable with these data to predict even one suicide! When applied to the high-risk subgroup with a rate of 747/100,000 persons, correct instruction as to base rates again led to a prediction of no suicides.

Discriminant analysis was unequal to the task. Both for the high-risk group and for the patients as a whole, the simple prediction of "no suicides" would have yielded a higher numerical rate of correct prediction than the computer was able to accomplish using all that clinical data. To apprehend the magnitude of the prediction problem, bear in mind that prediction was made on the same population from which the predictors were extracted. It could only be worse, with another, similar population. Obviously, this is unsatisfactory.

**Clinical Models as Predictors**

Motto (3, 4) took a different approach to the problem of forecasting suicide. Bypassing conventional clinical diagnosis, he proposed that "certain kinds of people constitute clinical models in that they tend to respond to a given constellation of stresses in a similar way with regard to suicidal behavior." His data base was 3,006 persons admitted to a psychiatric inpatient unit because of a depressive or suicidal state. The patients were interviewed extensively and 186 items of psychosocial behavior were gathered and entered into a computer. Two thousand nine hundred and fifty-three patients were followed up after two years to determine who had committed suicide. Before searching for patterns among the suicides, Motto took a courageous step. He divided his population into an index sample and a replication sample. This allowed him to extract predictor models from his first sample and to try them for predictive power on the second.

Using suicide as the outcome variable, Motto's computer chose the variables showing the most significant associations with this outcome. Then stepwise linear discriminant analysis selected the best predicting variables. Three models have been reported: one is a subjectively diagnosed group of alcohol abusers (criteria for the diagnosis are unstated). The others are characterized as "males under forty" and "stable with forced change." The prediction sets for two of these models performed expectedly less well on the replication set of subjects, but the deterioration was not as striking as might be expected for the "stable with forced change" model.

## Limitations of the Computer

What was interesting was the difference between how a computer thinks and how a clinician thinks. In concert with Pokorny's expectations, one factor common to all three models was the seriousness of suicide attempt or ideation at the time of index admission. It was important in one model but not in the others that the attempter actively sought help after the act. Being either a high-level executive or semiskilled worker was predictive in two of the models, leaving white-collar workers unaccounted for. Severe physical problems were predictive in one model, while in another it was safer to be either well or seriously ill, as opposed to having a minor impairment that was getting worse. Stresses, reactions to stresses (e.g., suicide attempt) and personal behavior (e.g., unfriendly to examiner) were all included in each list of predictor variables. They clearly depend on a computer assist, as many items were quite restricted; e.g., "severe stress, other" (presumably other than interpersonal or job loss). No single predictor was as prevalent as 14 percent in these specially selected suicide models. The highest sensitivity achieved in an index subsample was 93 percent, with an 82 percent specificity. In the validation set, the greatest sensitivity was 64 percent with 66 percent specificity. These values are far too low to possess utility for predicting suicide in a clinical population.

To be sure, Motto does point out that the purpose of the exercise was to identify persons at increased risk of suicide, rather than to predict suicide. But two of his three clinical models are fundamentally nonclinical. In addition to the problem of large numbers of false positives, they raise the question of what one is to do with such persons when clinical diagnosis is ignored.

These undertakings are interesting, and what both Pokorny (2) and Motto (3, 4) have demonstrated is the insuperability of the problem of long-range suicide prediction, given the low base rate. The problem does not lie so much in the inadequacy of the data base or its analysis, as in the characteristics of infrequent events (1). Prediction in the first sense, of suicide at some future time, is not merely difficult but rather clearly out of the question. In any case, information that a person is likely at some uncertain future time to take his/her life, would be of little help in deciding what to do now. Another approach is called for.

## THE CLINICIAN'S TASK

### Clinical Risk Assessment

As Pokorny (2) points out, the identification and treatment of the suicidal patient in clinical practice consists of a sequence of small decisions. The first decision might be based on some alerting sign or clinical configuration, and the decision would be to investigate further. After further investigation, one might stop, if no additional alerting or confirming indicator were found. Or one might decide to explore the situation even further; perhaps to hospitalize, for example. "In each case, the decision is not what to do for all time, but rather what to do next, for the near future." (2) In the clinical context, then, the problem of false positives is not what it is in the laboratory. The decisions made are investigation and treatment decisions, involving much more than the issue of suicide. There is the continuing opportunity for feedback, and thus for modification of risk assessment and intervention.

Retrospective studies of suicide have the supposed disadvantage of relying on secondary informants. But structured interviews with family members and others following suicide allow reconstruction of the terminal clinical status and of life changes close to the suicide. In this sense they are more immediate than anterospective studies. They tell less about the former life of the suicide, but much more about the circumstances antecedent to the event. Five independently conducted systematic studies in four different countries have conclusively shown that not only are nearly all suicides clinically ill, but also they are recognizably psychiatrically ill in the period just prior to self-destruction (5–9). They show that depressive illness is found in around half, alcoholism in about a fourth, and schizophrenia in three (5) to twelve percent (6) of unselected cases. They show where the risk is greatest. Clinical diagnosis is a robust alerting note.

Such studies have further shown that persons with a history of depression are nearly all, if not all in a depressive episode when they commit suicide (5, 8, 10). They are at little risk of suicide between episodes, so periods of risk are finite. By contrast, alcoholism is a chronic disorder, with suicide risk increasing as time goes on (5). Loss of a close interpersonal relationship marks a period of heightened risk. It has been shown to closely precede suicide in upwards of a third of alcoholics (11, 12). If a similar association occurs in ex-alcoholics, it has not yet been documented. It seems clear that effective treatment of these underlying disorders is the best suicide prevention available. One cannot say at this time that there is an effective treatment for schizophrenia.

The clinician as well as the researcher, must be concerned with false positives. He must consider the potential harm of his interventions. If our procedures for suicide prevention are very intrusive (such as involuntary hospitalization or ECT) and the only target is suicide prevention, they might be difficult to justify. But is suicide prevention the only target? Unless suicide-prevention efforts include the remediation of the underlying condition, a suicide aborted may or may not be a suicide prevented. The psychopathological foundation for the suicide would still be intact.

### Are We Preventing Suicides?

How do we know that we are not actually preventing suicides? Perhaps our concern about prediction stems from our failure to prevent *all* suicides. Many psychiatrists know the frustration of losing a patient to suicide despite their best efforts. More physicians know the dismay of learning of a suicide that was unexpected. Several studies show that many of these patients have been undiagnosed or underdiagnosed and, therefore, undertreated (7, 8, 10).

While inadequate diagnosis and treatment is the hallmark of suicides under the care of physicians, these are the cases that have fallen through the diagnostic net. It is likely that many more suicidal patients are recognized and successfully treated. How do we know this? Half of the suicides are among depressed persons, as a number of studies show (5, 7–9). A majority had been either undiagnosed, untreated or both (7, 9, 10). We know that depression is one of the most frequent conditions encountered in clinical practice. The huge numbers of antidepressant prescriptions written annually tells us of the growing recognition of clinical depression. In addition, there has been psychotherapy. In these days of "brand name" treatments, much of it might be considered "generic." But it embodies significant elements of hope and of human caring, elements that are by no means made obsolete by medication or electricity. Some patients must have received adequate treatment for their depression, or at least had hope sustained while the depression resolved.

Granted that not every depressed patient is suicidal, a majority have thought of suicide. The idea does not grow from its conception to fruition in a day. It develops, evolves, waxes and wanes. When the depression is substantially relieved the thought of suicide goes underground, not to return until depression returns. Early treatment will often forestall the development of the suicidal urge. Further, if the patient is recognized as severely depressed and suicidal, the physician will exert every effort to keep the patient out of harm's way and to treat the depression as well. Primary prevention occurs both at the level of removing a substrate of suicidal thinking and at the level of direct interruption of the developed thought. If it is successful, the patient will live. A suicide will have been prevented. Yet to quantify this effect is impossible. It is important to realize that *the absence of a suicide generates no data.* Thus, we can never prove what has been accomplished. Yet we can hardly doubt that it occurs.

This argument would be more satisfying if there had been a gradual reduction in the national suicide rate since studies of the late 1950's clearly linked suicide to psychiatric illness or if it had paralleled the growing use of antidepressants. It might then be concluded that physicians had learned from these studies and were more alert to the indicators of risk, or at least that they were recognizing and treating more depressions. In fact, the suicide rate has risen during that period of time. But it has not done so uniformly. It has actually fallen among the older age groups, those most likely to see a physician. It has risen most—and considerably—among adolescents and young adults. Evidence that is fragmentary at present suggests that this group is far less likely to have been under a physician's care. Thus, the opportunity to treat may not have occurred in many of these cases. It must also be said that neither the clinical characteristics nor other possible alerting features of this young suicide population have yet been demonstrated to be the same as for older groups.

## The Detection of Prevention

The argument that declining suicide rates in the 40-and-over age group reflects greater treatment efforts is not a totally persuasive one, since suicide rates have been known to fluctuate over long periods of time without obvious cause. Changes have occurred both according to age and according to sex, as well as more globally. That may be the case now. But the huge excess of treated depressions over suicides must mean something, and that something generates no data. The overall lack of reduction in the suicide rate shows that there is much to do. At the same time, consider that however difficult suicide is to *prevent*, suicide *prevention* is more difficult to *detect*.

Suppose that we could greatly improve detection and prevention. What would we have to do to prove it? Assume that of the 27,000 suicides in 1982, half, or 13,500, consulted a physician. Assume that half of them, 6,750, were clinically depressed. Assume that we correctly diagnosed 80 percent of them (5400) rather than the present 20 percent. Assume that we could improve our treatment success rate for depression from around 50 percent to 90 percent. Since all of the suicides represent failure of diagnosis or treatment failure (not necessarily failure to treat), this would represent a salvage rate of 40 percent (90 percent-50 percent) at best, of the 5400 diagnosed suicidal depressives, or 2160 suicides. That number prevented would produce an 8 percent reduction in suicides overall. If it were to happen all at once, and in conjunction with a known breakthrough in both diagnosis and treatment, it might be noticeable. Occurring over a period of several years, it would be viewed as a secular trend of familiar magnitude. Suicide prevention efforts would be unlikely to get the credit.

For the present we know that the risk of suicide lies chiefly in two clinical conditions. We know that these occasion much suffering and that they merit vigorous treatment even in the absence of suicidal intent. We know that we can ask about such thinking and that we can sometimes intervene still more vigorously. But we will rarely have the luxury of knowing that our efforts actually prevented a suicide. The statistical constraints of the prediction of infrequent events prevent it.

## SUMMARY

Methods for selecting those persons in a clinical population who will later commit suicide inevitably include large numbers of false positives—persons with similar characteristics who will not take their lives. This is true because of the absence of unique predictors and the statistical properties of infrequent events. At a clinical level, the focus is on risk detection rather than on specific behavior prediction. Since suicide is intimately related to certain psychiatric illnesses, effective treatment of those illnesses can prevent suicides. This must already be taking place. Prevention, however, generates no data. If suicide is difficult to predict, its prevention is even more difficult to detect.

## REFERENCES

1. Galen, R. S., and Gambino, S. R. *Beyond Normality. The Predictive Value and Efficiency of Medical Diagnoses.* John Wiley and Sons, New York, 1975.
2. Pokorny, A. D. Prediction of Suicide in Psychiatric Patients. *Arch. Gen. Psychiatry,* 40:249–257, 1983.

3. Motto, J. A. The Psychopathology of Suicide: A Clinical Model Approach. *Am. J. Psychiatry* 136:516–520, 1979.

4. _____ . Suicide Risk Factors in Alcohol Abuse. *Suicide Life Threat Behav.* 10:230–238, 1980.

5. Robins, E., Murphy, G. E., Wilkinson, R. H., Jr., et al. Some Clinical Considerations in the Prevention of Suicide Based on a Study of 134 Successful Suicides. *Am. J. Public Health* 49:888–899, 1959.

6. Dorpat, T. L., and Ripley, H. S. A Study of Suicide in the Seattle Area. *Compr. Psychiatry* 1:349–359, 1960.

7. Barraclough, B., Bunch, J., Nelson, B. and Sainsbury, P. A Hundred Cases of Suicide: Clinical Aspects. *Br. J. Psychiatry* 125:355–373, 1974.

8. Beskow, J. Suicide and Mental Disorder in Swedish Men. *Acta Psychiatr. Scand.* [Suppl] 277:1–138, 1979.

9. Chynoweth, R., Tonge, J. I., and Armstrong, J. Suicide in Brisbane–A Retrospective Psychosocial Study. *Aust. NZ J. Psychiatry* 14:37–45, 1980.

10. Murphy, G. E. The Physician's Responsibility for Suicide, II. Errors of Omission. *Ann. Intern. Med.* 82:305–309, 1975.

11. Murphy, G. E., and Robins, E. Social Factors in Suicide. *JAMA* 199:303–308, 1967.

12. Murphy, G. E., Armstrong, J. W., Jr., Hermele, S. L., et al. Suicide and Alcoholism: Interpersonal Loss Confirmed as a Predictor. *Arch. Gen. Psychiatry* 36:65–69, 1979.

# 4 The Deromanticization of Death

## Edwin S. Shneidman, Ph.D.

One of our basic assumptions is that death is best understood as a complex event with dual aspects: intrapersonal and interpersonal. This paper attempts to explore some ideas relating especially to the *inter*personal aspects of death; what might be termed the social or, more particularly, the dyadic view of death—and the implications of these ideas in the approach to the suicidal person.

During the Spring 1969 semester, I was Visiting Professor in the Harvard Department of Social Relations where I taught a course on the Psychology of Death. During the term, I invited a few colleagues to be guest lecturers in the course.[1] I now wish that I had tendered an invitation to Arnold Toynbee, the distinguished historian and philosopher. His recent book on death (1)—written in his eighties—qualified him completely as an active thanatologist. It is about his personal and moving epilogue to that book that I wish to make most of my comments in this paper.

With some passionate emphasis, Toynbee makes the points that death is essentially a dyadic (namely, a *two*-person) event and that, as such, the survivor's burden is the heavier.

> . . . The spectacle of insanity and senility has always appalled me more than witnessing or hearing of a physical death. But there are two sides to this situation; there is the victim's side, as well as the spectator's; and what is harrowing for the spectator may be alleviating for the victim. . . . This two-sidedness of death is a fundamental feature of death—not only of the premature death of the spirit, but of death at any age and in any form. There are always two parties to a death; the person who dies and the survivors who are bereaved. . . .

> If one truly loves a fellow human being, one ought to wish that as little as possible of the pain of his or her death shall be suffered by him or by her, and that as much of it as possible shall be borne by oneself. One ought to wish this, and one can, perhaps, succeed in willing it with one's mind. But can one genuinely desire it in one's heart? Can one genuinely long to be the survivor at the coming time when death will terminate a companionship without which one's own life would be a burden, not a boon? Is it possible for love to raise human nature to this height of unselfishness? I cannot answer this question for anyone except myself, and, in my own case, before the time comes, I can only guess what my reaction is likely to be. I have already avowed a boastful guess that I shall be able to meet my own death with equanimity. I have now to avow another guess that puts me to shame. I guess that if, one day, I am told by my doctor that I am going to die before my wife, I shall receive the news not only with equanimity but with relief. This relief, if I do feel it, will be involuntary. I shall be ashamed of myself for feeling it, and my relief will, no doubt, be tempered by concern and sorrow for my wife's future after I have been taken from her. All the same, I do guess that, if I am informed that I am going to die before her, a shameful sense of relief will be one element in my reaction.

> My own conclusion is evident. My answer to Saint Paul's question "O death, where is thy sting?" is Saint Paul's own answer: "The sting of death is sin." The sin that I mean is the sin of selfishly failing to wish to survive the death of someone with whose life my own life is bound up. This is selfish because the sting of death is less sharp for the person who dies than it is for the bereaved survivor.

> This is, as I see it, the capital fact about the relation between living and dying. There are two parties to the suffering that death inflicts; and, in the apportionment of this suffering, the survivor takes the brunt.

The students at Harvard provided some empirical data relevant to Toynbee's assertions. Two items from a class questionnaire are related to this topic. One item in the questionnaire was *"If and when you are married, would you prefer to outlive your spouse or would you prefer your spouse to outlive you? Discuss your reasons."* Table 4-1, which reflects the responses of 89 Harvard men and 29 Radcliffe women—mostly single—gives the percentages of preference in relation to one's own and one's (future) spouse's death.

TABLE 4-1
Percentages for Men and Women of Preference
for *Timing* of Own and Spouse's Death

|  | Together | First | Second | Indifferent; Uncertain |
|---|---|---|---|---|
| Men (N = 89) | 12 | 16 | 49 | 22 |
| Women (N = 29) | 24 | 34 | 21 | 21 |

The data of Table 4-1 indicate that more women than men want to die together with their spouses or first, before their spouses; and that more men than women want to die second, after their spouses. This difference is significant at the 0.02 level, that is, this finding could hardly occur by chance. It was clear that the modal male response was to prefer to die second; the modal female response was to prefer to die first. Toynbee's pronouncements, at the age of eighty, seem consistent with the younger Harvard people of the same sex. An appropriate question would be to ask what Mrs. Toynbee would have written on this same topic.

Following are a few sample male responses—in which they state a preference for dying second, namely, they prefer to outlive their wives:

Outlive spouse. No grief to her. Could always choose to follow her in death. (M, 18)

I think I would rather have my spouse die before me because I don't like the idea that something I do (like die) should be a burden on the shoulders of another person. (M, 19)

Here are some sample female responses, in which they prefer to have their husbands outlive them, that is, to die first or to die at the same time:

I think I would probably, selfishly, prefer to die first. I tend to be a rather dependent person and I will probably be very dependent on my husband. In that case, I could be extremely grief stricken at his death, more than I could handle. (F, 18)

I want us to die at exactly the same time. (F, 21)

Ideally, I wish my husband and I would die together, provided that there are no small children involved. (F, 20)

A few of the Harvard and Radcliffe students recognized the essentially romantic flavor of the question and responded to that aspect of it:

I really don't know. I tend to be rather fatalistic about such things. The whole question seems awfully romantic. (M, 18)

I would like to die together with my spouse but that's a little too romantic to be true. (F, 20)

Table 4-2, which presents the percentages of the various reasons given for the timing preference, shows that more women than men mentioned their wish to avoid loneliness or grief (as their reason for their timing choice); that more men than women gave, as their reason, wanting to spare their spouses the anguish of bereavement or feeling more capable of coping with life following the death of the spouse. The

TABLE 4-2
Percentages for Men and Women of *Reasons* for Preference of Timing

|  | Spare the Other Loneliness | Avoid Loneliness | Spare Grief | Avoid Grief | Better Coping Ability |
|---|---|---|---|---|---|
| Men (N = 45) | 4 | 13 | 31 | 4 | 46 |
| Women (N = 15) | 13 | 40 | 20 | 26 | 0 |

eighteen- to twenty-two-year-old Harvard male is, at least in his fantasy, protective of his spouse. In summary: the typical male response was to choose to die after his wife, believing that a widower can do better than a widow; the typical female response was to choose to die first, giving as her reason the desire to avoid the loneliness of widowhood.

This is a difficult question since both the alternatives are pretty bad. I *think* that I would prefer to outlive my spouse: (a) I think that an adjustment of this sort is more difficult than dying (that is, learning to live without a loved person whom you have lived with so long) and would prefer to take the burden upon myself; (b) I believe that a woman has a harder time after her husband's death than a man does after his wife's death. He has a job to bury himself in while a woman often has no comparable consuming commitment other than family. (M, 19)

I want to die first because I don't want to be lonely. I can't imagine surviving the grief I would have for my husband. Men are strong and less emotional. (F, 19)

Another item in the questionnaire read: *"Rank the following statements about the consequences of your own death from 1 to 7, where 1 indicates the least distasteful and 7 the most distasteful."* Table 4-3 presents the mean, mode, and rank order of the seven items for males and females. What is to be noted is although items 1, 2, 3, and 5 were ranked identically for the two sexes, the item "I could no longer care for my dependents" is ranked as third most distasteful by the males (after "I could no longer have any experiences" and "My death would cause grief to my relatives and friends") and was ranked as fifth most distasteful by the females. This result is consistent with the previous item and Toynbee's assertion about males in relation to death in a dyadic relationship.

Harvard undergraduate males are, compared with Radcliffe females, far more (at the 0.01 level of significance) sympathetic to Toynbee's assertion that "the sting of death is less sharp for the person who dies than it is for the bereaved." Males, far more than females, expressed the wish to spare their spouses the difficulty, anguish, and grief of loss and bereavement and so, by Toynbee's criteria, would seem more truly to love their

TABLE 4-3
Ranking of Consequences of Death

| | Male | | | Female | | |
|---|---|---|---|---|---|---|
| | Mean | Mode | Order | Mean | Mode | Order |
| I could no longer have any experiences | 4.8 | 7 | 1 | 5.7 | 7 | 1 |
| I am uncertain as to what might happen to my body after death | 2.8 | 1 | 7 | 2.0 | 1 | 7 |
| I am uncertain as to what might happen to me if there is a life after death | 3.7 | 2 | 6 | 2.5 | 2 | 6 |
| I could no longer care for my dependents | 4.5 | 5 | 3 | 4.2 | 5 | 5 |
| My death would cause grief to my relatives and friends | 4.6 | 5 | 2 | 4.8 | 4 | 2 |
| All my plans and projects would come to an end | 4.2 | 4 | 4 | 4.4 | 6 | 3 |
| The process of dying might be painful | 4.1 | 4 | 5 | 4.3 | 3 | 4 |

potential spouses. Perhaps this is a reflection of a psychologic set on the part of the males relating to their protective masculine role in the marriage.

> I am married and I think I know my wife well enough to know how she'd react. I'd be much more durable I think, which is to say she is more dependent. So I would prefer to outlive her. I just hate the idea of her grieving. That is one of my greatest fears about death. (M, 22)

In focusing on the importance of the dyadic relationship in death, Toynbee renders a great conceptual service to all those concerned with death, particularly with suicide. Suicide is typically an intensely dyadic event. In suicide prevention, the crucial role of the "significant other" in the total rescuing process is only now being appreciated. Indeed, much of what is new in suicide intervention is precisely the techniques which focus on the active involvement of the significant dyadic partner: the spouse, parent, sibling, or lover. Nor does it appear different in questions relating to death in general:

This is a difficult question for me since I have had very few really close relationships which could approximate the type a marriage would be. At this time in my life I have two very close friends, both girls, and I know I would be terribly upset if either were to die tomorrow, but I would be able to continue living. I have never had a heterosexual affair and the only real lasting homosexual affair I've had would have affected me in approximately the same way if the other had died. The question of "outliving" implies for me that both are in an old age, when the problem would be greater than if both were middle-aged or young. With the latter, another mate could be found or one could at least still have many years of productivity to look forward to; with the former (old age) neither of these alternatives would be possible and I'm sure whoever dies first would be the luckier of the two. (M, 20)

Although it is difficult to take a stance counter to Toynbee's persuasive position, nevertheless I believe that in emphasizing the dyadic aspect of death he seems to have jumped from a sentimental attitude of burden-sharing in a love relationship — the noble husband's wish to save his beloved wife from the anguish of bereavement over his death, to bear it on his own shoulders by living beyond her — to an unnecessarily romantic view of death itself. In cases of absolutely sudden and precipitous deaths, all of the total sum of dyadic pain is borne by the survivor (inasmuch as the victim has no opportunity to experience any of it); but in protracted dying, as occurs in most cases, the present pain and anguish involved in the frightening and lugubrious anticipations of being dead may well be sharper for the dying person than the pain suffered then and afterwards by the survivor. The algebra of death's suffering is a complicated equation.

I am occasionally bothered by dreams or imaginings of the death of a loved one and, of course, these thoughts are very upsetting. The idea of living after someone you love dies is disturbing. I have trouble imagining myself living after my parents die, but I know I will. Similarly, it is difficult to see myself continuing to live after a man I'd lived with for perhaps 50 years was gone, but, then again, I would be able to, even though it's momentarily inconceivable. Whether I want to die first or have him die first is a difficult question. It's similar to whether it's worse to be hurt by someone or to have to hurt someone. Both alternatives are disturbing, but they involve different problems, emotions, different sorrows. Assuming that I had a good marriage, that both my husband and I would be very lost without the other, I guess I'd want to die first to avoid having to live without him. But by that time I might be so devoted to him that my selfish interests would be overpowered by my concern for him and I would rather be the one to have to live alone, rather than have him suffer. All this is, of course, assuming that we are both very old and near death anyway. I haven't really answered the question, I can't, I just don't know. Whenever you love someone there's a conflict between your selfish interests and the other person's happiness. (F, 18)

I would prefer that we die together but on the other hand I believe that I will outlive my husband. This has been the pattern of my family. I would accept that as the better alternative. My mother's mother was a great comfort to her children after her husband's death. She is a strong woman and has led an active life (member of various organizations and much travel) in the last 20 years since my grandfather's death. I would hope that if the need arose I could be like her. Neither do I eliminate the possibility of remarriage. My father's mother, on the other hand, seemed to lose her purpose for living when her husband died, especially since her children were grown. She lived with our family and I felt she was somewhat of a burden. I do not want to finish my life in that way. (F, 18)

*If* I got married, and my husband and I loved each other dearly and lived more or less happily, *then* I would *want* to die first, because it would be hard living without him (and I don't like pain), but I would *choose* to outlive him, so that he would not have the pain to bear—*unless* I felt that he were less in love with me than I with him, in which case he would not suffer so much, then I would choose to die first. And then there are other conditions, such as which of us is the stronger, and which of us would want to go on living just for the sake of life itself (not me, because for me life depends on the people who are in it; but maybe for him it would be different). Such hypothetical questions are damn difficult. (F, 21)

For all his wisdom, I believe that Toynbee is indulging unduly in what I would call the romanticization of death. In my view, the larger need is to *deromanticize* death and suicide.

Certainly one of the most remarkable characteristics of man's psychologic life is the undiluted and enduring love-affair that each of us has with his own consciousness. Trapped, as he is, within his own mind, man nurtures his conscious awareness, accepts it as the criterion for mediating reality, and entertains a faithful life-long dialogue with it—even (or especially) when he "loses his mind" or "takes leave of his senses." Often, man communicates with his mind as though it were a separate disembodied "other," whereas it is really himself with whom he is constantly in communication. Indeed, the self-other to whom he talks is what, in large part, he defines himself to be. In light of all this, the great threat of death is that, like a cruel stepmother shouting at the excited children near the end of a full day's adventure, it orders a stop to this fascinating conversation-within-the-self. Death peremptorily decrees an abrupt, unwelcome and final adjournment and dissolution of what Henry Murray has aptly called "the Congress of the mind." Death—being dead—is total cessation, personal naughtment, individual annihilation. Should one traffic with one's greatest mortal enemy, rationalize its supposed noble and saving qualities and then romanticize it as an indispensible part of dyadic life?

One main difficulty with death is that, within himself, each man is noble—indestructible and all-surviving. One can, as Eldridge Cleaver has in his own naked way put his "soul on ice" or, at the other thermal extreme, one can bank the fires of his own passions (as does Narcissus in Hesse's *Narcissus and Goldmund*), but, for a number of known and mysterious reasons, it is next to impossible to defect from one's loyalty to his own consciousness. Being conscious is all one has. That is what one's life is. Consciousness defines the dimensions of life: its duration (how long) and its scope (its richness or aridity, the latter relating to "partial death" which can occur long before death itself).[2]

Psychologically, our current attitudes toward death are unconscionably sentimental. The several notions of "heroic death," of "generativity" and of a "wise death" in mature old age, are culture-laden rationalizations—as though the cerebrator could ever be truly equanimous about the threat of his own naughtment or annihilation.

Although there are undoubtedly special circumstances in

---

[2]For more on the notion of "partial death" see my paper "The Deaths of Herman Melville" (2).

which some individuals either welcome (seek, pursue, initiate, or effect) their own cessation—or circumstances in which they are essentially indifferent to whether or not their cessation occurs—for most individuals, at any specific time in their lives, the heightened probability of their own cessation constitutes the most dire possible threat imaginable. By and large, *the* most distressing contemplation one can have is of his own cessation. Much of religion and perhaps all of man's concern with immortality (or his "post-self") are tied to this specter. "In a certain sense," writes Ernest Cassirer (3) "the whole of mythical thought may be interpreted as a constant and obstinate negation of the phenomenon of death." It is not enough simply to say, as do Draper and others (4) that "each man dies in a notably personal way"; as does Herman Feifel (5): "A man's birth is an uncontrolled event in his life, but the manner of his departure from life bears a definite relation to his philosophy of life and death." Nowhere is a man more characteristic of himself than in his dying. It is not even enough to say, as Professor Abraham Kaplan of Michigan has told me, that dying is the one act that man does not have to "do"—"it will be done for him." Rather, we must face the fact that completed dying (that is, death or cessation) is the one uncharacteristic act in which the typical individual is forced to engage.

In this context, the word "forced" has a special meaning. It implies that a characteristic of death—similar to a characteristic of torture, rape, kidnap, lobotomy, degradation ceremonies—is its quality of *impressment*. The threat of being naughted, of being annihilated, of being reduced to nothingness can only be viewed reasonably as the terrifying epitome of duress, the strongest and most perfidious of forced punishments.

With his own special crafty perspicacity, Tolstoy, in *Anna Karenina*, compares life to the flame of an occult candle which, once extinguished, no longer exists. As Anna, crushed by the wheels of the train under which she has thrown herself, loses consciousness, Tolstoy mystically writes: "And the candle by whose light she had read the book of life, full of conflict, treachery, sadness and horror, flared up more brightly than ever, lighting all the pages that had remained in darkness before, and then sputtered, flickered and went out forever."

In all this I do not believe that I am really saying what Dylan Thomas meant in his "Do not go gentle into that good night. Rage, rage against the dying of the light." Rather, I am saying that one should know that cessation is the curse to end all curses, and *then* one can, as he chooses, rage, fight, temporize, bargain, compromise, comply, acquiesce, surrender, welcome, or even embrace death—but at least one should be aware of the dictum; Know thine enemy.

Death is not a tender retirement such as a bright autumnal end—"as a shock of corn to his season"—of man's cycle. That notion, it seems to me, is of the same order of courtly rationalization as would be romanticizing the kidnapping and impressment of young sailors or the assault upon unwilling victims of rape.

Nor even, I think, does it meaningfully mollify the arcane terror of death to discuss it in the honorific and beguiling terms of maturity, post-narcissistic love, or ego-integrity, even though one can only be grateful to Erikson (6) for the almost perfectly persuasive way in which he has done so. How ennobling and nearly worthwhile he makes a "generatic"[3] death sound:

> Only he who in some way has taken care of things and people and has adapted himself to the triumphs and disappointments adherent to being, by necessity, the originator of others and the generator of things and ideas—only he may gradually grow the fruit of these seven stages. I know no better word for it than ego integrity. . . . It is a post-narcissistic love of the human ego—not the self—as an experience that conveys some world order and spiritual sense, no matter how dearly paid for.

What is implied by this is that the gracious acceptance of death is clearly the "in" thing for a hep oldster to do. I wonder. I wonder too if this attitude could not usefully be distinguished from understanding "generativity"—the unselfish interest in

---

[3]In another context (7), I have divided suicidal acts into three types: *egotic* (in which the suicide is primarily the outcome of an intrapsychic debate), *dyadic* (in which the death relates primarily to deep unfulfilled needs and wishes pertaining to a significant other) and *ageneratic* (in which the self-inflicted death relates primarily to the individual's falling out of the procession of generations, having lost any investment in his own "post-self").

the forthcoming generations—as reflecting a realistic sense of pride and gratitude in one's progenitors and perhaps reflecting an even greater sense of pride and faith in one's progeny; and, in all this, seeing oneself as only one step in a long march of generations—without the necessity illogically to derive any pleasure from the reflection of one's own finiteness and the prospect of his too-early demise. There is (or ought to be) a reasonable difference between experiencing justifiable pride in what one has been and is and has created, on the one hand, and, on the other hand, feeling an unwarranted equanimity when one reflects that he will soon no longer be. Maturity and ego integrity relate to the former; the latter is supported largely by romantic, sentimental rationalizations that one's cessation is a blessing. Such a rationalization is no less than psychologically willing the biologically obligatory. While accepting this fact, it may be more "mature" to bemoan and regret it, as we bemoan and regret most "endings" in our lives—divorce, loss of a limb, the deaths of others, and so on. What is the appropriate mourning for one's own aging? What is the appropriate *preliminary* grief-work for one's own omnipresently impending death?

For one thing, all this means that death is a topic for the tough and the bitter—people like Melville (in *The Lightning-Rod Man*): "Think of being a heap of charred offal, like a haltered horse burned in his stall; and all in one flash!" Or Camus (in *The Stranger*), especially Meursault's strange burst of anti-theistic and anti-death rage just before the end. Or Percy Bridgman (8): "There are certain kinks in our thinking which are of such universal occurrence as to constitute essential limitations. Thus the urge to think of my own death as some form of my experience is almost irresistible. However, it requires only to be said for me to admit that my own death cannot be form of experience, for if I could still experience, then by definition it would not be death." Or Charles Sanders Peirce (9): "We start then with nothing, pure zero. But this is not the nothing of negation. For *not* means *other than*, and *other* is merely a synonym of the ordinal numeral *second*. As such it implies a first; while the present pure zero is prior to every first. The nothing of negation is the nothing of death, which also comes *second to*, or after, everything." These name but a few of the candid unromantics on this theme.

A brief "cross-cultural" note: When I was in some dozen parts of Japan a few years ago, it seemed to me that the most pervasive religio-cultural feature of the country was the romantically tinged *animism* which infused the religious thinking of Japan—not a more primitive feeling surely, but rather a more personal, spirited, animated feeling about, especially, nature. For example, the Japanese feeling about Mt. Fujiyama, Kegon Falls, Lake Chuzengi (the latter two well-known sites of many suicides), or a cherry tree in its ephemerally beautiful bloom seemed totally different from the feelings which an average American could muster looking at—I would need to avoid the word "contemplating"—Mt. McKinley, Niagara Falls, Oregon's Crater Lake, or a blossoming apple tree in Yakima Valley. The Japanese closeness to nature, a reverential closeness almost akin to deification, leads, it seems to me, to a special Japanese feeling in relation to death—what I would have to call a romanticization of death.

From a number of different sources, I was told about a particularly famous suicide in Japan (which had occurred well over a half century before) of a young man named Misao Fijimura who committed suicide in 1903 at the age of twenty-five by throwing himself over the Kegon Falls, after he had carved his suicide note on a nearby cypress tree. The note is hardly what one would choose to term a typical note from an American suicidal twenty-five-year-old. At Lake Chuzengi, some friends translated the note for me as follows: "Feelings on top of the cliff, Kegon Falls: The world is too wide and history is too long to be evaluated by such a tiny being as a five foot creature. . . . The true nature of all being is beyond understanding. I have made up my mind to die with this problem. Now at the top of the cliff I feel no anxiety. . . ."

On another occasion, when I addressed a group of Japanese university students as they sat attentively in their uniforms, one youth, after the lecture was over, stood up and asked if I could give him any reason why he should not kill himself if he sincerely believed that by doing so he would then become one with nature. The very quality of this question (asked some 65 years after the date of the note of Misao Fijimura) illustrates this animizing and romanticization of death. Further, I recall a young student who sat next to me on the new Tokaido train— as we sped along between Tokyo and Kyoto at 150 kilometers per hour—and, in the almost perfect English he had learned in Japan, wrote out for me: "Cherry blossoms is blooming quickly and scattering at once. Better to come to fruition and die like the blossom." He added: "We have had many great men among our forefathers whose deeds remind us of the noble characteristics of cherry blossoms."

Are there any possible applications of these thoughts about the deromanticization of death to the practical arena of reducing the excessive number of homicidal and suicidal deaths? In this country, the romanticization of certain types of homicide is an especially proud part of our national heritage and culture. The honorifics go to the man with the gun. Our televersion of both the peace-officer and the killer of the West (who are not mutually exclusive) teaches us that the guy who wears the gun gets the girl. We have glamorized our rural bandits and our urban gangsters. The more villainous are somehow the more interesting. The romanticized myth of the Western frontier, built around the image of the man with a gun, has set its necessarily homicidal stamp on our culture. The key problem for television may not be that of the effects of violence but that of the effects of the romanticization of violence.

This romanticization of death goes to the beginnings of our national history. In our monuments to our revolutionary heroes we depict them as citizens with rifles—as though it were primarily guns that had won the war. Harvard Professor Bernard Bailyn (10) persuasively argues, on the basis of his intensive study of pamphlets relating to the American Revolution, "that intellectual developments in the decade before Independence led to a radical idealization and conceptualization of the previous century and a half of American experience, and that it was this intimate relationship between Revolutionary thought and the circumstances of life in eighteenth-century America that endowed the Revolution with its peculiar force and made it so profoundly a transforming event" (p. vii). Consider this letter from John Adams to

Hezekiah Niles in 1818, quoted by Professor Bailyn (p. 160): "But what do we mean by the American Revolution? Do we mean the American War? The Revolution was effected before the war commenced. The Revolution was in the minds and hearts of the people; a change in their sentiments, of their duties and obligations. . . . This radical change in the principles, opinions and affections of the people was the real American Revolution."

Perhaps more appropriate monuments, at the Lexington common and the Concord bridge—and is it not curious that "Concord" has become, for us, the symbol of armed dissent?— might have been statues of Paine and Jefferson, seated, with pens. Unquestionably, these representations would have served to imply quite different values and might have subtly shaped our culture in somewhat different directions. Our recent inability to amend our gun laws in the wake of a series of catastrophic assassinations has been a national disaster and an international grisly joke, highlighting our irrational tie to our own essentially anti-intellectual legends of romanticizable homicide.

Our romanticization of killing in peacetime and of being killed in wartime—see, for example, the descriptions of the recipients of the Congressional Medal of Honor (11)—is only one of the tragic paradoxes that results from our anachronistic and outmoded values. Metaphorically speaking, the current romanticization of killing and being killed are tides that need to be damned; netherlands that need to be reclaimed from seas of inappropriate affect.

Romantic notions of death are also obviously not unrelated to suicide. Individuals who are actively suicidal suffer—among their other burdens (and especially the burden of unbearable anguish)—from a temporary loss of this unromanticized view of death-as-enemy. This is the paradox and major logical fallacy of self-inflicted death. It capitulates to the decapitor. Thanatologist Jacques Choron (12) has described certain notions of death which he calls "suicide promoting" and others which he deems to be "suicide inhibiting." Further, he has suggested that therapists routinely conduct "an inquiry into a suicidal person's notions about and attitudes towards death." I would believe that overly romanticized notions of death are, in general, more suicide promoting than otherwise.

Suicidal folk have lost sight of the foe: they openly sail with full lights in the hostile night; they smoke and show themselves on combat patrol. They are unvigilant and forgetful. They behave in strange, almost traitorous and defecting ways. Whose side are they on? They attempt to rationalize death's supposed lofty qualities and, what is most difficult to deal with, to romanticize death as the noblest part of dyadic love. Loyal people (that is, loyal-to-life people) are inured against nefarious propaganda leading to defection. One should not traffic with the enemy. Suicidal individuals have been brainwashed—and by their own thoughts.

This seduction and beguilement has been described by Melville in *Moby Dick* in a passage that is concerned not with actual death or overt suicide but with the temporary and partial death of being buried alive in a life at sea:

> . . . to the death-longing eyes of such men, who still have left in them some interior compunctions against suicide, does the all-contributed and all-receptive ocean alluringly spread forth his whole plain of unimaginable, taking terrors, and wonderful, new-life adventures; and from the hearts of infinite Pacifics, the thousand mermaids sing to them—"Come hither, brokenhearted; here is another life without the guilt of intermediate death; here are wonders supernatural, without dying for them. Come hither! Bury yourself in a life which, to your new equally abhorred and abhorring landed world, is more oblivious than death.

What is the practicality of these ideas on the deromanticization of death for helping suicidal persons, especially among the young? For example, would it be salutary or beneficial to embark on programs of deromanticizing death in our schools—courses in "death education"—or in our public media? In the treatment of the acutely suicidal person, what would the effects be of directing his ambivalent mind's attention to a view of death-as-enemy? Would such a psychologic regimen have deleterious effects—hastening a suicide—or no effects at all, permitting the suicide, in some course of time, to occur? Youth, incurably romantic itself, requires, for its own life's sake, this deromanticization of death. But in my own mind, the nagging question persists: would not this type of effort, like practically every other earnest exhortium in this alienated age, itself be doomed to an untimely figurative death?

## REFERENCES

1. Toynbee, A., and others. *Man's Concern with Death*. McGraw-Hill, New York, 1968.

2. Shneidman, E. S. The Deaths of Herman Melville. In *Melville and Hawthorne in the Berkshires*, Vincent, H. R., Ed. Kent State University Press, Kent, 1968.

3. Cassirer, E. *An Essay on Man*. Yale University Press, New Haven, 1944, p. 84.

4. Draper, G., Dupertuis, C. W., and Caughley, J. L. *Human Constitution in Clinical Medicine*. Hoeber, New York, 1944, p. 74.

5. Feifel, H. *The Meaning of Death*. McGraw-Hill, New York, 1959, p. 128.

6. Erikson, E. *Childhood and Society*. Norton, New York, 1950, p. 231.

7. Schneidman, E. S. Classifications of Suicidal Phenonema. *Bull. Suicidology* July, 1968, pp. 1–9.

8. Bridgman, P. *The Intelligent Individual and Society*. Macmillan, New York, 1938, p. 168.

9. Peirce, C. S. *Collected Papers*, Vol. VI, 1931–1958. Harvard University Press, Cambridge, p. 148.

10. Bailyn, B. *The Ideological Origins of the American Revolution*. Belknap Press, Cambridge, 1967, p. 160.

11. *Congressional Medal of Honor*. U.S. Government Printing Office, Washington, D.C., August, 1943.

12. Choron, J. Mortality and Death. In *On the Nature of Suicide*, Shneidman, E. S., Ed. Jossey-Bass, San Francisco, 1969, p. 34.

# 5 The Third Wish

Harry S. Olin, M.D.

*A hypothesis is proposed that the nonpsychotic patient in the presuicidal state may have impaired reality testing in which the act of suicide is perceived as not leading to injury or death. Impaired reality testing may be enhanced by intense affects, drugs, and sleep deprivation.*

In 1933, Karl Menninger in his classic paper, *Psychoanalytic Aspects of Suicide*, (1) stated that two wishes can be observed in the suicidal person, the wishes to kill and to be killed. The third element of suicide was an inference, the wish to die. Regarding this wish, he said, "One gets the impression that for such people the suicidal act is sometimes a kind of insincere play-acting and that their capacity for dealing with reality is so poorly developed that they proceed as if they could actually kill themselves and not die." Menninger further commented that this wish may have had its origin in childhood when the child acts as if death were reversible. Trautman (2) has described a type of suicidal attempt, the "suicidal fit," as a sudden impulsive act during which the person did not think rationally and behaved as if in a "trance."

The purpose of this paper is to propose a hypothesis which is an elaboration of the third element in Menninger's triad and Trautman's "suicidal fit."

## HYPOTHESIS

It is posited that the nonpsychotic patient in the immediate presuicidal state may suffer from impaired reality testing in which the consequences of the planned suicide are distorted and minimized. Suicide then becomes a means of dying without terminal death.

The patient in the presuicidal state is in a state of emotional conflict generally marked by intense affects of depression, hopelessness, helplessness, frustration, guilt, and anger. Intense affects can promote ego regression in which reality testing can be diminished. The ego functions that maintain contact with reality may be subject to other influences, causing additional impairment. For example, insomnia leading to sleep deprivation, often a concomitant of depression, may contribute to impaired ego functioning. In some cases psychomimetics, drug reactions, or drug withdrawal can cause impaired reality testing. The presence or ease of regression and impairment are related to the individual's personality structure.

Therefore, that state of regression leading to decreased reality testing in the patient who "premeditates" or "impulsively" attempts suicide consists of the following factors:

1. The conflict leading to a state of intense affects.
2. The possible presence of and effects of:
   a. Sleep deprivation
   b. Drugs or drug related states.


## CASE EXAMPLES

"Evidence" for this hypothesis is suggested both from information gained from the patient and therapist in the following two clinical vignettes:

### Case 1

A twenty-year-old man half-heartedly pursued his professional training career in which he felt increasing competition with his highly successful father whom he both feared and admired. Although he had begun psychotherapy, he felt powerless to counter his mounting paralyzing anxiety and insomnia. He was on the verge of flunking law school. Walking to his psychotherapy appointment early one morning, he felt particularly beset with seemingly unsolvable problems. He crossed over a bridge and looked down into the deep water which in the past he had found a relaxing sight. However, this time, feeling so alone in the world, he was seized with the impulse to jump into the inviting river waters and quietly put an end to his troubles by a prolonged sleep. In another moment or two, he had crossed the bridge and continued on his way to his appointment, but he tucked away the comforting image of the beckoning waters in the back of his mind.

During the psychotherapy session, the patient related his specific suicidal thoughts as a "solution" to his problems. The therapist listened calmly and replied that, "such a solution would be so final." The patient's perception of the "inviting waters" changed. His conflict, based on entering the profession of his competitive, ungiving lawyer-father, seemed a difficult one, but solvable by means other than "so final" a solution as death. The therapist's comment, focusing on death as irreversible, stripped the solution of fantasy and thus illuminated the conflict between son and father for further examination.

At no time was this patient considered psychotic. The therapist in this case needed only to remind him of the consequences of his fantasied solution and the transient impairment in reality testing was decreased. In the following weeks, the waters became wet, cold, and uninviting.

## Case 2

A twenty-four-year-old borderline man, talented in scientific studies, was unable to complete his college work. He had keenly felt his family's high expectations of him, but had secretly rejected these expectations. He wanted to succeed, but detested doing so only to please his parents. He searched for something that was his and found little solace in just doing well. Consequently, his college career was a checkered one, marked by flunks and leaves of absence. Frequently he thought about suicide, and then with his family's support he had started in psychotherapy.

In spite of therapy as the semester went along, he began to recognize the familiar signs of his not working effectively in class; and he became driven in his efforts to gain stability and meaning in his increasingly fragmented life. He began to obsessively keep track of the time spent in various activities and wrote notes to himself with admonishments to be more efficient. He smoked marijuana and several times had tried small amounts of LSD to help him to concentrate. He attempted to have sexual intercourse but was rebuffed by the woman. His sleeping habits were affected by his restless, agitated state and for about two weeks he slept poorly, often only three to five hours a night.

One morning prior to his psychotherapy session he briefly placed his head in the kitchen oven and then superficially scratched his wrists. He mentioned these attempts to his therapist who asked him if he had "gotten all of the suicide attempts out of your system." The patient replied that he had, and then nothing more was said about his attempts. After his therapy hour, he wandered about in the snowy streets and thought about suicide. He walked to the midpoint of a bridge and looked down at the frozen river. He imagined that were he to jump he could easily break through the thick ice and drown. He jumped, fell thirty feet, and landed on very thick, very solid ice which did not crack. Immediately he felt severe back pain and crawled under the bridge "to die." After about ten minutes, the cold and pain were so uncomfortable that he crawled from under the bridge, shouted for help, and was taken to a hospital where multiple vertebral fractures and avulsion of nerve roots were diagnosed. What surprised this science student in retrospect was his misperception that he would suffer no harm from falling on the frozen river.

## Case 3

A woman jumped off a bridge 150 feet to the water below and sustained multiple fractures plus serious visceral trauma. She was given lifesaving surgical care and then after three months of painful recuperation was transferred to the psychiatric ward where she remained three more months. On her first arranged leave of absence from the hospital, she jumped off the same bridge at the same location and died. This case is included as a reminder that some patients despite intervention are intent on committing suicide.

## COMMENT

The therapist treating the suicidal patient is faced with the immediate clinical task of assessing the risk of suicide. How likely is the risk for this person? Is patient-therapist alliance strong enough to allow outpatient treatment? What are the immediate precipitants?

Earlier studies (3, 4) have helped to define statistical profiles of suicidal populations by studying such items as age, sex, race, psychosis, marital status, history of broken home, and so on. More recently, in addition to the generally recognized risk factors, Beck and Kovacs (5) have directed attention to the suicidal state *per se* and have pointed out hopelessness as an important predictor of suicide with implications for treatment. General outlines of treating the suicidal patient are covered in standard psychiatric texts.

The hypothesis advanced here is that in the presuicidal state there is ego regression with decreased reality testing of the effects of a suicide attempt. I have never encountered a nonpsychotic patient who related after a suicidal attempt that in the presuicidal state death was directly perceived as a reversible condition. Yet, the sleep frequently desired by the suicidal patient, as in Case 1, suggests that there is to be an awakening at a later time. In a regressed state, it would be likely that the reality of injury or death is submerged by the fantasy of death—the suicidal person entertains a wish to die, or in Trautman's (2) terms, seeks "emotional death." Such a defect in reality testing would seem intimately related to rescue fantasies often described in suicide attempters (6). Wahl's (7) description of suicide as "a magical act, actuated to achieve irrational delusional, and illusory ends" is in my opinion correct. I would add though that if the person's reality testing is impaired, then the distinction between magic and reality becomes difficult and suicide may become more probable.

The man's suicide attempt in Case 2 would seem to suggest a defect in reality testing in both his crucial misperception of the thickness of the ice and the effect of jumping on thick ice. A "soft landing" was implied, as opposed to permanent bodily injuries. His unsettled family conflict, school troubles, drugs, sleep deprivation, and psychotherapeutic management of his presuicidal state would all seem to have contributed to this suicide attempt. As Menninger (1) stated, "the paradox that one who has wished to kill himself does not wish to die" was reflected in the effects of a hard landing, pain, and cold that improved reality testing to the point where he called for help. My point, again, is that the wish to die is more acceptable to the individual if in the presuicidal state the death attempt is perceived as not leading to dying.

The patient in Case 3 demonstrated that despite months of painful reality experience with the effects of a fall—and it is hard to imagine a more severe teacher—she killed herself.

## TREATMENT IMPLICATIONS

If this hypothesis has some merit for some suicidal patients, then the following can be considered in the therapeutic approach for such patients.

First, what degree of ego regression does the patient show? How intense are the affects, for example, hopelessness, helplessness, depression? Are there present the regression-enhancing factors of sleep deprivation and/or drug effects?

Second, does the regressed patient show evidence of impaired reality testing regarding the consequences of any planned suicidal action? What did the patient think would happen to him after taking the suicidal action? Of course, retrospective investigation has been one of the major difficulties in suicide research. Usually the postsuicidal individual, now thinking logically, strongly tends to reject primary process presuicidal thoughts. However, hints can be gained. The TAT by providing the "convenient fiction" of talking about the individual in the picture is probably underutilized.

Third, therapeutic intervention, be it hospitalization or outpatient psychotherapy, drugs, or ECT, can be more sharply focused on the impaired reality testing.

The acute versus the chronic suicidal patient is an important distinction to make. I would suggest that the therapist treating any patient threatening suicide assess the patient as outlined above. But for the patient chronically threatening suicide, the impaired reality testing is more likely to be in the area of avoiding responsibility for his life with the expectation that the therapist will be responsible for him (8).

Taking poetic license, I am reminded of the contrast suggested by Dorothy Parker's life and poetry. This is the contrast between primary and secondary process. The primary process thought, the wish to die without death, is contained in Robert Benchley's quip when he said after a recent Dorothy Parker suicide attempt, that if she committed suicide much more, she would make herself sick. Secondary process thinking, the acknowledgement of the consequences of lethal behavior is in Dorothy Parker's poem "Resume":[1]

> Razors pain you;
> Rivers are damp;
> Acids stain you;
> and Drugs cause cramp.
> Guns aren't lawful;
> Nooses give;
> Gas smells awful;
> You might as well live.

## SUMMARY

Menninger's formulation of suicidal motivation has been expanded by an elaboration of his third element, the wish to die. The hypothesis is offered that the presuicidal patient may suffer from an impairment of reality testing in which suicide is not thought of as lethal. Suicide then becomes dying without death. The emotional crisis present in the presuicidal state, plus the possible effects of sleep deprivation and drugs can lead to ego regression in which primary process thinking can influence the person's concept of suicide, for example, injuries

---

[1]From *The Portable Dorothy Parker.* Copyright 1926, 1954 by Dorothy Parker. Reprinted by permission of The Viking Press.

are not realistically considered or death becomes reversible. Brief case examples are given which partially illustrate the hypothesis, and its clinical use are suggested.

## REFERENCES

1. Menninger, K. A. Psychoanalytic Aspects of Suicide. *Int. J. Psychoanal.* 14:376, 1933.

2. Trautman, E. C. The Suicidal Fit. *Arch. Gen. Psychiatry* 5:76, 1961.

3. Tuckman, J. and Youngman, W. F. Suicide Risk Among Persons Attempting Suicide. *Public Health Rep.* 78:585, 1983.

4. Bagley, C. and Grier, S. Clinical and Social Predictors of Repeated Attempted Suicide; a Multivariate Analysis. *Brit. J. Psychiatry* 119:515, 1971.

5. Beck, A. T. and Kovacs, M. Hopelessness and Suicidal Behavior: An Overview. *JAMA* 234:1146, 1975.

6. Jensen, V. W. and Petty, T. A. The Fantasy of Being Rescued in Suicide. *Psychoanal. Q.* 27:327, 1958.

7. Wahl, C. W. Suicide as a Magical Act. *Bull. of the Menninger Clin.* 21:91, 1957.

8. Olin, H. S. Psychotherapy of the Chronically Suicidal Patient. *Am. J. Psychother.* 30:570, 1976.

# 6 Rational Suicide

## Karolynn Siegel, Ph.D.

*In recent years a more permissive attitude has emerged concerning the choice of suicide as an alternative to some life situations. This trend is examined with particular focus on increased public acceptance of the notion of "rational suicide." The position of rational-suicide proponents is critically examined in light of existing clinical and research data.*

Suicide has been a subject of philosophical discourse since the inception of Greek philosophy and over the centuries has been a topic of sustained interest among anthropologists, sociologists, psychiatrists, theologicans, and statesmen. Furthermore, Western cultures have always sought to discourage suicide through the imposition of negative social sanctions. These have included assigning disgrace to the reputation of the deceased, mutilating or dismembering the corpse, denial of a Christian burial, confiscation of the suicide's estate, excommunication, and fines or imprisonment for anyone who survived a suicide attempt (1–3). These historical circumstances constitute persuasive evidence that while suicide is generally regarded as a highly individualistic act, it has important social meanings that transcend the individuals involved.

Originally, the justification offered for these sanctions was either religious (i.e., suicide was an interference with the work of Providence or a rejection of God's gift and thus sinful) or civil (i.e., suicide constituted a reneging by the individual of his obligation to the state). However, as society became more secularized and enlightened the grounds for suicide intervention gradually shifted. Over time, the suicidal individual came to be judged as temporarily insane. As such, he constituted a danger to himself and was regarded as more appropriately the object of concern and caring than of blame and punishment. It was reasoned that if the wish to suicide was an expression of mental illness, society had a moral obligation to interfere with the individual's attempt to end his life.

But, whether the grounds offered for suicide-prevention efforts were religious, civil or medical is less important than the posture toward suicide that they signified. They reflected a consensus that a high suicide rate was somehow inimical to society's collective interests. Despite this, current social policies providing for detention and involuntary commitment to avert a suicide have been increasingly contested over the past two decades (4). The most vociferous opposition has come from those who regard any unsolicited interference with a suicide attempt as an infringement of fundamental liberties. In the view of these civil libertarians, such assistance undermines personal autonomy and self-determination.

The purpose of this paper is to examine recent trends in social attitudes toward suicide with particular focus on increased public acceptance of the notion of rational suicide. This concept is examined in light of existing clinical and research evidence.

**Changing Public Opinion**

In recent years a trend toward greater public discussion of suicide as an acceptable option to certain life circumstances has emerged. An organization called Hemlock has been established to promote wider acceptance of the practice of rational suicide. Another, called Concern for Dying, has furnished thousands of individuals with copies of the "Living Will," a document which permits them to designate when, in the case of a serious illness, they would wish medical intervention to cease. A Society for the Right to Die lobbies for state legislation to safeguard the individual's right to refuse extraordinary life-preserving measures. Others have proposed schemes for regulating the act, presumably in an attempt to remove the stigma of suicide and diminish the fear of death (5). And a leading thanatologist contends that within a few years suicide may become the culturally preferred mode of death (6). Collectively, these activities and ideas constitute what has been labeled the "Rational Suicide" or "Right-to-Suicide" movement.

Perhaps the most important factor underlying changing attitudes toward suicide has been the development of life-support technology which enables physicians to extend the survival of critically ill patients, beyond the point where the conditions for a meaningful life exist. The prospect of someday being indefinitely sustained in a vegetative state is a particularly disturbing one for many people. It is largely in reaction to this technological prolongation of life (or, as some would say, of death) that many individuals have become supporters of the concept of the "right-to-die" and by extension, the "right-to-suicide." For once one accepts the principle that there are conditions under which it may be preferable not to sustain life, the idea of suicide must inevitably be viewed with more tolerance.

Technological advances have brought about another condition which is likely to promote a more permissive social climate for suicide. As Wood (7) has discussed, part of our aversion to suicide derives from its repudiation of a "natural death" which we seem to believe is somehow imbued with an appropriateness, a timeliness and an assured dignity. A natural death confers a seal of rightness on the time of death that suicide does not possess. However, Wood argues that the notion of a "natural death" is becoming more obscured as the time of death is with increasing frequency being determined by human decisions. As the distinction between a natural death and a planned death becomes less meaningful some of the traditional antipathy toward suicide may be expected to abate.

Life-support technology has also raised difficult ethical issues concerning death and dying which have created a resurgence of interest in suicide as a philosophical issue. The ascendancy of the philosophical perspective on the problem of suicide, over the psychiatric and sociological perspectives which have guided clinical practice and public policy for the past several decades, has facilitated acceptance of the rational suicide position. For it is undoubtedly easier to persuade others of the inherent logic of that viewpoint when it is presented in abstract concepts that permit them to avoid considering the pattern of self-destructive behavior and impoverished interpersonal relationships frequently characterizing the lives of those who choose suicide. As Maris (8) has stated, "the worlds of the philosopher of suicide and the healer of self-destructive individuals are vastly different." There is, he notes, little concordance between the rational, neatly ordered world of philosophy and the chaotic, disorganized world of actual suicides.

In addition, as religiosity has declined the deterring influence of religious proscriptions against suicide has waned. People's actions are less constrained by religious teachings concerning immorality and sin, causing these historical controls on suicide to lose force.

## RATIONAL SUICIDE

The defining characteristics of a rational suicide are: (a) the individual possesses a realistic assessment of his situation, (b) the mental processes leading to his decision to commit suicide are unimpaired by psychological illness or severe emotional distress, and (c) the motivational basis of his decision would be understandable to the majority of uninvolved observers from his community or social group.

Supporters of rational suicide have consistently offered the incurably ill cancer patient in the advanced stage of his disease and suffering from intractable pain as the paradigmatic case on which their position rests. This case is well chosen and lends considerable persuasive force to their argument; for the ravages of the disease and the harrowing side effects of treatment are so much a part of the popular image of cancer that most would agree it is rational for an individual with painful terminal illness to refuse heroic life-saving measures or more actively plan to end his life. In fact, public acceptance of suicide under such conditions has been growing. Between 1977 and 1983 the percentage of adults in the United States who reported that they held the opinion that "a person has a right to end his or her own life if he/she has an incurable disease" increased from 39 percent to almost 50 percent (9).

However, as Ringel (10) has pointed out such "understandable" cases account for only a very small percentage of all suicides. He notes that with few exceptions, the situations of most suicides are in no way helpless, or frequently even critical.

Nevertheless, once having established the principle of the right of self-termination, some rational suicide proponents would extend that right to all individuals who decide their life is not worth living, for whatever reason. Among the groups for whom it has been explicitly argued this right should obtain, are the elderly who "no longer have great desire to live," (11) the incurably mentally ill, (12) and children who decide they will not be able to achieve a life for themselves that would be sufficiently satisfying (5). Rational-suicide advocates also wish to establish legal safeguards to insure that the rights of such individuals to end their lives will be protected from societal interference.

While the argument for rational suicide may appear reasonable, when its elements are examined critically, serious limitations of the position become evident. These are discussed below.

## Cancer and Suicide

While admittedly few empirical research studies exist which examine the relationship between cancer and suicide, and the findings are not consistent, the preponderance of evidence does not suggest that cancer patients are at increased risk for suicide (13). Clinical experience supports the same conclusion. Weisman (14) has observed that there are oncologists who have never known any patient who attempted suicide and contend that the suicide rate among cancer patients is lower than among the general population.

Stengel (15) asserted that those who are impressed by the

apparent compelling logic and reasonableness of the motives for suicide presented in some cases have to account for the absence of suicidal intention in the vast majority of cases suffering comparable or worse misfortunes. That is, if suicide is such an obviously rational alternative to enduring the painful consequences of a disease running its expectably torturous course, why do so few cancer patients attempt or commit suicide? The rarity of suicide among terminally ill cancer patients calls into serious question the assumption implicit in the rational-suicide position that most individuals suffering from such an illness would want to end their lives.

A recent study by Brown et al. provides further grounds for the rejection of this assumption (16). Forty-four terminally ill patients were studied (all but one were diagnosed with neoplastic disease) to determine if they "desired death." Of these, thirty-four had never had suicidal thoughts or wished that death would come early. Only one of this group was suffering from clinical depression. The remaining ten who had desired premature death or had contemplated suicide were all found to be suffering from severe depressive illness. This data suggests that the wish to die among terminally ill patients is not a rational adaptive response, but rather is associated with the presence of an emotional disorder.

The low suicide rates among cancer patients is all the more compelling given that the usual societal proscriptions governing suicidal behavior have been relaxed in the case of the terminally ill. On this basis alone we would expect a significantly higher suicide rate among individuals with neoplasms. That this does not occur suggests that in cases of suicide among this population, the actual physical distress of the illness may be of less significance in determining a suicidal outcome than the basic adaptive pattern of the individual and the responses of those around him.

Available research supports this conclusion. In a study which compared thirty-two terminal cancer patients who committed suicide with a control group who did not commit suicide but died of the disease, Farberow et al. (17) discovered distinctive psychosocial patterns that characterized the suicide group. Among these were: the experiencing of emotional distress over and above the physiologic aspects of the disease; the exhaustion of physical and emotional resources (including a feeling of lack of family or hospital staff support); and a history of prior suicide threats or attempts.

Weisman (14), who has carried out extensive research on cancer patients, contends that the few who do attempt suicide are characterized by a pattern of extreme family strife, alcohol abuse or a paranoid hatred of others. He concludes, "Hopelessness about cancer is never offered as a sufficient reason." There is also clinical evidence that the cancer patient at greatest risk of suicide is generally at a very advanced stage of his illness and is likely to have given previous indications of deficient psychological resources and difficulties in adjusting to his illness (18).

The behavior of significant others toward the cancer patient can also be an important factor in his adjustment to his illness. Weisman (19) has argued that death is an interpersonal crisis which affects the future survivors as well as the dying individual. They often suffer from feelings of anticipatory grief, apprehension, and guilt brought on by a belief that the illness might have been prevented or at least made more comfortable. In response to these feelings, family and friends of the terminally ill patient may start to withdraw from the patient. This social isolation and "emotional quarantine," as Weisman calls it, often leads to secondary suffering for the patient. Such circumstances can create a psychosocial void and contribute to a greater sense of hopelessness and despair in the terminally ill. In light of these observations, it must be considered that the reactions of significant others in the patient's environment can set in motion interpersonal dynamics which themselves engender the conditions associated with suicidal behavior.

### Extension of the Right-to-Suicide

Proponents of rational suicide would not limit the right of self-termination to the incurably ill. They contend that any individual who after thoughtfully assessing his life found it intolerable or without adequate satisfactions to render it meaningful should be permitted to choose suicide as an alternative.

The idea of "Bilanz-Selbstmord" or "balance-suicide" was proposed by Alfred Hoche, the German psychiatrist, at the beginning of the century (20). He used this term to refer to instances where presumably mentally unimpaired individuals take stock of their social and emotional assets and liabilities in life and finding themselves bankrupt and foreseeing no improvement choose to die.

Hoche's concept of a carefully evaluated and reasoned decision to commit suicide points up a number of problems with the rational suicide position. The first is its emphasis on cognition. It is in the realm of emotions – about one's self-worth and one's relationships with significant others – that the urge to suicide originates and must be stemmed. It is through restoring feelings of self-esteem, acceptance, and attachments to others that the clinician seeks to expunge suicidal ideation and behavior.

Second, to the extent that effective unimpaired reasoning is implicit in the notion of a rational suicide, suicidal individuals are generally not capable of such a considered action. Depression rigidifies their thinking and hinders their ability to envision alternatives or make judgments concerning the probable outcomes of different available options. It constricts and narrows their view concerning future possibilities. Their thinking reflects a twisted sense of values and impoverished insight. An objective, rational view of life is rarely present (21-23).

Additionally, as Brandt (22) has pointed out, even when suicidal individuals can be made to acknowledge that their circumstances may improve significantly at some future time, distant events or opportunities tend to exert a small motivational force on present behavior. Current circumstances and options loom large, while future possibilities, far off in time, seem remote and inconsequential. This is similar to the perceptual phenomenon that distant objects appear small.

The point is, we must be careful to not too readily affirm the individual's right-to-suicide or hastily remove the negative social sanctions attached to this act. Many people experience a transitory wish to die in response to a very stressful life event (e.g., the death of a loved one or loss of limb) or a developmental crisis (e.g., the onset of senescence). At the time they evaluate suicide as a reasonable solution to their problem. Fortunately, in the majority of cases these individuals eventually achieve a satisfactory adaptation to their circumstances. Obviously it is impossible to assess the role societal proscriptions play in preventing suicide attempts in such cases. It is, however, likely that they have served to avert some potentially tragic suicides, if only by heightening the individual's ambivalence about ending his life, forestalling action, and allowing him to arrive at a more realistic appraisal of his situation.

At the present time widespread public acceptance of the concept of rational suicide is largely restricted to instances where suicide is chosen as a means to escape extreme pain and suffering. However, Battin (24) points out that recent changes in societal attitudes concerning acceptable grounds for not prolonging life, what some would call passive euthanasia, are likely to foreshadow future extensions in the justifications proposed for rational suicide. Among the reasons already advanced for the withdrawal of treatment of the chronically or terminally ill are: to end or prevent the extreme physical dependence that causes degradation; to prevent the extraordinary financial burdens of long-term care; to spare the family the agony of a protracted death; and to conserve scarce medical resources for more promising cases. Battin (24) notes that while at the present time all proposed justifications for not extending life are limited to medical or quasi-medical situations, there is no reason to assume this will continue to be the case in the future.

### Safeguarding the Right-to-Suicide

Advocates of rational suicide seek both the removal of all social sanctions prohibiting the act and the institution of a law which would protect the individual's right to end his life. They argue that these conditions are necessary to remove the stigma associated with suicide as well as to facilitate the assistance from others (i.e., family, friends, physicians) that the individual wishing to end his life often requires.

Several potential abuses of such a law are obvious. First, once such a right was legally protected the means for successfully completing suicide would inevitably become much more readily obtainable. As a result, many tragic deaths might occur among individuals for whom the suicidal urge was transitory and irrational. Under the present circumstances most such cases would receive no encouragement or assistance in their plans to suicide and would make unsuccessful attempts to end their lives. This is a fortunate situation as the available evidence clearly suggests that a suicide attempt is generally a highly ambivalent action. It has been estimated that attempts outnumber completed suicides by more than 8 to 1, a failure rate supporting the view that most individuals who contemplate suicide are not resolved to die (25). Similarly, studies show that only about 1 to 2 percent of those who survive a suicide attempt go on to kill themselves within one year, the period of greatest suicidal risk (26, 27).

Advocates of the rational suicide position assert that they seek to protect the rights of the terminally ill and the aged to have the option of ending their own lives. The dying and the elderly, however, are among the weakest members of the social structure. Social approval of suicide for these groups could have profound unanticipated consequences. It is not difficult to imagine the right-to-suicide becoming the obligation to suicide. Once taking one's own life becomes an acceptable alternative, how can the terminally ill individual who still finds value and meaning in life elect to refrain from exercising his option if his illness has made him an emotional and financial burden to his family? How could he justify not choosing a socially approved alternative which would end their hardship, especially if they seemed somehow to be communicating he should do so?

If anyone doubts the likelihood that those close to an individual would in any way encourage his suicide, consider this. Although we now regard suicidal individuals as more deserving of treatment than punishment, many states retain statutes making suicide a criminal act, although not punishable. For if an act is not criminal, the courts have reasoned, how can it be a crime to assist in completing the act. These states want it to remain a criminal act to aid and abet a suicide in order to forestall the actions of those who might encourage or instigate a suicide to realize some personal gain. They recognize that because most suicides are ambivalent, active assistance or support might cause many to complete the act who otherwise would not have been able to do so (28).

Battin (24) has also expressed concern about the far-reaching consequences of removing societal proscriptions on suicide. She discusses the seductive qualities of recent shifts in ideology which have expanded the situations under which suicide is judged to be a rational solution to life problems. Battin cautions what while it is possible to maintain the appearance that suicide is a voluntary act, changes in ideology make it easier for people to arrive at the conclusion that suicide is a reasonable alternative. Inevitably, by expanding our definition of what constitutes a rational suicide to include more circumstances, more people will find it difficult to resist considering this option, thus making suicide a more frequent occurrence. She refers to such decisions to end one's life as instances of "manipulated suicide."

Many terminally ill individuals in severe pain make private preparations to end their lives. Freud, who suffered for many years with cancer, arranged with his physician to terminate his life when the distress of his disease prevented him from carrying on his work (29). It does not seem that the individual's or society's interests would be better served by protecting such arrangements through a law. The current policy of tacit acceptance and non-intervention adequately expresses society's attitude on this matter at this time. The formal institutionalization of that position into law could open the door for those who would seek to continually expand the classes of suicides to which society removes negative sanctions, or attaches positive ones, as part of the right of every individual to terminate his own life.

## Other Problems with Rational Suicide

Another problem with the right-to-suicide position, even in some so-called terminal situations, is dramatized by the case of Jo Roman that received public attention several years ago. Ms. Roman, a social worker, who for years had advocated choosing the time of one's own death ended her life by taking a fatal overdose of pills. She was 62 and had been diagnosed with breast cancer approximately fourteen months earlier. At the time of her death the disease had spread to the local lymph nodes, but she was not terminal or in severe pain. In a letter sent to the *New York Times* following her death, she explained that she was carrying out her suicide "more than a decade earlier than planned." She revealed that even before her cancer had been diagnosed, she had intended to end her life around 1992 (at about the age of 75) to avoid the dependency and infirmities of old age. She also left material to be presented as a television documentary on her advocacy of the right of "self-termination."

A book by Roman, published posthumously (5), reveals a lifetime preoccupation with death. As a child, she used to accompany her father, a fundamentalist minister, to funerals. She describes being quite fascinated by the corpses and devising a childhood game of turning them "on and off." Following her first husband's death, when she was 26, she became very depressed, started using Seconal and began contemplating suicide. At this time she also gave her young children to a former college roommate to raise because she wanted to protect them from her "underlying wish to die." The children were eventually legally adopted by this friend and her husband. Roman actually made a rather serious suicide attempt several years later. Describing her feelings just before the attempt, she wrote, "I did not feel depression or desperation or panic," implying that she also regarded that suicide decision as a rational choice. Nevertheless, by her own assessment the years following that unsuccessful attempt were perhaps the most fulfilling, productive, and rewarding ones of her life.

She also explains that it was about 1965 when she first began putting into writing her fantasies about an Exit House, an institute devoted to studying and helping people execute rational suicide. Clearly Roman's engrossment with death, dying and suicide long predated any serious physical illness or approaching senility.

At the time of her death, the media accepted uncritically Roman's contention that her purpose in preparing the documentary and letter for publication in the *Times* was to raise public consciousness of suicide as a nonpathological option to life. A closer examination, however, reveals that she and others like her who insist on their right-to-suicide are in a number of ways psychodynamically quite similar to the vast majority of suicides whose acts are clearly desperate and tragic and receive little media attention.

A preoccupation with killing oneself, even at some future time, is common among suicidal individuals. Many of them derive a feeling of comfort from the knowledge that they will determine the time and circumstances of their death. A sense of controlling exactly how and when they will die appeals to the omnipotent strivings of these individuals (30). As Hendin has observed, the potentially suicidal individual is likely to be someone for whom death is a necessary part of his adaption to life and who is reassured in the knowledge that he can end his life if circumstances seem too difficult (30).

Another quality frequently observed in those who demand their right-to-suicide is an inability to tolerate uncertainty in life, such as is introduced by a serious illness. The need to control death is an effort to deal with the anxiety associated with such uncertainty. Roman wrote that once one decided on a planned death by suicide, "life perspectives clouded by vagaries and fears of open-endedness become crystal clear "(5).

While suicide advocates charge that others are unwilling to enlarge their awareness concerning the "life-enriching value of suicide" (5) because of fears of confronting death, their own need to idealize and transfigure the experience of suicide into a creative act appears to be a defense against underlying feelings of helplessness and dread of death. The emphasis on thought processes seems to also serve a defensive function for rational suicide proponents. In a maneuver akin to the mental mechanism of dissociation, these individuals attempt to detach the idea of death from the underlying painful emotional feelings and affect associated with it.

Rigidity is another trait common among suicidal individuals (31). They often experience difficulty adapting to new demands or reformulating their roles and goals. An unwillingness to accept life on any terms but their own characterizes these individuals. They often set conditions on life: "If you don't save me, I'll die," "If I don't succeed, I'll kill myself," "If you don't love me I won't live" (32). "Why should I have pain. I don't want a day of pain," asserted Roman (33). These individuals often seem conditionally attached to life and willing to continue living only if their conditions are met. As Maris puts it, "Paradoxically much suicide is not the wish-to-die, but rather the wish-to-live in some way that is blocked" (34). Suicide, in his view, is the consequence of not being able to accept and adapt to in a satisfying way the inevitable miseries that are part of the human experience.

Shortly before he committed suicide Ernest Hemingway told his friend and biographer, "Hotch, if I cannot exist on my own terms, then existence is impossible. Do you understand? That is how I lived and that is how I must live" (35).

## CONCLUSION

In recent years society has adopted a more permissive stance concerning suicide as an acceptable option in some life circumstances. Unfortunately, however, "rational suicide" has been becoming a less differentiated concept over time. Not only has there been a tendency toward defining an increasingly diverse range of suicidal acts as rational, but previously distinct concepts of rational suicide and euthanasia are becoming increasingly blurred (36, 37). Because there currently is considerably greater public support for the practice of euthanasia than suicide (9), the loss of a clear distinction between the two concepts may contribute to the perception of greater social acceptance of suicide.

It is not necessary to argue whether rational suicides—in the most restricted use of the term—exist. They do. A recent example is the case of her mother's suicide presented by Betty Rollin in the book, *Last Wish* (38). Rollin's mother was terminally ill with ovarian cancer. She was in chronic pain and had exhausted available therapies. Due to an intestinal blockage she was for a long period of time unable to keep down food or control her bowels. She was confined to her apartment. In apparently full command of her mental facilities, she asked her daughter to assist her in committing what most would agree was a rational suicide.

Such true instances of rational suicide are, however, too rare to justify establishing a law protecting the right to terminate one's own life. While the existence of such a statute would have facilitated Rollin's task of obtaining the information she needed to provide her mother with the means to carry out her suicide, little else would have been gained. Her close friends seemed to understand and support her mother's decision, as well as Rollin's desire to assist her. It now seems clear that no legal action is likely to be taken against Rollin for her assistance in a suicide. In short, society's tolerance of such understandable suicides is adequately expressed in its posture of non-interference and tacit acceptance. The further removal of social proscriptions concerning suicide is only likely to result in more irrational and tragic deaths. It is sufficient to acknowledge in principle that rational suicides exist. To elevate such an acknowledgment to a law does not seem necessary or judicious.

As the societal norms concerning suicide are rendered increasingly ambiguous, an important countervailing force to the suicidal tendencies of a large number of people is weakened. Therefore, it is imperative not to further erode the negative social sanctions attached to suicide. It may, however, be no longer sufficient to arrest the trend toward an increasingly permissive atmosphere concerning suicide. Society must seize every opportunity to unequivocally affirm the value of each human life, even those that may be compromised by illness, disability or in some other way.

Finally, it is important to remember that psychodynamic investigation into the motivations of suicidal individuals reveals that they are not pursuing a predominantly rational act to attain rational ends, even when executed by individuals who appear notably rational. Rather, it is a magical act intended to achieve an irrational, delusional and deceptive end (39, 40). It is also important to recognize that a variety of clinical syndromes, personality traits and social circumstances characterize suicide. It is a symptomatic act and not a discrete psychologic entity. The dynamics leading to such an act are diverse and it is likely that more than one motive is operative in virtually all individuals who kill themselves (41).

## SUMMARY

In recent years a more tolerant attitude has emerged concerning suicide as an acceptable alternative to some life situations. This trend is attributable in large part to the growth of the "Rational Suicide" movement.

Proponents of rational suicide have consistently offered the terminally ill cancer patient in intractable pain as the paradigmatic case on which their position rests. Once having established the principle, however, they would extend the right-to-suicide to any individual who felt his life was not worth living, for any reason. They would also wish to institute a law to protect the individual's right to end his life.

While the basic argument for rational suicide may seem reasonable, serious limitations in the position are demonstrated when it is examined in light of existing clinical and research findings. Unanticipated adverse individual and societal consequences that can result from extending and legally safeguarding the right-to-suicide were reviewed. Evidence was also presented that individuals who contemplate what they regard as a rational suicide may have much in common psychodynamically with the much more numerous suicides that occur each year and which are clearly desperate and tragic acts.

## REFERENCES

1. Diggory, J. C. Suicide and Value. In *Suicidal Behaviors: Diagnosis and Management*, Resnick, H. L. P., Ed. Little Brown and Company, Boston, 1968.

2. Lonsdorf, R. G. Legal Aspects of Suicide. In *Suicidal Behaviors: Diagnosis and Management*, Little Brown and Company, Boston, 1968.

3. Silving, H. Suicide and the Law. In *Clues to Suicide*, Shneidman, E. S. and Farberow, N. L., Eds. McGraw Hill, New York, 1957.

4. Siegel, K. Society, Suicide and Social Policy. *J. Psychiatr. Treatment and Evaluation* 4:473–482, 1982.

5. Roman, J. *Exit House*. Seaview Books, New York, 1980.

6. Kastenbaum, R. Suicide as a Preferred Way of Death. In *Suicidology:*

*Contemporary Developments*, Shneidman, E. S., Ed. Grune and Stratton, New York, 1976.

7. Wood, D. Suicide as Instrument and Expression. In *Suicide: The Philosophical Issues*, Battin, M. P. and May, D. J., Eds. St. Martin's Press, New York, 1980.

8. Maris, R. Suicide: Rights and Rationality. *Suicide Life Threat. Behav.* 13:223–228, 1983.

9. National Opinion Research Center. *General Social Surveys*, National Opinion Research Center, Chicago, Illinois, 1977, 1978, 1982, 1983.

10. Ringel, E. Suicide Prevention and the Value of Human Life. In *Suicide: The Philosophical Issues*, St. Martin's Press, New York, 1980.

11. Barrington, R. M. Apologia for suicide. In *Suicide: The Philosophical Issues*, St. Martin's Press, New York, 1980.

12. Slater, E. Choosing the Time to Die. In *Suicide: The Philosophical Issues*, St. Martin's Press, New York, 1980.

13. Siegel, K. and Tuckel, P. Rational Suicide and the Terminally Ill Cancer Patient. *Omega* 15:263–269, 1984–85.

14. Weisman, A. D. *Coping with Cancer*. McGraw Hill, New York, 1979.

15. Stengel, E. *Suicide and Attempted Suicide*. Penguin Books, Baltimore, 1964.

16. Brown, J. H., et al. Is It Normal for Terminally Ill Patients to Desire Death? *Am. J. Psychiatry* 143:208–211, 1986.

17. Farberow, N. L. et al. Suicide among Patients with Malignant Neoplasms. In *The Psychology of Suicide*. Shneidman, E. S., Farberow, N. L. and Litman, R. E., Eds. Science House, New York, 1970.

18. Holland, J. Psychological Aspects of Cancer. In *Cancer Medicine*. Holland, J. F. and Frei, E., Eds. Lea and Febiger, Philadelphia, 1973.

19. Weisman, A. D. Misgivings and Misconceptions in the Psychiatric Care of Terminal Patients. *Psychiatry* 33:65–81, 1970.

20. Chronon, J. *Suicide*. Charles Scribner's Sons, New York, 1972.

21. Neuringer, C. Rigid Thinking in Suicidal Individuals. *J. Consult. Psychol.* 28:54–58, 1964.

22. Brandt, R. B. The Rationality of Suicide. In *Suicide: The Philosophical Issues*. St. Martin's Press, New York, 1980.

23. Mayo, D. J. Irrational Suicide. In *Suicide: The Philosophical Issues*. St. Martin's Press, New York, 1980.

24. Battin, M. P. Manipulated Suicide. In *Suicide: The Philosophical Issues*. St. Martin's Press, New York, 1980.

25. Pokorny, A. Myths about Suicide. In *Suicidal Behaviors: Diagnosis and Management*. Little Brown and Company, Boston, 1968.

26. Dorpat, T. L. and Ripley, H. S. The Relationship between Attempted Suicide and Committed Suicide. *Compr. Psychiatry* 8:74–79, 1967.

27. Paerregaard, G. Suicide among Attempted Suicide: a Two-year Follow-up. *Suicide Life Threat. Behav.* 5:140–144, 1967.

28. Douglas, J. The Absurd in Suicide. In *On the Nature of Suicide*, Shneidman, E. S., Ed. Jossey Bass, San Francisco, 1969.

29. Schur, M. *Freud: Living and Dying*. International Universities Press, New York, 1972.

30. Hendin, H. *Suicide in America*. W.W. Norton and Company, New York, 1982.

31. Breed, W. Five Components of a Basic Suicide Syndrome. *Suicide Life Threat. Behav.* 2:3–18, 1972.

32. Hendin, H. Suicide: The Psychosocial Dimension. *Suicide Life Threat. Behav.* 8:99–117, 1978.

33. Jacoby, S. *Hers. New York Times*, July 3, 1980, p.C2.

34. Maris, R. Rational Suicide: an Impoverished Transformation. *Suicide Life Threat. Behav.* 12:4–16, 1982.

35. Hotchner, A. E. *Papa Hemingway*. Random House, New York, 1966.

36. Pohlmeier, H. Suicide and Euthanasia: Special Types of Partner Relationships. *Suicide Life Threat Behav.* 15:117–123, 1983.

37. Tonne, H. Suicide: Is It Autoeuthanasia? *Humanist* 39:44–45, 1979.

38. Rollin, B. *Last Wish*. Simon and Schuster, New York, 1985.

39. Wahl, C. W. Suicide as a Magical Act. In *Clues to Suicide*. McGraw Hill, New York, 1957.

40. Meissner, W. W. Psychoanalytic Notes on Suicide. *Int. J. Psychoanal. Psychother.* 6:415–447, 1977.

41. Jackson, D. D. Theories of Suicide. In *Clues to Suicide*. McGraw Hill, New York, 1957.

# 7 Attempted Suicide in Manic-Depressive Disorder

Ngaere Goldring, Ph.D.
Ronald R. Fieve, M.D.

*Self-report of past suicide attempts was studied in 123 affectively ill outpatients. The highest frequency of attempts was found in bipolar women with a history of hospitalization for depression and outpatient treatment for hypomania (BP II), confirming prior studies. The suicide attempters were younger than the nonattempters. Treatment implications of the data were discussed.*

A major American study of completed suicides in the general population conducted by Robins and his colleagues (1) found that 47 percent of those people whose death by suicide they investigated were clinically depressed at the time of their act. Granted that this figure may vary somewhat in different parts of the country or from year to year, it nevertheless represents an enormous number of deaths that are potentially preventable through treatment for depression. Looking at the figure the other way, Guze and Robins (2) judged that about 15 percent of all deaths in manic-depressive patients were due to suicide (i.e. about 30 times more than in the general population). With such statistics in mind, it is not surprising to find that the study of suicidal behaviors in manic-depressive patients has accelerated in proportion to the development of treatments for depression, although firm data on the phenomenology of suicide and attempted suicide in the affectively ill are still sparse.

This paper will discuss available estimates for rates of attempted suicide and completed suicide in carefully diagnosed unipolar and bipolar affective disorder patients. We present data from the outpatient population of the Foundation for Depression and Manic Depression in New York City in an effort to clarify some clinical and psychosocial characteristics of the suicidal patient, particularly with regard to subtype of affective diagnosis. Treatment implications of the findings will then be discussed.

Beyond the statistics just quoted, there are a number of reasons to see primary affective disorder as closely linked to suicidal behaviors. Shneidman (3) has quoted a ratio of eight to one between suicide attempts and completed suicides. While the majority of completed suicides are by men, women more frequently make attempts. Similarly, two to three times more women than men suffer unipolar depression. In bipolar disorders the sex ratio is much smaller, although women still predominate. The periods of greatest risk for unipolar disorder in women are around the ages of 40 to about 55, and again above the age of 65. The age distribution for suicide in women is also bimodal, with peaks at 40 and between 50 and 65. For men, on the other hand, the risk of depression increases directly with age, as does the risk of suicide (4). Among the few direct relationships between depression and sociological variables, it is found that the incidence of depression is somewhat higher in single and divorced individuals, or those without social support (5, 6).

## Suicide in Manic-Depressive Patients

Estimates of the rate of death due to suicide in manic depressives vary greatly and are undoubtedly influenced by factors such as country of origin, the diagnostic criteria used, source of the sample, and so on. Epidemiological studies of communities report on all diagnosable cases, whether or not they were treated for the disorder. Helgason, for example, in his major study of Icelanders, found that 51 percent of manic depressives died by suicide (7). In contrast, Slater (8) obtained a figure of 15 percent. Follow-up studies of hospitalized patients deal with those cases that have at least been exposed to potentially effective treatment, whether or not they continued with it. An example here is the study of Dunner et al. (9) who found that within nine years of discharge from an inpatient unit at the National Institute of Health two of seventy-three unipolar patients, and eight of ninety bipolar patients had committed suicide.

Manic depression is a disorder where treatment may not permanently cure, but can radically change the course of the illness. Reduction in suicide rate is often cited as a striking consequence of the introduction of lithium carbonate. Reviewing three major lithium centers in the United States, including our own at the Foundation for Depression and Manic Depression, Goodwin and Jamison (10) found only four deaths by suicide in the whole group of patients—more than 9000 people—treated over a five-year period. At the Foundation Depression Clinic, from which the present sample was drawn, there have been no suicides in seven years, although we know of deaths by suicide in patients who have left treatment.

Data on self-report of past suicide attempts in manic depressives are available from a number of studies including the Dunner et al. paper, and those of Winokur, Woodruff, Johnson and Hunt, and Stallone et al. (11-14). In this group of similar studies rates of reported attempts in manic-depressive patients range from 20 percent to 56 percent. The previous study by our own research group, Stallone et al. (14), is particularly relevant because it reports data from the Lithium Clinic of the New York State Psychiatric Institute, a sample closely parallel to that of the Foundation.

Some researchers have also reported on the frequency of suicidal ideation in affective-disorder patients. In the Winokur study, for example, 82 percent were found to have thoughts of death or wishes to die. We chose not to include data on suicidal thoughts because we believe they cannot be characterized adequately from responses to a single question. It is an important area, however, and we are developing a more in-depth study on our population at the present time.

## METHOD

Data were collected over a two-year period by interviews at the time of intake on 123 patients at a clinic specializing in the affective disorders (The Foundation for Depression and Manic Depression, New York City). This interview, the Schedule for the Affective Disorders and Schizophrenia (SADS)—Lifetime Version (15), was administered as a matter of policy to all new patients in 1981 and 1982. In 1983 it was used in cases where precise diagnosis was uncertain. Because of the retrospective procedure, it is not possible to state how accurately the resulting sample reflects the overall clinic population. However, the administration of the SADS interview was determined blind to the subject's history of suicide attempts and the rater was unaware of the purposes of the present study. We feel that these data are representative enough to provide meaningful conclusions, particularly since the resulting distribution of diagnostic groups and sex is consistent with estimates of the overall clinic population. The slight predominance of females over males (66 versus 57) is to be expected from a mixed unipolar/bipolar group and the age range was broad: Seventeen to seventy-three years. Thus the sample reflects our clinic population over the last two to three years, including patients seen for consultation, those admitted to treatment but since terminated for any reason, and those remaining in treatment up to the present.

"Attempters" for the purposes of this study were all patients who responded in the affirmative to the SADS question, "Have you ever tried to kill yourself or done anything that could have killed you?" SADS diagnoses were categorized into three bipolar groups and one unipolar group in accordance with the criteria of Fieve and Dunner (16). These criteria are as follows: Bipolar I (BP I)—hospitalized for mania; Bipolar II (BP II)—hospitalized for depression only (outpatient treatment for mania or hypomania); BP O—outpatient treatment for depression or hypomania. Because of the small numbers all unipolar patients were combined into one group regardless of the history of hospitalizations, and patients with diagnoses cyclothymic or depressive personality were not included.

## RESULTS AND DISCUSSION

Table 7-1 presents the initial data. The overall percentage of suicide attempters in this sample was 34 percent, with the females having the higher rate: 39 percent as opposed to 28 percent. These figures are very close to the overall figures reported by Stallone et al. (14) which were 43 percent for females and 26 percent for males. Our data are also in line with those of Dunner et al. (9) at N.I.H. who reported a rate of 32 percent overall in primary-affective patients, but discrepant from Winokur et al.'s (11) finding of 23 percent in an apparently similar sample. The generally higher frequency of attempts in women confirms previous findings and we also concur with Johnson and Hunt (13) in seeing attempt rates in males and females as roughly equal within the BP I group. Johnson and Hunt, however, had a small group of inpatients and considered only suicide attempts leading to treatment. They found an overall attempt rate of 20 percent in these circumstances.

Stallone et al.'s data (14) are the most comparable with the present study. Since both studies used the SADS interview the definition of attempts was identical. The "contemplators" group in the Stallone study was not repeated in our more

TABLE 7-1
Past History of Suicide Attempts
in Primary Affective Disorder Patients

| | BP I | | BP II | | BP O | | UP | | Total | |
|---|---|---|---|---|---|---|---|---|---|---|
| | M | F | M | F | M | F | M | F | $M^a$ | $F^b$ |
| **Attempters** | | | | | | | | | | |
| N | 9 | 15 | 2 | 4 | 1 | 4 | 4 | 3 | 16 | 26 |
| % | 52.9 | 55.6 | 50.0 | 66.7 | 7.1 | 28.6 | 18.2 | 15.8 | 28.1 | 39.4 |
| Average | 54.5 | | 60.0 | | 17.9 | | 17.1 | | 34.1 | |
| **Nonattempters** | | | | | | | | | | |
| N | 8 | 12 | 2 | 2 | 13 | 10 | 18 | 16 | 41 | 40 |
| % | 47.1 | 44.4 | 50.0 | 33.3 | 92.8 | 71.4 | 81.8 | 84.2 | 71.9 | 60.6 |
| Average | 45.5 | | 40.0 | | 82.1 | | 82.9 | | 65.9 | |

(% are column-wise)
$^a x^2 = 10.26$ df $= 3$ p $< 0.05$
$^b x^2 = 9.94$ df $= 3$ p $< 0.05$

recent data collection. The highest suicide-attempt rate in the Stallone data was for BP II patients (51.6 percent in BP II women), just as in the present study, but there are some differences between the two sets of data. They show similar rates for BP and unipolar (UP) groups (35 percent and 35.4 percent respectively), whereas in the present study there was a considerable difference; 42.6 percent for BP versus 17.1 percent for UP patients. Dunner's group found a 44 percent attempt rate among similarly diagnosed bipolar patients and an even lower rate for unipolar patients—9 percent—but their subjects were inpatients at the time of the interview and it is hard to say how much difference that may make.

Some possible explanations for the variations between the Stallone et al. (14) data and our present findings are:

1. The diagnostic criteria were identical but the sample selection was not. The New York State Psychiatric Institute Clinic is part of a state hospital with a catchment area in Upper Manhattan. Patients are treated free. They may have felt some apprehension about admitting suicidal intent or past attempts at a clinic associated with an inpatient facility and so produced an overall suicide-attempt rate lower than that at the Foundation, which is a freestanding outpatient clinic. Since the Foundation charges low fees it attracts patients of a somewhat higher socioeconomic status than does the state clinic and this factor may have directly or indirectly influenced either the rate of suicide attempts or the reporting of them.

2. Our present data were collected at the time of admission to the clinic. Interviews for the Stallone et al. (14) study, however, took place either at intake or during the course of treatment, perhaps some years after admission, so we can suppose that their sample was a rather more stable group, the treatment-resistant cases having had the opportunity to drop out or be admitted to that or another hospital.

3. Despite these factors, another possibility deserves consideration. Stallone et al.'s (14) data were collected in the seventies, ours over the last two and a half years. In the interim there have been notable advances in the identification and treatment of the affective disorders. While the increased success of treatment for depression may have contributed to the apparent

drop in suicide attempts for unipolar patients, the lapse of years between the studies probably showed up a different pattern in the referrals for treatment of bipolar disorder. All psychiatrists and many general practitioners prescribe antidepressants or psychotherapy for depression. During the seventies, however, lithium treatment was largely confined to those psychiatrists or psychopharmacologists who were specially trained in or familiar with the techniques. In recent years the availability of lithium treatment has become more widespread and so referral to a specialist may be made now only when the case is seen as severe or difficult to treat.

The patients in the present sample were on average somewhat younger than Stallone's (mean of roughly 37 years versus 46 years). As noted before, suicide risks for males and females in the general population vary with age. It is unfortunate that we have no direct data on the age of our patients at the time the suicide attempts were made. This is not one of the questions on the SADS protocol from which the data were obtained. Since we did collect data on current age and the age at which patients were first seen for treatment of their disorder we can address the latency from onset of treatment to the time of interview. The mean age for all patients was 36.8 years, with a latency of 11.9 years. Suicide attempters were an average of 33.8 years old at the time of interview, with an average latency from treatment onset of 11.3 years. In other words, suicide attempters were seen at about the same delay after their first professional contact, but the attempters were slightly and significantly younger (mean age of attempters and nonattempters 33.8 and 38.3 years respectively; t = 2.02, p < 0.05). Population statistics usually show that the risk of suicide for men increases with age. If that were so in the manic-depressive population as sampled here there would be a tendency for male attempters to fall within the higher age categories, which would show up as a higher mean age for male attempters. Such was not found and we can therefore add some indirect support for the contention of Johnson and Hunt (13) that the risk of attempted suicide, at least for men, is highest during the early part of the illness course in bipolar patients.

Table 7-2 shows the age-of-onset data for patients by diagnos-

TABLE 7-2
Age of Onset: Attempters and Nonattempters

|  | BP I | BP II | BP O | UP | Total |
|---|---|---|---|---|---|
| **Attempters** |  |  |  |  |  |
| N | 24 | 6 | 5 | 7 | 42 |
| Mean age at first treatment | 22.2 | 28.3 | 20.0 | 20.3 | 22.5 |
| **Nonattempters** |  |  |  |  |  |
| N | 20 | 4 | 23 | 34 | 81 |
| Mean age at first treatment | 24.7 | 28.0 | 26.0 | 27.1 | 26.3 |

tic group and attempt history. There are many possible trends in these data but one observation we thought worthy of note is the apparent tendency for the unipolar patients who have attempted suicide to have a rather earlier age of onset. This is in fact a significant finding ($p < 0.05$) but with $N = 7$ it is very tentative. Furthermore, it emerges here that our unipolar sample may not be entirely typical of the unipolar population at large, since the average age at first treatment is in the twenties. While the years from twenty to thirty are often a peak period for the onset of bipolar disorder, unipolar disorder often does not manifest until later in life. With these considerations in mind we suggest that the age of onset of unipolar depressions be studied further in relation to suicide and suicide attempts because there are indications that unusually early onset may be a risk factor in suicidal behavior.

In discussing these data it should be noted that although the attempted-suicide and completed-suicide populations do over-lap, there are some important distinctions that restrict gener-alization. In predicting characteristics of completed suicides, this study is of limited value since the sample is highly selected in ways we do not fully understand. That is to say, even those with multiple past suicide attempts are still alive. They have also sought treatment, which is another selection factor, and cause and effect are necessarily confounded in its relationship to suicidal behavior and the outcome of suicide attempts. To truly generalize we would also want to know the full treatment history of these patients, their degree of compliance, and the source of the referral. Efficacy of treatment is perhaps particu-larly hard to evaluate. For example, Robins (1) reported that over 70 percent of the completed suicides in this study were by people who had received professional care in the last year of their lives. However expert and appropriate that care it was obviously unsuccessful in one sense at least.

Several authorities have reported that the risk of suicide is higher among those who are single or divorced than in married people. In our data, attempters did not emerge as significantly more often single or divorced than nonattempters. Most of the sample were single people (including divorced, separated, and widowed) with only 23.8 percent of the attempters and 31.1 percent of the nonattempters married. Marital status alone is probably too gross a measure to reflect social adjustment and support structures, and again these data give the status at the time of interview, not at the time of the attempt or attempts.

The last series of measures available from the SADS interview material has to do with the number and nature of attempts. The mean numbers of attempts were 3.9 for males and 2.78 for females. These figures may be slightly distorted because any number of attempts over 8 is coded as 8 on the protocol but the loss of information is slight and no significant difference was found. The most serious attempt reported by the patient is then coded for seriousness, from 1 ("obviously no intent, purely manipulative gesture") to 8 ("extreme—careful planning and every expectation of death"). Lethality refers to the actual outcome of the suicide attempt from 1 ("no danger") to 6 ("extreme, e.g., respiratory arrest or prolonged coma"). We found no significant difference between males and females on these measures, confirming Stallone et al. (14). Mean seriousness for males was 3.00 and for females it was 3.08. Mean lethality for males was 3.81 and for females it was 3.85. These ratings were comparable with those reported by Stallone et al., who used the same scales, but we found somewhat lower ratings of intent and higher ratings of lethality in both sexes than did Stallone et al.

## CONCLUSIONS

It is important to recognize that suicidal behavior is multiply determined and that the present data focus on a single element in the pattern: the psychopathology of the individual seen as a

lifetime diagnosis or predisposition rather than as a characterization of mental status at the time of the act. Durkheim's
famous treatise on suicide (17) amply reviews the sociological
influences on suicide rates. The psychoanalytic writers [Freud
(15); Menninger (19)] developed an understanding of the
antecedents of suicide and the symbolism of self-death. In
another vein, several researchers have reported a higher than
normal frequency of suicide in the close relatives of suicidal
probands [reviewed by Roy (20)] or a similarly high frequency
of suicidal behavior in the families of manic-depressive patients
[e.g., Leonard (21), Pitts and Winokur (22), and Mendlewicz et
al. (23)]. Most recently serotonin metabolism has been implicated in violent acts including suicide (24) and there are
indications that seasonal variations in suicide rates, as in the
onset of affective episodes, may be linked to such biological
factors as pineal function (25). Suicidal behavior must be seen
as representing the final common path of all these factors:
genetic, biological, sociological, inter- and intrapersonal.

Our understanding of suicide in manic depression is in its
infancy. We have yet, for example, to adequately incorporate
what is known of such behaviors as drug and alcohol abuse,
what Menninger called "chronic suicide," into the overall
picture of self-destructive acts. On the clinical or applied level,
there is an urgent need for detailed information on the patient
at risk for suicide. Some general parameters are known: Male
gender, single or divorced status, presence of depression, and
concurrent medical illness, for example. Stallone et al. (14),
using discriminant function analysis, demonstrated also that
socially isolated females with a positive family history of
suicidal behavior and either unipolar or bipolar affective illness
(excluding the Bipolar Other group) are often suicide
attempters. We can suggest also that early age of onset of
affective illness is a risk factor for some patients. But however
valuable statistical approaches are, they fall short of identifying
the individual patient who will take his or her life (26).

Identification of the BP I and especially BP II groups as
suicide prone provides a starting point for research along
several lines. Family history and epidemiological data suggest
that suicidal behavior is even more closely associated with

affective disorder than previously recognized, for example through suicides in individuals at risk for manic depression but not meeting the criteria for a clinical disorder, or through the disrupted family environment produced by the presence of a manic-depressive member. Pharmacological studies may identify a subtype of manic-depressive illness where suicidal behavior is a prominent feature and which is transmitted genetically.

From the point of view of treatment, we would emphasize the following indications from the data:

1. Bipolar patients are apparently at high risk for suicide in the early stages of the disorder. About half our bipolar sample had attempted suicide within ten or eleven years of their first treatment contact, that is, by their mid-thirties. This trend may be particularly marked for men. The implication is that prophylactic treatment should be pursued promptly, even if the patient has had few episodes. Lithium obviously has enormous potential for the prevention of suicides in these patients.

2. Particularly early onset of depressive disorder, especially when this is in the adolescent or early adult periods, may be associated with higher suicidal risk. An effort should be made to ascertain when the patient had his or her first experience of mood swings, whether or not treatment was given and whatever the patient's current age.

3. When the diagnosis is major bipolar disorder the clinician should be aware that men seem as likely to attempt suicide as women and should explore suicidal intent fully.

4. Careful diagnosis is obviously crucial. A partial reason why BP II patients have such a high frequency of suicide attempts may be their lack of adequate treatment. Patients who do not display the full manic pattern may be mistakenly treated for depression alone. In fact, recent evidence suggests that tricyclic antidepressants can speed up mood cycling in bipolar patients, with very destructive results. So a careful review of possible hypomanic symptoms should be made. BP II patients frequently respond well to lithium but should be urged to persist in taking it even if the first result is the loss of the often pleasurable hypomania, before the depression is relieved.

5. An important guide to diagnosis is a thorough family

history. Suicide in close relatives should be an indication to consider seriously suicidal ideation in the patient.

6. Perhaps the simplest and most effective treatment approach once a thorough diagnosis is made is education of the patient and his family, not only about the course of the disorder, but about the efficacy of treatment.

We are at present designing and implementing studies of the genetics and phenomenology of suicide and attempted suicide within our clinic population and in large data set accumulated in our seven-year family study of manic depression (27). An important goal in this endeavor is to further characterize the suicidal patient in diagnostic and psychosocial terms and to establish whether suicide proneness is a consistent attribute of a subtype of affective disorder. Referring back to the present data, it should be emphasized that any behavior occurring in 50 percent or more of patients in a homogeneous diagnostic group is worthy of careful investigation. When this behavior is attempted suicide the need for further understanding of its causes is major indeed.

## SUMMARY

Structured interviews were used to study rates of past suicide attempts among 123 outpatients treated for affective disorders. Subjects met the Feighner criteria for major affective illness, and bipolar and unipolar groups were identified in accordance with the Fieve-Dunner criteria. Although a small group (N = 6), the women with a history of hospitalization for depression and outpatient treatment for hypomania (BP II) had the highest rate of past suicide attempts (66 percent). This confirms previous findings. Women showed higher rates overall (39 percent vs. 28 percent for men). Suicide attempters were found to be significantly younger than nonattempters, which is in line with previous reports that suicide risk is high early in the course of bipolar illness. A trend for attempters to have received their first treatment at a younger age suggests that early onset may be a risk factor. No differences in marital status were found between attempters and nonattempters. Males and females did not differ in number, seriousness, or lethality of attempts.

# REFERENCES

1. Robins, E., Murphy, G. E., Wilkinson, R. H., et al. Some Clinical Considerations in the Prevention of Suicide Based on a Study of 134 Successful Suicides. *Am. J. Pub. Health* 49:888–899, 1959.

2. Guze, S. B. and Robins, E. Suicide and Primary Affective Disorders. *Br. J. Psychiatry* 117:437–438, 1970.

3. Shneidman, E. S. Current Overview of Suicide. In *Suicidology: Contemporary Developments*, Shneidman, E. S., Ed. Seminars in Psychiatry, Greenblatt, M., Series Ed. Grune and Stratton, New York, 1976.

4. Linden, L. L. and Breed, W. The Demographic Epidemiology of Suicide. In *Suicidology: Contemporary Developments*, Shneidman, Ed.

5. Weissman, M. M. and Myers, J. K. Affective Disorders in a U.S. Urban Community. *Arch. Gen. Psychiatry* 37:519–523, 1980.

6. Braverman, J. and Roux, J. F. Screening for the Patient at Risk for Post-partum Depression. *Obstet. Gynecol.* 52:731, 1978.

7. Helgason, T. Epidemiology of Mental Disorders in Iceland: A Psychiatric and Demographic Investigation of 5395 Icelanders. *Acta Psychiatr. Scand.* Suppl. 1973, 1964.

8. Slater, E. Zur Erbpathologie des manisch-depressive Irreseins: Die Eltern und Kindern von Manisch-Depressiven. *Z. Ges. Neurol. u. Psychiat.* 163:1–47, 1938.

9. Dunner, D. L., Gershon, E. S., and Goodwin, F. K. Heritable Factors in the Severity of Affective Illness. *Biol. Psychiatry* 11:31–42, 1976.

10. Jamison, K. Suicide in Manic-Depressive Illness. In *Manic-Depressive Illness*, Goodwin, F. K. and Jamison, K., Eds. Oxford University Press, New York (forthcoming).

11. Winokur, G., Clayton, P. J. and Reich, T. *Manic-Depressive Illness.* Mosby, St. Louis, 1969.

12. Woodruff, R. A., Guze, S. B. and Clayton, P. J. Unipolar and Bipolar Primary Affective Disorder. *Br. J. Psychiatry* 119:33–38, 1971.

13. Johnson, G. E. and Hunt, G. Suicidal Behavior in Bipolar Manic-Depressive Patients and Their Families. *Comp. Psychiatry* 20:159–164, 1979.

14. Stallone, F., Dunner, D. L., Ahearn, J. and Fieve, R. R. Statistical Predications of Suicide in Depressives. *Comp. Psychiatry* 21:381–387, 1979.

15. Spitzer, R. L. and Endicott, J. *Schedule for Affective Disorders and Schizophrenia—Lifetime Version.* Biometrics Research, New York State Psychiatric Institute, New York, 1978.

16. Fieve, R. R. and Dunner, D. L. Unipolar and Bipolar Affective States. In

*The Nature and Treatment of Depression*, Flach, F. F. and Draghi, S. C., Eds. Wiley, New York, 1975.

17. Durkheim, E. *Le Suicide.* (Translated and published as "Suicide," Glencoe, Illinois, 1951).

18. Freud, S. Mourning and Melancholia (1917). In *Standard Edition of the Psychological Works*, Vol 14. Hogarth Press, London, 1965.

19. Menninger, K. A. *Man Against Himself.* Harcourt Brace and Co., New York, 1938.

20. Roy, A. Family History of Suicide. *Arch. Gen. Psychiatry* 40:971–974, 1983.

21. Leonhard, K., Korff, I. and Schultz, H. Die Temperamente in den Familien der monopolaren und bipolaren phasischen Psychosen. *Psychiatria et Neurologia* 14:416–434, 1962.

22. Pitts, F. N. and Winokur, G. Affective Disorder III: Diagnostic Correlates and Incidence of Suicide. *J. Nerv. Ment. Dis.* 139:176–181, 1964.

23. Mendlewicz, J., Fieve, R. R., Rainer, J. D. and Fleiss, J. L. Manic-Depressive Illness; A Comparative Study of Patients with and without a Family History. *Br. J. Psychiatry* 120:523–530, 1972.

24. Asberg, M., Traskman, L. and Thoren, P. 5-HIAA in the Cerebrospinal Fluid: A Biochemical Suicide Predictor? *Arch. Gen. Psychiatry* 33:1193–1197, 1976.

25. Wirz-Justice, A. and Arendt, J. Plasma Melatonin and Antidepressant Drugs. *Lancet* i:425.

26. Pokorny, A. D. Prediction of Suicide in Psychiatric Patients. *Arch. Gen. Psychiatry* 40:249–257, 1983.

# 8 Death by Suicide in the Hospital

Michail Rotov, M.D.

The current therapeutic strategies in the management of hospitalized suicidal patients evolved gradually through the past 25 to 30 years. Numerous papers have contributed useful observations and suggestions on the intramural handling of suicidal subjects. A crucial issue still under debate, especially when tragedy occurs, is the degree of limitation of freedom imposed upon the suicidal patient by the hospital. In the 1930's opinions were voiced advocating a nearly total control of formerly suicidal patients by having them under constant observation as long as they were "psychotic." Banen has made reference to this (1). Such a simplistic solution reflects both the fear of responsibility and the fear of failure. This is why even today one finds proponents of total control among the less secure. Woolley and Eichert faced this painful problem in 1941, as they had met it at the Sheppard and Enoch Pratt Hospital, and came to the significant conclusion that, "The correction of this [suicide] does not seem to lie in the general curtailment of parole privileges, but rather in developing more accurate criteria for determining the immediacy of the danger in the individual instance" (2). Today every modern hospital accepts this dictum.

Another major observation has been that a suicidal patient

should not be kept in isolation. Beisser and Blanchette (3) noted that between 1916 and 1958, 52 per cent of suicides at the Metropolitan State Hospital, Norwalk, California occurred in seclusion rooms. When their paper was published in 1961, the seclusion of suicidal patients was still a common practice in many mental hospitals. A paper published in 1945 by Wall (4) had underlined the fact that many patients commit suicide in the early morning hours.

The small number of cases in this study does not allow it to be of a statistical nature. What is offered here is a post-factum examination of the circumstances of suicides as they are reflected in patients' hospital records. This examination includes: (a) the therapeutic regime, (b) the doctor-patient relationship, (c) the adequacy of preventive measures, and (d) missed clues of suicidal intent or suicidal potential.

Before beginning this analysis, I wish to point out that this study would not have been possible had it not been for the absolute honesty of the physicians who recorded what they saw as they saw it, and who made no attempts to correct the records after the fact. That such improvements of records do occur was noted by Litman (5), who stated that in his investigation of the therapists' reactions to suicide "They forgot details of the history, or they unconsciously omitted or distorted relevant features of the case."

## The Problem of Causation

Here, to some extent, the problem of causation must be examined because an implication might be read into this work that the physicians in some cases were responsible or "had caused" the suicide. Such a conclusion I wish partly to deny and partly to neutralize.

In modern medical textbooks a distinction is made between *necessary* and *sufficient* causes. Necessary causes are those in whose absence the effect cannot occur, as for example, tubercle bacillus in tuberculosis. Sufficient causes, on the one hand, are those which are capable of precipitating the event. The tubercle agent, accordingly, is a necessary but not a sufficient cause for generalized infection. It can only cause such infection when combined with a sufficient factor, such as malnutrition, with the concomitant low body resistance. Malnutrition by itself cannot produce tuberculosis, since it is not a necessary cause. Transposing this system into the realm of psychology, we will benefit in clarity by referring to the necessary causes as those that make an event possible, and to sufficient causes as those that make the event probable. Thus, suicide is made possible by psychosis, depression, social mores in certain cultures, prolonged stressful life situations, brain disorders, and so on. Suicide is made increasingly probable by such additional factors as lack of environmental support, unavailability or inadequacy of therapy, constitutional or temporary ego weakness, various intercurrent stresses, and the like.

The examination of causation in the psychologic realm reveals one essential characteristic. While in the field of body functions and ailments—as in the physical world in general—the sufficient causes are relatively constant, in psychology the factors which make the event probable change from case to case and even from episode to episode in the same person. Promotion, for example, is usually a cause for celebration. But in one of the cases to be referred to later, it led to depression and suicide. In each instance a multitude of factors are in operation supporting or working against each other in determining the occurrence of a psychologic event. The examination of obvious precipitating factors, their interconnectedness with less obvious dynamic forces and their logical extension into the distant genetic roots strongly suggests that the patient's whole past is "the cause" of the fateful action. The search for cause in psychology under these circumstances remains an unproductive task.

If we take the case of a patient who became depressed and suicidal after an incident on the turnpike when he was nearly hit by another car (the actual contact between the vehicles did not occur)—we must postulate the presence of an active possibility factor. We must further postulate an extremely precarious emotional balance with "pro and con" forces canceling each other out, until the trivial turnpike incident, representing the last critical probability component, overthrew the balance. Nobody would seriously regard the turnpike incident as the cause of his suicidal attitude. Similarly, a physician by his managing or mismanaging the case can only increase or decrease the probability of suicide; he can never cause it.

Classifying the factors into those that make the psychologic event possible and those that make the psychologic event probable may provide a meaningful methodological guideline to the analysis of behavioral manifestations.

## Therapeutic Regime

The question whether therapeutic attention had been adequate can, in every case here discussed, be answered affirmatively. All patients had had the appropriate admission work-up, had received proper medication, and were closely followed by their physician and the nursing staff. Many were having group and individual therapy. The striking feature common to all these cases is that not one of the patients was receiving electroshock treatment immediately prior to his death. This seems to support the argument of those who hold that electroshock is the most effective measure in severe depression, as its action is faster than that of other therapies. Admittedly, the electroshock treatment does not resolve the underlying conflict; it only postpones its consequences. There are public mental hospitals, or sections within such hospitals, where the electroshock treatment has been abolished, since it was regarded as too drastic a measure. The error of such an attitude, when consistently applied, lies in the fact that the hospital in such instances does not supplement the resources of the community. Certain therapeutic measures can best be applied during hospitalization, and frequently patients are admitted because these special possibilities are unavailable on the outside. A hospital which just writes off certain therapies loses a considerable degree of its usefulness.

## Doctor–Patient Relationship

A particularly sensitive variable under examination is the doctor-patient relationship. In the psychiatric literature this aspect has received very little attention. The reasons are

obvious: inadequate records, or the doctors' defensive attitudes. Bloom (6), the author of a recent and perhaps the only
study along these lines, encountered considerable difficulties
in his investigation when he interviewed the doctors. He was
able to obtain adequate data on six patients only, but even there
the validity of the information was open to question since he
based his conclusions on the doctor's verbal after-the-fact
comments.

By contrast, the examinations here presented are based
wholly on recorded material that is available to any other
investigator. A case of negative countertransference, for example, may be reflected in the patient's folder in the following
manner: (a) The doctor writes that the patient, in his opinion,
had signed in repeatedly for insufficient reasons, and he
instructs the admission office to refuse her next application for
admission; (b) after she had been admitted by another doctor
subsequent to threatened suicide, he dictated the following
note: "We will transfer this patient to the geriatric section, in
order to make her stay here unpleasant. Hopefully, this will
prevent her from signing in next time for insignificant reasons." Another doctor's punitive pattern toward his patient is
illustrated, among others, in the following note: "Patient
refuses to work. His courtesy card, therefore, will be taken
away."

On the other hand, a case of positive countertransference, or
excessive empathy, was documented as follows: (a) After
making all the preparations for the needed ESTs, the doctor
postponed them because "Patient is afraid of them and she
pleaded with me not to give her shock"; (b) in spite of the
evidence of her poor adjustment at home on weekend visits
and his own notes that she is suicidal, he repeatedly gave in to
her pleas to let her go home. On one such visit she hanged
herself.

Other authors who mentioned, but did not elaborate on the
question of countertransference were Hand and Meisel (7). In
1966 they wrote, "The doctor's hostile feeling toward the
patient, or his failure to recognize the patient's importance to
him, may precipitate the act." Admittedly, complex and intimate aspects contribute to the formation of countertransference

proper. In this series the term "countertransference" is used rather broadly, and is not intended to convey that the involved physicians were re-experiencing a particular neurotogenic relationship from their own infancy. What I wish to indicate is that the dominant emotional attitude was unprofessional, determined as it was by the physician's needs, his primary and secondary gains, rather than by the needs of the patient. On the record, there is not enough evidence for the assertion that a full-fledged countertransference occurred in any of the cases.

The sample of 20 cases here discussed was drawn from two public mental hospitals. Nine cases from one hospital were spread over a 10-year period. They showed no particular pattern with respect to specific wards or physicians. The 11 cases from the other institution were dated between 1962 and 1966, with seven of the suicides occurring in one hospital section which we will call the South Section. During the same period the Central Section had three suicides, and the North Section, one. If one counts the number of suicides that occurred somewhat later, after discharge, that is, a total of three cases in the South Section, it becomes obvious that the South Section personnel was vulnerable in this respect during those years.

Through personal knowledge and by discussing the matter with other physicians and nurses familiar with that section, I am convinced that a peculiar and in many ways extraordinary constellation of circumstances had caused this vulnerability. Specifically, one of the ward physicians who was responsible at the time for four patients who eventually committed suicide (three are not included in this series), had left psychiatric practice in a somewhat discouraged mood. Furthermore, a young physician was active on those wards at the time, who not much later himself attempted suicide, and barely survived. He was attending two of the seven patients in the South Section, although not during the final stages of the patients' hospitalizations. On the staff of the South Section there was furthermore a woman psychologist who eventually committed suicide. She was actively involved with two of the cases, in one instance until the end. I keep asking myself, what subtle exchanges occurred between these kindred souls under the guise of evaluation, therapy, or interview. What can a frightened therapist tell a patient whose frankly stated intentions are resonant with the doctor's own hidden impulses?

One of the patients, a twenty-seven-year-old housewife and mother of two, had the misfortune of being the center of attention of all the above people at approximately the same time. In addition, she was a very close friend of a girl who had committed suicide while on a week-end visit. Maybe a more resistant individual would have survived the risk but this patient throughout her life showed depressive attitudes, with several serious suicidal attempts. She came very close to the type of people considered to be suffering from thanatophilia (8)—a lifelong preoccupation with the idea of death. She kept referring to her depression as "my old feeling," and spoke frankly about wanting to die. Nevertheless, her own physician kept denying that she was suicidal. It was obvious to nurses—as they stated to me in interviews—that an odd relationship developed between these two, inasmuch as they irritated each other but yet continued with their scheduled meetings. The patient insisted that she was not well and kept asking for electroshock treatment; the doctor insisted that she did not need it and that she "just wanted attention." The patient was allowed to go home week ends, although the nursing personnel was very apprehensive of this. The young doctor, who later himself attempted suicide and who at that time was on another service, continued seeing the patient. The suicidal psychologist kept on with her visits, even though the formal evaluation was already filed. Finally, the doctor, impatient and exhausted, presented the patient to the staff for discharge. The staff, recognizing the patient's serious condition, turned down the request for her release. Home for the week end, she woke up early in the morning, telling her husband that it was too hot. He then fell asleep again. The patient took a pesticide, went to the garage, and died there.

Another patient in this series came from the same section. He was a forty-six-year old man who for nine years had had difficulties walking. He developed depression, became moody, aggressive, and beat his wife. Neurologic consultants including a college professor, brought in the diagnosis of amyotrophic lateral sclerosis. The patient's last admission to the hospital was voluntary, due to depression, crying spells, and suicidal ideation. The hospital progress notes indicated that the doctor-patient relationship was unsatisfactory. The doctor insisted on discussing the patient's feelings toward his wife, while the patient angrily protested that his problems were physical. Finally, he signed out and at the staff conference referred to his physician and the hospital in abusive terms, stating that he had been neither helped nor understood. He went home and hanged himself. It is of interest that the attending physician offered a diagnosis of psychophysiologic reaction, despite the clear-cut diagnosis made by prominent neurologists. The physician was as fixed in his views on the patient's problem as was the patient himself. Neither would concede the point, and what happened was that the weaker one perished.

In a case from the Central Section, the doctor-patient relationship deteriorated catastrophically, leading to the patient's suicide. Here we come closer than in any other case to where one can say that the doctor "caused" the suicide. The collapse of the relationship, however, was not due to the doctor's undue involvement with the patient, but rather to his inexperience. Actually, his interest in the patient, his perseverance, and his ability to establish rapport with a malignant psychopath, were exemplary. The patient was a twenty-four-year-old male Negro with a stormy life history and continual involvement with the law. His last commitment had been accompanied by a detainer because he had severely injured his wife with a brick when he surprised her *in flagrante* with another man. The patient had left home at the age of sixteen, had traveled extensively as far as Cuba where he learned Spanish and acted as an interpreter to tourists. There he married, had two children, but abruptly abandoned them and returned to the United States. Here he married again, this time a white girl who made her living by prostitution.

The patient appeared to be a curious mixture of extreme egocentricity with an ability to empathize, at times excessively, with the sufferings of others. He could shed tears for a patient in a seclusion room and become emotional over some little boys on the ward. He protested if anyone used profanity in front of a nurse. At the same time he felt no guilt regarding the fate of his wife and children in Cuba nor showed any interest in them. His several suicidal attempts were in connection with his second wife who "did him wrong." The patient's doctor, an excellent young resident, succeeded in stabilizing him to some degree and getting him interested in individual psychotherapy sessions. This was by no means easy, but it appears that their meetings were becoming constructive. An unfortunate and unexpected occurrence destroyed the good relationship. Someone on the ward stole something of value and the patient was accused. The nursing personnel reported the incident to the doctor, who questioned the patient about it. Even though the doctor claims that he did it tactfully, the patient became angry, requested transfer to jail, and there hanged himself.

**Preventive Measures**

Of the preventive lapses the most significant were those when patients were placed into seclusion rooms. Of the two such cases, one occurred in 1957 and the other in 1962. As already mentioned, the awareness of the dangers inherent in this measure had emerged fully by 1961. In some public mental hospitals the seclusion of suicidal patients, after they have been denuded, is today still an accepted practice. Ironically, this is being done also in institutions where the administration of electroshock is apparently considered to be inhuman. A denuded patient certainly cannot hang himself, but he can hit his head against the wall, and he can break lighting fixtures and cut his wrists. Apart from these dangers, Beisser and Blanchette point out that the depressed person in isolation, having nobody around, turns to his internalized objects, thus intensifying and prolonging his conflict (3). Psychiatrists, when they stop to think about it, find it difficult to rationalize the limitation of freedom of a suicidal nonpsychotic patient. It seems as if in the minds of many, occasional loss of life is preferable to the organized control of one group over the other, even for the noble cause of preserving mental health.

## Missed Clue of Suicidal Intent or Potential

Lipschutz reported on a suicidal patient who prior to her death expressed concern that someone might harm her children (9). In three cases in this series similar coded disclosures of suicidal intention were recorded. The dynamics in each case were significantly different, deserving brief discussion. The first case was that of a relatively young man in his late thirties, a college graduate and educator, who developed his schizophrenic paranoid condition in crescendo fashion. Unrealistic and bizarre actions appeared gradually over a period of time. He began to work on grandiose plans, requested large sums of money, became oversensitive and oversexed, and finally became totally irrational. In the hospital he was argumentative and legalistic. Although very tense, he was without depression. The physician recorded the patient's concern that his wife might commit suicide. Unfortunately, the message was not decoded. The patient went home for the week end, and hanged himself. In this instance the mechanism of projection was used, reflecting the true paranoid nature of his disorder.

In the second case, a young man was hospitalized because of depression following charges and incarceration for a rather serious offense. No overt suicidal behavior was in evidence, but the patient kept saying that his wife would die. This apparently groundless concern was not further investigated. In this instance the intended self-destruction with the concomitant destruction of the internalized object (his wife) caused intense guilt feelings. The inability to absorb more blame for the intended symbolic violent act toward his wife caused the patient to express his concern for his wife, as though the danger to her was coming from another source.

In yet another case, an elderly depressed man was repeating obsessively that he was dying and would soon be dead. He did eventually kill himself, to the consternation of the personnel who had thought that death was precisely what the patient was afraid of. The sources of this apparent paradox were rooted in the acute disintegration of ego content, due to intense repressive process. The self-destructive tendencies became alien forces from the unconscious threatening the self. The patient, therefore, was paraphrasing his intention to kill himself. Summarizing the above three cases, it can be said that the common denominator in all was the concern of the patient for his own or his internalized object's well-being, as if the danger was not coming from himself. This formulation should be sufficient for recognition of future similar cases in medical practice.[1]

## Tic Suicide

Before going over to the assessment of doctors' personalities, I should recount a case that stands somewhat apart from the others and which is remarkable for two reasons. First, the breakdown and hospitalization occurred following promotion on the job; second, the case is a good illustration of so-called "tic" suicide, discussed by Kubie (10). He refers to it as a "suicidal effort which acquires the independent clock-like automatism of a tic." It occurs in persons who do not necessarily appear depressed but who obviously harbor some significant psychopathology. They belong in the broad category of "depression sine depression" syndrome, a term coined by Lesse (11).

The patient in question was a thirty-three-year-old married man, employed in a business firm of which his father was president. The father was a difficult man, tense, irritable, and often away from home. The mother did not compensate for his deficiencies in any way, being often intoxicated and prone to use profanity. Early in life the patient went through a religious crisis when, after graduation from high school, he converted to Catholicism. He often expressed the feeling of being oppressed by his successful father. On two occasions he was hospitalized for depression and treated with electroshock. The last episode and commitment followed his promotion on the job. He felt depressed, worthless, expressed suicidal ideas, and presented numerous bodily complaints. After an apparent improvement

---

[1]Newspaper accounts of various tragedies are frequently suggestive of the above depicted dynamics. Thus, *Newark Star-Ledger* carried a story on Tuesday, April 8, 1969, of a school principal who committed suicide after killing his wife and three young children. Previously he had publicly expressed concern about the rise in the number of suicides among juveniles.

had set in, he was allowed to go home on a brief visit. He seemed to be doing well, attended to some errands, and played with the children. In the afternoon, when he and the whole family were putting up a tent in the back yard, he went down to the basement to get a rope. After a while his wife followed to see what the delay was, and found he had hung himself.

Albeit aware of Bleuler's warning about the unpredictability of patients recovering from depression, the practicing psychiatrists, nevertheless, find such cases very disturbing. When a psychiatrist can identify his errors, he feels strengthened so that he is able to handle subsequent cases. But histories such as above, where the clues and motivations are completely hidden from view, do not contribute constructively to the psychiatrist's therapeutic skills. They rather tend to discourage him. Reflecting upon the above and similar cases, I have come to the conclusion that the clue to the tic-like suicide lies in the nature of its primary mechanism of defense, namely, the dissociation.

As a rule, persons who commit tic-like suicide have been depressed and suicidal in the past. Then, an apparent improvement sets in when the routine examination and observation does not disclose any significant psychopathologic process. The patient's statements about his subjective feelings are also satisfactory. He is calm, denies depression or conflict, he socializes and pursues what appears to be a regular life course. In this condition he is either discharged or permitted repeated visits home. Typically, the tragedy is not triggered off by any overt or hidden stress. The trigger mechanism is usually an unexpected and convenient opportunity for self-destruction: somebody's loaded gun lying around, a rope in the basement, a razor blade.

An examination of the patient's circumstances and attitudes prior to his death discloses that the patient expected to live. He may have announced his plans to visit his mother on her birthday, bought tickets for a ball game, made vacation requests, and the like. Presumably, the patient would have been surprised himself by his sudden act. By what psychic process does he arrive at such a state of mind? Obviously something very significant happens between the phases of overt depression and apparent recovery. This significant step is regression, in terms of changing over to the use of more primitive mental mechanism. In earlier phases, when the patient was struggling with repressing his conflict, the repressed material made its presence felt by seeking substitutive ways of expression. Consequently, there were clinical signs and symptoms testifying to the presence of the illness: the feeling of discomfort and depression, preoccupation, possibly restlessness, and some physical complaints. At some point under the pressures of conflict, the patient changed his tactics and employed massive dissociation. Dissociation is a radical operation. The dissociated material—in the case of amnesia, the whole past—is completely severed from the ego. It coexists with it, so to speak, without making its presence felt in any detectable way.

The formerly suicidal patient who uses dissociation has a twin-ego, popularly called "dual personality," who does not know when the other segment might emerge. Neither does his doctor, who does not even suspect the state of dissociation. This hypothetical state of more or less chronic dissociation ties in logically with the observation made by Stengel, that acute depressions may cause a transitory state of fugue or "pathological wandering" (12). The question, then, is—how can we identify a chronically dissociated suicidal patient, and how can we say whether the improvement in any depressed patient is genuine or spurious, reflecting only ego fragmentation?

## The Physicians

All the physicians involved in this study were trained psychiatrists, except for one general practitioner and one psychiatric resident. To my knowledge, none had undergone personal analysis and only one was Board-certified at the time in question. Only three had been in prior private practice. Five could be considered to have been of above-average ability. The majority were rather young, their average age being somewhere between thirty-four and thirty-six years. Five were American graduates, a proportion which reflects the 30 per cent of American graduates in our state hospitals during those years. I want to make it clear that the evaluation of physicians' personal characteristics reflects my own opinion. It is, therefore, the most speculative part of this study, even though in about half of the cases it was confirmed by other co-workers.

Nevertheless, I am struck by the apparent fact that four physicians who were responsible for four cases had very similar character make-ups. They represented the type who is very quiet, friendly, noncompetitive on the job, and very benevolent toward his patients. This to the degree that they would let themselves be easily manipulated by psychopaths and could be led astray by their sentiments in cases where there is a need for firm control and rapid, accurate therapy. There would be repeated and unnecessary postponements of unpleasant therapeutic measures, changes in previously made orders and decisions, and prolonged hesitation. Inevitably, sooner or later the patient perceives this lack of direction and realizes that he is on his own.

The other characteristic group consisted of five physicians who were responsible for six cases in this series. This type of doctor has a very raw, sharp-edged personality that is at times explosive, and otherwise spends much energy to control its own aggression. His involvement on the job is limited to the performance of routine duties. He has little interest in advancing his own psychiatric knowledge, mainly because of his underlying cynical and nihilistic attitude toward the effectiveness of therapy. Consequently, he is bored at work and unable to use advice and criticism. This type of physician can become quite destructive if he is permitted to manage his ward without supervision. Individualized treatment, one-to-one relationship, and continuity of care are all useful concepts if the particular physician is to fit the particular event.

Another observation, on a more philosophical level, concerns the theoretical posture of the involved physician. It has been my impression, based on a generalization from three doctors personally known to me, that a considerable number of these physicians were suffering from a prejudice typical of the pre-Freudian era of psychiatry. They seemed to subscribe to the view that the neurotic patient is capable of arresting his disorder if only he decides to exert an effort in this direction. Accordingly, any unimproving neurotic under their care was liable to cause irritation.

## SUMMARY

1. Seclusion of suicidal patients has to be abandoned as an antitherapeutic anachronism. An immediate preceptorship type of doctor-patient relationship should be established, implying frequent personal contacts and 24-hour availability. In the doctor's absence the preceptor role may be delegated to another member of the psychiatric team. At no time should the patient have the occasion to feel abandoned.

2. Countertransference and other anomalies in relationship toward patients frequently immobilize the hospital physician. It is imperative that he be helped and guided through consultation and team work.

3. Electroshock treatment should be retained by the hospital as a treatment possibility for selected patients.

4. In weighing the strength of suicidal potential, it may be helpful to conceptualize the patient's mental state by breaking all the significant factors into two groups: (a) the factors that make the suicide possible; (b) the factors that increase or decrease such a possibility (factors that make the suicide probable).

5. An important clue to a patient's hidden suicidal impulses is a projective concern over his relatives or his own well-being, as if the danger stemmed from someone else.

6. Tic-like suicide, an impulsive (sometimes repetitive) suicidal attempt, may reflect a state of chronic dissociation. At the time of the attempt the dissociated material breaks through.

7. A significant proportion of physicians responsible for the cases included in this paper fall into two distinct characterological types: the one, a benevolent, indecisive, meek physician; the other, an aggressive, nihilistically oriented physician.

## REFERENCES

1. Banen, D. M. Suicide by Psychotics. *J. Nerv. Ment. Dis.* 120–355, 1954.

2. Wooley, L. F. and Eichart, A. H. Notes on the Problems of Suicide and Escape. *Am. J. Psychiat.* 98:114, 1941.

3. Beisser, A. R. and Blanchette, J. E. A Study of Suicides in a Mental Hospital. *Dis. Nerv. Sys.* 22:368, 1961.

4. Wall, J. H. The Psychiatric Problem of Suicide. *Am. J. Psychiat.* 101:405, 1944.

5. Litman, R. E. When Patients Commit Suicide. *Am. J. Psychother.* 19:573, 1965.

6. Bloom, V. An Analysis of Suicide at a Training Center. *Am. J. Psychiat.* 123:918, 1967.

7. Hand, M. H. and Meisel, A. M. Dynamic Aspects of Suicide. *Dis. Nerv. Sys.* 27:373, 1966.

8. Assael, M. I. Thanatophilia. *Dis. Nerv. Sys.* 26:777, 1965.

9. Lipschutz, L. S. Some Administrative Aspects of Suicide in the Mental Hospital. *Am. J. Psychiat.* 99:184, 1942.

10. Kubie, L. S. Editorial. *J. Nerv. Ment. Dis.* 138:6, 1964.

11. Lesse, S. Apparent Remissions in Depressed Suicidal Patients. *J. Nerv. Ment. Dis.* 144:4, 1967.

12. Stengel, E. *Suicide and Attempted Suicide.* MacGibbon & Kee, London, 1965, p. 115.

# 9 Fantasized Companions and Suicidal Depressions

Kenneth Seeman, M.D.
Leslie Widrow, A.B.
Jerome Yesavage, M.D.

*Two acutely suicidal adult patients with fantasized companions integral to the formation of suicide intent are presented. The phenomenon of the fantasized companion is reviewed, differentiated from true hallucinatory or psychotic phenomena, and related to other fantasy and dissociative states, such as daydreaming and multiple personalities. In this regard, the concept of hysterical psychosis is discussed. The functions served by the fantasized companions and their involvement in the successful treatment of the patients are described.*

It is not infrequent that patients presenting with dramatic imaginative phenomena, including accounts of voices and appearance of spirits and other visions, are erroneously diagnosed as schizophrenic and treated on that assumption. Many of these patients, however, are not describing hallucinations in the sense that would characterize a schizophrenic decompensation, but rather discretely formed figures or imaginative creations that relate to the patient in a purposeful and symbolic fashion. Spiegel and Fink (2) differentiate what they refer to as hysterical psychosis from true schizophrenia. Patients suffering from such a psychosis tend to be extremely sensitive to external cues, often decompensating readily in response to severe environmental stress, may recompensate rapidly, are nonresponsive to neuroleptics, and tend to be good candidates

133

for treatment employing hypnosis. Such a presentation is distinguished from the true schizophrenic, whose illness may lack responsiveness to external factors, who is more likely to respond to pharmacologic intervention, and whose mental processes are typically so fragmented that he is unlikely to be a good hypnotic candidate.

It is apparent that many of these patients presenting with "voices" are describing not hallucinations as such, but rather communications from fantasized figures. These figures may be amorphous and spiritlike, or may be well defined with specific personalities and physical features. They differ from true hallucinations in that they perform specific symbolic functions for the patient, who often requires them as a means of working through conflicts. These figures, who interact in meaningful ways with the patient, show considerable coherence, in contrast to the relative fragmentation of true schizophrenic hallucinations. It becomes essential to understand these figures in order to most effectively help the patient resolve his disturbance and return to normal functioning. One may speculate that it may be these more coherent phenomena that are described by Jungian theorists (2) in working with hallucinations and artistic creations of "schizophrenics."

The imaginary figures may become so well defined as to attain clearly assigned personalities and physical attributes, often conversing actively with and influencing the patient. Thus, we are dealing with the phenomenon of the fantasized companion.

The most frequently cited definition of fantasized or imaginary companions is that of Svendsen, describing their appearance in children: "an invisible character, named and referred to in conversation with other persons or played with directly for a period of time, at least several months, having an air of reality for the child but no apparent objective basis. This excludes that type of imaginative play in which an object is personified or in which the child himself assumes the role of some person in his environment (3)."

Typically fantasized companions occur during childhood, usually appearing between ages two and five, and tending to disappear by early adolescence (3, 4). Persistence into adulthood is seldom reported, although Harriman (5) mentions several cases of fantasized companions appearing as late as adolescence, and remaining into early adulthood. Proskauer et al. (6) describe fantasized companions among Navajo late adolescents. Hilgard's material (4), drawn primarily from interviews with college students, shows an occurrence of fantasized companions during childhood in 17 percent, while Svendsen (3), studying children from varying socioeconomic groups, reports an occurrence of 13 percent. Other studies, however, suggest that the phenomenon is far more common. Harriman (5) believes it to occur in one third of children, and Kirkpatrick (7) suggests that it occurs in nearly all children in one form or another. Nagera (8) believes that fantasized companions are abandoned as the child passes through appropriate developmental stages, and that memories of them are poorly recovered, even in analysis. It may be that the phenomenon is ubiquitous, persisting in some individuals in response to specific internal or external stresses. Incidence is more common among girls than boys in most samples. Rucker (9) analyzes this higher frequency among girls as representing different demands for separation and gender identification between the sexes during the Oedipal phase. Fantasized companions tend to be more prevalent among more intelligent subjects (3), and subjects with higher IQs are also more capable of describing those companions (10).

While the presence of imaginary companions is regarded as a normal phenomenon, it is clear that they help defend against a variety of stresses. Most common are the experiences of loneliness, isolation, and neglect, particularly in preschool years, leading to their eventual disappearance as the child enters into stages of increased socialization. Where such socialization is impeded, there is greater tendency for those companions to persist. They also serve as mechanisms for dealing with forbidden impulses or aggressivity (11) by allowing for a splitting off of the undesired or prohibited feeling. In psychoanalytic formulations, the fantasized companion may allow for a separation of superego from ego and id functions, where the child is unable to integrate them (note the Jiminy Cricket type of fantasy). The fantasized companion often represents an idealized image, becoming what the child is not, and sometimes rebuking the child for not being better. In discussing the functions of the fantasized companion, Nagera (8) includes acting as a consultant with instruction to control behavior; serving as a "superego prop"; justifying "naughty" behavior; serving for drive discharge; acting as a scapegoat whom the child can berate or blame; prolonging feelings of omnipotence and control; personifying ego-ideals; providing relief from loneliness; alleviating guilt; helping to avoid regression and symptom formation; allowing for externalization of painful experience; and helping to deal with loss. He points out that the companion typically appears in situations of special stress of traumatic character. Benson and Pryor (12) refer to functions of protection from potential narcissistic injuries and rebuffs; enhancing sense of perfection and self-worth; offering reassurance, reminiscent of the mirror on the wall in *Snow White*; and serving in a similar way to the transitional object in development, persisting until object-love becomes safe and tolerable. Manosevitz et al. (13) refer to the function of aiding the child in developing social and language skills that might otherwise develop more slowly. Bach (14) discusses the functions of helping with a narcissistic blow, acting as a transitional object, and providing a sense of mastery or competence.

The form of the fantasized companion can vary. It is typically of the same sex, but need not be, and indeed need not even be human (15, 16). The companion may act as a playmate, a commentator or a responsive audience, a boyfriend or girlfriend, among other roles, and its function may be both pleasant and unpleasant. Usually there is explicit imagery connected with the fantasized companion, who has specific attributes and can be physically defined. By the age of five, the child is usually aware of the imaginary nature of the companion, although he may be experienced as more real at earlier ages.

Other phenomena involving fantasy and dissociation may be related to that of the fantasized companion. Singer (17) discusses the importance of daydreams, the capacity for which he regards as a fundamental characteristic of the human constitution. Nagera (8) refers to the similarity of fantasized companions to daydreams, in that both are attempts at wish fulfillment, are fueled by the pleasure principle and can ignore the reality principle, and yet reality testing remains unimpaired. Unlike daydreams, the fantasized companion is perceived as space-occupying, and it allows the person the opportunity not to withdraw into fantasy but to return with his fantasy to real life. More specifically than typical daydreams, it fills the emptiness, neglect, loneliness or rejection which is experienced, satisfying a need for attention, love, and companionship. Proskauer (6) postulates a developmental sequence from daydream through imaginary companion to multiple personality and beyond, perhaps to schizophrenia.

Of particular significance is the continuum between the phenomenon of the fantasized companion and that of a true multiple personality. Hilgard (4) describes one subject who traded places periodically with the companion, thus becoming both herself and the other person. In both phenomena, the tendency toward dissociation characterizes the subject. Describing the transition from fantasized companion to multiple personality, Bliss (18) points out that all of the later personalities first appear as friends or allies or as invited guests. Congdon et al. (19) describe the transition from fantasized companion to dual personality through role-playing. Ludwig et al. (20) further demonstrate the nature of the continuum in discussing variations between subjects in whom the various personalities coexist, aware of each other (i.e., lying toward the fantasized companion end of the spectrum), and those in whom the personalities are independent of each other with separate consciousness (i.e., more completely multiple personalities). Bowers and Brecher (21) discuss the hypnotic treatment of a patient in which the primary personality referred to itself in the first person, while other personalities remained in the third, suggesting another intermediate between the fantasized companion and multiple personalities.

Interestingly, the alter personalities, similar to the fantasized companion, tend to develop early, typically at four to six years (18), but sometimes as early as 2½ (22). The alter personality may continue to develop or others emerge even as late as 40 (24). As in many cases of fantasized companions, they arise in response to specific stresses (22), allowing repression of the trauma. They may be only transient, or eventually become so dominant as to take over the body and exclude the original personality. As with fantasized companions, the expression of the multiple personalities may be confused with schizophrenia, with manifestations of what may be interpreted to be actual hallucinations or delusions (18). It should also be noted that other serious clinical problems may develop, including major depressions and suicide attempts.

With respect to treatment, the literature generally considers the more pervasive phenomenon, that of the multiple personalities. The presence of fantasized companions, often regarded as a normal phenomenon, may be considered generally in treating a patient, but the object of treatment is not to remove them. It is far more common, however, to attempt to treat multiple personalities, often by aiding the patient in integrating the personalities, or by strengthening either the original or the healthiest personality (22). Even when the personalities are treated separately, some form of integration is hoped for. Although various methods of both psychodynamic and organic therapies, including electroshock therapy, have been used, most clinicians treat the condition through the use of hypnosis. Nemiah (23), in his comprehensive discussion of multiple personalities and other dissociative states, describes the use of hypnosis in uncovering environmental precipitants and inner conflicts that have contributed to the psychogenesis of the disorder. Bliss (18) and Spiegel and Spiegel (24) point out the element of self-hypnosis in the multiple-personality syndrome, and Morton Prince (25) describes the spontaneous emergence of one of the earliest described multiple personalities, "Sally Beauchamp," in the course of a hypnotic session. There is considerable rationale for the use of hypnosis in approaching individuals with fantasized companions as well, especially when these companions have become part of a malignant psychopathologic process.

Although multiple personalities are often assumed to be rare, with a total of slightly over 200 documented cases, there has been an increasing incidence of reports, particularly since

1970, suggesting that the condition often is unrecognized and may be far more common than ordinarily assumed.

Similarly, it is highly likely that the presence of fantasized companions, a phenomenon that may be antecedent to the development of a true multiple personality, may also be more common than recognized, even in adults. It is also likely that these companions may be integral to the manifestation of psychopathology, often being confused with other disease entities, as has been demonstrated in our clinical experience (K.S.) in a variety of treatment settings.

In this paper, two patients will be described, both of whom presented with severe depressions, and in both of whom a fantasized companion was integrally involved in a suicide attempt leading to admission to a high-security psychiatric unit at the Palo Alto Veterans Administration Hospital. Each patient was previously diagnosed as schizophrenic, and may indeed have manifested schizophrenic pathology in the past. Communications from the fantasized companion were in both instances misinterpreted by admitting physicians as auditory hallucinations, which were considered to confirm the diagnosis of a currently active schizophrenic reaction. In each patient, extreme interpersonal dependence and a consequent sense of helplessness were crucial in the despair that led to the resolve to commit suicide. Anger or reproach directed toward the patient by the companion was the direct precipitant in forming the suicide intent. In one case, this intent was actually acted on prior to admission, and in the other, it was seriously threatened but not yet acted out. In each case, subsequent to admission, the patient was determined (by K.S.) not to be actively schizophrenic, and the reported "voices," not true hallucinations. Rather, it became obvious that the "voices" were conceived by the patient as emanating from well-defined fantasy figures, in effect alter egos, who almost always accompanied the patient, and bore major responsibility for defining motivation and determining behavior. In one of the patients, the companion at one point threatened to "possess" the patient if he did not behave appropriately, thereby possibly foreshadowing the development of a dual personality.

With ample precedent in previous work with multiple personalities, and considering the closeness of the two phenomena in general and in the two patients in particular, treatment of each of these patients using hypnosis was decided on. More specifically, it was considered that access to each of the patients and opportunity to influence both the feelings of despair and the suicide intent, would be best accomplished by entering the patient's metaphor and communicating directly with the fantasy figures, as could occur through a hypnotic trance. Furthermore, since the fantasized companions of the two patients had become so prominent as to direct behavior, it was felt that a process of integration similar to that often attempted in treating multiple personalities might be worth considering.

Each patient was induced according to the method described by Spiegel and Spiegel (24), and his hypnotic profile and induction score were determined. After the initial session, the hypnotic-trance state was used as the medium of working with each patient and his fantasized companions in all sessions.

## Case 1

A., a 37-year-old man with a diagnosed history of schizophrenic illness, was admitted for a suicide attempt with ingestion of thioridazine. He described what the admitting physicians interpreted to be unremitting voices commanding him to commit suicide. He was living with his former wife and their five-year-old child, and was feeling humiliated by his continuing dependence on this woman and over the fact that his daughter tended to ignore him, not relating to him as her father. Seeing no way to overcome his defeating feelings of dependence, he made his suicide gesture.

A.'s initial decompensation occurred while in the service, when he heard threatening voices, and attempted to attack some of the other men. He was successfully treated with neuroleptics, and ultimately discharged with a diagnosis of schizophrenic reaction, paranoid type. Since then, A. had remained on small doses of thioridazine, and though there had been no further episodes suggestive of an overt schizophrenic process, he had made two suicide attempts, and reported often feeling on the verge of suicide.

A. came from a family dominated by a strong mother, and with no father available since he was an infant. He had a younger and more successful brother, who, he felt, was favored by the mother. He expressed considerable separation difficulties from the mother. At time of admission, while remaining in an untenably strained situation, living with his estranged wife, he was conscious of his preference to stay with the mother. The mother had told him that it would be better for him to live independently of her, and while agreeing, this was obviously difficult for him. Clearly, he would have preferred to be cared for, with minimal demands, by one of these two women.

On closer interviewing, it was determined that the "voices" described on admission were in fact one voice, which was well formed. It emanated from a figure that had been an imaginary companion since A. was five, and who was given a name, and could be described in minute detail, both in physical appearance and personality. Signs of disorganization or fragmentation that one might expect in a true schizophrenic presentation with auditory hallucinations were absent.

A. told us that his companion was a "ghost," named Jeremiah David De Saul. He was a Civil War lieutenant, sent to A. on his fifth birthday by the "general." In effect, De Saul, as A. referred to him, was everything that the patient was not and wished to be. A. looked years older than his stated and documented age, was gray and balding, and told us that he knew himself to be ugly and repulsive to women. De Saul was dashing, always smartly dressed in his Confederate uniform and sword or in the clothes of a Southern gentleman, with a well-kept black beard and wavy black hair. The current crisis was triggered by De Saul's abrupt departure on "pay day," after having been constantly present since he had first appeared 32 years ago. Apparently pay day represented a point of departure for A., when he felt he had to express his independence and move away from his estranged wife and daughter. A. had been told by De Saul only that A. needed to be independent now, and to achieve this, De Saul had been recalled by the general. A. told us that if he could regain contact with De Saul, he might not feel the compulsion to commit suicide. Accordingly, it was decided to use hypnosis and age regression to enable A. to reach De Saul, and for the therapist also to contact De Saul directly. It was hoped thereby to gain more insight into the dynamic factors affecting the patient, and in the process to influence suicidal ideation and intent.

A. was hypnotized, with a hypnotic induction profile (HIP) grade of 1–2 increment, and an induction score of 13 out of a possible 16. It was apparent that he had considerable motivation and ability to use hypnosis in his therapy, despite his low-to-moderate eye roll which might have predicted a lower hypnotic potential.

A. was regressed to the time immediately prior to De Saul's departure. He described him in detail. By special signal, De Saul was called upon to speak to us in the patient's voice. De Saul told us that A. desperately needed to be on his own, and particularly to establish relationships with women other than his wife. He told us that the general was recalling him because A. no longer needed him, and that indeed, his presence made A. excessively dependent and was therefore detrimental. Unless De Saul left, A. could not achieve "maturity." The decision of the general was final and irrevocable. It was asked whether A. might call on De Saul in an emergency. De Saul said that the general would permit this if he were not required to be there all the time. When out of his trance, A. was advised that he now had an alternative. Although he had reached such a point in his life that De Saul could not be available to the extent that he previously had, A. would be able to call on him for brief periods by placing himself in a trance, and using a signal that he was instructed to use. He was told to do this two to three times per day, for brief periods, until our next session. This arrangement was immensely reassuring for A., who now felt he could proceed toward his independence. Clearly, the need to separate himself from his wife and mother had become confused with the need to separate himself from his "ghost." A. could now be separate from De Saul, and still call on him for brief contacts. A. was also relieved to feel that he was now in greater control, with the option of choosing his own contact with the ghost, rather than being passively visited. This was also helpful to him in view of his feelings of lack of control when dealing with his feelings of dependence.

In the following session, A. was regressed to various birthdays. The common element in describing these occasions was the presence of his brother, with whom he felt in intense competition for the attention of his mother. Even though it was

A.'s birthday, the brother also received presents and this was deeply resented. De Saul would sit in the background, known and available only to A., and apparently provided a caring and attentiveness that was not shared with the brother.

During this second hypnotic session, De Saul advised us of what apparently was the primary precipitant to both A.'s suicide attempt and De Saul's departure. The estranged wife, in whose home the patient remained, was now involved with another man, and a marriage was planned two months in the future. The patient had told us nothing about this in direct interviewing. It was now obvious that he felt both wounded and under time pressure to arrange his affairs. Within two months it was now imperative for him to gain his independence, both emotionally and in his living situation, and this crisis was displaced in his awareness by a crisis with De Saul.

Between the hypnotic sessions, A. continued to establish his own contact, briefly and infrequently, with De Saul, as instructed. At the third session, he advised us that De Saul had now assured him that, rather than disappearing precipitously, he would remain available for a year, thereby allowing A. time for adjustment and a means of gradually establishing the independence that he felt he needed. This construct allowed him to continue his dependence on his fantasized companion, while seeking greater autonomy, and without having to experience the insult to his self-esteem that his awareness of dependency had engendered.

During the fourth session, De Saul confirmed that he would remain available, particularly during times of crisis, and if needed would be in especially close contact with A. to prevent him from implementing suicidal impulses. He further presented for us a plan for A. to gradually move away from the estranged wife, and guaranteed that this would be in A.'s best interest. Accordingly, we were assured that A. could leave the hospital with no danger, and that the precipitating crisis was now resolved.

A. was again hospitalized at a later time, when his feelings of rage over his extreme dependence were directed outward. By this time he no longer lived with his wife, but shared an apartment with a roommate. When his roommate suggested that he might still be leaning too much on his estranged wife, A. assaulted him, following De Saul's encouragement to be more aggressive. He was again treated through hypnosis to establish contact with De Saul. This time the fantasy became much more elaborate and indeed grandiose, with De Saul receiving contrary messages from a variety of generals throughout global history, including Ghengis Khan, Alexander, Napoleon and Patton. Some of the generals were counseling a supportive approach from De Saul, who now was constantly present, suggesting that he bring the patient along easily. Others were instructing De Saul that if the patient did not "shape up" rapidly, he was to possess the patient. Were this to have occurred, we would have been dealing with a true multiple personality, which rarely commences at so mature an age. On this occasion, behavioral techniques incorporating some assertiveness training were used, to help the patient feel that he was expressing himself more effectively. This process apparently satisfied the patient, thereby appeasing De Saul and all the generals, and he was ultimately discharged again, feeling hopeful and in greater possession of himself. Significantly, the essential messages about what the patient was feeling and needing were conveyed through the fantasy figure, De Saul, the patient being unable to communicate so effectively about "himself."

## Case 2

B., a 24-year-old man, was admitted with alleged "voices" commanding him at various times either to kill himself or his mother. The mother was perceived as punishing and often taking advantage of B. The father was distant and minimally involved. B. felt in competition with his two older sisters, two older brothers, and a twin sister for whatever minimal parental attention might be available.

Prior treatment consisted of one visit by the entire family to a psychiatrist 12 years earlier, at which time B. was the identified patient. The chief complaint involved the patient's inability to sleep. No treatment was recommended. Two years prior to admission, after four years of military service, B. was hospitalized in a military hospital, because he "couldn't handle stress." He was regarded as a borderline patient, with schizophrenia as a possible underlying disturbance, and was ultimately discharged with a psychiatric disability. Subsequent treatment was on an outpatient basis in his home community.

B.'s admitting diagnosis at the current hospitalization was listed as schizophrenic because of the presence of the command "voices." He was placed on neuroleptics and referred to the acute treatment unit. On closer evaluation, it became apparent that the "voices" emanated from a well-defined fantasy figure, whom he referred to as "Alex." It was Alex who told him alternately to kill himself and his mother, and who had become so intrusive that B. felt he had lost control over him. Alex instructed him to do away with himself because he was insufficiently assertive with women in general but specifically and most relevantly with his mother. B. was clearly depressed and anxious at times to the point of agitation, but there were no overt psychotic symptomatology. Because of the importance of this fantasy figure, and the fact that the phenomena belonged ' more in the arena of fantasy than hallucination or delusion, it was decided to use the patient's metaphor to approach and treat him through hypnotherapy.

B. was hypnotically induced with a profile grade of 1 increment, and an induction score of 12 out of a possible 16. The profile of 1 might predict a low degree of hypnotizability. In fact, as reflected in other responses to hypnotic induction, B. revealed considerable motivation and ability to use hypnotic trance. Once hypnotized, he followed suggestions easily, allowing us to work with his fantasy figure and eventually to produce additional figures, and continued to work on his own between sessions. Interestingly, he professed amnesia to the events during the trances, but remembered all commands and suggestions nearly verbatim.

During the first hypnotic session, he was age-regressed to the time of Alex's first appearance. B. was in the army at the time, and some of the interpersonal difficulties that ultimately led to his psychiatric discharge were especially active. His unit was expecting a visit from the Inspector General, and B. was being yelled at by his sergeant for not having handled his paper work correctly. Shortly after this, B. noticed a figure in the corner, dressed in a blue suit and top hat. In subsequent sessions, Alex was further described as being approximately 5" 8' tall, 150 lb., and 24 to 25 years old. These specifications easily fitted B. himself. Shortly after the dressing down by the sergeant, the patient began to drink, and was discharged from his job by the captain. He was furious at both the sergeant and the captain, but even more so at himself for not overtly expressing his anger and for being so obsequious. Alex, who was initially silent and observing, berated B. for not expressing his anger and ordered him to yell back at the sergeant.

During the following session, B. was regressed by two weeks, to a crucial time of confrontation with his mother. This was an event which largely precipitated his current depression and ultimately led to his hospitalization. While in the trance, he acted out in minute detail his quarrel with his mother. The mother was characterized as making unreasonable demands of him. Alex remained in the background, but told the patient that he should slap or stab the mother. B. resisted this command with some effort. He became intolerably anxious at this point in the session, and was allowed to retreat to a calm and neutral situation. He was further instructed to take this refuge whenever he required it during our meetings, so that he would not have to experience more anxiety than he could effectively deal with. Before the conclusion of the session, he was asked to explore by himself ways to effectively deal with his mother, without being passive or subservient, but also without acquiescing to Alex's demand for violence. It was suggested that since he now had a clear task and direction ahead of him, he would find himself feeling more hopeful and brighter in mood. This means of concluding sessions was repeated in most subsequent contacts, so that B. felt he could use our meetings to deal with his problem constructively.

During the third session, B. spoke to Alex while in a trance, and was advised by Alex that he needed both to separate himself from his mother and to leave the hospital. Both attachments gave him a humiliating sense of dependence. B. was then given a signal that would allow Alex to speak to us directly in the patient's voice. Alex now told us that the best advice that he had for B. was that he kill himself or the mother. B. later rejected the idea of killing his mother, in the process making it clear that he felt ready to follow Alex's advice to kill himself. Attempts were made to see if Alex could act in a more supportive capacity, but this role was rejected. The session was concluded by instructing B. to enter trances on his own prior to the next meeting, and to use these trances to see if he could discover another figure who would offer him a different kind of help and in effect compete with the malevolent influence of Alex.

During the next session, B. defined someone sitting behind Alex, in his shadow, dressed in a black suit, white patent leather shoes, with a funny hat. He was born in 1826, was described as 4' 8" tall, and weighed 95 lb. Alex refused to allow him to come out from his shadow. B. agreed at this time to resist any destructive messages from Alex, and to see if he could help this new figure to become stronger and more developed.

At the next session, the new figure became more crystalized. He was named "Jay," had now grown in stature to 5' 5", and was dressed more casually than at the previous interview. B. recognized Jay as being similar to his best friend as he entered puberty. Alex had resisted Jay's arrival by trying to murder the patient and B. in fact attempted to smother himself between the interviews.

In the series of interviews that followed, the figure of Jay became more developed. He gradually increased in size to a maximum of 6', and gained weight as well. His age became fixed at 30. B. had forgotten his initial reference to a birth date of 1826, could not explain that date, and mention of it did not recur. Jay, with assistance during hypnotic sessions, gradually emerged from behind Alex's shadow, becoming more identifiable as a figure in his own right. Accordingly, B. now had dichotomized the influence that he felt, with Alex being entirely malevolent and desiring B.'s suicide, and Jay being supportive, particularly of his desire to become more assertive and independent.

B. gradually improved in mood and assertiveness, and achieved some ability to formulate plans for a future, involving greater independence. Ultimately, when he felt a weakening of the part that desired independence and which was represented by Jay, B. discovered a third figure, also standing behind Alex. When I asked to speak to the newcomer, he presented himself as "George," age 43, over 6', and about 230 lb. He subsequently also emerged from Alex's shadow, and his function was to assist Jay in the battle against Alex. Since Jay was relatively light and weak (his stature had diminished from his maximum of 6'), he required an ally who could physically overpower Alex. Jay had summoned George, and needed to bring him out of the shadow carefully, so that Alex would not rebel by harming B.

In subsequent sessions, our emphasis was on helping B. to link Alex's destructiveness to his own feelings of rage and fear toward his mother. Alex's destructiveness became more prominent at times of separation and confrontation with the mother. We succeeded in binding Alex's suicide commands by pointing out the paradox that were B. to be killed, Alex would no longer have a vehicle to continue living himself. Accordingly, it was in Alex's interest to keep B. alive at all costs.

Shortly after this, B. became comfortable with his own ability to deal effectively with Alex. In the process he retained Jay to aid him and George was discarded as unnecessary. B. explained that Jay was now strong enough to contend with Alex, a message we interpreted as indicating that B. felt better able to deal with his own feelings and to work on areas of relationship, both with his mother and others. Having felt and demonstrated considerable improvement, B. was clearly no longer suicidal, and was feeling quite hopeful. With Jay's assistance, we worked toward a disposition that would assure B.'s independence.

Interestingly, at time of discharge, B. also seemed to be incorporating the image of his therapist (K.S.), dressing in similar styles, assuming more of a therapist's role in group meetings, and managing to have the other patients address him as "doctor." This incorporation, in addition to having his fantasy figures controlled and enlisted in his own service, seemed helpful to him in achieving a separation that previously would have been difficult for him. In feeling better about himself, his companions also became less intrusive, so that he was less aware of their presence and more able, as it were, to act in his own behalf.

In summary, B.'s self-esteem suffered in connection with feelings of helplessness in interpersonal relationships, particularly involving his mother. He felt worthless because of his inability to assert himself and to achieve independence, and externalized the anger that he felt at himself by adopting a malevolent fantasy figure (Alex). He was able to keep this figure, representing his low self-esteem and suicidal impulses, controlled by working directly with "him," and by constructing two competing benevolent fantasy figures: one primary (Jay) and one auxiliary (George). The outcome was substantially augmented feelings of confidence and self-esteem, and the alleviation of the depression and self-destructive inclinations.

A postscript may be added regarding B., who returned to

the unit approximately half a year later, having again become acutely suicidal while living in his home community. Once again, conflicts with his mother had led to Alex becoming dominant over Jay. Jay had almost entirely disappeared by this time, and Alex had the patient attempting to kill himself with a razor. Another figure appeared now, called "Billy," who was six years old. Billy was conceived of in part as a companion of the patient at that age, but also as B. himself, thus bringing the presentation closer to that of a dual personality. Billy was also a symbol for B.'s desire at the time to regress to that age. In a trance, B. was encouraged to find Jay again, and to have Jay become allied with Billy. He was able to do so and in the process, Alex disappeared again. B.'s mood immediately brightened, and he became hopeful about the future with no concerns about suicide.

## DISCUSSION

Both of the patients described, because of the presentation of voices commanding suicide, were admitted and initially treated as schizophrenics. Although one of them had in fact had a previous schizophrenic episode, and required neuroleptics, his particular presentation at this instance was not truly schizophrenic. Rather, both patients were dealing with dissociative phenomena, falling more appropriately in the general category of "hysterical psychoses" (1). More specifically, they were influenced by communications from fantasized companions that also presented some of the features of multiple personality. These features were apparent as the fantasized companions began to assume several of the ego-functions of each patient, threatening to do for the patient what he could not do himself. Thus, Alex would have discharged B.'s hostility toward his mother, Billy *was* B. at age 6, and De Saul would have possessed A. to insure his independence. In addition, it was evident that the companions were clear constructs for features of each patient's own personality, allowing him an opportunity to split these functions off from his primary personality.

What was particularly unusual in the fantasized companions in each patient was the persistence into adulthood. Still more unique was the fact that B. created his companion during adulthood. Even in multiple personalities, as discussed above, the initial emergence of the alter personality generally occurs at earlier ages. In discussing the occurrence of fantasized companions in Navajo adolescents, Proskauer et al. (6) suggest that this may arise because of poor opportunities for positive identification with adults. Each of the patients described here had hostile relationships with their mothers, poor or nonexistent relationships with their fathers, and were unable to find friends among peers of either sex.

Each of the patients was able to make use of his imaginative capacities in treatment and thus in the service of the ego. Since they are so consumed in the fantasies and personalities of the companions, failure to deal with the companions would have missed the essential issues faced by the patients, and in particular the suicidal danger might not have been as readily controlled. Rather than attempting to ignore or eliminate the companion as an unwanted "hallucination," the companion was addressed directly and his involvement in the treatment process was encouraged. This allowed for a partial integration of the companion into the patient's primary personality, especially in B.'s case.

It should be pointed out that the style of treatment described is not necessarily expected to produce a final resolution of the patient's problems. Additional crises may arise, as happened with both patients presented. At these times, dealing with the fantasized figures through hypnosis may provide the most effective means of approaching the current conflicts.

While fantasized companions are frequently expected to be playmates or otherwise pleasant or supportive figures, Hilgard (4) points out that they may also be unpleasant or hostile. This was certainly so with each of the above patients—the companion threatening A. alternately with abandonment and possession and B. with murder of the primary self.

While A.'s companion for the most part cooperated with us, B.'s entirely malignant companion refused to do so, and ultimately was best influenced by encouraging the creation under hypnosis of competing, benevolent companions. In effect, these were complementary and supportive personalities. There is some precedence in the hypnotic induction of multiple personalities, both in experimental situations (26, 27), and in therapy (28). Leavitt (28) described the induction of both a superego- and an id-like personality, the latter providing information in therapy that greatly enhanced the course of treatment. We are not aware of previous therapeutic inductions of fantasized companions in the literature. The use of hypnosis in therapy was also important in enabling each patient to establish control over his own experience. In the process he was able to overcome feelings of helplessness, and deal with his dependency and bolster his self-esteem.

The theme common to both patients was the feeling of weakness and ineffectiveness in dealing with the external environment, particularly in interpersonal contexts. Each tended to be isolated, and felt humiliated by his dependence on others. With feelings of inadequacy and difficulty with assertiveness, each experienced extremely low self-esteem combined with resentment and rage. The fantasized companion allowed for a splitting of ego and superego functions, and in the superego role, threatened dire punishment to the patient in the form of abandonment, possession, or death. On some occasions, however, the companion acted to goad the patient into becoming hostilely assertive, with murderous rage directed at the mother by B. and at a roommate by A. The patient in each case was thus freed from his burden of guilt, in that the companion assumed all responsibility for the prohibited rage and its discharge.

Each patient had an especially poor sense of his own identity, and seemed to require the fantasized companions to provide him with an intimate figure with a more defined identity. With A., that identity had been clear and unchanging since the age of 5. B.'s primary companion, Alex, was also relatively stable, although the two induced companions tended to vary according to need or circumstance. Interestingly, this patient was very specific about details, that could then be entirely abandoned or forgotten (e.g., the mention of a birth date for Jay that never recurred). The stronger identity of the companions often served an ego-function for each patient, encouraging a shaping of the environment or dealing with interpersonal problems in ways that were too frightening for him to undertake by himself. Thus A.'s companion instructed him in how to deal with his wife and make living arrangements, and B. was encouraged to establish an independent residence by the benevolent companion, Jay. Of further interest was the tendency exhibited by this patient to adopt other personalities perceived as strong and benevolent, as he did when he assumed that of his therapist. One may speculate on the extent to which being a twin contributed to his identity confusion. A not uncommon form of fantasized companion is that of the fantasy twin (11). Alex's appearance was not unlike that of the patient himself, and may have allowed for a perpetuation of the feeling of being half of a pair of twins. The fantasized companion was of the same sex, and thus perhaps a more compatible twin that the real twin sister.

Another function served by the companions was that of ego-ideal, more strikingly so in A., but also in the appearance of the benevolent and powerful George for B. Proskauer et al. (6) write that the experience of the fantasized companion "cannot survive the successful forging of a unified identity later on." Indeed, as B. came to identify the nature of his conflicts, primarily regarding his mother, his need for his companions diminished and they appeared less intrusively and less frequently. A., however, never reached such a point. In many respects, the companion, as a powerful ego ideal, was the preferred personality, but the patient, by the time of the second discharge, had not reached a sufficient level of self-esteem to allow for its integration into his own identity.

The functions of offering companionship and caring were served in each patient. A., feeling neglected and less loved than his brother, could be watched over and cared for by this somewhat parental companion, while B., in finding the figure of Jay, regained a lost pal of his adolescence. A. was additionally able to establish his own importance, even to the point of grandiosity, in that his companion was specially sent by powerful generals.

Issues of loneliness were also addressed with each patient.

Leiderman (29), in his discussion of pathological loneliness, suggests a difficulty in self-object differentiation. When significant individuals, including a mother or sibling, for example, are lost to these patients, they feel incomplete and will appear depressed. It may be speculated that A., forced to be separate from his mother and his wife, and B., separated from his mother and a twin during military service, could not replace the lost relationships with others external to themselves, and instead relied upon their fantasized companions to reestablish a sense of completeness, and thus redress their loneliness.

In both cases the companions, as typically occurs, were means of dealing with stresses and trauma, often involving threatened separation. At the point of hopelessness about dealing with these traumata, the companions became malignant. By bringing to the therapy context the same imaginative capacity that had created the companions, the conflicts could be approached, and the patients felt more hopeful about eventual resolution.

While the primary focus in this paper has been on fantasized companions who have expressed pathology, and have been addressed in the treatment of that pathology, the phenomenon needs to be recognized as a normal one as well. As in multiple personality, there is likely to be a range of experience from the normal and appropriate to the severely pathological. One may say, in recalling an act that was atypical of himself, that "That's not the kind of thing I would do," or "I just wasn't myself." At the other end of the spectrum, one may dissociate himself entirely from that foreign part of himself. Similarly, most people address some sort of fantasized companion, for example in the form of a personal God with whom one converses, or perhaps as a responsive audience that one carries with him. At the other end of this spectrum are fantasized companions who become so dissociated from the person that they acquire independent behavior, as in the patients presented here.

## SUMMARY

Two cases of adult men, with well-established fantasized companions integral in suicidal ideation, both admitted to an acute psychiatric inpatient service, have been presented. The persistence of a fantasized companion this late in life is unusual, and the original occurrence, as in Patient B., even more so. Each patient was initially regarded as actively schizophrenic, and treated accordingly. The relationship of the described condition to hysterical psychoses, multiple personalities and other fantasy states is discussed. Because of that relationship, treatment employing hypnosis was regarded to be appropriate, and outcomes are described. The fantasized companions served the functions, in varying degrees with each patient, of relieving isolation and loneliness; enhancing self-esteem; punishing the patient in a superego role; acting as an ego-substitute to help deal with the external environment; alleviating guilt in the experience and discharge of rage; enhancing and complementing a sense of identity, in effect joining with the patient's primary personality to form one total identity; acting as ego-ideal; and providing a means, even though destructively, of dealing with unacceptable stresses and threatened separation.

The importance of differentiating conditions, in which fantasy and dissociative elements are integral, from true psychosis, is emphasized.

*Acknowledgment:* Greatest appreciation is expressed to David Spiegel, M.D., Associate Professor, P. Herbert Leiderman, M.D., Professor, and C. Peter Rosenbaum, M.D., Professor, all of the Department of Psychiatry and Behavioral Sciences, Stanford University School of Medicine, for their critical reading and invaluable comments.

## REFERENCES

1. Spiegel, D., Fink, R. Hysterical Psychosis and Hypnotizability. *Am. J. Psychiatry* 136:777–781, 1979.

2. Perry, J. *The Self in Psychotic Process: Its Symbolization in Schizophrenia.* University of California Press, Berkeley and Los Angeles, 1933.

3. Svendsen, M. Children's Imaginary Companions. *Arch. Neurol. Psychiatry* 32:985–999, 1934.

4. Hilgard, J. R. *Personality and Hypnosis.* The University of Chicago Press, Chicago, 1979.

5. Harriman, P. L. Some Imaginary Companions of Older Subjects. *Am. J. Orthopsychiatry* 7:368–370, 1937.

6. Proskauer, S., Barsh, E. T., and Johnson, L. B. Imaginary Companions and Spiritual Allies of Three Navajo Adolescents. *J. Psychiatr. Anthropol.* 3:153–174, 1980.

7. Kirkpatrick, E. A. *Fundamentals of Child Study.* Macmillan, New York, 1929.

8. Nagera, H. The Imaginary Companion. Its Significance for Ego Development and Conflict Solution. *Psychoanal. Study Child* 24:165–196, 1969.

9. Rucker, N. G. Capacities of Integration, Oedipal Ambivalence, and Imaginary Companions. *Am. J. Psychoanal.* 41:129–137, 1981.

10. Jersild, A. T., Markey, F. V., and Jersild, C. L. Children's Fears, Dreams, Wishes. *Child Devel. Monograph, 12.* Teachers College, Columbia University, New York, 1933.

11. Myers, W. A. Imaginary Companions, Fantasy Twins, Mirror Dreams and Depersonalization. *Psychoanal. Q.* 45:503–524, 1976.

12. Benson, R. M., and Pryor, D. B. "When Friends Fall Out": Developmental Interference with the Function of Some Imaginary Companions. *J. Psychoanal. Assoc.* 21:457–473, 1973.

13. Manosevitz, M., Prentice, N. M., and Wilson, F. Individual and Family Correlates of Imaginary Companions in Preschool Children. *Develop. Psychol.* 3:72–79, 1973.

14. Bach, S. Notes on Some Imaginary Companions. *Psychoanal. Study Child* 26:159–171, 1971.

15. Fraiberg, S. *The Magic Years.* Scribner's, New York, 1959.

16. Freud, A. *The Ego and the Mechanisms of Defense,* rev. ed., International Universities Press, New York, 1966.

17. Singer, J. The Importance of Daydreaming. *Psychology Today* 1:18–27, 1968.

18. Bliss, E. L. Multiple Personalities: A Report of 14 Cases with Implications for Schizophrenia and Hysteria. *Arch. Gen. Psychiatry* 37:1388–1397, 1980.

19. Congdon, M. H., Hain, J., and Stevenson, I. A Case of Multiple Personality Illustrating the Transition from Role-Playing. *J. Nerv. Ment. Dis.* 132:497–504, 1961.

20. Ludwig, A., Brandsma, J., and Wilbur, C. The Objective Study of Multiple Personality, or, Are Four Heads Better than One? *Arch. Gen. Psychiatry* 26:298–310, 1972.

21. Bowers, M., and Brecher, S. The Emergence of Multiple Personalities in the Course of Hypnotic Investigation. *Int. J. Clin. Exp. Hypn.* 3:188–199, 1955.

22. Greaves, G. B. Multiple Personality 165 Years After Mary Reynolds. *J. Nerv. Ment. Dis.* 168:577–596, 1980.

23. Nemiah, J. C. Hysterical Neurosis, Dissociative Type. In *Comprehensive Textbook of Psychiatry, vol. 1, 2nd ed.* Freedman, A. M. et al., Eds. Williams and Wilkins Company, Baltimore, 1975.

24. Spiegel, H., and Spiegel, D. *Trance and Treatment.* Basic Books, New York, 1978.

25. Prince, M. *The Dissociation of a Personality.* Longmans, Green, New York, 1906.

26. Kampman, R. Hypnotically Induced Multiple Personality: an Experimental Study. *Int. J. Clin. Exp. Hypn.* 24:215–227, 1976.

27. Harriman, P. L. The Experimental Induction of a Multiple Personality. *Psychiatry* 5:179–186, 1942.

28. Leavitt, H. C. A Case of Hypnotically Produced Secondary and Tertiary Personalities. *Psychoanal. Rev.* 34:274–295, 1947.

29. Leiderman, P. H. Pathological Loneliness: A Psychodynamic Interpretation. In *The Anatomy of Loneliness*, Hartog, J. et al., Eds. International Universities Press, New York, 1980.

# 10 Double Suicide

## Patricia A. Santy, M.D.

*This chapter reviews the literature on double suicide and presents two cases: a suicide pact between two young women, and a pact between an older married couple. The cases are unique in that all four participants were in psychotherapy prior to their successful suicides, thus making antecedent histories available for review. Using these two detailed cases and two other cases reported in the literature, some general observations on the psychodynamics of suicide pacts are discussed.*

Double suicide is an agreement between two people to end their lives. It is a rare occurrence, accounting for only one in 400 completed suicides (1). Cohen (2) found that of 20,788 completed suicides in England between 1955–1958, there were only 58 double suicides; 42 of these involved husbands and wives whose mean ages were 60 and 56 years, respectively. Characteristic of these couples was social isolation, with dependence and devotion to one another. Unemployment and serious physical illness in one or both partners were common. Other authors (3, 4) have discussed instances in which the two people, under threat of separation by forthcoming death or other circumstances, have entered into a suicide pact. An exception to this is the study of double suicide in psychiatric hospital patients (5, 6) where there was no "pact" between the people, but one patient's suicide seemed to stimulate another's.

157

Tabachnick (7) in discussing interpersonal relationships where one member is suicidal, remarks on the dependent and masochistic aspects of the relationship, and the conflictual feelings that arise from this dependence. He felt that often both members of the unit were suicidal, although only one acted out these feelings.

Hemphill and Thornley (4) point out that very few cases exist where the psychiatrist has had the opportunity to investigate the personalities of the people involved in suicide pacts, apparently due to their very high success rate. Also, little seems to be known of the participants' lives or relationship to one another, since survivors are rare. In fact, of the approximately 10 cases mentioned in the literature, only two of the cases could be examined in depth, and the personalities of the parties described.

Noyes et al (1), in an in-depth study of conjugal suicide pact noted a striking resemblance between the conjugal suicide pact and folie à deux (7–10), in which delusional ideas or abnormal behavior are transferred from one individual to a second individual with whom the first is close. Typically in a folie à deux, a dominant, psychotic partner provides delusional development in a relatively dependent, submissive mate. Upon separation from the dominant partner, the dependent partner generally gives up his or her erroneous beliefs. It has been speculated that the dependent partner is so overwhelmed by fears of losing the mate that the psychotic behavior is accepted as a means of maintaining the relationship. Conjugal suicide pacts also appear to have developed out of the dynamics of the relationship and "not primarily of the stresses which were common accompaniments of life. . ." (4).

The two new cases presented in this article are unusual in that all members of the pacts were involved in psychotherapy at a large general hospital. In fact, in the first case to be presented, the two female participants met while involved in therapy.

## Case 1

S. was a 25-year-old, single, college-educated Caucasian. female. L. was a 30-year-old, Caucasian female. They were admitted a week apart to an inpatient psychiatric ward because of suicidal ideation. They had not known each other previously, and on the ward they became friends. Throughout the course of hospitalization both improved markedly and eventually were transferred to a Day Treatment service. Both women had the same doctor on that service; S. was seen in individual therapy with the doctor, and L. was seen in individual therapy with the social worker on the treatment team. When she left the Day Treatment service, S. continued in individual therapy, while L. and her therapist terminated. L. was then referred to an outpatient group.

S. had had no previous psychiatric hospitalizations but had made several suicide attempts over the previous two years. She dated her problem back two years when she began to experience feelings of isolation and depersonalization. Her background was extremely stormy. She was the illegitimate daughter of a well-known evangelist who was married, but who provided financially for S. and her mother. The father, who was idolized by S., was a rather promiscuous man and was finally shot and killed by a jealous husband when the patient was twelve years old and living away at school. S.'s mother married when S. was thirteen years old, and S. and her stepfather apparently had a good relationship. This relationship was abruptly terminated when the stepfather also was killed by neighbors, who though he was breaking into their house. Both S.'s father and stepfather had been alcoholics.

S. had left home at age seventeen and began a series of relationships with older men. She had made one suicide attempt after the breakup of one of those relationships several years earlier. At the time of her hospitalization, she was living with a forty-four-year-old, divorced college professor; she was extremely dissatisfied with the relationship, but unable to leave it.

S. did well in Day Treatment and individual therapy, and plans were made for discharge with continued individual therapy. Her therapist, however, left the Day Treatment service three weeks prior to S.'s discharge date. This signaled the beginning of serious acting-out behavior, which led to S.'s premature discharge from the service, thereby disrupting treatment. However, individual therapy was continued once a week. S. began to push her therapist for more frequent sessions, and after much discussion between them, as well as because of her progress over the next two months, it was decided to increase the sessions to twice a week. At that time, S. was not feeling suicidal and had just started taking classes at a local college.

It was also L.'s first psychiatric hospitalization. She was admitted to the ward after she had taken an overdose of her father's sleeping medication. Her problem dated back one year, when she had become dissatisfied with her job as a drug salesperson. With the encouragement of a male supervisor whom she idolized, and who was leaving the firm, she applied and obtained a better job at a rival company. After starting work there, however, she realized that the new job was beyond her capabilities, and she longed intensely for her old job and supervisor. Also at this time, she was informed that her father was dying of cancer and had only a few months to live. She precipitously quit her job and moved in with her parents. Her father soon could not be cared for at home and was placed in a convalescent home. During one of his "home visits," L. took his medicine in a deliberate attempt to kill herself. "I just couldn't watch him slowly deteriorate like that," was her statement on admission. Often she would describe her symptoms as a "cancer that is eating me up." She repeatedly expressed feelings of identification with her dying father to the point of fearing she was a man. An endocrine disturbance appeared at this point, increasing her body hair and her fears that she was "becoming a man." L. was diagnosed as having a psychotic depressive reaction, because her intense preoccupation with her body was thought to be a delusion. She was not started on any antipsychotic drug, however, since it was felt that it might worsen her endocrine problem.

L. responded well to individual pyychotherapy and was soon transferred to the Day Treatment service. Her prognosis was considered good, and she was seen in short-term individual therapy that focused on her feelings related to her father's imminent death. Her father died while she was on the Day Treatment service. She went through a grief reaction, and it looked as if her depression was resolving. Eventually she obtained a menial job, not wanting to go back to her old profession, and she was discharged from the service with follow-up group therapy planned in the outpatient clinic. L. expressed much disappointment at the termination of her individual therapy. Shortly after starting outpatient group therapy, L. found out that her mother had been diagnosed as having cancer of the bladder. Already angry that she had been assigned to group instead of individual therapy (something she talked about in group), she quit the group. She contacted S., and they disappeared. They were found four days later in a hotel room, lying clothed on separate beds with liquor bottles and various pills scattered over the floor. They had disappeared together the day after S. and her therapist had made the decision to increase the number of sessions per week.

S. and L. had become fast friends during their inpatient hospitalization, and their friendship continued while they were on the Day Treatment service. S. seemed to idealize L. and would continually urge her to drop out of therapy because she was really "healthy." L., on her part, supported and encouraged S.'s destructive acting out; for example, several times when S. would decide to "play hooky" from Day Treatment, L. covered up for her. L. was seen by the staff as a "good patient" meaning high-functioning, obeying the rules and "not causing trouble." L. very rarely expressed anger and was easy to get along with.

The two spent much time together while they were in Day Treatment. S. talked of wanting to commit suicide to "teach her mother a lesson," L. who talked of being "bored with her life," felt sorry for S. and her plight. The staff would often comment on the bizarre preoccupation with suicide the two women expressed in their conversations and interactions.

## Case 2

Mr. and Mrs. D., ages 52 and 49 respectively, were first evaluated at our facility after discharge from another hospital, where they had been admitted following an unsuccessful suicide attempt by taking an overdose of barbiturates. When they presented to our outpatient department seeking psychiatric help, they were started in conjoint therapy.

Mrs. D. and her husband were both alcoholics. Mrs. D. had a history of a prior suicide attempt three years earlier. At that time, their sixteen-year-old twin sons had just been placed on probation for burglary and drug charges. She and her husband had been planning a trip, but the night before they were to go, Mrs. D. decided she could not trust her sons alone and stayed home. Mr. D. then went on the trip alone. She related her suicide attempt as an impulsive act with no real planning or intent.

Mrs. D. was an only child who grew up in Texas. Her mother died when she was three years old. She described her father as "distant." Her father remarried when she was eleven years old. She disliked her stepmother and after two years left to live with an aunt and uncle. At age nineteen she married a compulsive gambler and bore two daughters. When she was pregnant with the third child, her husband left her. She put the third child up for adoption, sent the other children to the paternal grandparents, and had not seen them since. Four years later she married Mr. D. She then had a stillborn son, followed by the twins. After her first suicide attempt, she was told that she had impaired liver function and a borderline diabetic condition. She was uncooperative about having psychiatric treatment and left against medical advice, refusing any follow-up planning.

Mr. D. denied any previous psychiatric history. He had been a longshoreman for many years and claimed to be a nondrinking alcoholic when he and his wife contacted our clinic. He had been arrested the year before for allegedly acting as an accomplice in a homicide, but was released for lack of evidence. In therapy, he came across as very uncompromising and hostile. There was suspicion that he beat his wife, and her feelings vacillated toward him—sometimes referring to him as "tyrannical" and other times as "a very gentle man."

Mr. D. had been the instigator of the unsuccessful first suicide pact, and he related to the therapist that he had done it because he was "bored with his life" and because he was "disgusted" by his twin sons' laziness and the "way the world was going." Mr. and Mrs. D. were willing to give the therapy a try, and after two and a half months appeared to be feeling better about their lives. Mrs. D. was even thinking of going to work. At this point, the therapist, who Mr. and Mrs. D. had remarked, reminded them of their twins in appearance, informed the couple that he would be rotating off the service and that they would be transferred to a new doctor. When they did not show up for the last scheduled appointment with the therapist, he called and found out that on that day Mr. and Mrs. D. had successfully committed suicide by shooting themselves.

## DISCUSSION

Since the suicide pact seems to arise out of the relationship between the two parties, it is interesting to speculate exactly what features in the relationship play a part in the development of a suicide pact. What is (symbolically) expressed by committing suicide together? Cases 1 and 2 could be presented in detail only because the participants in the pacts were involved in psychotherapy for some time before their suicides. The conjugal suicide pact presented by Noyes, et al. (1) and the report by Hemphill and Thornley (4) of a pact between two adolescent boys, both of whom lived through the attempt and one of whom was followed in therapy, are the only other cases presented in some depth in the literature. These two previous examples of suicide pacts show a striking similarity with our new cases in several aspects.

Certain personality features appear to be significant in all four cases. The "dominant" members (the instigators of the pact) shared many similar qualities, as did the "passive" members; the former exhibiting features of Orgel's "fusion with the victim" (11), and the latter, what I would call, a "destructive desire for fusion" (Table 10-1 lists comparative features of these suicide-pact members).

In discussing suicide in general, Orgel describes "fusion with the victim," as a state considered to be the opposite of identification with the aggressor. In these suicidal individuals, the idealized love object is seen not as omnipotent and powerful, but as victimized and destroyed, i.e. helpless against the hostility of the world. Their suicidal feelings can be thought of as a symbolic fusion or identification, it may serve to keep the suicidal individual from awareness of his own hostility and aggression, as well as his own feelings of being victimized. The dominant members of the pacts all seem to view their partners in this light in order to protect themselves from the hostility they often have toward what their partners represent.

Three of the four dominant members had a history of antisocial behavior, some bad enough to draw jail sentences, for which they were not repentant, but openly blamed someone else. Mr. D. may have been projecting his own hostility onto his sons, whose antisocial actions might have been unconsciously encouraged by Mr. D.—much like the mechanism Johnson (12) described for parental sanctions of superego lacunae in adolescents. In the same way L. encouraged S. to

TABLE 10-1
Comparison of the Members of Four Suicide Packs

| Dominant Member | Passive Member |
|---|---|
| 1. Regressive identification with love objects (victims) | 1. Ambivalence toward love objects |
| 2. Projection is major defense | 2. Splitting as major defense |
| 3. Projection of hostility onto the "world" (homicidal?) | 3. Suicidal (hostility projected onto the self) |
| 4. Able to act successfully on suicidal impulse (instigator) | 4. Unable to act successfully (alone on suicidal impulse due to ambivalence) |
| 5. Aggressive/destructive fantasies projected onto the world (Identified with the victims of the world's hostility and safe from awareness of their own) | 5. Aggressive/destructive fantasies entwined with fantasies of "merging" with the loved object |
| 6 Encourages others to "act out" his own anger | 6. Express anger through "acting-out" behavior |
| Past History | Past History |
| No prior psychiatric history. History of antisocial behavior and involvement with police. | History of suicide gesture(s) and prior psychiatric treatment. History of severe depression and loss dating back to childhood. |

"act out" for her. While L. appeared healthy to the staff, it was discovered later that she had encouraged S. to leave treatment and to act on other destructive impulses, at the same time that she would cover up for and protect S. All four dominant partners were thus overtly or covertly angry, hostile persons (two of them may have had psychotic depressions). All had projection as a major defense and identified with the "victim" in their respective partners.

The passive members of the pact appeared to exhibit a different pathology (but one that fits with their partners like that of a "lock and key" mechanism). These members have the characteristic features of splitting, with extremes of good and bad, demonstrated by borderline personality disorders (the two passive partners of the pacts presented in this article carried this diagnosis on the chart). Three of the four passive partners had made previous suicide gestures. All four had early histories of object loss and emotional deprivation, resulting in markedly ambivalent feelings toward love objects and extreme splitting. S. would describe fantasies with the theme of destroying a love object and simultaneously reuniting with it ("destructive desire for fusion"). The suicide gestures may be viewed as an attempt to reunite with the lost, idealized love object, and at the same time to discharge the hostile, aggressive feelings toward these same objects. They did this via the mechanism of splitting. Their dominant partners, conversely, denied any hostility toward loved ones and identified via projection with their love objects as victims, whom they would rescue from the world's hostility.

The suicide pact represents one method for these two types of people to resolve the underlying psychodynamic conflicts in their relationships. For the dominant members, who view their partners as the helpless victims doomed by the world, and do not recognize that it is their own hostility that continues to victimize their partners, the regressive identification leads to a strong suicidal impulse. The deaths of the loved ones/victims coupled with their own deaths cement in reality this symbolic fusion and make them simultaneously the "rescuers" and the fellow-victims. The passive partners are dependent and feel massive ambivalence, while their dominant partners are relatively unambivalent and therefore able to act as instigators.

An important aspect of this author's two cases is the observation that the two double suicides occurred at significant points in the psychotherapeutic process. This, of course, is of practical concern to the therapist. How did the therapeutic relationship touch on or activate the dynamic conflicts in each of these persons? There seem to be no other cases in the literature except for the two presented here, where the members of suicide pacts were in therapy prior to their successful double suicides. Both dominant members L. and Mr. D., were faced with the *loss of the therapist* to whom they had become attached. We can speculate that this mobilized the hostile-aggressive feelings, which then were dealt with by inducing their partners to act out with them, convinced that they were actually "rescuing" the loved ones and themselves from the cruel and hostile world, as symbolized by the "cruel, rejecting" therapist.

As far as the passive members are concerned, S. was to have increased the number of sessions per week and this intensified closeness (merging) with the "good" object simultaneously stimulated the need to destroy the "bad" (herself) and made her particularly vulnerable to L.'s need to see her victimized. Mrs. D. had reported feeling much better in the therapy, and we can speculate that the anticipated loss of the "good" therapist suddenly transformed him into the "bad" therapist, again mobilizing Mrs. D.'s anger toward bad objects and stimulating the suicidal impulses which then made her receptive to Mr. D.'s plan.

The therapeutic relationship will reflect significant aspects of the pathology of the suicide-pact relationship. The dominant partner will inevitably project his anger and hostility onto the therapist, or he may be manipulative and uncompromising in his view of the world, making the therapist uncomfortable (or even angry) and likely to push away the patient (13). This action, conscious or unconscious by the therapist, may reinforce the patient's identification as a victim, and stimulate the suicidal impulse. Separation issues cannot be played down and should be dealt with directly, over a long enough time to permit their working through by the patient. It might be very difficult to handle such cases in short-term therapy.

The passive partner's ambivalence toward objects needs to be kept constantly in mind by the therapist. Often the therapist's own rescue fantasies toward such patients as well as the desire to be the "good" mother, can make the therapist blind to the destructive feelings present in the patient that may be mobilized in the transference. Thus, increasing the number of sessions, as well as decreasing or terminating them, might result in the desire of the patient to destroy the "bad" object, i.e. himself.

The high success rate for this type of suicide leaves the therapist little room for miscalculations. It is hoped that the two cases presented here will help to make therapists more aware of the dynamics involved in potentially suicidal relationships.

## SUMMARY

The author suggests that the dominant and passive members of suicide pacts may each have specific psychodynamics which, when brought together, make a suicide pact more likely. The dominant partner's "fusion with the victim" and the passive partner's "destructive desire for fusion" may be keys to help the therapist identify these potentially suicidal relationships.

It is emphasized that these psychodynamics are also played out in the relationship with the therapist, and that therapists should be alert for actions on their part that may unwittingly stimulate the pact. In being able to identify the individual psychopathologies that, when combined, may lead to double suicide, the therapist can more accurately predict the suicide pact and prevent it.

## REFERENCES

1. Noyes, R., Frye, S., and Hartford, C. E. Conjugal Suicide Pact. *J. Nerv. Ment. Dis.* 165:72, 1977.

2. Cohen, J. A Study of Suicide Pacts. *Medico-legal J.* 29:44, 1961.

3. East, N. A Study of Suicide Survivors. *J. Ment. Sci.* 59:428, 1913.

4. Hemphill, R. E., and Thornley, F. I. Suicide Pacts. *S.A. Med. J.* 43:1335, 1969.

5. Crawford, J. P., and Willis, J. H. Double Suicide in Psychiatric Hospital Patients. *Br. J. Psychiatry* (493):1231, Dec. 1966.

6. Sacks, M. and Eth, S. Pathological Identification as a Cause of Suicide on an Inpatient Unit. *Hosp. Comm. Psychiatry* 32:36, 1981.

7. Tabachnick, N. Interpersonal Relations to Suicidal Attempts. *Arch. Gen. Psychiatry* 4:42, 1961.

8. Lange, E., and Ficker, F. Suicide à deux and Folie à deux. *Arch. Gen. Psychiatry* 5:257, 1961.

9. Gralnick, A. Folie a deux—Psychosis of Association. *Psychiatr. Q.* 16:230, 1942.

10. Pulver, A. and Brunt, M. Deflection of Hostility in Folie à deux. *Arch. Gen. Psychiatry* 5:257, 1961.

11. Orgel, S. Fusion with the Victim and Suicide. *Int. J. Psych-Anal.* 55:531, 1974.

12. Johnson, A. Sanctions for Superego Lacunae of Adolescents. In *Search-lights on Delinquency*. K. R. Eissler Ed., International Universities Press, 1949.

13. Tabachnick, N. Countertransference Crisis in Suicidal Attempts. *Arch. Gen. Psychiatry* 4:64, 1961.

# 11 Erotized Repetitive Hangings

## H. L. P. Resnik, M.D.

> Razors pain you;
> Rivers are damp;
> Acids stain you;
> And drugs cause cramp.
> Guns aren't lawful;
> Nooses give;
> Gas smells awful;
> You might as well live.
> Dorothy Parker, *Résumé*

This paper will consider a syndrome in which some nooses give, and other take, lives. Erotized repetitive hangings, as best I can ascertain by a review of the professional literature, have to date not been considered as a psychologic entity.

The study of self-destructive behaviors is a multidisciplinary task. This was the case for both myself and Dr. Robert Litman, who independently working with receptive Medical Examiners[1] and utilizing the technique called the "psychological autopsy" were invited by them to explore the entity referred to as a "sex hanging," a syndrome well known to Medical Examiners and police investigators (1, 2).

---

[1]Medical Examiners: Joseph Davis, M.D., Dade County, Fla.; Theodore Curphey, M.D. (Retired), Los Angeles, Calif.

169

These deaths by hanging or asphyxiation involved men who seemed to be engaged in autoerotic activity, judged by such features as partial nudity, binding of the genitals, and pornographic materials. Although they are bizarre, these cases are not medical rarities or forensic curiosities. Stearns (3) reported one or two a year from Massachusetts, between 1941 and 1950. In Virginia, six such deaths occurred in five years, and in Fort Worth, Texas, seven in five years (4). There were 20 fatal cases in Los Angeles between 1958 and 1968. From these data, Litman and I estimated that there are *at least* 50 erotized hanging deaths yearly in the United States. Yet, what one cannot estimate is even more important! How many young men engage in this activity and how frequently do they suspend themselves?

This paper will attempt (a) to draw this potentially lethal form of sexual behavior to the attention of clinicians in the hopes that both patients and parents can be cautioned about the danger of self-suspension; and (b) to stimulate clinical study of patients who have before, or are currently, engaged in such behaviors, in order to better understand and treat it. I shall also attempt to conceptualize this syndrome psychodynamically and to relate it to neurophysiologic mechanisms. Since living persons with this syndrome are so rare[2] it will be important for others who will treat such patients to evaluate the hypotheses and formulations I have derived from the literature and a study of *les faits accomplis*. I would have much preferred one living patient but have been unable to locate one in the ten years of my interest. Increasing requests by colleagues to share my thoughts have moved me to write this paper without actual clinical experience with the syndrome.

## DESCRIPTION OF THE SYNDROME

The elements of the "erotized repetitive hanging" syndrome are as follows:

---

[2]William H. Masters, M.D. has informed me that such sexual behavior has never been reported by patients he has studied.

1. An adolescent or young adult male (it is in adolescence that the behavior begins; if the practitioner lives to adulthood, the syndrome can become less lethal as partners may become involved);

2. Ropes, belts, or other binding material so arranged that compression of the neck may be produced and controlled voluntarily;

3. Evidence of masturbation (for example, semen);

4. Partial or complete nudity;

5. A solitary act;

6. Repetitive behavior that the deceased had tried to insure would leave no visible mark on his person;

7. No apparent wish to die;

8. The presence of erotic pictures or literature; and less frequently

9. Binding of the body and/or the extremities and/or genitals with ropes, chains or leather; and

10. Female attire may be present.

## LITERATURE REVIEW

The association of priapism and suspension, sometimes with ejaculation, has been reported following execution by hanging. An old English poem dramatically bears evidence of this:

In our town the other day
They hanged a man to make him pay
For having raped a little girl.
As life departed from the churl
The townsfolk saw, with great dismay
His organ rise in boldest way
A sign to all who stood around
That pleasure e'en in death is found.

In his last work, completed only five months before his death, Melville directs to the medical profession the question of the origin of priapism in hanging. Following the hanging of Billy Budd (" to the wonder of all, no motion was apparent . . .")

the Purser advanced to the ship's Surgeon his theory that the absence of an erection was secondary to Billy Budd's will power. The Surgeon's reply is no less appropriate now than it was in 1891: "I do not with my present knowledge pretend to account for it at all" (5).

In 1911, Hanns Heinz Ewers, the German novelist who wrote of the erotic and grotesque, produced a novel called *Alraune* (The Mandrake) based upon a folk superstition that semen emitted from a hanged man when spilled upon the ground will fertilize the growth of a mandrake plant (6). Sterba (7) cites one of Ewers' short stories involving the elements of masturbation and a young man's suicide by hanging, this time associated with the fear of oral incorporation by mother as symbolized by the spider who both hangs, binds, and bites.

In *Waiting for Godot* (8), Beckett also had something to say about erotized repetitive hangings (pp. 12–13).

*Vladimir:* . . . What do we do?
*Estragon:* Wait.
*Vladimir:* Yes, but while waiting.
*Estragon:* What about hanging ourselves?
*Vladimir:* Hmm. It'd give us an erection.
*Estragon:* (highly excited) An erection!
*Vladimir:* With all that follows. Where it falls *mandrakes grow*. That's why they shriek when you pull them up. Did you now know that?
*Estragon:* Let's hang ourselves immediately.

There follows a discussion of who will go first, and, as throughout the play, no action is taken.

In published erotica, hanging is described as an act connected with sexual stimulation and intense excitement. For example, in de Sade's *Justine* (9), Roland introduces Thérèse to "Cut-the-Cord." One version of this occurs when Roland himself is haltered. He masturbates, kicks the stool from under himself and is cut down by his female partner. The association of masturbation, sexuality, and the gamble with death are clear from the text: "I am as firmly persuaded as I can possibly be that this death (by the rope) is at least sweeter than cruel. . . .

It is in person I wish to be acquainted with the sensation. . . . By way of experience itself, I want to find out whether it is not very certain this asphyxiation impels, in the individual who undergoes it, the erectory nerve to provide an ejaculation." De Sade offers us the most graphic description of this behavior short of that one would encounter clinically. Thérèse speaks: "Nothing but symptoms of pleasure ornament his countenance and at practically the same instant rapid jets of semen spring nigh to the vault. . . . I rushed to cut him down. He falls unconscious. Thanks to my ministrations, he quickly recovers his senses." Upon reviving, Roland exclaims, ". . . Oh, those sensations are not to be described; they transcend all one can possibly say."

Prostitutes who are specialists in catering to the diverse needs of their clientele have been known to have at their disposal ingeniously constructed hanging contrivances by means of which they procure for the client the pleasure of strangulation so controlled as not to endanger his life. Hirschfeld (10, p. 273) reported a case in which "the masochist had himself hauled up by pulleys; that excited him and while he was suspended, he went blue in the face and had a discharge."

The musician, Kotzwarra, regarded by Bach as the best bass player in Europe, died in 1791 as a result of a similar episode. He had a prostitute hang him for five minutes. However, upon release, he could not be revived. The girl was tried, acquitted, and "took resolutions for a better life." The facts revealed were so extraordinary that the court requested ladies in the audience to leave and all records to be destroyed (10).

The medical literature has far fewer references. Stearns (3) reviewed suicides in Massachusetts during the ten-year period, 1941–1950, and found that 97 of those involved were under twenty-one years of age. Of those, 25, or one-fourth, were variously attributed to either probable suicides in young persons without obvious motivation, accidental death, or sex hanging. Stearns' review of the literature identified reported cases by the English forensic pathologist, Simpson, and by the French psychiatrist, De Boismont. A review of De Boismont's 1856 monograph (11) reveals that he reported 30 percent of the males (197 of 656 cases) who died by hanging had associated erections or ejaculations (p. 525).

Anthropologists have reported that Eskimo children hang themselves in some game, probably sexual, and that the Yahgans in South America tied the neck to induce partial strangulation and exhilaration, at which time they saw beautiful colors (3). De Sade also traces erotized hanging behavior back to the Celts (9). Shoshone-Bannock Indian children have among their games several involving risk-taking and suffocation experiences. These are called "smoke-out," "red-out," and "hang-up."[3] I too have noted several games in which excited children choke each other by compressing the neck or chest.

Stearns posed the question of whether these hanging deaths are accident or suicide, but without a psychodynamic conceptual framework, he was unable to go further (3). The former Boston Medical Examiner, Richard Ford, reported six such cases in which he concluded the deaths were accidental; his determination was that the intention was autoerotic and not suicidal (1). All forensic pathologists indicate perplexity and ask for psychologic evaluation of the syndrome in order to better understand how to classify the death. Furthermore, I believe that most physicians are unaware that choking sets free in certain individuals feelings of pleasure, erections, and even an orgasm.

## NEUROPHYSIOLOGY

Hormonal influences bringing about the maturation of the genitals are probably accompanied by unconscious instinctual influences subjectively perceived as sexual fantasies, images, and impulses. In the male such cortical stimuli will result in penile erection via subcortical limbic structures; cortical inhibitions such as "fear of performance" will produce impotence as Masters and Johnson have so clearly described (12).

Responses mediating sexual arousal probably travel through the pedunculi cerebri, the pons, and cervical portions of the

---

[3]Larry H. Dizmang, M.D. personal communication.

cord to lumbar reflex centers for vasomotor innervation and ejaculation. Nervous impulses are conveyed from these centers via the nervi erigentes composed of fibers from the first three sacral nerves to the capillaries of the corpora cavernosa with resulting penile distension. Contraction of the bulbo-cavernosus and erector penis muscles over the dorsal penis further impede the return of blood. Masters and Johnson have described the process of erection as well as orgasm in more detail (12, Chapter 12).

The lumbar cord reflex center, which mediates both erection and ejaculation, is under the influence of excitatory as well as inhibitory innervations arising from the cerebral cortex. This would explain erections immediately following a hanging when inhibitory impulses have been suddenly severed.[4]

## Neck Constriction

In erotized hangings, I believe that constriction of the neck (secondary to suspension) results in (a) a disruption of the arterial blood supply resulting in a diminished oxygenation of the brain (a condition of anoxic anoxia) and (b) an increased carbon dioxide retention (a condition of relative hypercapnia). *Either will heighten sensations* through diminished ego controls that will be subjectively perceived as giddiness, light-headedness, and exhilaration. This reinforces masturbatory sensations. In fact, ejaculatory pleasure is often accompanied by holding the breath or contracting the neck strap muscles. Variations on the impaired blood flow theme have been recognized where death has occurred from a plastic bag tied about the neck, inhalation of gasoline or spray deodorizers, and the use of gas masks in the pursuit of sexual sensory elevated excitations. Giddiness, "highs," and "good feelings" have also

---

[4]Reflex penile erections have been reported in neonatals (13) as one of several spontaneous behaviors secondary to endogenous afferent stimulation (during the period when such stimulation may be critical for the developing central nervous system), during REM stage sleep (14) (the association of penile erections and REM activity are both indications of limbic system excitation), during anesthesia associated with urologic procedures, in patients with paraplegia secondary to low cord transection, and to high cord transections during hangings.

been reported by skin divers – due to increased carbon dioxide retention – as well as pilots whose oxygen supply has been impaired. Some effects of nitrous oxide ("laughing gas") are heightened fantasy formation, giddiness, and "well-being." Louria (15) reported that amyl nitrite capsules (a potent cerebral smooth muscle relaxant and vasodilator) have been inhaled at the moment of orgasm with exaltation of the sexual sensations and the creation of a sexual dreamy "high." The common element would appear to be a method to alter the cerebral blood flow resulting in a transient hypoxia (or relative hypercapnia) sufficient to produce an exhilarating potentiation of the individual's fantasy.

There is another and more immediate consequence of neck constriction. Bilateral pressure upon the carotid sinus will reflexly result in immediate unconsciousness. Thus, pressure applied slowly to the neck may result in enhanced sensations. When by inexperience, excitement, or accident the pressure is sudden or exaggerated, so, too, may be the result – carotid sinus reflex, unconsciousness, asphyxia, and death. Berlyne and Strachan (16) have reviewed the literature on the neuropsychiatric sequelae of hanging. They cite Polsen's experimental work on the pressure needed to obstruct the carotid circulation. A pull of as little as seven pounds will diminish flow through the common carotid artery to a mere trickle. That is more than sufficient to produce rapid unconsciousness within seven seconds. Even the vertebral artery, although in a bony tunnel, is vulnerable to occlusion in its first part, as it courses between the scalenus anticus and longus cervicis muscles.

Practitioners of erotized hanging control pressure on the neck in a variety of ways – by relaxing the body weight progressively, by manipulating the tension on the neck through ropes tied to the legs (primarily) and the arms (secondarily), and by increasing weights tied to the neck. Bruises to the neck may result from accidents or slipped padding; any such marks on an adolescent patient should alert the physician to inquire about this syndrome.

In summary then, giddiness secondary to cerebral hypoxia due to carotid artery compression may result in impaired control. Suspension may follow a loss of balance and control of position, brought about by physical contractions of the body, associated with ejaculation (or even in the absence of ejaculation). The real danger appears to be unconsciousness following carotid sinus reflex. If death does not ensue, chronic brain damage may result in those who go too far too long.

## GENERAL CONSIDERATIONS

Loewenstein (17) has summarized the various mechanisms by which masochistic perversions can occur—through castration fear, through fear of the loss of the object of its love, and through superego anxiety. Because of *castration* anxiety, libidinal and aggressive impulses directed at forbidden (incestuous) objects may be turned against the self as punishment. The feminine posture of passivity and helplessness places the subject completely in another's power, removing responsibility for any sexual gratification. The anxiety can be understood by viewing the gamble with death as an index of the forbidden wish itself. At times, then, a suicide may be the ultimate payment for the guilt of separation or the fear of punishment for an incestuous wish. To anticipate actively (hanging behavior) what one passively fears or wishes is understandable.

Freud (18) has described the origin of beating fantasies in the boy's wish to assume a passive receptive feminine (hence, castrated) role with the father. This theme is repeated by Kronengold and Sterba, who report a patient whose "childhood attempts at hanging had to be considered as a passive instinctual satisfaction in connection with Father" (19). That castration anxiety is present in this syndrome seems clear; whether the anxiety is generated from a fear of mother or father (or both) is less important.

The dominant aim of the hanging behavior—to be suspended by the neck—(or cut off) allays the castration anxiety. The hanging may also be a punishment for masturbation; in this way, superego derived anxiety may be allayed. There are also indications of castration concerns from notes reported by Stearns (3). A college sophomore found hanging with evidence of ejaculation penciled in an open textbook: "Jodphur girl. If I lose, I will wear breeches, but if I win, I will go as a cowboy . . . Signed, Breeches Boy." The note of another decedent had to do with a fear of a forthcoming rhinoplasty.

## Pregenital Influences

Melitta Sperling (20), among others, has indicated the influence of the mother-infant relationship on perverse sexual behavior. Litman (21) has elaborated these pregenital (separation anxiety) determinants for suicidal behavior as well. I feel that emphasis in the erotized hanging syndrome should be placed upon the oral incorporative-oral aggressive conflict, as well as the adolescent's anxiety at separation. Weisman (22) has reported psychoanalytic case material of a patient who attempted suicide by hanging, behavior later followed by subjugation, suffocation, and overtly sadomasochistic sexual behavior. The patient was able to recover an early memory associated with smothering and the patient's wish for her mother's breast.

I have analyzed a young schoolteacher who experienced an Isakower phenomenon (23) which was associated with early breast feeding. This patient was struggling with his own oral incorporative wishes toward the nipple and breasts; a slip of the tongue revealed his sadistic fantasy of biting off the nipple. (The nipple has infrequently been recognized as an aggressive extension of the body, somewhat similar to the phallus, by virtue of its erectile nature, intrusive quality, and capacity to discharge contents. Since the nipple [or breast] is often aggressively placed into the infant's mouth, or he is firmly clasped to it, such associations are not surprising). The description of my patient, Mr. K., of his detached feeling as "being separated, cut-off, suspended" sounds similar to the description of a hanging involving the separation of the head from the body. During his fantasies, Mr. K. *held his breath* in order to heighten his body awareness, lay with his arms at his side, had an erection, and fantasied himself an erect phallus.

Azima and Wittkower report about a patient with a spider phobia who also experienced an Isakower phenomenon in the course of therapy (24). Little's elabortion of the spider as a symbol ranges from separation themes involving the pregenital orally incorporating mother to fears of phallic castration by an aggressive biting mother (25, 26). Newman and Stoller report the use of spider symbolization in a conflict over bisexuality (27). Adolescents behaving as I have described, may, in part, act out their male-female conflicts by hanging as spiders (and some by dressing in women's underclothes).

Repressed oral sadism is the theme in Sterba's analysis of a young man's spider phobia (7). The unconscious relationship was clarified for him by recalling a short story of Ewers (to which I alluded earlier) involving a young man's death by hanging. In this story, the male spider (an adolescent male in both the story and in the syndrome under discussion) is first sexually drawn to and then bound by the many-legged spider mother who ultimately sucks him dry. The student was found hanging by the neck with a spider clamped between his teeth. Sterba's analysis pointed out the young man's conflict over masturbation with incest fantasies; he concludes that the fear of spiders in his patient was the defensive use of projection as a substitute for the wish to orally incorporate mother. Sterba's thesis that suicide by hanging could represent oral incorporation fantasies parallels my observation of several erotized hangings in which a brassiere was found wrapped around the face, and in another, stuffed in the mouth. The fear of being swallowed reveals itself as the original wish to incorporate the mother. Ewer's student was found hanging, both as the victim of the spider-mother and as the spider-mother whom he had incorporated between his teeth. Some persons have also been found thoroughly bound, as if encased in the web of the spider-mother, as described in the short story (7).

Thus the theme of incorporation and separation-individuation is a very important one. Clinical material from Little (28) illustrates the utilization of the erect penis alone and the erect penis plus the extended body, as with Mr. K. (I would add the suspended erect body) as unconscious representations of the umbilical connection to mother.

Evidence for the separation hypothesis in this syndrome may

be derived indirectly from Loewenstein's classic paper on masochism in which he mentions being told by Dr. Harry August of a case in which a man was found dead by hanging, while engaging in complicated masochistic behavior involving masturbation. Loewenstein (17) indicated he had never seen such a case, but that such cases may be known to the police. He comments only that such a death may result either from an unconscious wish or an accident. Dr. August informed me that he learned of the man's activities from the latter's mother who was his patient. He described her as a controlling, possessive woman who was unable to tolerate attempts on the part of her son to separate. Identification with the aggressor or with a lost object, or both, as a defense in coping with loss has been well summarized by Krupp (29). It may well be that the total defensive identification with the mother from whom he separates is to be female. This is acted out by wearing women's clothing, while at the same time the femininity and castration are denied by manipulating the penis.

Bondage may accompany or occur independently of hanging. Progressive elaboration of bondage behavior to include the neck is illustrated in Krafft-Ebing's case No. 91 in which a mother reports that her six-year-old son, from earliest childhood, bound himself in various ways with her clothing, eventuating in "the curtain cord around his neck like a noose" (30).

On a primitive level, bondage does recreate the most constricting of environments—that reminiscent of the infant blanketed and swathed tightly and securely in the firm hold of its mother. Recall the spider symbolism with union represented by encasement in the web or by inclusion in the mouth (or womb). Krafft-Ebing reports the case of a man who bound himself hand and foot while lying blindfolded in a darkened room (30). To be restricted or controlled can be reassuring. On a symbolic basis, the binding is overdetermined and appears as a punishment for masculinity, with the hanging (binding the neck) a castration of the erect body-penis. The genitals may also be constricted by bands placed about the shaft and scrotum. Here, castration anxiety is of a more overt and less symbolic language, although the sensations associated with the penile distension may have a physiologically based enhancing effect.

In the only clinical report of the circumstances surrounding a first hanging episode, Shankel and Carr describe a patient who, at the age of ten or eleven, became depressed ("I wasn't really trying to kill myself") and *wondered* what hanging would be like; he then experimented with it. In this initial hanging, he developed an erection and found the experience exhilarating (31). Why did he select hanging to wonder about? My explanation for this selection is the overdetermination of the neck as the focus for castration anxiety and being suspended as the focus for separation anxiety. The erection and the exhilarating experience associated with the hanging were probably influenced by the physiologic mechanisms I have described. This boy began his hanging behavior two years *prior* to his ability to ejaculate, which again confirms that the cerebral sensations *per se* while hanging are important, and that the ejaculation is of secondary reinforcement. The boy's fantasies would help us immeasurably, but they are not reported. I would speculate that they involve a separation theme. Furthermore, I think that smothering (while feeding), or breath-holding experiences while crying, may be early determinants of the search for exalted sensations resulting in neck compression behavior.

How do young men learn of such hanging behavior? In the literature review, I noted that sexual "highs" by strangulation have been reported in many cultures. Is this behavior "accidentally" learned? Shankel and Carr suggest it is overdetermined (31). I have information that one young man had seen a televised movie involving hanging earlier on the evening of his own hanging. Patients in the course of their treatment have reported sexual arousal upon reading pornographic literature showing sadomasochistic hanging behavior. Sex thrill magazines may serve as advertisements and encouragements to various experiments. Discovered at the feet of their victims, they serve as mute testimonies to trials by example. I am concerned that the ready availability of erotic literature with illustrations involving suspension and hanging may introduce such potentially lethal behaviors to susceptible adolescents.

## Psychodynamic Themes

Figure 11-1 is a schematic representation of separation and castration components in erotized repetitive neck bindings. I acknowledge its speculative and theoretical nature. The elements of the erotized repetitive hanging syndrome can occur independently, or in combinations.

Why is this syndrome reported to occur only with boys? I believe boys experiment with neck binding play as an upward displacement of castration concerns. The exciting feelings will lead to erection and this may or may not be associated with masturbation. As the behavior becomes more elaborated, bondage and/or fetishism may be added. The absolute absence of females reinforces the theoretical position that this syndrome is related to phallic anxiety concerns. Females do engage in other

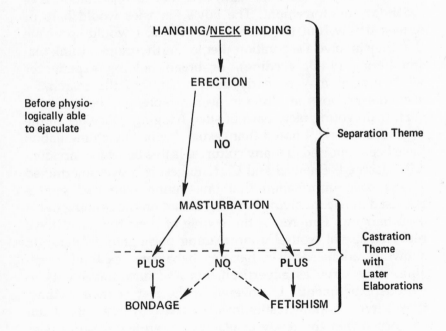

Figure 11-1 *A schematic representation of the behavioral manifestations of separation and castration components in the erotized repetitive hanging syndrome*

behaviors that enhance sexual sensations but without neck specificity. One example of highly sublimated male neck cathexis may be the social institution of the necktie, until recently solely a male fashion hallmark. There is an associated behavioral component—knotting and tightening the tie (noose) about the neck, and later releasing it!

Two levels of psychosexual conflict are formulated (Fig. 11-2). At the genital level, castration is feared. The subject feels inhibited with girls and in his fantasy imagines himself as feminine. By repeatedly constricting the neck, symbolic amputation of the neck and head of the penis occurs; castration is meted out and survived again and again. The simultaneous masturbation reifies the presence of the penis, thus denying castration, the equivalent of which is actually occurring. With the untying of the rope, the castration is undone, and the oedipal guilt assuaged through the masochistic brush with death. During the course of the fantasy, compression of the

| LEVEL OF PSYCHOSEXUAL CONFLICT | COMPONENTS | | |
|---|---|---|---|
| | Rope | Masturbation/ Emission | Female Clothing |
| Oral (Separation Anxiety) | Umbilicus Dropline | Well-being and Contentment | Unity with Mother |
| Genital (Castration Anxiety) | Agent of Punishment | Phallic Potency | Identification with the aggressor; defense against castration fears |

Figure 11-2 *The relationship between level of psychosexual conflict and components of the erotized repetitive hanging syndrome*

neck produces a relative hypoxia which heightens subjective sexual sensations. The hanging behavior may be necessary for ejaculation. (For instance, I do not know whether these boys can have erections without hanging.) Sandler reports a patient whose fear of erection was resolved by his fantasy that when lying in bed he was the erect penis (32). It would be helpful to know the fantasies these young men have while hanging. Thus, the fantasy which serves to defend against separation and/or castration anxiety becomes pleasurably associated with hanging behavior. The masturbation complemented by exalted fantasies secondary to the physiologic influences, adds to the heightened sensations (33).

At the oral level, the conflict is over separation from the mother. Immobilization and asphyxia contribute to the fantasies of feeding, reunion, and rebirth. The male infant, while feeding (whether at the breast or the bottle), has been observed to develop erections. The neonate may experience a relative asphyxia in association with the sense of well-being derived from feeding; these sensations may then be accompanied by a gastrourethral reflex resulting in erection. The continued choice to be learned while feeding may be: feed and remain somewhat short of breath at the risk of letting go of the nipple, or breathe completely and lose the good visceral feelings, and the associated erection. Mothers may often interpret the child's relinquishing of the nipple as a personal rejection rather than as a very real choice against asphyxiation. The child's conflict may well be that erection feels good just as feeding does. The conflict, then, is one between separating (to breathe) and strangling (while feeding). A permissive mother will allow the infant to separate from the source of food (and her) as he needs; an intrusive mother can control by forcing the breast (and herself)—she becomes the "smother mother." The gastrointestinal sensations (producing reflex erections) accompany the well-being associated with feeding and become unconsciously associated with the separation-strangle conflict.[5]

One might look to Mahler's formulation of the infant's progress through the developmental phases of symbiosis,

---

[5]Catherine L. Bacon, M.D., personal communication.

separation-individuation, and bisexual identification in order to establish sexual identity (34). The symbiotic psychosis syndrome in children may help us here. Mahler states that the ego's ability to reality test becomes greatly impaired under the threat of separation (and annihilation) such as stimulated in childhood by mother's illness or the child's going off to school. The child's symbiotic psychotic syndrome aims at restoring the child's oneness with mother. In the repetitive hanging syndrome the early separation threat becomes unconsciously reactivated with the adolescent's sexual fantasies and ability to ejaculate with pleasure that usually leads to a search for genital female objects. Blos has characterized adolescence as the *second* separation phase (35). I would suggest that the original conflict while feeding—separate or smother and experience sexual feelings—is reawakened. The repetitive hanging behavior allays the separation anxiety thus engendered. Whereas the nursing infant concludes, "I'll strangle a while to feed," the choking adult masturbator concludes, "I'll strangle a while to get sexual."

### Is this a Suicidal Syndrome?

When the gamble with death is erotized, the probability of death is greatly enhanced. The symbolic realization of approaching death closely and then escaping it, exemplified by the repetitive hanging behavior, has its deepest roots in fantasies of uniting with mother. By escaping from the rope, whether by the knife as Roland did, or through the untying of knots, unity with and separation from mother are acted out as rebirth fantasies. Such fantasies are not at all uncommon in suicidal patients. I believe that the process of separating *per se* has been erotized, and it is therefore this behavior which is repetitively reenacted. These people are not suicidal in the sense that they seek death as much as they seek the dying experience to deny their fear of separation. It is the erotization of leaving and returning, appearing and disappearing, dying and being reanimated. A close parallel may be those patients who constantly doze off, but can never fall asleep, or even children who hold their breath and refuse to breathe (on their own) for periods of time. Thus it is while actively seeking a dying experience (as motivated by their separation anxiety) that these men hasten toward their self-destructive ends.

Farewell notes indicate that in some cases, self-rescue is made progressively more difficult by complicated bindings or the use of candles burning escape ropes, thus making death inevitable. Others unconsciously set up the stool or the ropes in such a manner that they will tip over or bind themselves without an opportunity for a safe release. Although dying, rather than death, appears to be the end-game, this would not seem to mitigate the self-destructive and suicidal nature of the behavior. The repeated episodes of high death-risk sexual activity attempt to bind or avert anxiety. They are maneuvers to ward off overwhelming feelings of depression.

Ejaculation has also been equated with symbolic death. That is, in each orgasmic experience one loses a part of the self. This loss has been associated with expiring; one feels spent, empty, and frequently lapses into a deep sleep from which one awakens alive and rejuvenated.

There are any number of self-destructive behaviors (ranging widely in severity) in which there is no obvious risk-taking; yet, when they result in the death of the actor, he has, indeed, killed himself, even though his goal may have been to coerce, frighten, seduce, or punish. At the root of the behavior, there is usually anxiety, the etiology of which may be similar to that I have described in this paper. The significant variables of intent, timing, opportunity for detection, choice of method, and the recognized risk of death as manifested by precautions against it, all must be evaluated in reaching a judgment of the lethality of the self-destructive behavior. These all appear to be significantly high in this syndrome. In addition, the nature of any self-destructive act must take into consideration unconscious dynamic factors, as I have outlined. When this is done, it would seem appropriate to consider this a suicidal syndrome of life threatening behavior, involving erotization of dying brought about in order to escape overwhelming anxiety, rather than "accidental death." The latter term appears to be a sterile solution which disregards complex psychologic influences and multiple determinants. The "erotized repetitive hanger" commits suicide for the same reason the alcoholic or the repetitive overdose-taker, or the psychotic does—because he is compelled by unconscious forces to take risks that endanger his life.

## SUMMARY

A syndrome of erotized repetitive hangings has been described in which adolescent males and young men engage in masturbation titrated to increasing self-manipulated neck pressure. Although the actual prevalence is unknown, at least 50 deaths annually result from its practice. The psychodynamic elements of castration anxiety, separation anxiety, and erotization of dying appear most important. Neurocirculatory mechanisms, especially cerebral hypoxia, reinforce the hanging behavior by enhancing the masturbatory pleasure. However, unexpected death may result from unconsciousness due to carotid sinus reflex and gradual asphyxia resulting from complete body suspension. These mechanisms add a physiologic basis for understanding the overdetermination of the neck in this syndome. Clinicians are alerted to question any unusual neck bruises on their male patients.

## REFERENCES

1. Ford, R. Death by Hanging of Adolescent and Young Adult Males. *Forensic Sciences* 2:171, 1957.

2. Gonzales, T., Vance, M., and Halpern, M. *Legal Medicine and Toxicology*, Appleton-Century, New York, 1940.

3. Stearns, A. Cases of Probable Suicide in Young Persons without Obvious Motivation. *J. Maine Med. Assoc.* 44:16, 1953.

4. Henry, R. Unpublished Manuscript.

5. Melville, H. *Billy Budd, Foretopman*. In *The Shorter Novels of Herman Melville*, Evans, B., Ed. Fawcett Publications, Greenwich, Conn., 1928.

6. Ewers, H. H. *Alraune*. John Day, New York, 1929.

7. Sterba, R. On Spiders, Hanging and Oral Sadism. *Am. Imago* 7:21, 1950.

8. Beckett, S. *Waiting for Godot*. Grove Press, New York, 1954.

9. De Sade, The Marquis. *The Complete Justine, Philosophy in the Bedroom and*

*Other Writings.* Trans. by Seaver, R., and Wainhouse, A. Grove Press, New York, 1965.

10. Hirschfeld, M. *Sexual Anomalies: The Origins, Nature and Treatment of Sexual Disorders.* Emerson, New York, 1948.

11. De Boismont, A. B. *Du Suicide et de la Folie Suicide.* Germer Bailliere, Paris, 1856.

12. Masters, W. H. and Johnson, V. E. *Human Sexual Response.* Little Brown, Boston, 1966.

13. Korner, A. F. Neonatal Startles, Smiles, Erections and Reflex Sucks as Related to State, Sex and Individuality. *Child Develop.* 40:1039, 1969.

14. Fisher, C., Gross, J., and Zuch, J. Cycle of Penile Erection Synchronous with Dreaming (REM) Sleep. *Arch. Gen. Psychiat.* 12:29, 1965.

15. Louria, D. B. Sexual Use of Amyl Nitrite. *Med. Aspects Human Sexuality* 4:89, 1970.

16. Berlyne, N. and Strachan, M. Neuropsychiatric Sequelae of Attempted Hanging. *Brit. J. Psychiat.* 114:411, 1968.

17. Loewenstein, R. A Contribution to the Psychoanalytic Theory of Masochism. *J. Am. Psychoanal. Ass.* 5:197, 1957.

18. Freud, S. A Child is Being Beaten: A Contribution to the Study of the Origin of Sexual Perversion. In *Collected Papers,* Vol. 2. Jones, E., Ed. Basic Books, New York, 1959.

19. Kronengold, E. and Sterba, R. Two Cases of Fetishism. *Psychoanal. Quart.* 5:63, 1936.

20. Sperling, M. A Study of Deviate Sexual Behavior in Children by the Method of Simultaneous Analysis of Mother and Child. In *Dynamics of Psychotherapy in Childhood,* Jessner, L. and Pavenstedt, E., Eds. Grune & Stratton, New York, 1959.

21. Litman, R. Freud on Suicide. *Psychoanal. Forum* 2:206, 1966.

22. Weisman, A. Self-Destructive and Sexual Perversion. In *Essays in Self-Destruction.* Shneidman, E., Ed. Science House, New York, 1967.

23. Isakower, O. A Contribution to the Pathopsychology of Phenomena Associated with Falling Asleep. *Int. J. Psychoanal.* 19:331, 1938.

24. Azima, H. and Wittkower, E. Anaclitic Therapy Employing Drugs; A Case of Spider Phobia with Isakower Phenomenon. *Psychoanal. Quart.* 26:190, 1957.

25. Little, R. Oral Aggression In Spider Legends. *Am. Imago* 23:169, 1966.

26. _____ . Spider Phobias. *Psychoanal. Quart.* 36:51, 1967.

27. Newman, L. and Stoller, R. Spider Symbolism and Bisexuality. *J. Am. Psychoanal. Ass.,* 17:872, 1969.

28. Little, R. Umbilical Cord Symbolism of the Spider's Dropline. *Psychoanal. Quart.,* 35:587, 1966.

29. Krupp, G. Identification as a Defense against Anxiety in Coping with Loss. *Int. J. Psychoanal.,* 46:303, 1965.

30. Von Krafft-Ebing, R. *Psychopathis Sexualis,* Trans. by Klaf, F. Stein and Day, New York, 1965.

31. Shankel, W. and Carr, A., Transvestism and Hanging Episodes in a Male Adolescent. *Psychiat. Quart.,* 30:478, 1956.

32. Sandler, J. The Body as Phallus: A Patient's Fear of Erection. *Int. J. Psychoanal.,* 40:191, 1959.

33. Lewin, B. The Body As Phallus. *Psychoanal. Quart.,* 2:24, 1933.

34. Mahler, M. *On Human Symbiosis and the Vicissitudes of Individuation, Vol. 1: Infantile Psychosis.* International University Press, New York, 1968.

35. Blos, P. *On Adolescence: A Psychoanalytic Interpretation.* Free Press of Glencoe, New York, 1962.

# PART II

# Treatment

# 12 The Range of Therapies With Severely Depressed Suicidal Patients

## Stanley Lesse, M.D., Med. Sc.D.

*The treatment of patients with suicidal drives and ideas is often less than adequate due to theoretic and technical prejudices. This chapter describes the requirements that one who treats suicidal patients should meet. The phases of treatment and aims of each phase are outlined. Finally the combined antidepressant drug-psychotherapy technique and electroshock procedures are described in detail.*

During the past decade and a half, heightened interest has been shown in suicidal behavior. This is evidenced by the number of papers that have appeared in psychiatric and psychologic journals, in the number of national and international meetings dedicated to a discussion of suicidal behavior, the formation of suicide prevention centers throughout the country, and the emergence of a new psychiatric and psychologic subspecialist, namely, the suicidologist. In reality, this heightened interest has led to a greater understanding of the sociodynamic and to a lesser degree of the psychodynamic mechanisms behind suicidal ideation and gestures. Many new theoretic conceptualizations have been evolved, some of which have dealt with the philosophic and moral aspects of suicide, particularly with regard to a patient's rights to terminate his or her own life. Others have theorized about the psychiatrist's or psychotherapist's obligation in dealing with patients with suicidal behavior.

Despite the veritable renaissance of interest in suicidal patients, there has been a most pathetic and dangerous void in the development of pragmatic guidelines and techniques in the managment of patients who have suicidal ideas or drives. Most of the therapeutic measures considered in the literature have dealt with the very specialized procedures evolved in suicide prevention centers. These techniques are stop-gap procedures intended to "contain" the patient's self-destructive ideation and drives until the patient entrusts himself or herself to a trained psychiatrist or psychotherapist. Papers directed at the development of step-by-step pragmatic techniques designed for optimum application in different types of depressed, suicidal patients have been scarce.

In part, this therapeutic void is due, theoretically and technically, to the anachronistic and dangerous schism between those psychiatrists who employ only organic therapies and those psychiatrists and psychologists who limit themselves solely to various psychotherapies. The problem is further complicated among the organicists by the fact that there is a divergence of opinion between those who use electroshock therapy and those who do not.

The greatest scotomatized therapeutic void in the management of suicidal patients exists among psychotherapists. Too often, in this group, the therapeutic problem ranges from lack of concern to ineptness, resulting at times in suicidal acts and even death. Psychotherapists frequently fail to evaluate the intensity of a depression. They are particularly lax in their evaluation of the intensity of a patient's suicidal preoccupations and drives.

There is a very dangerous misconception among many psychotherapists that an understanding of the psychodynamics of a depression is equivalent to a penetrating awareness of a patient's clinical psychopathologic manifestations. As I have pointed out in previous papers, *the psychodynamics of a patient with a mild depression may be exactly the same as of one who is actively contemplating suicide* (1, 2).

The inadequacy and naiveté on the part of psychotherapists

in the management of suicidal patients have been fanned by philosophic concepts held by some therapists which may severely limit their ability to react to the emergency of an impending suicidal act (3). These philosophic concepts may be legalistic in nature, such as those proposed by Szasz, to the effect that an individual must have the right to kill or injure himself (4). Other therapists have expressed the opinion that overconcern with regard to the possibility of suicide might interfere with effective therapy (5, 6). Still others have stated their indifference with regard to the patient's possible death; some even contend that the therapist has no responsibility for the patient's death by suicide (7).

In addition to these suicide-enhancing philosophic concepts held by some psychotherapists, an increase in the culturally determined romanticization of death has occurred, as pointed out by Shneidman (8). He parallels this with the romanticization of certain types of homicide which is an especially proud part of our national heritage and culture, and equates it with anachronistic and outmoded values. Shneidman relates the romantic notions of death to suicide and suggests that we must have an effective approach to the deromanticization of death, particularly among the young.

### Requirements for Therapists Who Treat Suicidal Patients

For a therapist to be optimally effective in the management of depressed, suicidal patients, a number of fundamental requirements must be met. The therapist must be thoroughly acquainted with the range of treatment procedures that are available and must be trained in the appropriate application of the proper type of therapy or types of therapies for a given patient at a given time.

Not all psychiatrists, psychotherapists, psychologists, or social workers are equipped by personality or training to manage severely depressed patients, let alone those who have suicidal preoccupations or drives (9). This pertains to senior personnel and residents alike. Senior personnel should not place residents in charge of suicidal patients. It is imperative that they should be extremely closely supervised by a highly trained and motivated senior staff.

Therapists who have depressive propensities should not take on the treatment of severely depressed patients. Similarly, those who are threatened by aggressive patients or who have difficulties in the management of emergency situations should not take on the responsibility of severely depressed individuals. The same may be said of hostile therapists. Hostility on the part of a therapist toward a patient, particularly one with a long-standing, unyielding therapeutic problem may blind the therapist to the urgency of that patient's psychic state. Finally, severely depressed persons should not be managed by individuals who do not have the capacity for intensive, psychopathologic investigation.

Ideally, those who undertake the treatment of severely depressed patients should have a broad-spectrum training background, including an understanding of the benefits and limitations of the various organic therapies and an active awareness of the benefits and limitations of various psychotherapeutic approaches, either alone or in combination with organic treatments. Any individual who undertakes the management of severely depressed patients must have ready access to appropriate hospital facilities should institutionalization become imperative as a life-saving measure.

A competent therapist also must comprehend the various meanings of suicidal ideas and behavior (9). Suicidal behavior does not always have death as its goal. The suicidal gesture may be a means of verbal or nonverbal communication by the patient to a "significant other person." It may be "a cry for help" by patients who react as if they were not receiving the support, recognition, love, or understanding they feel is necessary or to which they are entitled. This is usually on an unconscious level. The suicidal gesture may also be a communication of overwhelming feelings of guilt or guilt-linked rage.

Finally, the therapist must have a positive feeling with regard to the value of life. *There should be no confusion between the act of saving the person's life and the long-term psychotherapeutic re-education of a severely depressed patient.* The therapist must have the capacity to psychically transfuse the severely depressed patient during the initial phases of treatment (1).

At this point, I would like to emphasize that there can be

iatrogenically produced deaths in severely depressed patients, particularly those who have suicidal ideation and drives. Stone, in 1971, pointed out that psychotherapy often has a powerful impact which can be either benign or malignant (10). He presented three types of "malignant psychotherapy" which fostered suicidal attempts. In Stone's experience, these three examples illustrated how suicide attempts were precipitated when patients were forcibly induced to see their reality situation as being empty of any gratification. This type of forced awareness is not the only type of psychotherapeutic procedure that is fraught with danger.

*One may say without being in significant error that if a patient with suicidal ideation or drives is accepted by a psychiatrist or psychotherapist for active treatment, a suicidal attempt by the patient, while in active treatment, may often be the psychiatrist's or psychotherapist's fault, since suicidal attempts can be prevented and suicidal drives can be blunted and eliminated in most acute suicidal situations.*

## Aims of Treatment with Suicidal Patients

There are different goals in the treatment of severely depressed, suicidal patients depending upon whether the suicidal process is acute or chronic.

*Phase I. The purpose here is to save a patient's life, nothing more, nothing less.* This means that the patient's suicidal drives must be blunted and ameliorated. At this point long-range therapy is not given any consideration. All treatments in this phase are emergency procedures, comparable to life-saving surgical procedures or the utilization of life-saving medical measures for a patient who is having a coronary occlusion.

*Phase II.* After the suicidal drives are blunted, one must become aware of the suicidal preoccupations and ideas, for the patient remains in a potentially precarious situation if the suicidal drives are blunted but the suicidal ideas are still in evidence. A patient who has suicidal ideas is in an urgent situation. This fact is not taken with sufficient seriousness by psychiatrists and members of allied professions. The overt or subliminal expression of suicidal ideation is often accepted in a very cavalier fashion by therapists whether they are primarily organically or psychotherapeutically oriented (11).

*Phase III.* Following the amelioration of the suicidal drives and suicidal preoccupations, the third phase of treatment is devoted to the modification of the underlying depression. As I have previously and repeatedly stressed, *the use of psychotherapy alone in the treatment of severely depressed patients who have or had suicidal ideas or drives is anachronistic, dangerous, and cruel in the light of our current knowledge of depressions* (1). Severely depressed patients in Phase III should be treated either on an outpatient or inpatient basis with psychotherapy in combination with antidepressant preparations. Some require electroshock.

*Phase IV.* Following the significant amelioration of the underlying depression, the long-term therapy of patients with severe depressions is designed to raise their ego capacities and to help them live optimally within these ego capacities. The repressed hostility that is an intimate part of almost all severely depressed personalities must be gradually unfolded in a cautious fashion. One must also help these patients to recognize the earliest evidence of depression that is unique to them as individuals. In this way, they can actively attempt to modify or correct adverse behavior and to obtain effective help with minimum delay.

## APPROPRIATE TECHNIQUES
## FOR SUICIDAL PATIENTS

### Active Suicidal Drives

As noted above, *patients with active suicidal drives are true emergencies requiring immediate, life-saving procedures.* This is a fundamental concept. It is for this reason that a psychiatrist who undertakes the responsibility for such patients must have a broad range of facilities and techniques available to him.

Most of these patients should be hospitalized without delay. Under certain circumstances, some may be treated on an outpatient basis with electroshock therapy. Some such patients may also be treated on an outpatient basis with antidepressant drugs combined with specifically designed psychotherapeutic techniques. I have outlined in detail, in many other papers, the nature of this combined drug-psychotherapeutic procedure (1, 12).

The question of whether any type of therapy should be attempted on an outpatient basis in patients with active suicidal drives depends upon a number of clinical phenomena:

1. Intensity of the suicidal drive.
2. The intent behind the suicidal ideation and drive.
3. Rate of change of the intensity of the suicidal drive.
4. Recent history of a suicidal gesture.
5. History of previous suicidal acts.
6. History of suicide in the family.
7. History of acting out as a prime expression of increased anxiety.
8. Intensity of guilt feelings.
9. Intensity of overt or covert hostility.
10. History of anhedonia.
11. Availability of family or friends to care for the patient during the acute phase.
12. Hostility and reliability of family members or friends.
13. History of poor results with electroshock therapy, psychotropic drugs, or psychotherapeutic procedures.
14. Hostility to drug therapy or psychotherapeutic procedures.
15. Presence of a debilitating physical disorder.
16. Regressed schizophrenic patients, in whom severe depression is a major factor, are poor candidates, in general, for drug therapy and/or psychotherapy on an ambulatory basis. Electroshock therapy remains the preferred treatment in these instances. Usually severely depressed schizophrenic patients should be hospitalized without delay.
17. Patients who manifest severe anxiety and depression in the matrix of an organic mental syndrome should not be treated by drug therapy alone or in combination with psychotherapeutic techniques on an outpatient basis. In most instances, such patients should be hospitalized without delay.
18. I would like to flag, at this point, another serious clinical situation. Patients with a manic-depressive psychosis who have been in a hypomanic state and who are rapidly changing

into a severe depressed state accompanied by suicidal preoccupations and drives, must be considered as being in an emergency situation, for they are extremely prone to carry out suicidal acts.

19. *Patients with Masked Depressions.* As I have described in many previous publications, approximately 42 per cent of the patients who appear with masked depressions have suicidal preoccupations or drives (13). The masks of depression or depressive equivalents may be in the form of acting-out behavior, hypochondriasis, somatic syndromes, drug addiction or habituation, alcoholism, the use of psychedelic drugs, hostile behavior, homosexual problems, etc. (14). One must be extremely careful with these patients, since there is a tendency to underestimate the intensity of the underlying depression. This will very frequently cause psychiatrists or psychotherapists to prematurely lower their vigil, at times leading to active suicidal behavior. These patients are poor subjects for psychotherapy alone on an outpatient basis.

I have emphasized on many previous occasions that a suicidal act is an excellent, temporary, antisuicidal, and antidepressive therapeutic procedure, if the patient survives the suicidal act (9, 11). The postsuicidal "amelioration" is, in reality, a "pseudoamelioration," and the patient must be considered as being in a masked depressed state. The apparent improvement in the underlying depression is untenable and rarely lasts for any significant period of time. A large number of fatal suicides have occurred when naive psychiatrists have misinterpreted these apparent remissions.

I have also pointed out that there are other types of maskings of severely depressed patients, even patients with suicidal preoccupations and drives. For example, patients may appear to be vastly improved, if they have made their final decision to commit suicide. Similarly, schizophrenic patients who are actively hallucinating may appear to be significantly improved, if they have decided to kill themselves in response to directives by "voices."

Therapists must be extremely cautious lest they prematurely relax careful vigilance in a severely depressed patient, particularly one who has had suicidal drives or ideas. Many patients will respond either through specific therapeutic effects of a procedure or drug or through a placebo effect of this procedure or drug. The improvement may only be transitory and, in reality, exaggerated. This is particularly true during the early phases of treatment. Patients such as these are likely to have marked rapid exacerbations of depression and suicidal drives, often ending in a precipitous suicidal gesture.

## TECHNIQUES WITH SUICIDAL DRIVES OR PERSISTENT IDEATION

### Electroshock Treatment

Electroshock treatment remains the most reliable and effective method of rapidly ameliorating suicidal drives and ideations. Once the decision to utilize electroshock treatment is made, the psychiatrist should simultaneously decide as to whether the electroshock treatment should be given on an outpatient basis or in a hospitalized setting. This decision must be made promptly and decisively. In these instances, electroshock is the equivalent of emergency surgery and its purpose is the same, namely, to save the patient's life. It is not a time for therapeutic ambivalence.

Prior to 1958, electroshock treatment was the only approved effective treatment for depressed, suicidal patients. It remains the treatment of choice in a number of situations, as I have noted above. Schizophrenic patients, in whom depression is a prominent manifestation, are, in general, poor candidates for drug and/or psychotherapy on an ambulatory basis. All schizophrenic patients with suicidal ideations should be hospitalized without delay. If the suicidal ideations are accompanied by strong suicidal drives, the patient should be under constant observation by special-duty nurses. Intensive electroshock therapy should be instituted as soon as it is possible following admission.

Patients who have depressions in the matrix of a manic-depressive psychosis and who have suicidal preoccupations also respond best, on a short-term basis, to electroshock therapy in a hospital setting. As I have already noted, there are also severely depressed, nonschizophrenic, nonmanic-depressive patients who are too ill for ambulatory treatment with antidepressant drugs and/or psychotherapy and who optimally should receive electroshock, either on an ambulatory or inpatient status.

Electroshock treatment in suicidal patients must be given on an *intensive basis*. The treatment should be administered daily until there is clear-cut evidence that the suicidal drives and preoccupations have cleared. If the psychiatrist is less vigorous in his use of ECT in these situations, he runs the risk of a suicidal gesture occurring during the initial period of treatment (11). With some actively suicidal patients, it may be advisable to give more than one treatment per day during the first few days of hospitalization.

In my experience, it usually requires five or six electroshock treatments to effectively blunt suicidal drives. In some patients, the suicidal drives may be blunted even after one, two, or three treatments. However, one must be extremely cautious if there is an apparent amelioration of suicidal propensities after so few treatments. After all suicidal ideation is ameliorated, the treatments then may be spaced to three times per week until all the direct and indirect clinical evidence of depression has disappeared, including symptoms such as insomnia, anorexia, hypochrondriasis, and so forth.

Electroshock treatments should not be stopped precipitously in patients with a history of suicidal drives or ideation. Usually ten or more treatments are necessary to complete the series. The dangers in the use of electroshock treatment with such patients is not overtreatment but undertreatment. I do not subscribe to statements purporting that suicidal patients may require only five or six treatments. This concept is fallacious and dangerous and too often results in avoidable exacerbations.

After all symptoms of depression have cleared, I taper the electroshock treatments, with the patient receiving two treatments per week for one or more weeks, and then once per week for one or two more weeks. This regime is particularly applicable in suicidal schizophrenic patients, in whom the end points of depression may be difficult to delineate. A total of 10 to 15 electroshock treatments, spread over a four-to-eight-week period may be necessary, depending upon the patient.

A word of caution is in order. Electroshock therapy, while it is a very effective method of treating depressed patients with suicidal drives, may occasionally just blunt or mask the suicidal impulses, particularly if the frequency or number of treatments is inadequate. As a result, the psychiatrist prematurely may lessen his careful vigil in the course of treatment, at times with tragic results. Also, in some instances, as the organic mental syndrome secondary to electroshock clears, residual self-destructive drives may mushroom rapidly and end in a suicidal attempt. One cannot stress too urgently that during the early phases of electroshock therapy with suicidal patients, there must be very close nursing care until all suicidal ideations have been ameliorated.

Following the completion of an intensive series of electroshock treatments in depressed suicidal patients, a careful psychopathologic evaluation of the patient must be undertaken. Any residuals of the underlying depression, whether they are overt or masked, must be recognized for what they are; namely, they indicate that the patient's ego capacities are severely limited and that they are the nidus for a full exacerbation of depression, perhaps with recurrent suicidal behavior.

Too often patients are prematurely discharged and returned to active vocational and social activities by psychiatrists who administer electroshock therapy. One of the reasons is that very few of them are sufficiently well trained in appropriate psychotherapeutic techniques. Patients who are returned to vocational and social activities prematurely have a very high rate of exacerbation of depression and suicidal ideation. This is particularly true if the patient faces an impending or actual significant adverse circumstance.

After a patient has demonstrated effective amelioration of the underlying depression secondary to electroshock treatment, the decision must be made as to the nature of the psychotherapeutic procedure, if any, that should be utilized. Some patients or patients' families will reject any and all types of psychotherapeutic help. This occurs if people are rather primitive with regard to the concept of psychiatry and psychotherapy. It also occurs among patients with obsessive-compulsive personality patterns who must be in control of themselves at all times and who are massively dominated by feelings of inadequacy. Psychiatrists and psychotherapists must be sufficiently modest to appreciate that not all patients are good candidates for psychotherapeutic help, no matter how much they really need it.

The question also arises whether these patients should automatically be placed on antidepressant drugs following the completion of a successful series of electroshock treatments. In most instances, it does not make much sense to start patients who are free of depression on antidepressant drugs. All antidepressant drugs work optimally on severely depressed patients.

There are some exceptions to this general rule. Ideally if the patient has a history of recurrent depressions drug therapy should be combined with effectively designed psychotherapy. (I am referring to unipolar types of depression, not to bipolar types. Bipolar patients should be placed on a regimen of lithium carbonate.)

One must be very modest and careful in instituting psychotherapy in patients who have demonstrated significant improvement from electroshock treatment. As I have noted above, many of the patients are not good candidates for psychotherapy per se. They should not be brought into psychotherapy as captive individuals. The patient's ego capacities must be evaluated very closely.

There should be no massive, aggressive attempt to unfold to the patient the psychodynamic mechanisms behind the depression too rapidly. Some psychotherapists hold the mistaken belief that following successful electroshock therapy the patients automatically have strong ego capacities. Nothing could be further from the truth.

There should be no uncovering of psychodynamic mechanisms just for the sake of uncovering. The therapy initially should be tentative, probing, and supportive in nature. Similarly, one must be very cautious not to bring underlying hostility into focus too rapidly and too precipitously. This can be extremely dangerous and may provoke an exacerbation of the depression. Quite often, directive, environmentally manipulative types of psychotherapy may be initially optimal. The therapist should not be inappropriately too ambitious.

*Another word of caution is in order. There is no clear-cut evidence that any one psychiatric technique or combination of procedures has been more successful than any other technique in the prevention of recurrent suicidal acts* (15).

### Antidepressant Drugs in Combination with Psychotherapy

Antidepressant drugs combined with specifically designed types of psychotherapy have a significant place in the treatment of severely depressed patients, even those with suicidal ideas or inconsistent suicidal drives (1, 16). They must be utilized only by those who have a very intensive understanding of the benefits and limitations of the psychotropic drugs and of the benefits and limitations of the briefer types of psychoanalytically oriented types of psychotherapy. I would even go beyond this description. One must have training in utilizing these combined techniques, for this combination has unique qualities that differ from drug therapy alone and psychotherapy alone.

I have already indicated that psychotherapy in combination with antidepressant drugs is not indicated in all severely depressed, suicidal patients, particularly on an ambulatory basis. I have specifically indicated which patients should be hospitalized or treated with electroshock therapy either on an inpatient or outpatient basis.

However, in some patients the combined drug-psychotherapy technique has many advantages even over electroshock treatment. In some patients, this combined therapy may be more rapid in its positive effects. Some patients may respond in from 24 to 48 hours after the introduction of antidepressant drugs. Others may be dramatically improved within a period of a week. Also this type of therapy avoids the strong prejudices toward electroshock treatment held by some persons or families. The organic mental deficits that are secondary to electroshock treatment are eliminated. Quite often a patient can return to meaningful activities in a shorter period of time.

I cannot emphasize too forcefully that when this combined technique is employed in severely depressed patients, particularly those with suicidal ideas or suicidal drives, *the therapist must have emergency facilities available.*

Most psychiatrists use antidepressant drugs in splendid isolation, the aim being to ameliorate symptoms, with the implication that if the symptoms are ameliorated, the patient will have the capability to adapt to this environment. This is an anachronistic concept in view of our current understanding of the dynamics of emotional illness and in the light of our knowledge of the need for a planned program of psychosocial adaptation as an integral part of the treatment of emotionally disturbed individuals.

I do not consider psychotropic drugs as being an end in themselves; rather they are a vehicle by means of which the patient can better function in a cooperative fashion in a psychotherapeutic relationship. Drugs in themselves do not enlighten patients to the sources of their illnesses; nor do they demonstrate to them the manner in which they should adapt to the surrounding milieu. Medications do not make them appreciative of their emotional limitations. Also drugs do not make the patients aware of the need to avoid certain stresses or how to utilize the beneficial aspects of their environment. This psychosocial awareness can best be learned through a type of dynamically oriented psychotherapy.

Having said this, I would reiterate that initially the total thrust in the use of the combined treatment in the management of severely depressed, suicidal patients is to blunt and then eliminate all suicidal drives and ideation. If this is not accomplished during the first week of treatment, the patient should be treated with electroshock either on an outpatient or inpatient basis.

*It is dangerous, primitive, anachronistic, and cruel to treat severely depressed, suicidal patients with psychotherapy alone. I will go further; it is reprehensible on an outpatient basis.* I call to the reader's attention that most persons who make suicidal attempts have been seen by a physician, psychiatrist, psychotherapist, counselor, clergyman, or others, some time before the suicidal act is carried out.

In utilizing the combined treatment procedure, *the therapist must be very aware that a knowledge of the psychodynamics of a depression per se does not indicate the severity of the depression at a given moment. The psychodynamic modus operandi may be the same in a mildly depressed patient as in a patient with intense suicidal drives.* A meticulous investigation of the patient's daily environmental adaptations, his symptoms, and his affective behavior, is necessary before one can ascertain the intensity of a depression at any particular point.

The therapist must also carefully weigh the meaning of the suicidal preoccupations or attempts to determine whether the suicidal behavior in a given patient has death as its goal. This is a most delicate decision requiring persistent, sensitive clinical probing into the psychopathologic manifestations, psychodynamic, and sociodynamic forces that are involved.

## Technique of Combined Therapy

I have treated more than 600 severely depressed patients with antidepressants in combination with analytically oriented psychotherapeutic techniques. Approximately 35 percent of these patients had suicidal ideas. A far smaller number had suicidal drives of varying intensity. This experience has been gained over a period of more than 18 years.

## Selection of Drugs

During the first 12 years I utilized only three antidepressant drugs. They were (a) iproniazid (prior to 1960), (b) imipramine hydrochloride (Tofranil), and (c) tranylcypromine (Parnate) with a phenothiazine drug, usually trifluoperazine (Stelazine). During the past few years, I have used other tricyclic drugs as well. On the basis of this extensive experience, I have found that only very rapidly acting antidepressant drugs can be safely utilized when treating depressed suicidal patients on an outpatient basis. In most instances, only tranylcypromine reacts with sufficient rapidity to be utilized in the combined technique in the depressed suicidal patient.

## Initial Phase of Treatment

The initial psychotherapeutic aspect of combined therapy is supportive in nature. The sole purpose of the combined technique, at this phase of treatment, is to eliminate the suicidal drives and ideation. It is a life-saving procedure. The goal during this aspect of treatment is also to produce a marked improvement in psychomotor activity and in the depressed mood. This phase of therapy is always brief, one to two weeks at the very longest. With patients who have suicidal drives, this initial phase is limited to one week or less. Suicide is the omnipresent danger in this stage of treatment and all patients are treated accordingly.

Therapy is conducted in a face-to-face setting in all instances. The early aspect of combined therapy, namely during the first or at the very most two weeks of treatment, is directive and strongly ego-supportive in character. This is necessary, since all of the patients demonstrate an extremely limited ego capacity and are dominated by their painful, depressive affect in a manner that is so unique to the depressive syndrome. The patients are usually helpless and infantile in their dependency. Most have lost hope of recovery. Many do not feel that they deserve help, even though they continue to plead for assistance. Most of the patients have an overpowering, obsessive guilt mechanism which is rage linked, in that the conscious and unconscious hostility that can be detected readily in almost every depressed patient serves as a constant source of fuel for their paralyzing guilt.

During this initial phase of treatment, the underlying psychodynamic mechanisms are not brought into focus. *One cannot deal with the psychodynamics of depression until the actual depression has been greatly ameliorated.* The patient's ego capacities in this particular phase are too fragile to accept discussion of any unconscious mechanisms that may be quite vague or overwhelmingly painful.

A type of "ego tranfusion" technique is utilized during this initial emergency phase of treatment. These patients have childlike, magical expectations, and it is necessary for the therapist to be direct, giving, and protective. During this period of therapy the severely depressed patient requires and should receive repeated reassurance to the effect that he will improve. In general, these are not idle or false reassurances, for the vast majority of severely depressed patients do remit in response to the combined technique, and most of those who do not, respond to electroshock treatment. Therefore, it is not false to reassure the family and the patient that the outcome of treatment is usually very satisfactory, at least with regard to the current depressive episode.

If a very strong positive transference relationship is not fostered, combined therapy must be terminated and the patient started on electroshock therapy or be hospitalized without delay. In the absence of a marked positive transference reaction, combined therapy on an outpatient basis is too precarious with severely depressed patients.

The agitated depressed patient will frequently "confess" to real or imagined wrongs. At this phase of psychotherapy, the patient should receive prompt, sympathetic "expiation" of these real or imagined "sins." Many patients with severe depressions are vocationally or socially accomplished individuals who have functioned on a very high plane prior to their illnesses. Those with agitated depressions often are meticulous, overly conscientious persons who are in positions of authority and who are highly respected. These patients are given recognition for their past accomplishments. It was found effective to imply in general terms that "your illness is due to exhaustion, emotional exhaustion."

This strongly ego-supportive technique is extremely effective in temporarily containing or reducing the overwhelming feelings of worthlessness and guilt that plague these patients. This in turn temporarily contains the strong guilt-linked rage mechanisms that are an intimate part of many and even most depressions.

During the first two weeks, particularly during the first week, the patient is seen in frequent interviews. During each visit the patient is evaluated minutely. Of particular importance is the degree of psychomotor activity, the intensity of the depressive affect, the intensity of feelings of hopelessness, the frequency and intensity of suicidal preoccupations, and above all, the frequency and intensity of suicidal drives. These points must be kept sharply in focus. Similarly, it is imperative that the therapist evaluate the degree of overt or covert hostility. Other factors of importance are the degree of insomnia, anorexia, hypochrondriasis, or psychosomatic disturbances. These all give evidence, directly or indirectly, of the degree of depression present. Changes in the intensity of psychomotor activity have a special importance, for a change in the direction of psychomotor activity to a more normal pattern, in my experience, is almost always the first sign of improvement in a depressed patient.

The patient's family plays in intimate role in the treatment of the depressed patient in this early emergency phase. They are consulted closely to obtain information concerning the patient's background and personality matrix. The therapist also obtains from them a detailed description of the quality and intensity of the patient's current behavior pattern.

At the time of the initial visit, the family is briefed on the severity of the patient's ailment, and they are informed in precise terms that if the suicidal drives and ideas would not respond effectively in a matter of days to the combined drug therapy-psychotherapy technique, or if the patient appeared to become worse during this period, then hospitalization or ambulatory electroshock therapy would be recommended. The family is made sharply aware that suicide is an omnipresent and real danger in all patients with severe depression. Many families will refuse to accept the concept that a member of their family could commit suicide. Unfortunately, some family members unconsciously will the death of a patient.

Although I clearly recognize that the family is of very imperfect assistance in the treatment of the depressed patient, they are advised to observe the patient carefully during this initial phase of treatment and to report to the therapist at any time. The patient and the family are encouraged to report by telephone at specifically designated times during the initial week or ten days but particularly during the first few days. The patient's medication is managed by the family during the initial week. The possible side effects of the drugs are described in detail to the family and to the patient.

Finally, the therapist admonishes the patient in the presence of the family that he or she should severely curtail all vocational and social responsibilities until such time as the therapist advises him or her to do otherwise. This tends to relieve the strong guilt feelings and feelings of self-derogation that stem from a patient's inability to function due to the overwhelming depressive affect. The therapist's directive to this effect, coming as part of the medical regime, is eagerly grasped by the patient.

Combined drug and psychotherapy in the ambulatory treatment of severely depressed patients requires a great deal of time, and the therapist must be available to the patient at all hours. Half-hearted measures may result in precipitous suicidal attempts. At all times, it should be recognized that this is emergency treatment paralleling emergency medical and surgical procedures.

Strong, positive tranfusion techniques, such as those described above, are effective for very limited periods of time. If the patient does not demonstrate a definite improvement in his suicidal drives and ideas during the first few days, if the over-all depression is not significantly helped during the first seven to ten days, or if the patient's clinical status deteriorates, then the combined procedure must be terminated and the patient either hospitalized or be given ambulatory electroshock treatment. Once a decision is made to terminate combined therapy, it must be done with definiteness and consistency. Indecisiveness on the part of the family or psychiatrist may expose the decompensated, depressed patient to the risk of suicide.

The time limit of approximately seven days allowed for the first symptoms and signs of improvement was established for valid reasons. It has been my experience that if severely depressed patients treated on an ambulatory basis did not begin to respond in approximately one week's time, it was unlikely that a significant change would occur. There is reason to believe that the concept that antidepressant drugs may require many weeks to be effective may be fallacious and that the changes that occur after a long period may be accounted for by many unintended or placebo factors. In the outpatient treatment of severely depressed suicidal patients, a drug must work quickly or it must be discontinued and be considered as an ineffective therapeutic agent in a given patient.

Finally, the initial emergency phase of the combined therapy technique was limited to a period of one or one-and-a half weeks, because the "magic" of supportive psychotherapy in markedly ill patients becomes very tenuous after a short period of time. If a severely depressed patient does not begin to experience beneficial results in a short period of time, a strongly negative attitude toward the psychiatrist and the treatment quickly replaces the positive transference relationship.

**Psychoanalytically Oriented Phase of Treatment**

When definite evidence exists that suicidal drives and suicidal preoccupations have disappeared and that feelings of hopelessness and the intensity of the depression have decreased, then the scope of the psychotherapeutic procedures can be broadened. It should be remembered that the patient's improvement at this point is due to either the effects of the drug, the strong supportive psychotherapy, or to placebo effects. It is not possible at this point to determine the relative importance of these factors. Indeed, one must be cautious lest the improvement be more apparent than real. The psychotherapeutic process remains ego supportive in nature with the degree of support being decreased gradually in proportion to the increase in the patient's ego capacity. The patient has little or no insight at this point as to the causes of the illness. He is literally dependent upon the drugs and the therapist for his very existence, and any appearance of "recovery" is extremely tenuous.

I stress once again that at this point suicidal attempts are not uncommon during the states of apparent remission. Bleuler first described this state in 1924 as a "reactivation phase" (17). I have described this situation in many papers dealing with apparent remissions in depressed suicidal patients (9, 11). It occurs often when the therapist is lulled into a false sense of security and relaxes his vigil too quickly. This danger can be avoided, if one will continue to probe for evidence of the residual symptoms and signs of depression in the patient.

The extremely positive transference relationship is reduced gradually to prevent a "permanent atrophy" of the ego. This pattern, that simulates infantile dependency, inhibits effective psychotherapy if permitted to remain. The therapist's support is removed cautiously, the rate dependent upon realistic evidence of an increase in the patient's adaptive capacities.

Therapy at all times is carried on in a face-to-face setting. Free association is encouraged, but it is "controlled" free association in which the therapist actively points out the psychodynamic and sociodynamic relationships between the events, thoughts, and emotions that occur in the patient's daily pursuits and their counterparts from the patient's past. Free association is encouraged only when I feel the patient's ego capacities are sufficiently strong to tolerate them. This active interpretation is necessary to prevent the development of a state of free-floating anxiety, which from experience I have found can act as the nidus for an exacerbation of a depression, if the patient is permitted to ruminate too freely without trying the ruminations to the "here and now"; more specifically, to the patient's emotional reaction to the events taking place in his or her daily life. Dreams are studied very intensively, for they offer very important information. Dream material can be at times sources of data heralding an exacerbation or improvement in the patient's clinical status (18–20).

After the patient attains a greater degree of stability, the patient's unconscious hostility is gradually permitted to unfold. In some patients this hostility is covert, while in others it is overt. In most instances, as I have intimated above, this anger is strongly linked to guilt mechanisms. Until all latent hostility is brought into consciousness and the patient is able to react appropriately to anger-producing situations without experiencing guilt, the patient remains extremely vulnerable to a recurrence of depression. I would like to emphasize that exposure of the guilt-linked rage mechanisms should be handled very cautiously. If not, explosive abreactions can occur resulting in a severe exacerbation of the depression and even a suicidal act. Some patients were so terrified in their early formative years that they are unable to express anger and literally must be taught to express it. This must be done very gradually and not with any cavalier "break-through" on the part of the therapist.

Much of the psychoanalytically oriented phase of treatment is spent in pointing out to the patient that the depression was the result of long-standing maladaptations to the environment. Therapy is directed toward helping to alter adverse habit patterns. It is emphasized to the patient that drugs alone, or the mere parroting of the psychodynamic formulations quoted in treatment do not safeguard him from future illnesses. In addition to helping the patient to adapt more realistically to his or her environment, a pointed attempt is made to make the patient poignantly aware (a) of the earliest manifestations of emotional decompensation as they occur, and (b) that often emotional problems are readily reversible if the environmental stresses are confronted as soon as they become evident.

During the past 20 years I have treated more than 500 patients who have had suicidal ideas or suicidal drives either with electroshock or antidepressant drugs in combination with psychotherapy. In all, eight patients made active suicidal attempts while they were under treatment during this 20-year period. Fortunately, none of these suicidal acts resulted in a fatality. Six of the patients took overdoses of medications; two took large amounts of tranquilizers, two others overdoses of an antidepressant drug, and two an excessive amount of soporifics. In none of these instances could the amount of drug taken have caused a fatality, indicating marked ambivalence with regard to the purpose of the suicidal acts. This ambivalence was documented by very intensive studies immediately following the suicidal gestures and as a result of a long period of intensive treatment. Two other patients attempted suicide by slashing their wrists.

Four of the patients were individuals who entered treatment with long-standing, chronic masked depressions. Three had atypical facial pains of psychogenic origin (faciopsychomyalgia). Two additional patients had recurrent agitated depressions superimposed upon a schizoid matrix. Both were relatively anhedonic. The two remaining patients were hyperactive, menopausal, obsessive-compulsive, suburban housewives who had histories of chronic agitated depressions. They had demonstrated excellent initial responses to treatment. Both decompensated precipitously, when contrary to strenuous advice, they returned to their self-defeating pattern of racing about and to their compulsive home and community activities.

None of the eight patients made a suicidal attempt during the acute or subacute phase of treatment. Five occurred 30 to 60 days following the onset of the combined drug-psychotherapy procedure. All five initially demonstrated very significant improvement. Three suidical attempts followed 30 to 60 days after extensive electroshock treatment.

The five patients who initially had been treated with the combined antidepressant-psychotherapeutic technique were given electroshock treatments followed by several months of antidepressant drugs combined with psychotherapy. None of these five has had any further exacerbation of their depressions. The three who had again become depressed following a series of electroshock treatments were given a second series. All three were then treated with antidepressant drugs in combination with psychotherapy. One patient has had no further recurrence of depression. Two of the patients who had agitated depressions superimposed on relatively anhedonic, schizoid personalities have had recurrent depressions despite their exposure to multiple therapies administered by several psychiatrists.

## SUMMARY

Suicide is one of the more common causes of death in the United States. Suicidal ideas and drives are realities faced by all psychiatrists and psychotherapists. However, too often therapy is less than adequate due to ideologic, theoretic, and technical prejudices. Not all psychiatrists and psychotherapists are equipped emotionally or technically to manage suicidal patients.

This paper describes in detail requirements for therapists who treat suicidal patients. It outlines the various phases of treatment and the therapeutic aims of each phase. The clinical decision as to when patients may be treated on an outpatient basis and when they should be hospitalized is discussed.

The limitations and advantages of electroshock treatment and antidepressant drug therapy in combination with psychotherapy are discussed. The author describes in detail his combined antidepressant-psychotherapy technique and his guidelines for electroshock treatment.

## REFERENCES

1. Lesse, S. Psychotherapy in Combination with Antidepressant Drugs. *Am. J. Psychother.* 16:407, 1962.

2. _____ . Management of Depressed Suicidal Patients. In *Current Psychiatric Therapies*, Vol. 8. Masserman, J., Ed. Grune & Stratton, New York, 1968.

3. Litman, R. E. When Patients Commit Suicide. *Am. J. Psychother.* 19:570, 1965.

4. Szasz, T. S. *Law, Liberty and Psychiatry.* Macmillan, New York, 1963.

5. Basescu, S. The Threat of Suicide in Psychotherapy. *Am. J. Psychother.* 19:99, 1965.

6. Kubie, L. S. Multiple Determinants of Suicidal Attempts. *J. Nerv. Ment. Dis.* 138:3, 1964.

7. Litman, R. E. Immobilization Response to Suicidal Behavior. *Arch. Gen. Psychiat.* 18:360, 1959.

8. Shneidman, E. S. On the Deromanticization of Death. *Am. J. Psychother.* 25:4, 1971.

9. Lesse, S. Apparent Remissions in Depressed Suicidal Patients: A Variant of Masked Depression. In *Masked Depression*, Lesse, S., Ed. J. Aronson, New York, 1974.

10. Stone, A. A. Suicide Precipitated by Psychotherapy. *Am. J. Psychother.* 25:18, 1971.

11. Lesse, S. Apparent Remissions in Depressed Suicidal Patients. *J. Nerv. Ment. Dis.* 144:291, 1967.

12. _____ . *Anxiety: Its Components, Development and Treatment,* Chapter 15. Grune & Stratton, New York, 1970.

13. _____ . Hypochondriasis and Psychosomatic Disorders Masking Depression. *Am. J. Psychother.* 21:607, 1967.

14. _____ . The Multivariant Masks of Depression. *Am. J. Psychother.* 124 (Suppl.):11, 1968.

15. Stengel, E. and Cook, N. G. Attempted Suicide: Its Social Significance and Effects. Maudsley Monograph No. 4. Chapman Hall, London, 1958.

16. Lesse, S. Psychotherapy plus Drugs in Severe Depressions—Technique. *Compr. Psychiat.* 7:224, 1966.

17. Bleuler, E. *Textbook of Psychiatry.* Macmillan, New York, 1924, p. 492.

18. Mintz, R. S. Psychotherapy of the Suicidal Patient. *Am. J. Psychother.* 15:348, 1961.

19. Gutheil, E. *The Handbook of Dream Analysis.* Liveright, New York, 1951.

20. Lesse, S. Experimental Studies on the Relationship Between Anxiety, Dreams and Dream-like States. *Am. J. Psychother.* 13:440, 1959.

# 13 The Use of Electroconvulsive Therapy

Fred H. Frankel, M.B. Ch.B., D.P.M.

*ECT is valuable in the treatment of appropriately selected cases of suicidal behavior. These are patients with major affective illness. The suicidal threats and concerns of patients with personality disorders are not likely to respond to ECT except in the presence of a complicating depressive illness.*

In the literature on suicide (1, 2), statements supporting the use of electroconvulsive therapy (ECT) in the treatment of suicidal patients can be found. The seriousness of the intent, the risk, or the need for a more immediate treatment are generally given as indications for ECT. The inference is clear that in the presence of major illness, especially depressive illness, the treatment of choice for suicidal behavior might well be ECT.

In the literature on ECT recommendations for its use in the management of suicidal patients are included (3) (p. 161); (4) (p. 27); (5, 6). Those authors emphasize the increased death rate among depressed patients who are not treated with ECT. The fatalities are due to exhaustion, inanition, and intercurrent infections in addition to suicide. The findings are quite compelling in demonstrating the improved outcome when ECT is used in major affective illness.

What needs to be stated, even though already implied, is that for many instances of suicidal behavior ECT is not the appropriate treatment, and in many cases of major affective illness requiring ECT there is no clear evidence of suicidal ideation or behavior. This absence of a direct correlation is challenging and commands our attention. We cannot assume that the higher the potential for suicide in any patient, the greater the need for ECT. We are confronted by other dimensions which must be drawn into the overall clinical evaluation of the individual case. It might be useful to start this paper with a brief review of ECT.

## Electroconvulsive Therapy

The use of convulsive therapy, that is, the induction of a seizure to combat severe psychiatric illness, was introduced by Meduna, a Hungarian psychiatrist, in 1934 (4) (pp. 8–11). The agents first used were chemical, such as camphor and pentylenetetrazol. In 1938 two Italian psychiatrists, Cerletti and Bini, first introduced the application of electrical energy to the scalp to induce the seizures. Although the initial use of this therapy, also known as electroshock therapy or electroplexy, was aimed at improving schizophrenia, its value as a treatment for major affective illness has persuaded even the great majority of its critics to concede its importance as a therapy in that disorder. Rational discourse about it has not always prevailed, neither in clinical practice nor in the published literature (3) (pp. 132–50); (7). Hostile political developments and open antagonism to the treatment have often baffled the clinicians who have witnessed dramatic improvements attend its appropriate use.

The primary goal of the treatment procedure is to produce a generalized cerebral seizure which can be discerned on EEG. The seizure is achieved by applying a minimal electrical stimulus to the scalp. For over three decades efforts have constantly been directed toward improving the procedure and reducing its adverse effects. The method now used differs considerably from that employed in the 1940s and 1950s. The routine use of general anesthesia, muscle relaxation, and ventilation with pure oxygen has transformed a treatment that once terrified patients and disturbed witnesses into a comfortable and relatively safe procedure.

After preparing the patient with an anticholinergic agent, such as atropine, a short-acting anesthetic agent is introduced. Ventilation with 100 percent oxygen is provided through an anesthetic face mask, and maximal muscle paralysis is then achieved with succinylcholine, a rapidly metabolized muscle paralysant. A mouth gag is used to protect the teeth and structures of the mouth. The patient is thus temporarily deeply asleep, oxygenated, and virtually incapable of anything other than minimal musculo-skeletal activity. Electrodes covered with moistened cotton pads are applied to both temples (for bilateral ECT) or the temple and parietal region on the same side as the dominant hand (for unilateral ECT over the nondominant hemisphere). A minimal electrical stimulus is administered for a fraction of a second, and a modified convulsion follows. This is very often extremely difficult to detect from observation of the body and limbs because the movements are usually very slight. The essential therapeutic event, however, is the generalized cerebral seizure which is recordable on EEG.

After a matter of minutes the patient begins to waken, and frequently within fifteen to thirty minutes is wide awake. Temporary mild confusion is often present after bilateral electrode placement but considerably less evident after unilateral application. The treatments are usually administered three times a week on alternate days, and the average ECT series consists of eight to twelve treatments.

With regard to short-term adverse effects, it is useful to remember that the experienced anesthesiologist can manage the potentially adverse effect on cardiac conduction and respiration of either the electrical current or the drugs used in ECT. Patients with cardiac disease thus generally tolerate ECT better than they do high doses of tricyclic antidepressants. ECT is time limited, and the patient is under constant medical observation during the whole of the procedure. This cannot be said of antidepressant medication.

The imputed long-term adverse effects of ECT continue to draw attention and criticism. Although opponents of the treatment have argued that the treatment permanently impairs memory, recent evidence suggests that patients experience very little memory disability, and few persistent memory complaints with unilateral electrode placement over the nondominant hemisphere.

Although bilateral placement is sometimes associated with greater anterograde amnesia and more extensive retrograde amnesia for remote events than is unilateral placement, patients recover a substantial portion of their new-learning capacity within six to nine months after completing either type of ECT, and also largely recover their memory of events that occurred long before ECT. Events that occurred just days prior to and during the treatment might be permanently lost (3) (pp. 57–71).

Formal testing reveals no evidence of lasting impairment of memory six to nine months after the treatment. This could be due to the limitations of the tests. It should be borne in mind, however, that many professionals, academicians, and business executives who have had ECT rarely complain of a lasting memory deficit.

The efficacy of ECT in major affective illness is compelling. Studies strongly suggest that there exists a population of depressed patients who clearly respond to ECT but not to drugs.

The APA Task Force on ECT concluded that ECT is an effective treatment in cases of:

1.  Severe depression where the risk of suicide is high and/or where the patient is not taking food or fluids and/or where the use of drug or other therapy entails high risks and/or will take an unacceptably long period to manifest a therapeutic response;

2.  Severe psychoses characterized by behavior which is a threat to the safety and well-being of the patient and/or others and which cannot be controlled by drugs or other means, or for which drugs cannot be employed because of adverse reactions or because of the risks which their use entails;

3.  Severe catatonia under special circumstances;

4.  Severe mania under special circumstances.

ECT is probably effective in less severe depressions with vegetative or endogenous elements where drug therapy has been ineffective or contraindicated; and in less severe psychoses, particularly those with an endogenous affective element where drug therapy has been ineffective or is contradicted (3) (pp. 161–62).

The psychoses referred to include conditions classifiable as schizophrenia, although the need for further studies of the efficacy of ECT in that condition has been emphasized (8).

In the absence of clearly defined conditions such as those already mentioned, ECT should not be used solely to control symptoms or violent behavior. While ECT is recommended for the treatment of affective disorders, and possibly some cases of schizophrenia, it is not recommended as a method to prevent suicide per se. The essential step to be mastered is the evaluation of the suicidal behavior within the context of the overall clinical picture.

## Understanding the Nature of Suicidal Behavior in Relation to ECT

The criteria generally used in the assessment of suicidal behavior, while not all central to the role of ECT, are nonetheless highly relevant. Every effort should be made during the evaluation to accumulate information about the seriousness of the situation and the potential risks to the individual's life. From the history and clinical interview the examiner determines the pervasiveness and the intent of the suicidal thoughts; the presence or absence of concrete plans; the lethal nature of the attempt or the ideation; and the degree of hopelessness about the future. These are read in conjunction with the demographic characteristics known to correlate with a high incidence of suicide, and also with the circumstances of the act if a failed attempt has already been made.

The available rating scales (9–13) can provide considerable additional assistance in assessing the real danger of a threatened suicide, and will even contribute to a deeper understanding of the overall clinical picture. However when general treatment decisions are to be made, including those relating to the immediate handling of a suicide threat, the clinical picture should take precedence. Experience constantly reaffirms the paramount importance of the clinical interaction. The final evaluation should still take into account whatever other useful information can be culled from whatever source, structured or otherwise. The nature of the suicide threat sometimes influences, but does not of its own determine the clinical diagnosis.

It should be emphasized that ECT has a proven record in the management of major affective illness. Its efficacy under other circumstances has been more questionable. Where major affective illness is suspected, the treatment options are clear. The choices are primarily antidepressant medication or ECT, preferably within a supportive and psychodynamically sensitive management plan. The selection of ECT depends on the nature of the depression, which in turn may establish the seriousness of suicide as a possible complication.

Admission to an adequate inpatient facility capable of providing the emotional support and the necessary vigilance, plus the opportunity for building a reliable therapeutic relationship, might well permit a reasonable trial of antidepressant medication even in the presence of thoughts about suicide. In general, a trial of antidepressant medication is frequently favored in most cases of major depression provided that the necessary supportive structure is in place. There is, however, accumulating evidence that patients suffering from delusions and severe vegetative signs such as insomnia, weight loss and agitation probably respond better to ECT than to drugs (14, 15). In the current therapeutic climate, few have been bold enough to state that such patients should be treated *ab initio* with ECT. The time might not be too distant when such an assertion could be made with confidence. We still await the develoopment of reliable clinical or laboratory predictors to place treatment decisions on a firmer footing.

In the presence of very serious suicidal preoccupation it must be remembered that neither ECT alone nor drugs alone will take care of the problem. The necessary supportive and vigilant environment is essential if patients in treatment and on the road to recovery are to be prevented from committing suicide. Clinical experience attests to the numbers of patients who achieve suicide after the commencement of antidepressant drugs or ECT in an inpatient setting.

In the choice between drugs and ECT, the seriousness of the affective illness is measured by taking into account several factors. These include criteria generally considered to be descriptive, in addition to whatever else emerged during the clinical interaction. An appreciation of both the phenomenological and the psychodynamic factors are needed for the richest understanding of the problem. Integrating the biological, the psychological, and the social aspects leads to the best assessment and involves an evaluation of the intensity, the persistence, the content, and the meaning of the depressive symptomatology. A family history of affective illness is similarly important. In the overall evaluation one also takes into account the presence of psychosis, bizarre suicidal acts, suicidal symptoms in response to delusions and hallucinations, or the pathological identification with an individual who died by suicide; when present, such factors mandate the use of either medication or ECT, or ultimately both.

We know from epidemiological surveys that lonely, socially isolated, unmarried, and unemployed elderly white males are among the most vulnerable to suicide. We are also learning of the constantly increasing suicide among adolescents and young adults. Generally speaking, isolating social conditions, progressive immobilization, and gradual depletion of internal and external resources predispose to suicidal behavior. These might well be reflective of major affective illness responsive to biological treatments. However, they might also be the direct consequence of a socio-economic reality that could respond to broader environmental and psychological manipulations. Neither ECT nor drugs will be the treatment of choice under such circumstances.

**Relative Contraindications to ECT in Suicidal Behavior**

This leads us to the other categories of illness that might masquerade as major depressive illness or be interpreted as such. I refer here to the depression of a characterologic kind, the depressive reaction to psychosocial stress, and the tearful expressions of anger that carry with them declarations of despondency and sometimes impulsive, manipulative suicide attempts. We enter here the challenging arena of the neuroses and personality disorders, most of which respond poorly to ECT unless there is evidence of an affective illness of major proportions superimposed on the other substrate.

The early history of ECT is sadly replete with instances of its inappropriate use. Driven by the enthusiasm accompanying a new and relatively safe treatment that was clearly effective in some conditions, psychiatrists were tempted to try it in others. This was at a time prior to the development of the neuroleptics and antidepressant drugs when effective remedies were rare. In retrospect, many inappropriate categories of illness were treated with ECT, including the neuroses, and the troublesome acting-out behavior of characterologically disturbed patients. Only very few therapists might still be persuaded that such an approach is justified (3) (pp. 161–62).

Depression in response to psychosocial stress and disappointment is not amenable to treatment by ECT, unless the events trigger a more pervasive, more enduring depression of biological proportions. Similarly, a tearful rage or brooding vengeful fantasies demand the consummate skill of a compassionate psychotherapist. ECT does not easily dissolve deep feelings of loneliness, abandonment, humiliation, and frustration, especially when these have their roots in overwhelming narcissism, entitlement or reality. These deserve a sympathetic understanding and examination; neither judgment nor punishment is an effective remedy. ECT under such circumstances is often seen as punishment, and in all candor must many times have been used as such, particularly when a negative countertransference went unrecognized. Borderline patients or those viewed as primitive and hysterical can be sorely trying to both relatives and therapists by threatening or attempting suicide. Rarely, and only if one strongly suspects the presence of a superimposed affective illness, should one resort to the use of ECT. Perhaps antidepressant medication, if the possibility of overdose can be monitored, would be a preferable first step.

## CONCLUSION

In sum, this paper tries to emphasize the importance of the clinical diagnosis in evaluating the role for ECT in suicidal behavior. It is especially helpful in the treatment of severe affective illness, schizoaffective illness, and in some instances of schizophrenia. If the suicidal ideation and behavior are a part of those conditions, the role of ECT should be considered side by side with that of medication. It should also always be borne in mind that the biological intervention deals only with certain aspects of the crisis, improving matters to some extent while containing the behavior. In almost all instances, a compassionate and watchful milieu, in addition to a supportive relationship with a therapist are essential if tragedy is to be averted in the further unfolding and management of the patient's problems.

## SUMMARY

Publications on the subjects of ECT and suicide stress the importance of ECT as a valuable treatment in appropriately selected cases of suicidal ideation or attempted suicide. There is no direct correlation between the degree of suicidality and the usefulness of ECT. In the management of cases with major affective disorder, particularly those showing delusions and vegetative signs, ECT should be considered early in the treatment. The presence of the potential for suicide provides an added incentive. However, suicidal threats or attempts on the part of patients with severe personality disorders are not likely to respond to ECT unless the picture is complicated by major depressive illness. In the absence of such affective illness, understanding and skilled psychotherapy are likely to be more effective. Antidepressant medication and ECT should be administered within a supportive, watchful, and compassionate setting.

## REFERENCES

1. Schoonover, S. C. Pharmacotherapy of the Suicidal Patient. In *Lifelines: Clinical Perspectives on Suicide*, Bassuk, E. L., Schoonover, S. C., and Gill, A. D., Eds. Plenum Press, New York, 1982. pp. 67–68.

2. Kahn, A. The Moment of Truth: Psychotherapy with the Suicidal Patient. In *Lifelines*, p. 89.

3. American Psychiatric Association Task force Report 14, *Electroconvulsive Therapy*. APA, Washington, D.C., 1978.

4. Fink, M. *Convulsive Therapy: Theory and Practice*. Raven Press, New York, 1979, p. 27.

5. Avery, D. and Winokur, G. Mortality in Depressed Patients Treated with Electroconvulsive Therapy and Antidepressants. *Arch. Gen. Psychiatry* 33:1029-1037, 1976.

6. Avery, D. and Winokur, G. The Efficacy of Electroconvulsive Therapy and Antidepressants in Depression. *Biol. Psychiatry* 12:507-524, 1977.

7. Frankel, F. H. Reasoned Discourse or a Holy War: Postscript to a Report on ECT. *Am. J. Psychiatry* 132:77-79, 1975.

8. Salzman, C. The use of ECT in the Treatment of Schizophrenia. *Am. J. Psychiatry* 137:1032-1041, 1980.

9. Beck, A., Kovacs, M., and Weissman, A. Assessment of Suicidal Intention: the Scale for Suicide Ideation. *J. Consult. Clin. Psychol.* 47:343-352, 1979.

10. Beck, A., Weissman, A., Lester, D., et al. The Measurement of Pessimism: The Hopelessness Scale. *J. Consult. Clin. Psychol.* 42:861-865, 1974.

11. Beck, A., Schuyler, D., and Herman, I. Development of Suicidal Intent Scales. In *The Prediction of Suicide*, Beck, A., Resnick, H., and Lettieri, D., Eds. Charles Press Publications, Baltimore, Md., 1974, pp. 76-78.

12. Weissman, A. and Worden, W. Risk-rescue Rating in Suicide Assessment. *Arch. Gen. Psychiatry* 26:553-560, 1972.

13. Tuckman, J. and Youngman, W. A Scale for Assessing Suicide Risk of Attempted Suicides. *J. Clin. Psychol.* 24:17-19, 1968.

14. Glassman, A., Kantor, S. J., and Shostak, M. Depression, Delusions and Drug Response. *Am. J. Psychiatry* 132:716-719, 1975.

15. Horden, A., Holt, H. F., Burt, C. G., and Gordon, W. F. Amitriptyline in Depressive Cases. *Br. J. Psychiatry* 109:815-825, 1963.

# 14 Guidelines for "Suicide-Proofing" A Psychiatric Unit

Howard S. Benensohn, M.D.
H. L. P. Resnik, M.D.

A recent California Court decision held that a hospital was responsible for the suicide of a patient on its grounds. In reaching its decision, the Court had to consider what reasonable suicide precautions the Institution had taken (1). Yet, it would seem that this should not be a judicial decision but one based on psychiatric opinion.

Nearly all hospitals have a standard series of "suicide precautions." These usually include having ward personnel know the patients' whereabouts at all times, permitting access only under close supervision to articles that might be used for self-harm, and making sure that a patient is not isolated in a room [Beisser and Blanchette (2) noted that 52% of suicides at Norwalk State Hospital occurred in seclusion rooms], and assigning a staff member to "special" the patient in a one-to-one situation (3). Margolis *et al.* (4) instituted an "attend at all times" order for the protection of both the suicidal patients and the integrity of their ward as an "open unit." Banen (5) pointed out that in the 1930's a near total control of previously suicidal patients by having them under constant observation was advocated.

Wooley and Eichart (6) stated that "The correction of this (suicidal ideation) does not seem to lie in the general curtailment of parole privileges, but rather in developing more accurate criteria for determining the immediacy of the danger in the individual instance." Rotov (7) recommended continuing consultation and close teamwork to deal with countertransference issues and suggested clinical clues such as projecting concern over a patient's own well-being or a state of chronic dissociation to alert a staff to a possible impending suicide attempt.

Maintenance of custodial-type "suicide precautions" of high-risk persons, that is, total observation, limitation of belts, shoelaces, blankets, no access to public areas, is impossible to maintain for long periods of time. There is usually insufficient staff to sustain such high level, ongoing precautions. Often a suicide attempt will occur once precautions have been discontinued, as a patient seems to be improving. When several patients require such precautions simultaneously, as is frequently the case, the drain on staff can become extreme. The staff then becomes exhausted and often resentful of the quasi-control the suicidal patient exerts over them. (This is not unlike the control the suicide attemptor fantasizes or realizes in this control of "significant others.")

Of course, one might feel that with the advent of tranquilizers and antidepressant medications, the need for precautions is time-limited. Yet, the onset of action of antidepressants often is a week or more. Only electroshock treatment is currently available for immediate relief, and patients have been reported to have committed suicide after a course of EST (8). To believe that suicidal precautions exist as a holding action until treatment (of whatever nature) commences can be a serious error. The care and interest of a staff and clinician are the common essential ingredients of precautions and treatment. The treatment starts with the custodial relationship.

Reports of circumstances of death by suicide in the hospital are limited. Kayton and Freed (9) describe a woman who suffocated herself with a plastic bag; however, the major emphasis of the paper was the study of reactions to the death on the different hospital wards. Margolis et al. (4) describe a young man who hung himself on an overhanging doorstop in his room and, as mentioned, that unit's attempts to deal with the dilemma posed to the therapeutic community by such a patient. Rotov (7) analyzes 20 cases of death by suicide in the hospital; however, patients described all committed suicide while on pass or after contact with the hospital had been terminated.

Suicide attempts in the hospital occur in the context of variable treatment settings depending on the nature of the therapeutic milieu, orientation of the staff, and physical setting of the unit. The orientation of the staff and therapeutic milieu is usually difficult to change, and the advisability of drastic alterations in those parameters on any given unit would be questionable. However, the physical setting of a unit can often be altered minimally and yet decrease the number of potentially lethal options available to any patient intent on committing suicide. To our knowledge, this has never been systematically investigated. The purpose of this paper is to: (a) examine some methods that could be, or have in the past been, used by hospitalized patients to attempt suicide, and (b) propose some guidelines that physicians and administrators might follow, regardless of orientation or milieu, to further "suicide-proof" their unit, whether in a general or psychiatric hospital. However, this is NOT to suggest that by following these guidelines ALL suicide behavior can be avoided.

## THE STUDY METHODS

Although clinicians have considered this topic at some length, none have reported involving their patients in the task of "suicide-proofing" their unit. Yet, it seems that there is no better way to plan a "suicide-proof" unit than by involving patients whose suicidal drive will test their surroundings. Because of its concentration of suicidal patients, the Suicide Studies Unit (SSU), a treatment-research-training Unit run jointly by the Center for Studies of Suicide Prevention and the St. Elizabeth's Hospital Division of the National Institute of Mental Health, was an ideal place to conduct such a project. Only patients who have made a serious suicide attempt are admitted. Since this is a research Unit located within St.

Elizabeth's Hospital, most of those referred have been in treatment for a long time, often years, with little or no modification of their chronic suicidal ideation. Consequently, most have been hospitalized in more than one other facility at some point in their life, and several have made suicidal attempts in these hospitals. Because of the patient population, the SSU is a locked unit, so it does differ from many psychiatric units in general or psychiatric hospitals. However, we believe that our observations are also applicable to such units.

The purpose of this study was explained to our patients, and permission to record a meeting was obtained. The question of how one might kill oneself on the SSU was posed to separate groups of nine inpatients, seven former inpatients receiving outpatient therapy, and finally to the Unit's staff. This was followed by a discussion of how patients have attempted suicide elsewhere. Suggestions as to how to make units more "suicide-proof" were then solicited. Patient cooperation was excellent.

## RESULTS

The Suicide Studies Unit is geared to dealing with suicidal patients exclusively. The staff, quite expert in dealing with such patients, had taken into account some of the more obvious methods discussed, but the variety of methods introduced by the patients and not even considered by the staff was astounding. What follows is a summary of the patients' observations. It is not intended to be an all-inclusive list.

1. *Hanging:* Perhaps the one method most frequently mentioned by our patients was hanging. A variety of materials could be used including wire hangers, ties on robes, belts, yarn, electrical cords, bed linen, guitar wires, clothing, and string. These could be attached to shower rods, ventilating ducts, grates, bedposts, door handles, clothes hooks, or other fixtures. One patient had removed the cord used to tie a laundry bag and attempted to hang herself over a shower curtain rod.

2. *Jumping:* A second major cateogry for attempts is jump-

ing. Most reports of suicide from general medical-surgical hospitals list jumping as the most prevalent method (10). Every patient participating in the discussions had independently checked the windows and screens throughout the Unit. The inpatient group discussed at some length how much strength it might take to penetrate the screens, whether they could be cut with sharps, or whether they could be removed. The fact that the windows were partitioned was noted by several patients who felt that they were not thin enough to be able to slide between the frames. All doors to stairwells had been carefully checked, as had heating ducts, pipes, and elevator doors, both on the Unit and in the corridors just outside the doors to the Unit.

3. *Cutting:* Cutting is a common suicidal behavior, though rarely lethal, and stabbing has been included in this category. The patients noted that scissors could be signed out for Occupational Therapy assignments, and knives were available in the dining room and could be used even though they were counted to prevent secreting them. There is, of course, much glass on the Unit, in the nursing station, light bulbs, mirrors, and so on, and it was noted that it would be an easy matter to find glass for cutting oneself. Phonograph records and ashtrays, when broken, also could be used for cutting.

4. *Ingestion:* Most of the patients had attempted suicide by drug overdose, so it is not surprising that ingestion was another frequently mentioned method. Placing tablets under the tongue and not swallowing is a common way to accumulate pills. Also, on occasion, pills were left unattended in the nursing station. The patients, but not staff, noted that when medicines are delivered, those for other units are left unattended on the delivery cart while the pharmacist checks his list in the nursing station. It would be easy for patients to take entire bottles of medication from these carts.

Ingestion of nonmedical materials was also mentioned. The housekeeping employees have a portable cart on which they keep lye-containing mixtures, ammoniated cleaning compounds, and other compounds potentially fatal if ingested. Perfumes, colognes, and lighter fluid could also be ingested. A surprising method pointed out was the use of aerosol cans either to spray directly into the lungs with damage resulting from pressure, or breathing into a bag while simultaneously spraying.

5. *Other forms:* These include drowning in the bathtub, smothering oneself with a plastic bag (for example, those from the cleaners), banging one's head against the wall, and setting oneself on fire, a rare method but one which recently occurred in epidemic form in the psychiatric unit of the E. J. Meyer Memorial Hospital in Buffalo, N.Y. Although smuggled firearms was a concern of the staff, this was never mentioned by the patients.

Precautions noted on other units included absence of matches, records, no smoking in patient rooms, no belts, and, in one instance, no shoelaces. Plastic eating utensils had been tried in one facility but abandoned as too costly.

Afterwards the patients were asked for their reactions to the discussion. Their first concern was whether we would tighten our procedures by depriving them of some of the items usually permitted on the SSU, namely, matches, yarn, phonograph records. No radical alteration in Ward policy was initiated, although we did lock up the housekeeping cart, shorten electrical cords, and alter the pharmacy's distribution of medicine on the Unit. Perhaps we can rationalize this somewhat belated action as showing our patients we did care enough about them to take such steps.

Though there was some concern by the staff, prior to posing this problem, that such a discussion might result in increased patient anxiety and acting out that might include a suicide attempt, the opposite was found to be the case. The acknowledgement by the staff that the patients knew how to kill themselves in the hospital "if they really wanted to" simply reaffirmed a self-evident truth. Most patients felt relieved that they had the opportunity to share their observations. They noted that it was reassuring that others had made similar checks of the Unit, and the fact that the nursing staff took some of their suggestions (but none that would alter the extent of their personal freedom) was frequently mentioned positively. Though some tended to project their relief onto either other patients or a "future admission," most were able to identify the feelings as their own. Finally, all patients reported being pleased that we asked them to participate in this project, and no suicide attempts have occurred on the Unit since the discussion.

## DISCUSSION

From our results certain facts are immediately apparent. First, suicidal patients will and do test the physical layout of their ward. If the unit is locked, as it may be with several actively suicidal patients, doors will be tried, screens examined, windows checked, the unit thoroughly inspected. However, we believe that nonsuicidal patients in similar situations might also test their physical setting. Somehow, suicide precautions and settled limits invite testing. This suggests to us that patient participation in limit-setting is desirable. Second, patients are aware that no unit can be made completely "suicide-proof," yet they are reassured by the efforts taken to protect them from harming themselves.

The patient material reported herein, coupled with our clinical experience, highlights the fact that the institution of simple guidelines in an attempt to "suicide-proof" psychiatric units does decrease the number of options available to a patient intent on trying to kill himself. We feel such plans are requisite in affording satisfactory psychiatric care. We have indicated that no technique is perfect, nor can it be maintained reasonably for a long period, but perhaps for 48 to 72 hours. Fortunately, the majority of hospitalized suicidal persons do respond, primarily to the reinforcement of their own weakened ego controls, in such time. However, in the event a patient somehow is successful despite these safeguards, we would consider the hospital had taken reasonable steps in conformance to our experience.

It should be understood that all of the guidelines are meant to supplement "usual" suicide precautions. These include:

1. A thorough clinical evaluation of the patient with the question of suicidal ideation being raised specifically and recorded on the patient's chart.

2. Staff specials when indicated. Suicidal patients should not be left alone.

3. Counting silverware and, when permitted on the unit, "sharps" such as scissors, nail files, and so forth.

4. Specific education of personnel about suicidal patients and their management in the context of their ward orientation.

From our studies the following additional guidelines are strongly suggested:

5. Patients should spend a minimum amount of time in their bedrooms, one of the places where suicide is most likely to occur. Private rooms should be eliminated. This does not necessarily include a seclusion room although, as mentioned, suicides do occur there. An analysis of 30 cases of inhospital suicide by the Veterans Administration Research Unit shows that of these, 20 patients had jumped, 12 from a private room, and five had hung themselves, all in private rooms (11).

6. The bathroom is also a common location for suicide attempts. In the same VA study, six of 30 patients had jumped from bathroom windows. The opportunity for suicide by hanging is also high in bathrooms. Thus, all bathrooms should ideally be locked except perhaps a single, centrally located one for each sex. All curtain and shower rods should be of the "break-away" variety. These are available to "break away" under 50 test pounds. Shower nozzles should ideally be set into the wall or ceiling and never protrude. Pipes should not be exposed. Ventilating ducts should be at floor level.

7. All windows should have screens that are impenetrable and can not be removed except by special key or tamper-proof devices. Nonbreakable glass is an alternative although the efficacy of such glass has recently been the subject of some controversy.

8. Utility and storage rooms must be kept locked at all times and should not have windows.

9. All electrical appliances and lamps should be located near an outlet, and electric cords should be shortened to minimal length necessary.

10. Visitors, no matter how well intentioned, often bring in items potentially lethal in the hands of a suicidal patient, and while it is not reasonable to search them, they should be alerted

to report all gifts to the nursing staff. All patients on admission or returning from pass should be searched. This does constitute an infringement on rights and is repugnant to some, but it also eliminates a potential source for introducing lethal materials onto a unit. Taking into account that patients are often most suicidal as they begin to improve, which often accompanies receiving passes, at the very least, patients who have been suicidal should be searched on return from a pass.

11. The importance of locking all doors and windows should be stressed to all with access to a particular unit, including housekeepers, students, staff, and maintenance and construction personnel such as telephone repairmen or electricians who may not be familiar with a hospital's procedures.

12. Often suicide precautions are strictly adhered to on a unit but are largely ignored just outside the door. Stairwells, utility rooms, offices, and kitchens are left unlocked, housekeeping carts are stored in corridors, and in some instances, windows are not fitted with protective screens or doors to roofs or solaria are left unlocked. Staff should be aware that often suicides occur in promixity to, and not on, a unit, and these can frequently be the source of much legal, as well as emotional grief (12). The off-unit surroundings are especially important on open units.

13. Consider enlisting the patients' help in "suicide-proofing." Ward administrators have at their disposal a potential wealth of information about their own facility's suicide precautions in their patient population and especially among their suicidal patients. This potential should be tapped by asking the patients questions, preferably in a group setting. It should be presented directly as an attempt to make the hospital more secure and thereby further the patients' welfare. Our experiences indicate that rather than producing increased anxiety and even suicide attempts, it had the opposite effect, to help the patients feel more secure in their hospital environment. Finally, in hospitals where suicidal ideation is not openly discussed by the patients in a milieu, such a project would provide the structure necessary for them to deal more openly with their impulses.

14. For new hospitals the following are recommended:

a. When possible, psychiatric units should be located on lower floors.

b. If windows can open, they should be partitioned so that a patient could not get through.

c. All windows should have tamper-proof screens including utility rooms and hallways, not just patient, day, or bathrooms.

d. All glass should be of the "shatter-proof" variety.

While most of the above should pose no problems for the locked unit, practical and theoretical questions can be posed for the open unit. Each unit must evaluate its therapeutic milieu setting and goals to determine at what point instituting the above guidelines will begin to threaten the unit's integrity. At this point the clinical judgment of the administrators becomes crucial. However, most items mentioned can be implemented without threatening the open unit, and such items as impregnable screens or locked utility rooms should be standard on all units. If an open unit is going to deal with seriously suicidal patients, the one-to-one staff specials will assume primary importance, and suicide-proofing the physical environment just beyond the limits of the unit becomes crucial.

The other major problem posed to the open treatment setting results from potential imposition of too many controls, assuming the role of providing those controls that the patient should be developing on his own. We believe that suicidal patients are reassured by the external controls on their self-destructive impulses, especially when they are first admitted, and it was viewed by our patients as evidence of caring, something they often felt was lacking from the "significant others" in their lives. The purpose of increased privileges, including passes, is to enable patients to assume increased responsibility for handling themelves, including their suicidal impulses, as they improve. This is true even in so-called short-term or crisis-intervention units and should not be considered as a valid contraindication to decreasing the availability of potential means of suicide on a unit.

Lastly, we have found that the enlistment of other patients in caring for a suicidal patient has the effect of increasing the staff size geometrically. Sensitizing one patient to another's needs provides the happy circumstance that caring about another is often the vehicle for psychologic growth. The often neglected asset, then, in suicide-proofing a unit, is to sensitize the other patients in sharing the responsibility so that no one can kill themselves on "our ward."

## SUMMARY

A recent court decision held a hospital liable for the suicide of a patient on its grounds. In reaching its decision, the Court had to take into account what measurable suicide precautions the Institution had taken. A review of the literature by the authors exposed a lack of information on what might be considered some "baseline" or "minimal" suicide precautions.

A group of patients and staff on a Suicide Studies Research Ward at St. Elizabeth's Hospital were asked to discuss how they might attempt suicide on the Ward or in the Hospital. Their responses indicated that all of the patients had given the matter considerable thought and had thoroughly checked the Unit. On the basis of these meetings plus the authors' experiences, 14 guidelines are proposed. The applicability of the technique is discussed.

## REFERENCES

1. Hospital Responsible for Self-Inflicted Injuries of Patients. *Psychiatric News*, September 15, 1971.

2. Beisser, A. R. and Blanchette, J. E. A Study of Suicides in a Mental Hospital. *Dis. Nerv. Sys.* 22:368, 1961.

3. General Instructions Manual, Saint Elizabeth's Hospital, Chapter 70. Washington, D.C.

4. Margolis, P., Meyer, G., and Louw, J. Suicidal Precautions: A Dilemma in the Therapeutic Community. *Arch. Gen. Psychiat.* 13:224, 1965.

5. Banen, D. M. Suicide by Psychotics. *J. Nerv. Ment. Dis.* 120:355, 1954.

6. Wooley, L. F. and Eichart, A. H. Notes on the Problems of Suicide and Escape. *Am. J. Psychiat.* 98:114, 1941.

7. Rotov, M. Death by Suicide in the Hospital. *Am. J. Psychother.* 24:216, 1970.

8. Dome, A. A. Treatment of the Hospitalized Suicidal Patient. In *Current Psychiatric Therapies*, Vol. IX. Grune & Stratton, New York, 1969, pp. 209–217.

9. Kayton, L. and Freed, H. Suicide in the Psychiatric Hospital. *Arch. Gen. Psychiat.* 24:216, 1970.

10. Pollack, S. Suicide in a General Hospital. In *Clues to Suicide*, Shneidman, E. S. and Farberow, N. L., Eds. McGraw-Hill, New York, 1957, Chapter 15.

11. Farberow, N. L., Banzler, S., Cutter, F., and Reynolds, D. An Eight-year Survey of Hospital Suicides. *Life-Threatening Behavior* 1:184, 1971.

12. Perr, I. N. Liability of Hospital and Psychiatrist in Suicide. *Am. J. Psychiat.* 12:631, 1965.

# 15 Psychotherapy of the Depressed Suicidal Patient

## Ronald S. Mintz, M.D.

The question I wish to consider can be simply stated: Given a helping person, a therapist, with knowledge, skill, and experience in general psychotherapy—what are the basic considerations of which he should be cognizant in order to undertake the psychotherapeutic treatment of a depressed suicidal patient. The question assumes that, from the experience of clinicians and from the vast published literature,[1] there exists some extractable core body of knowledge about suicide—suicidology—which is relevant and essential in the treatment of the suicidal person. I am convinced that this assumption is correct. It is this body of knowledge and the treatment implications stemming from it which constitute my subject.

The existence of such basic considerations in the psychotherapy of suicidal persons is a matter of far more than academic interest. The evidence is that many suicidal persons are seeking help. Retrospective studies of persons who have made suicide attempts indicate clearly that a large percentage have been in contact with their physicians during the period immediately prior to the suicide attempt (1–10). Persons who may be

---

[1]See Farberow, N. L. *Bibliography on Suicide and Suicide Prevention.* National Clearinghouse for Mental Health Information, Chevy Chase, 1969.

suicidal seek out professional help from a wide variety of helpers, including psychiatrists, nonpsychiatric physicians, psychologists, social workers, ministers, educators, lay counselors, and many others. Unpublished data from the author's survey of over 2,000 persons in Los Angeles City regarding suicidal thoughts and behavior reveal that persons who state they have made one or more suicide attempts have sought help for emotional difficulties five times as frequently as persons in the general population (11). There is, therefore, an urgent need for the selection, organization, and dissemination of available basic knowledge regarding the treatment of suicidal persons.

Although the majority of suicidal persons suffer from depression, not all do (12–14). For example, clinicians are encountering in increasing numbers a new category of suicidal individuals, young persons whose suicidal impulses and behavior are precipitated by a drug-induced panic. Many of the basic considerations I wish to discuss pertain to suicidal persons in general; some will focus specifically on the treatment of *depressed* suicidal persons.

In discussing the treatment of the depressed suicidal person, it is often difficult to separate psychotherapy and management; both are included in the following discussion.

## THE SUICIDAL IMPULSE

Where suicide researchers gather, the apocryphal story is told of a young man who attempted suicide by leaping from the San Francisco Bay Bridge. Quite miraculously, he rose to the surface of the water alive and unharmed. A policeman on a patrol boat ordered him to climb aboard. The young man refused. The policeman drew his revolver, pointed it at the young man, and warned, "If you don't climb aboard this minute, I'll shoot." The young man promptly climbed aboard.

The clinician familiar with the behavior of suicidal persons will recognize in this vignette the presence of several important characteristics of the suicidal impulse, including irrationality, ambivalence, and its episodic duration. An understanding of the nature of the suicidal impulse is essential to the therapist treating a suicidal person. The suicidal impulse is the precursor to suicidal behavior and suicide acts. Many of the characteristics of the suicidal impulse have important treatment implications.

1. *Symptomatic Nature.* The suicidal impulse is not pathognomonic of any specific psychiatric nosological entity. While it is true that persons in certain psychiatric or social diagnostic categories [for example, psychotic depressive reactions, schizophrenic reactions, alcoholic problems (14–16)] have a higher suicide attempt rate than the general population, the suicidal impulse is a symptom which can appear in persons with widely differing emotional problems (17). Effective treatment may require a corresponding diversity of treatment approaches.

2. *Motivation.* There is no one single motivation of all or most suicidal impulses. Research workers who have studied this question have enumerated about a dozen recurring motivations which clinically often appear in combination (18–29).

a. Hostility directed against an introjected lost love object.
b. Aggressive impulses turned back upon the self.
c. Retaliation, spite, and the wish to punish another by inducing guilt or pain.
d. Efforts to force affection or other narcissistic gratification from persons in the social environment.
e. Efforts to destroy intolerable feelings or impulses within the self, such as those related to hostility, heterosexuality, masturbation, homosexuality, or incest.
f. Efforts to escape from real or anticipated physical pain or deformity, loss of esteem, emotional distress, or emotional vacuum.
g. Efforts to achieve masochistic gratification.
h. Efforts to achieve atonement or expiation, to make restitution and/or reduce feelings of guilt.
i. Rebirth fantasies, including fantasies of reincarnation or of heaven.
j. Efforts to rejoin or merge with a dead or lost loved one.
k. Counterphobic response to fear of death.
l. Defensive regression to a state of infantile omnipotence.

3. *Duration.* The suicidal impulse is episodic, usually lasting minutes or hours, sometimes days. It may recur, but each instance is time-limited. This characteristic of the suicidal impulse underscores the therapeutic importance of helping the suicidal person get through the individual suicidal crisis.

4. *Irrational Nature.* One might reasonably anticipate that a person planning and making arrangements to kill himself would be aware that if his plans succeed he will be dead. Often, however, this is not the case. Wahl and others have discussed the suicide attempt as a magical act "actuated to achieve irrational delusional or illusory ends" (26, 30). The therapist may be surprised to discover that the suicidal person before him is discussing suicide with no recognition whatsoever that if he dies he will be permanently dead and gone, his children will be fatherless, he will not be around to hear others apologize, and so forth. Other aspects of the suicidal person's reasoning and understanding in discussing the anticipated sequelae of his own suicide may reflect clear-cut illogic. This phenomenon is by no means limited to persons suffering from psychotic delusions.

5. *Ambivalence.* Whether any suicidal person ever *only* wishes to die may be a matter of dispute, but it is a clinical fact that the suicidal person is usually highly ambivalent about committing suicide (25, 27). None would seek help if this were not so. Most persons recovering from suicide attempts of whatever degree of seriousness or potential lethality express relief that their attempts at self-destruction have failed (27). Although the subsequent suicide rate is higher for these persons than for the general population (31–33), it is worthwhile to reflect on the fact that most persons surviving a suicide attempt do *not* go on to ultimately kill themselves (9, 23, 31, 34–36).

6. *Communication Function.* The results of recent studies repeatedly confirm the fact that most persons making suicide attempts communicate their intention to one or several persons in their social environment prior to the actual suicide attempt

(1-3, 7, 10, 32, 37-39). Often the suicide attempt itself is so structured as to give others an opportunity to intervene. Stengel has called this the *appeal* aspect of the suicide attempt (25). This is the "Cry for Help" we have heard about. It may be a matter of life or death whether someone in the social enviroment recognizes and adequately responds to this cry.

7. *Adaptational Function.* The main and only purpose of the suicide attempt is not, as is commonly believed, self-destruction (25). The suicide attempt usually represents an effort, however misguided, on the part of a desperately unhappy human being to solve a current, intolerable, personal human problem of living, by bringing some intensely desired change in the external world or in the internal (psychic) world. If one considers the suicidal person in this light, one is apt to raise appropriate important questions, such as:

What is the problem in which this person feels so hopelessly caught?

What is it that this person is so desperately trying to change?

Why does he feel so hopeless about the possibility of being able to bring about any change?

## DETECTION AND ASSESSMENT OF
## SUICIDAL DANGER

The first task of the therapist is the detection and assessment of the degree of suicidal danger present. Two of the most important clues to the existence of suicidal danger are the presence of *depression* and indications of *conscious suicidal preoccupation or intent.*

1. *Depression.* As mentioned above, most suicide attempts are made by persons suffering from depression. Therefore, the diagnosis of this condition and evaluation of its depth may often be an important first step in the prevention of suicide. Depression is probably the most common emotional disorder encountered by the general physician. It is easily recognized when it appears in classical form, with anorexia and associated recent weight loss, insomnia, constipation, dryness of mouth,

amenorrhea in women, impotence and diminution of sex drive in men, psychomotor retardation or agitation, and the black mood of discouragement, despondency, and hopelessness, sometimes with severe guilt feelings and persistent worry. Frequently, however, the underlying depression is masked by preoccupation with a variety of vague and shifting physical symptoms. In such instances physical evaluation and laboratory studies reveal no basis for the symptoms, which subside with symptomatic medical treatment only to be soon replaced by a new set of complaints.

Often the diagnosis of depression may be tentatively made by careful observation of the person. The slowed gait, the downcast eyes, the dejected countenance, the absence of makeup, the limited and retarded flow of speech are all suggestive clues. Often there are complaints regarding memory or the ability to concentrate, boredom, loss of self-confidence, inability to make decisions.

When depression is suspected it must be asked about. Often roommates, relatives or co-workers will have observed recent changes in the personality and habits of the patient and will describe a course of progressive social withdrawal.

2. *Conscious Suicidal Preoccupation or Intent.*  Although most persons making a suicide attempt have previously communicated their intentions to family, friends, co-workers, physicians, therapists, or others, some studies suggest that there are those who will not do so unless someone makes a deliberate, direct inquiry (9). Some therapists have felt an understandable concern that asking a person about suicidal rumination may plant a suggestion in his mind and actually increase the suicidal danger. It is important to emphasize that clinicians with wide experience in the treatment of suicidal persons agree that this is not the case. All authorities seem in agreement that *a chief error in the detection and evaluation of suicidal danger lies in not asking the person about suicidal thought and impulses.*

There is no right way of inquiring about such thoughts. The wording and approach may vary according to the patient, the personality of the therapist, and the location and circumstances of the interview. In order to encourage maximum frankness, the conversation should take place in privacy. Some therapists first inquire about the patient's recent general mood with a question such as, "What kind of mood have you been in lately?" or, "How have your spirits been?" After the patient has spoken of his dejected mood, the therapist might ask, "Have you felt so low sometimes that you have had ideas of ending your life?" or simply, "Have you had thoughts about suicide?" The therapist must then draw upon his own clinical experience to evalute the person's response to this question. Let me, however, suggest some guidelines. In general, the most reassuring response is a qualified denial such as, "I have thought about it, but I love my children too much to desert them like that." A flat denial of suicidal thoughts is not at all reassuring. The therapist would do well to adopt the premise that most persons experiencing any prolonged period of despair and hopelessness, intense unremitting anxiety, or severe agitation, give some thought to suicide. One must suspect that a seriously depressed person who denies any such thoughts might well be attempting to conceal aspects of his frightening inner world from others. If the person responds to your inquiry with resentment and indignation, your index of suspicion must increase. A response such as, "I used to think about that, but I don't anymore" must be further evaluated.

There is a four-level hierarchy of increasing suicidal danger with which every therapist should be familiar: suicidal thoughts, suicide plans, suicide preparations, suicide attempts. On the lower level of danger are vague suicidal thoughts such as, "Sometimes I wish I were dead." On the next higher level is the formulation of a specific plan. The level above this consists of the suicidal person having taken preparatory action for a possible suicide attempt, such as saving up a particular number of sleeping pills. The highest level of danger is reached when an attempt has actually been carried out.

A variety of indicators may point to conscious suicidal preoccupation or intent: rumination about death; discovery of a suicide note, whatever the person's explanation may be; abruptly taking steps to put one's estate in order; giving away expensive gifts or objects of great sentimental value for no apparent reason.

A history of past suicide attempts increases suicidal danger (1, 9, 31–33, 40–41). The person has already demonstrated that one aspect of his coping style is a suicide attempt. It should be remembered that past suicide attempts are not always admitted by the person or the family. Therefore, transverse scars on the anterior aspect of the wrist must automatically be considered evidence of a previous suicide attempt.

3. *Other Factors.* There are a number of other factors, internal and environmental, which should be considered in assessing suicidal risk. All of the following contribute to increased suicidal danger:

a. The tendency toward impulsive behavior.

b. An inflexible stressful environment.

c. Fatigue, illness, drug ingestion, or excessive environmental demands. These factors diminish the individual's capacities to cope effectively with stress.

d. The presence of intense anxiety, fears of loss of control, or depersonalization experiences.

e. A paucity of positive relationships and meaningful involvements with other persons and life activities.

f. Unrealistic ideas or grossly inaccurate expectations concerning the reality consequences of a fatal suicide attempt.

g. Death or loss of one or both parents early in life.

h. Manifest dream content of increasing violence and destructiveness or themes of death and dying of idyllic surrender.

i. Unexplainable sudden changes in mood or behavior, regardless of whether they appear to be deteriorations or improvements.

I have discussed these factors in greater detail elsewhere (42). Obviously, the therapist must continually reassess the degree of suicidal danger throughout this treatment relationship with the patient.

## THE PRESERVATION OF LIFE

No form of treatment is effective with a dead patient. The first concern of the therapist in the management and treatment of the suicidal patient is the preservation of life. More than any other single concern, it is this damoclean danger of a possible irreversible act of self-destruction that gives rise to the need for special awareness, precautions, and techniques in the treatment of the suicidal person as distinguished from treatment in general. The therapeutic relationship, including a good working alliance between patient and therapist, is a powerful bulwark against the carrying out of suicidal impulses. All of the many factors which strengthen that relationship, such as the therapist's interest, concern, and understanding, contribute toward the preservation of life. In addition to these important general components of the therapeutic relationship, a number of specific procedures may sometimes make the difference between life and death.

1. *Initial Precautions.*   In 1931 Fairbank reported on a careful study, undertaken at the suggestion of Adolph Meyer, of 100 suicide attempts (37). In presenting her conclusions regarding suicide prevention she wrote: ". . . I would suggest the restriction of the loose-handling of firearms, poisons, and sedatives. . . ."

Twenty-five years later Ettlinger and Flordh reported on 500 consecutive cases of attempted suicide in Stockholm (43). Seventy-three percent had used barbiturates in the attempt. The authors state: "It should be possible to reduce the large number of serious narcotic poisonings. Our patients, as we have shown, very often used supplies they had at home."

In the United States, according to latest available figures, over 75 percent of all suicides are committed by use of poison, including barbiturates, or firearms and explosives (44). Indications are that this percentage is rising.

In reviewing the histories of persons who have made fatal and nonfatal suicide attempts while in treatment, I have repeatedly discovered instances where the therapist did not inquire from the suicidal person or from his family about the presence in the home of firearms and lethal supplies of drugs. One cannot rely on the assumption that family members of the suicidal patient will bring the presence of such suicidal dangers to the attention of the therapist. Indeed, spurred on by unconscious hostilities, family members sometimes bring such lethal weapons to the attention and availability of the suicidal patient.

Therefore, in the psychotherapy of a suicidal patient, it should be a matter of routine initial procedure to inquire from the suicidal person and from his family about the existence of firearms or potentially lethal medications and the therapist should make every effort to have these lethal weapons removed from the suicidal person's environment.

2. *Prescription Drugs.*  Obviously, it makes little sense to carefully bring about the removal of lethal quantities of drugs from the suicidal person's home and to then hand that same suicidal person a prescription for a lethal quantity of drugs. Yet, repeatedly, this is exactly what is done. This dangerous procedure of therapeutic illogic is seen among psychiatrists as well as nonpsychiatric physicians. Some years ago, Motto and Greene demonstrated that, in the San Francisco area, one out of three persons killing himself and two out of five persons attempting suicide did so with a drug available only on a doctor's prescription (6). I would anticipate that a repetition of that study today would reveal no change.

Davis recently reported a study of over 200 suicides involving barbiturates prescribed by physicians; over two-thirds of these victims had a history of previous suicide attempts (45). One might indeed ponder what kind of a nonverbal communication the suicidal person must feel he is receiving when he is handed a prescription for a potentially lethal quantity of drugs. Surely elementary prudence dictates that prescriptions should be limited to sublethal quantities of medication. Brophy has suggested that prescriptions for major and minor tranquilizers, with the exception of meprobamate, be limited to an average dosage 30-day supply; that prescriptions for meprobamate and the antidepressants be limited to an average dosage 10-day supply; and that prescriptions for barbiturates be limited to an average dosage two-week supply (46). In having to refill prescriptions more frequently, there is an additional valuable by-product: the early detection of regressive changes in the patient's condition, manifested by an increase in the quantity of medication being taken.

3. *Suicidal Crises.*  The preservation of life is most critically at issue when the suicidal person is undergoing a suicidal crisis.

During such periods the therapist must extend additional support, attempt to strengthen the patient's behavioral controls, and carefully evaluate whether any changes in the treatment program are indicated. The patient must usually be seen more frequently, even daily. The therapist must frequently take a more active role during such crisis periods.

It is often helpful to point out to the patient that suicidal *urges* will not interfere with the progress of the treatment so long as the patient maintains control of his *actions*, and that treatment will be interfered with only if the patient *does* something to harm himself. The patient should be told to contact the therapist if he feels unable to control his behavior in the face of increasing suicidal urges. He should be told that temporary voluntary hospitalization can be arranged. The therapist should point out, without anger, that he wants to help the patient but will be unable to do so if the patient is dead. The therapist should extend hope to the patient, verbally and by general attitude, on the basis of his experience with other patients, that the extremely distressing feelings and impulses being experienced by the patient are amenable to modification and change through treatment. Sometimes it may be quite clear that the patient does not really wish his own death, but escape from some problem or from certain feelings within. In such instances, the therapist should emphasize that the use of suicide in an attempt to achieve this goal will result in irreversible and final death.

4. *Hospitalization.* If the patient is judged to be severely suicidal or if, despite ongoing therapy, the suicidal danger continues to rise, hospitalization may be required. I have elsewhere suggested a number of factors to be considered in assessing the advisability of hospitalization: the degree of suicidal risk; the quantity and quality of supervision available in the patient's home; the skill and experience of the physician in treating such patients; the anticipated duration of the present crisis; what effect, if any, such hospitalization will have on the continuation of treatment; the degree of increased feelings of dependency expected in the patient in response to hospitalization; the desirability of electroconvulsive therapy in

cases of depression; the therapist's willingness and capacity to tolerate his own anxiety and uncertainty should he decide against hospitalization (47).

Although hospitalization may serve a variety of purposes, such as providing an opportunity for an evaluation of the patient, removing the patient from an environment with which he is currently unable to cope, permitting the establishment of an enforced therapeutic relationship or inducing effective involvement of relatives in the treatment program—the most frequent primary purpose of hospitalization is to lessen the possibilities of suicide. Several important points concerning hospitalization of the suicidal patient may be mentioned.

a. Once the therapist has made the decision that hospitalization is necessary, he should remain absolutely firm about it with the patient and his family. When a recommendation for hospitalization is made, the patient's first reaction may be one of protest and refusal to cooperate. In most instances the patient can ultimately be persuaded to enter a psychiatric hospital or a psychiatric ward of a general hospital as a voluntary patient.

b. As the patient's anxieties lessen or his mood improves in the hospital setting, he will attempt to enlist the support of his relatives in efforts toward an early discharge. Therefore, anticipate this, and begin early to discuss with the patient's relatives the danger of premature discharge from the hospital.

c. When the hospitalized suicidal patient begins going home on pass or is about to be discharged from the hospital, anticipate a reactivation of suicidal impulses and discuss this in advance with the patient and relatives. If the patient recognizes that a return of suicidal feelings is not unexpected by his therapist, he is less likely to be panicked by such feelings. If the family has been forewarned, they may remain more alert to suicidal dangers. Remember that most hospitalized suicidal patients who subsequently kill themselves do so during the months immediately following their discharge (23). Adjusting to the sheltering environment of a hospital community is quite different from developing the ability to deal effectively with the pre-hospital environment in which the current emotional stress developed.

5. *Patterns.* Often it is possible to perceive a specific sequential pattern of feelings and behavior in a given suicidal patient which repeatedly leads up to episodes of heightened suicidal danger. Sometimes such a pattern may be discernible even though its motivation is not yet understood by patient or therapist. The recognition of such repetitive cycles by therapist and patient may be life-saving, and the exploration and understanding of their genesis and meaning may contribute greatly toward a resolution of the problems for which the patient turns to suicidal solutions.

In this same category are so-called anniversary reactions. Anniversaries of such events as previous suicide attempts, the beginning of treatment, the death or birth dates of relatives or loved ones, the suicide of a friend or relative, the patient's own birthday are times when the therapist must be especially alert to the possibility of increasing despondency and growing suicidal danger.

6. *Personal Patient Data.* The therapist treating a suicidal patient must arrange to have available to him at all times such data about his patient as may be needed in an emergency situation. The necessity for this becomes painfully clear the first time the therapist is contacted at home by a severely lethargic patient with an unlisted telephone number who informs him he has just taken an overdose of sleeping pills. Examples of the kinds of information which might be desirable include the license number and description of the patient's car, the name of a particular bowling alley the patient frequents, the telephone number of the patient's close friends, the name of a motel the patient has mentioned, the names of other physicians the patient is seeing, and so on.

## THE ROLE OF RATIONAL HOPE

There is impressive evidence that rational hope is a potent force in sustaining the suicidal person's behavioral controls as he labors in treatment toward a workable, nonsuicidal solution to his problems (48, 49). Theocritus and Cicero and John Gay have told man, "Where there's life, there's hope," and that is true. Yet suicidal persons seem to paraphrase the poets as if to say, "Where there's hope, there can be life." Alexander Pope notwithstanding, hope does *not* spring eternal in the human breast and when it ceases to spring, suicidal behavior may be the result.

In the presuicide-attempt history of many depressed persons there is a common theme of progressive social withdrawal—a marked narrowing and limiting of social contact and social involvement. Whether the individual's feelings of social isolation are the result of external life-circumstances, or the result of his own social withdrawal secondary to an incipient depressive illness, they may be accompanied by the same subjective feelings of helplessness and hopelessness and a growing conviction that the situation will never change. In my judgment, one of the clinically most significant aspects of a depressive illness is the associated subjective conviction that the depression will never remit. Man seems able to endure periods of intense pain if there is an assurance that it will end. The crucial factor is not the darkness of the tunnel, but whether, however far in the distance, there is a glimmer of light.

When the depressed suicidal patient enters treatment, improvement may often be observed on the second or third visit. Strangely, this is often not subjectively reported by the patient but is evident objectively through such changes as less retardation in movement, more facial expression, improvement in grooming, and the like. No doubt certain irrational transference expectations contribute to this change, but can one not consider a portion of this response a realistic hopefulness? Long-term depressed suicidal patients who have been repeatedly hospitalized often arrive at a point where they are able to inform the therapist that they require a short period of hospitalization. They are sustained through such periods of difficulty and disappointment by an enduring hope in the ultimate resolution of their problems.

Some interesting suggestive support for the thesis that hope may provide "suicide antibodies" comes from an unpublished study by Gould (50). In investigating the natural history of attitudinal changes in individuals toward self, spouse, parents, children, and so on, with change of age, Gould has discovered a marked reorganization which occurs at about the age of forty-three. This change appears to include a new recognition of the brevity of life, a feeling that one's personality is pretty well set, abandonment of certain life goals, rigidification, and some feelings of bitter resentment. It is possible that this "normal" change bears some relationship to the corresponding increase in the suicide rate of males in this age range.

If there be merit in these considerations, the conclusion must be drawn that the therapist of a suicidal person must concern himself with the fostering and maintenance of the suicidal person's rational hope. Of course the therapist, by his very presence, attentiveness, concern, and understanding contributes toward a sustained rational hopefulness. As therapy continues, the recognition of patterns, the isolation and structuring of major problems, the gaining of insight, the progressive resolution of conflict all contribute toward awakening and maintaining a hopefulness. But are there not other specific measures which will assist in this effort?

1. *Depression.* The depressed person lives in a changed world. His appetite and interests may have vanished. His world is grey. His mouth is dry and his tears come slowly, if at all. He feels severed from his fellow man, trapped in a room without visible doors. It may relieve him considerably to be informed that he is suffering from an illness which is usually self-limited. It is often possible to point out that he has suffered from similar episodes in the past, with this same feeling that the future would bring no change, only to later experience genuine remission. Letting the patient know that suicidal thoughts and impulses are common and understandable in persons suffering from depressive illnesses may also reduce the level of panic and may open the door to a frank discussion of the patient's feelings of hopelessness and despair.

2. *Pharmacotherapy.* Most clinicians concur that medication has a role in the treatment of the depressed suicidal person. In addition to the supportive and placebo aspects of prescribing

medication, the reduction in severity of symptoms of major concern often allows the patient to reintegrate faltering ego functions. The three complaints of suicidal patients for which medications most frequently are prescribed are the depression itself, overwhelming anxiety, and insomnia.

Because the depressed patient generally feels better and is able to function better and do more if he can overcome his initial inertia in the mornings, some clinicians, myself among them, continue to find dextroamphetamine a helpful drug for these persons. Five or 10 mg are taken on awakening each morning; sometimes a smaller amount suffices. Methylphenidate hydrochloride (Ritalin), 10 mg on awakening, perhaps repeated once later in the day, may be similarly used.

The host of medications which have become available during recent years for the direct treatment of the depressive mood has been overwhelming. The literature on the so-called antidepressants has continued to be confusing and conflicting and the majority of studies continue to have serious deficiencies in design and execution. Experienced clinicians continue in disagreement over the relative merits of the various families of antidepressants and even over whether any merits, in fact, exist at all. We can hope that time will bring greater clarity in this matter. In the meantime, it is probably wisest to familiarize oneself with a limited number of established antidepressants and develop one's own clinical impressions about their efficacy.

In the reduction of overwhelming anxiety, I have found chlordiazepoxide (Librium) or diazepam (Valium) of value, in moderate dosage levels (for instance, 10 mg of Librium on arising and p.r.n.). In some depressed patients, especially those with unremitting agitation, promazine hydrochloride (Sparine) is particularly effective in dosages ranging from 25 to 150 mg twice daily.

Sometimes the problem of insomnia is resolved by the slight sedative side effects of antidepressive medication given at bedtime or by the anxiety reduction brought about by a phenothiazine. When sedatives are required, the quantity should be closely controlled. It should be noted that some of the once-claimed superiority of nonbarbiturate sedatives over barbiturates has now been demonstrated to be nonexistent. Warnings regarding psychologic and physical dependence and severe withdrawal syndromes, including delirium and grand mal convulsions, now appear in the product inserts for glutethimide (Doriden), etchlorvynol (Placidyl) and methyprylon (Noludar) just as with the barbiturates.

It is, of course, important in the treatment of depressed suicidal persons, as it is in the treatment of any patient, to caution about and to discuss common and possible serious drug side effects.

3. *Relatives and Significant Others.* Those closest to the suicidal person can often play a significant role in the patient's treatment. From the beginning they can supply crucial information regarding the patient's history and current functioning; they can contribute emotional support through trying periods; they can exercise supervision; they can explore and modify their own pathologic contributions to the patient's emotional difficulties.

The depressed suicidal patient may have a variety of awesome fears about the consequences of his spouse, parents, or friends finding out about his illness, and may urge the therapist to join with him in a compact of secrecy about the nature of his illness. Such a course is almost always ill advised. The patient himself usually experiences relief once the burden of his secret is shared with significant others in his life. As a general rule, the therapist should contact and meet personally with one or more close relatives at the very beginning of treatment. Communication between the patient and his relatives removes many of the patient's silent fears regarding what will happen if his condition becomes known.

4. *Activity.* Some clinicians have pointed out that a depressed patient often feels better if he has some active, constructive task to carry out on his behalf. Naturally, the nature of the task will have to be related to the severity of the condition. The therapeutic regimen itself may include such assigned activities as daily walks. Later, as the depression lessens, the therapist may encourage the patient toward a gradual resump-

tion of his normal social, household, and occupational involvements.

5. *The First Interview.* In the light of varied points made above, it may be of value to outline one suggested "check list" for the therapist to keep in mind during the initial interview with a depressed suicidal person.

a. *Bring the subject of suicide frankly into the open.* Help this suffering human being to share the helplessness and hopelessness which must underlie such desperate thoughts. Remember that one of the most potent supports at times of human crisis is the empathic presence of another human being.

b. *Insist on the removal of all firearms and potentially lethal medications from the home of the patient.* Usually this must be discussed not only with the patient but with the relatives as well.

c. *Notify and arrange to meet with one or more significant, responsible relatives of the patient.* Do this with the patient's knowledge. Enlist the help of these persons in your treatment program.

d. *Discuss the natural history and typically self-limited course of depressive illnesses with the depressed suicidal patient.*

e. *Offer realistic hope* that the extremely upsetting and disturbing feelings being experienced by the patient are amenable to modification and change through treatment.

f. *Formulate and communicate a specific initial treatment plan.* Your treatment plan will usually involve some combination of psychotherapy and chemotherapy. It is often appropriate for the physician to undertake a trial period of treatment for two or three weeks.

g. *Schedule a specific next appointment.*

## COUNTERTRANSFERENCE

Nowadays we are accustomed to acknowledging the important role which countertransference plays in any psychotherapeutic relationship. Intellectual or emotional attitudes of the therapist toward suicide, held knowingly or unknowingly, may interfere with his efforts to adequately assess the presence and degree of suicidal danger. In the psychotherapy of depressed suicidal persons, the therapist is often subject to a variety of particularly intense stresses which may give rise to hostility, denial, or other countertransference response. Foremost among these stresses is the ever-present danger of the patient carrying out an irreversible self-destructive act. In addition, depressed persons may make intense oral demands on the therapist or may in a variety of passive ways express marked hostility. Suicidal patients often make taxing demands on the therapist's time, skill, energies, and patience. They may telephone at inconvenient hours, require extra time, and in other ways interrupt the professional and personal life of the therapist. Some are highly skilled at sadistically playing on the therapist's own anxieties and may consciously or unconsciously attempt to provoke him into an angry rejection. It may become difficult, indeed, to refrain from taking the patient's unremitting castigations personally.

One valuable source of information regarding countertransference complications in the treatment of suicidal patients is the retrospective study of persons who commit suicide during or shortly after psychiatric treatment. Wheat presented the results of a study of the treatment of 30 patients who committed suicide while in inpatient treatment or within six months after discharge (38). Seventy per cent committed suicide after discharge, two-thirds of those during the first month. Most of the patients had a primary diagnosis of neurotic or psychotic depression; three were diagnosed as schizophrenic reactions. Thirty per cent had made previous suicide attempts.

In reviewing the treatment of these 30 patients, Wheat isolated several specific patterns between patient and therapist which acted as crucially important influences on the suicidal act. These included the following:

1. The refusal of the therapist to tolerate the patient's infantile dependency; rather, the therapist's conveying to the patient an expectation of mature behavior exceeding the patient's capacity.

2. Discouragement and pessimism of the therapist about progress in treatment.

3. An event or environmental crisis of overwhelming importance to the patient unrecognized by the therapist or beyond
control of the therapeutic situation.

The results of this study have important treatment implications. They stress the necessity for sensitivity and flexibility on
the part of the therapist. "All of these processes," writes
Wheat, "can lead to a breakdown in effective therapeutic
communication resulting in the patient's feelings abandoned
and hopeless, thus setting the stage for the disastrous result of
suicide."

"A therapist," he concludes, "may be seriously handicapped
in evaluating and treating a suicidal patient through: (a)
inability to weigh certain attitudes of the patient heavily
enough because his own attitudes devalue their importance;
(b) inability to comfortably tolerate grossly immature, dependent behavior; (c) inability to recognize and endure protracted
emotional bankruptcy of the patient and the therapeutic interaction; and (d) inability to curb therapeutic ambitions for the
patient and modify goals according to a realistic appraisal of the
patient's assets and abilities."

Bloom reports a similar review of known suicides of persons
in treatment at a training center during a 10-year period (51).
He writes: "These cases of suicide in patients who were in
psychotherapy reveal that in each case the suicide was preceded by rejecting behavior on the part of the therapist."
Included in such rejecting behavior were verbal and facial
expressions of anger, premature discharge from the hospital,
reduction of frequency of psychotherapy sessions, and lack of
availability.

In a previous communication, the present author has offered
two specific suggestions for attempting to minimize pathologic transference responses in the treatment of suicidal
persons (52).

1. Periodically review your treatment of suicidal patients
with a colleague. This may be done on a formal or informal
basis.

2. Limit carefully the number of seriously suicidal persons
for whom you accept treatment responsibility. If you have

more than two, or possibly three, patients in suicidal crisis at the same time, it is doubtful that you will be able to function with optimal clinical judgment.

## SUMMARY

Drawing from the experience of clinicians and from the vast published literature, this presentation reviews a core body of knowledge about suicide—suicidology—which is relevant and essential in the treatment of the depressed suicidal person. The author discusses clinically important characteristics of the suicidal impulse, detection and assessment of suicidal danger, special considerations regarding the preservation of life, the role of rational hope in the treatment process, and counter-transference problems in the treatment of depressed suicidal persons. The individual therapist must constantly strive to improve his clinical skills in the detection and psychotherapeutic treatment of this usually predictable and usually preventable condition which continues to result in the death of tens of thousands of persons each year.

## REFERENCES

1. Beisser, A. R. and Blanchette, J. E. A Study of Suicides in a Mental Hospital. *Dis. Nerv. Syst.* 22:1, 1961.
2. Delong, W. B. and Robins, E. The Communication of Suicidal Intent Prior to Psychiatric Hospitalizations. *Am. J. Psychiat.* 117:695, 1961.
3. Dorpat, T. L. and Ripley, H. S. A Study of Suicide in the Seattle Area. *Compr. Psychiat.* 1:349, 1960.
4. Dripps, R. D., Linden, M. E., Morris, H. H., and Phillips. W. A. Medical, Social and Legal Aspects of Suicide. *J.A.M.A.* 171:523, 1959.
5. Litman, R. E., Shneidman, E. S., and Farberow, N. L. Los Angeles Suicide Prevention Center. *Am. J. Psychiat.* 117:1084, 1961.
6. Motto, J. A. and Greene, C. Suicide and the Medical Community. *A.M.A. Arch. Neurol. Psychiat.* 80:776, 1958.
7. Ringel, E. *Der Selbstmord-Abschluss einer krankhaften psychischen Entwicklung.* Hollinek, Vienna, 1961.
8. Robins, E., Murphy, G. E., Wilkinson, R. H., Jr., Gassner, S., and Kayes,

J. Some Clinical Considerations in the Prevention of Suicide. *Am. J. Public Health* 49:888, 1959.

9. Schmidt, E. H., O'Neal, P., and Robins, E. Evaluation of Suicide Attempts as a Guide to Therapy. *J.A.M.A.* 155:549, 1954.

10. Shneidman, E. S. and Farberow, N. L. Clues to Suicide. In *Clues to Suicide*, Schneidman, E. S., and Farberow, N. L., Eds. McGraw-Hill, New York, 1957.

11. Mintz, R. S. A Pilot Study of the Prevalence of Persons in the City of Los Angeles Who Have Attempted Suicide. *Bull. Suicidology.*

12. Ayd, F. J., Jr. *Recognizing the Depressed Patient.* Grune & Stratton, New York, 1961.

13. Braaten, L. J. and Darling, C. D. Suicidal Tendencies among College Students. *Psychiat. Quart.* 36:665, 1962.

14. Dublin, L. I. *Suicide: A Sociological and Statistical Study.* Ronald Press, New York, 1963.

15. Pokorny, A. D. Suicide Rates in Various Psychiatric Disorders. *J. Nerv. Ment. Dis.* 139:499, 1964.

16. Stenback, A. and Blumenthal, M. Relationship of Alcoholism, Hypochondria and Attempted Suicide. *Acta Psychiat. Scand.* 40:133, 1964.

17. Darbonne, A. R. Suicide and Age: A Suicide Note Analysis. *J. Consult. Clin. Psychol.* 33:46, 1969.

18. Batchelor, I. R. C. Repeated Suicidal Attempts. *Brit. J. Med. Psychol.* 27:158, 1954.

19. Finn, M. E. Study in Suicidal Attempts. *J. Nerv. Ment. Dis.* 121:172, 1955.

20. Hendin, H. The Psychodynamics of Suicide. *J. Nerv. Ment. Dis.* 136:236, 1963.

21. Litman, R. E. and Tabachnik, N. D. Psychoanalytic Theories of Suicide. In *Suicidal Behaviors: Diagnosis and Management,* Resnik, H. L. P., Ed. Little, Brown, Boston, 1968.

22. Menninger, K. Psychoanalytic Aspects of Suicide. *Int. J. Psychoanal.* 14:37, 1933.

23. Moss, L. M. and Hamilton, D. M. Psychotherapy of the Suicidal Patient. *Am. J. Psychiat.* 112:814, 1956.

24. Palmer, D. M. Factors in Suicidal Attempts. *J. Nerv. Ment. Dis.* 93:421, 1941.

25. Stengel, E. and Cook, N. G. *Attempted Suicide: Its Social Significance and Effects.* Maudsley Monogr. No. 4. Chapman & Hall, London, 1958.

26. Wahl, C. W. Suicide as a Magical Act. *Bull. Menninger Clin.* 21:91, 1957.

27. Weiss, J. M. A. The Gamble with Death in Attempted Suicide. *Psychiatry* 20:17, 1957.

28. Zilboorg, G. Differential Diagnostic Types of Suicide. *Arch. Neurol. Psychiat.* 35:270, 1936.

29. _____ . Considerations of Suicide with Particular Reference to that of the Young. *Am. J. Orthopsychiat.* 7:15, 1937.

30. Jensen, V. W. and Petty, T. The Fantasy of Being Rescued in Suicide. *Psychoanal. Quart.* 27:327, 1958.

31. Ettlinger, R. W. Suicides in a Group of Patients Who Had Previously Attempted Suicide. *Acta Psychiat. Scand.* 40:363, 1964.

32. Pokorny, A. Characteristics of Forty-Four Patients Who Subsequently Committed Suicide. *Arch. Gen. Psychiat.* 2:314, 1960.

33. _____ . A Follow-Up of 618 Suicidal Patients. *Am. J. Psychiat.* 122:1109, 1966.

34. Batchelor, I. R. C. and Napier, M. B. The Sequelae and Short-Term Prognosis of Attempted Suicide. *J. Neurol. Neurosurg. Psychiat.* 17:261, 1954.

35. Robins, E., Gassner, S., Kayes, J., Wilkinson, R. H., Jr., and Murphy G. E. The Communication of Suicidal Intent. *Am. J. Psychiat.* 115:724, 1959.

36. Schneider, P. B. *La Tentative de Suicide.* Delacheux & Niessle, Paris-Neuchatel, 1954.

37. Fairbank, R. E. Suicide: Possibilities of Prevention by Early Recognition of Some Danger Signals. *J.A.M.A.* 98:1711, 1932.

38. Wheat, W. D. Motivational Aspects of Suicide in Patients During and After Psychiatric Treatment. *South Med. J.* 53:273, 1960.

39. Yessler, P. G., Gibbs, J. J., and Becker, H. A. On the Communication of Suicidal Ideas. *Arch. Gen. Psychiat.* 3:612, 1960.

40. Batchelor, I. R. C. Repeated Suicidal Attempts. *Brit. J. Med. Psychol.* 27:158, 1954.

41. Farberow, N. L. and Shneidman, E. S. Attempted, Threatened, and Completed Suicide. *J. Abnorm. Soc. Psychol.* 50:230, 1955.

42. Mintz, R. S. *Detection and Management of the Suicidal Patient.* Disease-A-Month (Chicago) 7:1, 1961.

43. Ettlinger, R. W. and Flordh, P. Attempted Suicide: Experience of Five Hundred Cases at a General Hospital. *Acta Psychiat. Scand.* (Suppl.) 103:1, 1955.

44. U.S. Bureau of the Census: Statistical Abstract of the United States: 1969. Table No. 212, Washington, D.C. 1969, p. 143.

45. Davis, J. H. *Quoted in* Many Suicides Traced to Careless Prescribing of Drugs. *J.A.M.A.* 211:1778, 1970.

46. Brophy, J. J. Suicide Attempts with Psychotherapeutic Drugs. *Arch. Gen. Psychiat.* 17:652, 1967.

47. Mintz, R. S. Psychotherapy of the Suicidal Patient. In *Suicidal Behaviors: Diagnosis and Management,* Resnik, H. L. P., Ed. Little, Brown, Boston, 1968.

48. Kobler, A. L. and Stotland, E. *The End of Hope: A Social-Clinical Theory of Suicide*. Free Press of Glencoe, New York, 1964.

49. Tabachnik, N. D. Two Types of Suicidal Behavior. In *Suicide Among the Indians*. National Clearinghouse for Mental Health Information, Chevy Chase, 1969.

50. Gould, R. L. The Phases of Adult Life: A Study in Developmental Psychology. Unpublished Manuscript, 1970.

51. Bloom, V. An Analysis of Suicide at a Training Center. *Am. J. Psychiat.* 123:918, 1967.

52. Mintz, R. S. Some Practical Procedures in the Management of Suicidal Persons. *Am. J. Orthopsychiat.* 36:896, 1966.

# 16 Psychotherapy and Suicide

## Herbert Hendin, M.D.

*Psychotherapy can be successful with suicidal patients if the therapist does not reduce therapy to management and control of the patient; understands the ways in which the patient uses his potential death as part of his adaptation; and avoids specific countertransference pitfalls. Case examples are provided.*

In reviewing articles written in the past thirty years on the treatment of suicidal individuals one is struck with how often the word "management" is used synonymously with therapy. Such articles are usually guides designed to help the therapist outmaneuver the potentially suicidal person. They contain a series of recommendations of a practical nature such as "Make every effort to have firearms and potentially lethal medications removed from the home of the suicidal patient," "Control carefully the prescription of potentially lethal drugs," "Advise the family to be watchful," and so forth (1–6).

Such precautions and warnings seem reasonable, but in practice they reflect a state of mind and a way of relating to suicidal patients that often make treatment unsuccessful. Since many suicidal patients are themselves preoccupied with management and control, therapy can become a contest with the suicidal patients usually obtaining their pills if they really want them, and the therapist reassuring himself that he has taken all

265

possible precautions. All the precautions and all the management may result in encouraging one of the most lethal aspects of the suicidal individual, that is, his tendency to make someone else responsible for his staying alive.

In most articles the approach to therapy itself is usually based on similar attempts at manipulation. In a widely recommended article on the subject it is suggested that the therapist encourage the patient to believe that his current mood will pass; hold out hope by telling the patient of others who felt as he does and have gotten better; point out that actual suicidal behavior will interfere with treatment; indicate that the treatment cannot help the patient if he is dead; and remind the patient of his feelings for his spouse, children, or pets (1).

Encouraging a suicidal patient to live for the sake of the therapy, the therapist, or his family is a reinforcement of what many such patients already feel, that is, that they are only living for the sake of others. Such feelings are more apt to encourage suicide than prevent it.

The warning issued in one form or another in most articles on the treatment of suicide is "No form of treatment is effective with a dead patient." A list of criteria for evaluating suicidal risk is likely to follow. In some cases the list is basically an evaluation of the degree of the patient's depression based on his mood, energy, performance—socially and vocationally— and degree of anxiety. A series of danger points may be listed: When the patient is on pass from the hospital, when he first goes home, when stress in his life increases, to name a few examples. Such a list usually includes the clinically axiomatic warning, going back to Manfred Bleuler, that a lessening of depression often precedes a suicide attempt. In other words, if the patient remains depressed be wary and if he is getting less depressed be even more wary.

These articles reiterate in some form or another an injunction, for "constant monitoring" to ascertain suicidal risk. They recommend that a judgment of increased risk should invariably be accompanied by more intensive management measures— hospitalization, medication, more medication or new medication, and electric shock. What such articles fail to include is any statement as to how lacking in evidence we are that such measures are effective in preventing suicide.

In any case it would be better for the therapist working in or out of a hospital to recognize that he is not likely to keep alive by surveillance, incarceration, or any form of precaution a patient who is determined to kill himself. The best chance for helping the patient lies in understanding and helping him with the problems that are making him suicidal, including most specifically the way in which he uses the threat of death.

## THERAPIST'S ANXIETIES

A therapist who is threatened by the fact that a patient may kill himself while under his care is in no position to be a therapist to the patient. The rationalization that emergency measures are necessary to prevent suicide and make therapy possible serves to conceal the fact that emergency measures, reflecting the therapist's anxiety, often make therapy impossible.

Only in psychotherapy does the nature of the suicidal individual's involvement with death and self-destructiveness become fully apparent. The therapist's own attitudes toward death, dying, and suicide, however, become almost as important as the patient's in determining the outcome. Fear of the responsibility for suicidal patients is a conscious motivation leading many therapists to avoid treating them. Among therapists who do treat suicidal patients, anxiety over a patient's possible death often serves unwittingly to deaden their perceptions. Such anxiety is as apt to derive from guilt or a fear of being blamed for the death as it is from any excess of compassion or empathy. Although suicide is a life-or-death matter for the patient, once the therapist begins to see the success of therapy as a life-or-death matter to his own self-esteem, his efforts are apt to be futile.

Suicidal patients, although they may deaden themselves to much else in life, are usually perceptive about such anxieties on the part of a therapist. Since so many of them (including those who eventually kill themselves) have learned to use the anxiety they can arouse in others about their death in a coercive or manipulative way, they will usually test the therapist to see if they can do the same thing with him. If the therapist meets unreasonable demands in response to death threats, the situation usually repeats itself with escalation of the demands and increasing angry dissatisfaction if they are not met. Unless these character attitudes and expectations of the patient are explored and understood, the therapist is apt to go into bondage to the patient—with bad results.

One therapist was coerced into calling a patient every morning for a year because of an implicit threat that if the therapist did not call, the patient might kill herself. This particular patient eventually did, despite the calls, leaving the therapist feeling both troubled and betrayed. Had more effort been spent in challenging and understanding the patient's attempt to structure how and in what manner the therapist was to show interest, rather than gratifying the patient's demands, the therapy would have had more chance of success.

## THERAPEUTIC INTERACTION

The suicidal person often makes conditions for life: if you don't save me I'll die; if I can't make you happy I'll end my life. Such attitudes are central to the patient's involvement with suicide; if their emergence does not arouse excessive anxiety on the part of the therapist, he is in a position to explore them to therapeutic advantage.

### Case 1

A succesful, forty-eight-year-old executive, whose wife had left him after years of an unhappy marriage, became depressed, began drinking heavily, and was suicidal. Although his wife seemed satisfied with the new life she was making for herself, he insisted he would not rebuild his own life until he knew she was happy. A dream he had when he was concerned about my leaving on vacation opened up some of the meaning of his wife's leaving him. He dreamed that his father had died and he was annoyed that his two brothers had not consulted him over the funeral arrangements. The dream helped make him aware that his response to his wife's leaving was centered around the issue of control—who determined the circumstances of separation or loss was as central to him as the loss itself. His need to set the conditions under which he would be happy was an outgrowth of his inability to determine the conditions of her happiness.

Therapy helped him to become aware of how much his response originated in fear of severing an unhappy relationship with his mother. He had felt frightened and despondent over his inability to influence her lack of interest in him, but had also felt responsible for her unhappiness. As he perceived the interconnections and origins of his need to control his relationships with his wife, his mother, and with me, and was able to use this insight constructively, his depression lifted, his excessive drinking stopped, and he was no longer suicidal. He was once again able to be productive at work although his difficulties in forming a close and satisfying relationship with a woman remained.

## Case 2

One young man had shot himself in the heart—the bullet grazed his heart, pierced his lung, and came to rest close to his spine. He came into treatment telling me that he would give me six months to make him less lonely, isolated, and depressed before killing himself. This kind of ultimatum, whether given to a therapist, a lover, or to oneself is designed not merely to bring about the end but to kill whatever relationship comes before it. This young man was treatable only when we focused on the ways in which he tried to make our relationship one in which he would be dead and therefore challenge or resist any efforts to bring him back to life. Life is not, as it seems, or as the individual often says, unbearable *with* depression, but may sometimes be inconceivable *without* it.

Sometimes the conditions the patient wishes to set in therapy include involving the therapist actively during a suicide attempt. A therapist's own inclination to see himself as the savior or rescuer of the suicidal patient can be responsible for perpetuating suicidal behavior, particularly in young people.

**Case 3**

One young woman had made five suicide attempts in her past therapy. She would call her therapist during her attempts and manage to have him come to one hotel or motel after another to save her. He dealt with his irritation with her behavior by a fierce determination to save her and pride in being her rescuer. His willingness to do so seemed to intensify the severity of her attempts. After her last attempt, which she was lucky to survive, her parents, her therapist, and the patient agreed on the need for some change in therapy.

This young woman came from a family where little interest, affection or attention was paid to her. She had learned to use illness or suicide attempts coercively to gain attention. She felt secure only when she was able to use crises to control the interest and attention given to her, and she had to learn to value affection of any other kind.

Despite progress in her therapy it seemed likely that she would eventually test me, as she had her parents and her prior therapist, with her coercive use of the threat of suicide. She did. She called one evening from a motel in the suburbs just after swallowing some sleeping pills. I told her to go to a nearby hospital and to have them call me. My knowledge of her and her progress made me feel that this decision was reasonably safe and necessary. Yet I was considerably relieved when the hospital called after having pumped out her stomach. She came in for her next appointment initially angry with me for not coming to her rescue, but this was the end of her suicide attempts and the beginning of a dramatic over-all therapeutic improvement. There is a risk in being misunderstood in relating such an incident. A therapist must know a patient well and have extensive experience in order to make such a decision. But there is a greater risk in allowing to leave unchallenged the widespread misconception that a therapist does such a suicidal patient a service by allowing himself to become a constant savior. A therapist in such a coercive bondage, no matter how well intentioned, is of little use to a patient.

## THERAPY WITH OLDER SUICIDAL PATIENTS

If suicidal young people arouse rescue fantasies in therapists, older people who are suicidal are more apt to arouse irritation and to be dealt with by medication or hospitalization without psychotherapy. Many make the unwarranted assumptions that little can be done with psychotherapy for older people in general and even less for older people who are suicidal.

Many older people who are suicidal have, despite their problems, demonstrated varying degrees of adaptive capacity throughout a lifetime. Past proven adaptive capacity is probably a better indicator than age in determining the prognosis in psychotherapy.

### Case 4

A sociology professor of sixty became suicidal after a stroke left him almost completely paralyzed on the left side. He was depressed, enraged, and unable to tolerate the decline in his physical and mental abilities. He told me, "When you came out to see me I watched you like a hawk. You can move your left arm and left leg and envy and anger just swells up in me." He became impossibly irritable with his wife and step-children, although he had had a good relationship with them previously. He was aware of being enraged by their ability to come and go as they pleased in contrast to the restrictions imposed by his own incapacity.

His past life had made him particularly vulnerable to what had happened. He had grown up with a powerful need for self-sufficiency and control that was fostered by his mother's indifference. A great deal of his self-esteem was tied up with his teaching. He was seen as the best teacher in his department, frequently received accolades for his performance, and was nominated several times for special teaching awards. His wife confirmed that the majority of his students would say that he was the best teacher they ever had.

He had had a recurrent dream during the last five years. He is teaching a class, then begins to move his arms like wings and rises to the top of the room where he flies around the room and then out the window and over some tall trees. He then becomes afraid of the height. In talking about the dream it is clear that he does get "high" on teaching and on the admiration and awe of his students.

His wife had treated him with similar awe and respect. Indeed she continued to do so. His own self-esteem was so tied to receiving admiration for his performance, knowledge, and ability to control situations that he could not conceive of his wife's continuing to love him in his partly disabled condition. As a result he became increasingly critical of her in a manner that was bound to push her away.

During a session when he related to me several instances in which he had helped to resolve some friction between two attendants in the hospital, I had responded positively to what he had done. He immediately replied that he used to be so much more capable. He compared any current achievement in a derogatory way to his past abilities. This attitude became a central issue in his therapy and as soon as he was able to change his mood improved.

Even more critical was a passive, resigned attitude he had toward his progress in rehabilitation therapy in particular and toward his life in general. He wanted greater mobility within the hospital grounds, yet he did not request such privileges. He was passive about caring for himself, waiting for his wife to visit to help him button his shirt. His passivity was in marked contrast to his prestroke behavior. When his behavior was pointed out, he became quite angry. The word "passivity" irritated him, but also challenged him, and he began doing everything for himself, becoming remarkably agile with his walker. He would begin many subsequent sessions by letting me know how much he had accomplished and how wrong I had been to see him as passive. His ability to resume a satisfactory relationship with his wife and children also became a challenge to him, which in time he met.

## Case 5

A fifty-five-year-old man who had built up his own accounting firm had come home from work ten years earlier to find his wife and only son—a boy of fourteen—had drowned. They had been visiting his wife's parents and he had asked his in-laws to make sure that his wife and child did not sail alone in a small boat he owned. They had done so anyway with the result that the boat overturned in rough water.

Two weeks after their death, this man turned on the ignition of his car in his closed garage with the intention of suicide. He would have succeeded if his neighbors had not seen him pulling into the garage without any lights going on subsequently in the house. They became suspicious and rescued him just in time.

In the ten years that followed the deaths of his wife and son and his suicide attempt, this man became progressively alcoholic. He gave up his business and worked on and off at menial jobs, some of which he lost because of his drinking. Contrary to the popular belief that people drink to forget, he claimed that he did not think of his wife and son except when he was drinking. He had broken off with his in-laws blaming them for what had occurred. His anger at them permitted him to avoid facing his anger toward his wife for not listening to him or his own guilt over having bought the boat for his son.

He had a recurrent dream during his drinking episodes. He was on a roof top (a place where he often drank) and two rats were trying to climb up the drain pipe to get up to the roof. He was pushing them down with a stick. His associations indicated that the two rats were his wife and son—rats for having abandoned him, rats because what had happened continued to gnaw away at him.

Despite his ten-year history of alcoholism and suicide attempts he made excellent progress in psychotherapy. When he was freer of the emotions that bound him to the death of his family, when he was able to feel entitled to live, his past ability to enjoy work and to care for other people were strengths that were soon in evidence.

## Case 6

Prior to the past few years when the loneliness and depression caused by her unhappy marriage had made her suicidal, a sixty-five-year-old woman who had come to this country from Austria had had a successful working career and a good relationship with her son (who lived in another state) whom she had raised virtually without help from her husband. Her situation was complicated because she viewed her unhappy marriage as just punishment for having left her mother and sister who later died in concentration camps.

In response to a question as to why she stayed with her husband if she was so unhappy with him she spoke of her childhood, telling first about her father who was killed in World War I when she was two, while her mother was pregnant with her sister. Her mother and the two daughters went to live in a household headed by her mother's bachelor brother, an Austrian newspaper publisher, and by the patient's grandmother. Her mother was something of a servant in the household, and, although they were treated well, they were all conscious of the need not to offend her uncle and her grandmother. She seemed to be indicating that her fear of being uncared for and abandoned had a long history.

She then went on to tell me that she is frequently preoccupied with the question of why she was spared when her mother and sister died. She feels that maybe God spared her in order to punish her—that she was destined to live an unhappy life ending up in suicide. She had one dream years ago which she regards as the most significant dream of her life.

Her sister, dressed as monk, was behind barbed wire and was trying to hand her a letter. She never gets to know what was in the letter. The monk's outfit suggested death to her, the barbed wire the concentration camp. The letter appeared to be a message from her sister, perhaps an answer to the question she had always wanted resolved as to why she lived and they died. What she appeared to need and had never received from her sister was permission to enjoy her life, permission that would free her from her sense that she had no right to live or was destined to live unhappily.

At first the patient needed the therapist to give her the permission to live that she had vainly and recurrently sought in her dreams of her dead sister. Even before the loss of her mother and sister, and despite her intelligence and ability, she had never felt entitled to shape the circumstances of her life. Since childhood, after her father's death, she and her family were dependent on her uncle's permission for every decision they wished to make. The major decision she had made independently—to leave Austria—saved her life, but left her feeling guilty for having survived.

As she came to understand the relation of her past life to her present situation, she was able to make a satisfying life for herself apart from her husband. She moved to where her son lived, became more involved with him, his wife, and her grandchildren, and was able for the first time in years to take a trip by herself to visit old friends in Vienna.

## Case 7

Even in older patients where the past adaptive capacity has been poor, psychotherapy can make suicide much less likely. A fifty-six-year-old man who suffered from chronic schizophrenia and nearly killed himself while a patient in the hospital is a case in point. Dependent on, but abused by, first his mother and then his two wives, he was unable to function on his own.

In the hospital he was treated primarily with medication for his anxiety with the dosage increased whenever he seemed more upset. His periods of disturbance were considered to be due to the vicissitudes of his schizophrenia and usually resulted in the hospital restricting his freedom to leave the ward because of the fear that he might kill himself. His response in turn was to become only more agitated.

When seen in psychotherapy it soon became evident that all his disturbed periods were triggered by episodes in which he felt rejected or abandoned by the hospital staff or by his brothers and sisters who refused to visit him in the hospital. His sensitivity to such rejection was great, but his agitated response and attempts at suicide only occurred when the staff's response to his difficulties was restriction, seclusion, or more medication rather than empathy with what he was feeling. When such empathy was provided in psychotherapy he changed from a nonfunctioning, angry, depressed suicidal individual to an active and productive member of the hospital community.

## COUNTERTRANSFERENCE PROBLEMS

Since many suicidal patients have been in psychotherapy at the time of their suicide, researchers have sought to examine such cases systematically to see what might have gone wrong. Wheat (7) did a retrospective study of therapeutic interaction in the cases of thirty patients who committed suicide during or after hospitalization. He emphasized three factors in attempting to explain these suicides: (a) the refusal of the therapist to tolerate infantile dependency so that the therapist conveyed to the patient an expectation of mature behavior exceeding the patient's capacity; (b) discouragement on the part of the therapist about the progress of treatment; and (c) an event or environmental crisis of overwhelming importance to the patient unrecognized by the therapist or beyond the control of the therapeutic situation such as the refusal by the family of the last patient to respond to his requests that they visit him in the hospital.

"All of these processes," Wheat writes, "can lead to a breakdown in the therapeutic communication resulting in the patient's feeling abandoned or helpless, thus setting the stage for the disastrous result of suicide." Bloom (8), in a similar review of known suicides in treatment at a psychiatric training center, identifies as significant precipitants rejecting behavior on the part of the therapist, including verbal and facial expressions of anger, premature discharge of the patient, reduction of frequency of psychotherapeutic sessions, and lack of availability of the therapist. Lowenthal (9) complains of a lack of empathy on the part of therapists treating suicidal patients. He lists a number of factors as responsible: The potential for guilt is greater if the therapist is close to a patient; shame over a potential suicide being a reflection on the therapist's capacity or competence; and most important the therapist's inability to come to terms with suicidal impulses in himself or in his patients as a possibly reasonable alternative to life's dilemmas. He implies that only a therapist who has seriously contemplated suicide can properly empathize with a suicidal patient. He provides no evidence for this conclusion, but is content to state his admiration for the empathy with suicidal patients which A. Alvarez expresses in his book on suicide, *The Savage God* (10), an empathy which Lowenthal believes stems from Alvarez having made a serious suicide attempt.

Although having been personally involved with a problem may be of aid in the treatment of others, providing the therapist has satisfactorily resolved it, it does not guarantee greater insight or empathy. I have seen many suicidal individuals, including therapists, who attempt suicide without gaining either insight into themselves or greater understanding of their own or others' desire for suicide. Case studies by suicide prevention centers suggest that counsellors who are not depressed nor suicidal, but are reasonably happy with their own lives, do best with suicidal patients.

I have long been impressed, however, by the fact that most articles on suicide, including Lowenthal's, seem more comfortable with abstractions than with people; they usually do not present a single suicidal individual with a view toward conveying a sense of the quality of the person's life or wish to die.

Such articles stand in startling contrast to articles on virtually any other clinical problem. The absence of such case descriptions does bespeak the distance and lack of empathy about which Lowenthal complains.

Maltzberger and Buie (11) in a fine article on the subject of therapy with suicidal patients (flawed only by the absence of any case illustrations) deal with many of the harmful countertransference reactions aroused in therapists by suicidal patients, particularly those who are borderline or psychotic. By their primitive attacks on the therapist, ranging from attempts to frustrate his therapeutic efforts to expressions of contempt for him as a person, such patients are often able to arouse "countertransference hatred." "The three most common narcissistic snares," they write, "are the aspirations to heal all, know all and love all . . . such gifts are no more available to the contemporary therapist than they were to Faust." The attack by the suicidal patient, who may sense the therapist's vulnerability, can lead to destructive reactions in the therapist varying from malice to aversion.

Maltzberger and Buie go on to point out that the therapist's repression of these reactions may lead him to lose interest in the patient or to reject the patient as hopeless. Conversely, projection of countertransference hatred taking the form of "I do not wish to kill you, you wish to kill yourself," leads to the therapist's paralyzing preoccupation with the danger of suicide by the patient. Reaction formation to such countertransference feelings can contribute to oversolicitousness, exaggerated fear of suicide, fantasies of rescue, and overprotection of the patient.

Lesse (12) pointed out that experience and competence as well as self-knowledge are vital if the risks in treating suicidal patients are to be minimized. He pointed out the necessity for competent supervision if inexperienced residents are to treat seriously suicidal patients.

In the past fifteen years I have been consulted on numerous occasions by therapists who wished help in understanding a patient's suicide attempts or suicide and their reactions to this behavior. In most cases, the problem was the therapist's failure to understand what was going on in the interaction between the patient and therapist, rather than any basic lack of concern for the patient. In fact, a major therapeutic difficulty often stems from the therapist's assumption that by simply supplying a care and concern that had been missing in the patient's life, that is, by not being rejecting, he will somehow give the patient the desire to live. Often the patient's hidden agenda, however, is an attempt to prove that nothing the therapist can do will be enough. The therapist's wish to see himself as the suicidal patient's savior may blind the therapist to the fact that the patient may have cast him for the role of executioner (12).

## Case 8

For example, one young woman jumped in front of a train and lost both her legs when her therapist was about to leave on a vacation. On the day she jumped she called a local TV station to tell them that at 8 p.m. a man—she gave her therapist's last name without indicating that he was treating her—would push a girl in a pink dress in front of a train at a particular station. Her warning was not heeded and at 8 o'clock, dressed in a pink dress, she jumped.

She considered she had "died" when her father left the family when she was eight or nine. She was preoccupied with death throughout her adolescence. She could recall the death scene in many novels, vividly recalling Anna Karenina's suicide in front of a train. Her relationships with men had been painful recapitulations of the earlier rejection by her father—and one unhappy love affair had been followed by a suicide attempt.

The following dream concerning her present suicide attempt made her wish to die more understandable. She was in a long, narrow tunnel and could see a light at the end of it. She walked toward the light, and there she saw a man and a woman standing over a manger. In her associations to the dream, the tunnel suggested to her the subway, where she had jumped with the train coming out of the tunnel and into the lighted platform area. Moving from the darkness of the tunnel and into the light she saw as like being born. The child in the manger was both the Christ child and herself. She particularly identified with the sense that the crucifixion reunited Christ with his Father. She saw her life as having been set on a course in which gratification of her fantasies was only possible through her death. One can see how much she accomplished in her death fantasy. She is reborn, is a boy, is reunited with her father and, finally is omnipotent. For a patient with such fantasies the thought of dying has a very strong appeal.

The grandiosity expressed in the dream of a rebirth as Christ is a common feature in the psychodynamics of suicide. It reflects the illusion of omnipotent mastery that suicide may provide, as well as suggesting the profound narcissistic injury that underlies the need for such grandiosity.

This young woman's therapist had tried to be available in the way that her father was not. He was uncomfortable with the way in which the patient had actually incorporated him into her suicidal fantasies but did not realize till later that she was determined to perceive him—like her father—as responsible for her death while binding him to her through death. She structured the relationship this way and used his leaving on vacation as an excuse for her suicide attempt. Even in the way in which she tried to kill herself, she appeared to be asking him to rescue her, but in fact was trying to make sure that he could not, and that he would be blamed for her death.

When seen in consultation after her suicide attempt she was still interested in punishing her therapist. She suggested that I should write up her case being sure to include her therapist's name. At the same time she behaved as if she had accomplished a rebirth. And paradoxically in her new life as a cripple with vastly reduced expectations she made a much better adjustment than she had previously. One suspects that her need for self-punishment may in some way have been permanently satisfied by the self-inflicted injury.[1]

Successful therapy cannot be conducted with the suicidal patient unless the therapist understands the ways in which the patient uses his potential death as part of his adaptation. Such knowledge may minimize the risk of suicide, but therapy requires that the therapist be able to accept and live with some risk. As Schwartz, Flinn, and Slawson (13) point out "the only

---

[1] Her response to the incapacity that followed her suicide attempt was paralleled by the suicide attempt of a man who had shot himself in the head as a college student, blinded himself, but survived. When I met him 25 years later he insisted his life had been changed for the better by the experience and had published a book detailing the transformation.

method of reducing the long-term risk of suicide may be one that risks its short-term commission."

As we have seen, suicidal patients often use the threat of suicide as a means of controlling the behavior of others. This is true of those who eventually kill themselves and those who do not. Szasz (14) points out correctly that many therapists respond to the patient's need to control with their own need to control. In order to avoid the risk of suicide, they coercively hospitalize the patient. Although hospitalization and involuntary commitment of the suicidal patient are subjects requiring a separate treatment, it should be noted here that ultimately, in or out of a hospital, successful psychotherapy cannot be conducted by a "policeman."

Psychotherapy with an experienced therapist is the treatment of choice for seriously suicidal patients. It should be supplemented by psychotropic drugs when necessary to relieve severe depression or paralyzing anxiety. Seriously suicidal patients are either too depressed, too withdrawn, or too fragile to tolerate the anxiety that is generated in the psychoanalytic process. Yet most suicidal patients, like most of the individuals discussed in this article, can work psychodynamically in psychotherapy and should be given the opportunity to do so.

## SUMMARY

In contrast to most current strategies for treating suicidal patients, which consist largely of intensive measures for management and control, psychodynamic psychotherapy is described as a potentially highly effective method of treatment for this patient population. Elaborating the thesis that successful therapy cannot be conducted with suicidal patients unless the therapist understands the ways in which the patient uses his potential death as part of his adaptation, several specific countertransference issues which often prevent such understanding are discussed. Numerous case examples are provided which illustrate approaches to successful psychotherapy with young, middle-aged, and elderly suicidal individuals.

# REFERENCES

1. Mintz, R. Psychotherapy of the Suicidal Patient. *Am. J. Psychother.* 15:348, 1961.

2. _____ . Some Practical Procedures in the Management of Suicidal Persons. *Am. J. Orthopsychiatry* 36:896, 1966.

3. _____ . Basic Considerations in the Psychotherapy of the Depressed Suicidal Patient. *Am. J. Psychother.* 25:56, 1971.

4. Shein, H. and Stone, A. Monitoring and Treatment of Suicidal Potential within the Context of Psychotherapy. *Comp. Psychiatry* 10:59, 1969.

5. _____ . Psychotherapy Designed to Detect and Treat Suicidal Potential. *Am. J. Psychiatry* 125:141, 1969.

6. _____ . Psychotherapy of the Hospitalized Suicidal Patient. *Am. J. Psychother.* 22:15, 1968.

7. Wheat, W. Motivational Aspects of Suicide in Patients during and after Psychiatric Treatment, *South. Med. J.* 53:273, 1960.

8. Bloom, V. An Analysis of Suicide at a Training Center. *Am. J. Psychiatry* 123:918, 1967.

9. Lowenthal, U. Suicide—The Other Side: The Factor of Reality among Suicidal Motivations. *Arch. Gen. Psychiatry* 33:308, 1975.

10. Alvarez, A. *The Savage God: A Study of Suicide.* Weidenfeld, Nicholson, London, 1972.

11. Maltzberger, J. and Buie, D. Countertransference Hate in the Treatment of Suicidal Patients. *Arch. Gen. Psychiatry* 30:625, 1974.

12. Lesse, S. The Range of Therapies in the Treatment of Severely Depressed Suicidal Patients. *Am. J. Psychother.* 29:308, 1975.

13. Schwartz, D., Flinn, D., and Slawson, P. Treatment of the Suicidal Character. *Am. J. Psychother.* 28:194, 1974.

14. Szasz, T. The Ethics of Suicide. *Antioch Review* 31:7, 1971.

# 17 Cognitive Therapy of Depression and Suicide

A. John Rush, M.D.
Aaron T. Beck, M.D.

*This chapter reviews the cognitive therapy of depression. The psychotherapy based on this theory consists of behavioral and verbal techniques to change cognitions, beliefs, and errors in logic in the patient's thinking. A few of the various techniques are described and a case example is provided. Finally, the outcome studies testing the efficacy of this approach are reviewed.*

Beck (1) reformulated the phenomenon of depression from a cognitive viewpoint. This formulation was designed to provide a model for understanding the relationships of the signs and symptoms of the depressive syndrome (e.g., guilt, difficulty concentrating, low energy, etc.). In addition, the cognitive framework was to provide a basis for a systematic psychotherapy of depression called "cognitive therapy."

This paper will review briefly the cognitive theory of depression. We will describe a few specific psychotherapy techniques used in the cognitive therapy of depression to change cognitions. A case example will illustrate the application of cognitive therapy. Finally, we will review the controlled psychotherapy research studies designed to test the efficacy of cognitive therapy with depressed patients.

## THE COGNITIVE THEORY OF DEPRESSION

The cognitive theory of depression is a formulation which grew out of careful clinical observation and experimental testing. This interplay of a clinical and experimental approach has allowed for careful evolution of this model and of the psychotherapy it has spawned (2).

The cognitive model postulates three specific notions to explain depression: cognitive triad, schemas, and cognitive errors. The cognitive triad consists of three major cognitive patterns that induce the patient to regard himself, his future, and his experiences in an idiosyncratic manner.

### Cognitive Triad

The first component of the triad revolves around the patient's negative view of himself. He sees himself as defective, inadequate, or unworthy. He tends to attribute his unpleasant experiences to a physical, mental, or moral defect in himself. The patient believes he is undesirable and worthless *because* of his presumed defects. He tends to underestimate or criticize himself because of them. Finally, he believes he lacks the attributes he thinks are essential to attain happiness and contentment.

The second component consists of the depressed person's tendency to interpret his ongoing experiences in a negative way. He sees the world as making exorbitant demands on him and/or presenting insuperable obstacles to reaching his life goals. He misinterprets his interactions with the world around him as evidence for defeat or deprivation. These negative misinterpretations are evident by observing that the patient negatively construes situations *even* when less negative, more plausible, alternative interpretations are available. The depressed person may realize that his initial negative interpretations are biased if he is persuaded to reflect on these less negative alternative explanations. In this way, he can come to realize that he tailored the facts to fit his preconceived negative conclusions.

The third component consists of a negative view of the

future. As the depressed person looks ahead, he anticipates that his current difficulties or suffering will continue indefinitely. He expects unremitting hardship, frustration, and deprivation. When he thinks of undertaking a specific task, he expects to fail.

The cognitive theory considers the other signs and symptoms of the depressive syndrome to be consequences of the activation of the negative cognitive patterns. For example, if the patient incorrectly *thinks* he is being rejected, he will react with the same negative affect (e.g., sadness, anger) that occurs with *actual* rejection. If he erroneously believes he is a social outcast, he will feel lonely.

The motivational symptoms (e.g., paralysis of will, escape and avoidance wishes, etc.) can be explained as consequences of negative conditions. "Paralysis of will" results from the patient's pessimism and hopelessness. If he expects a negative outcome, he won't commit himself to a goal or undertaking. Suicidal wishes can be understood as an extreme expression of the desire to escape from what *appears* to be insolvable problems or an unbearable situation. The depressed person may see himself as a worthless burden and consequently believe that everyone, himself included, will be better off when he is dead.

Increased dependency is also explicable in cognitive terms. Because he sees himself as inept and undesirable, the depressed person unrealistically overestimates the difficulty of normal tasks and expects things to turn out badly. The patient tends to seek help and reassurance from others whom he considers more competent and capable.

Finally, the cognitive model may also explain the physical symptoms. Apathy and low energy may result from the patient's belief that he is doomed to failure in all his efforts. A negative view of the future (a sense of futility) may lead to "psychomotor inhibition."

## Schemas

A second major ingredient in the cognitive model consists of the notion of schemas. This notion is used to explain why a depressed patient clings to painful attitudes despite objective evidence of positive factors in his life.

Any situation is composed of a plethora of stimuli. An individual selectively attends to specific stimuli, combines them in a pattern and conceptualizes the situation. Although different persons may conceptualize the same situation in different ways, a particular person tends to be consistent in his responses to similar types of events. Relatively stable cognitive patterns form the basis for the regularity of interpretations of a particular set of situations.

The term "schema" designates these stable cognitive patterns. When a person faces a particular circumstance, a schema related to the circumstance is activated. The schema is the basis for molding data into cognitions (defined as any mental activity with verbal content). Thus, a schema constitutes the basis for screening out, differentiating, and coding the stimuli that confont the individual. He categorizes and evaluates his experiences through a matrix of schemas.

The kinds of schemas employed determine how an individual will structure different experiences. A schema may be inactive at one time but can be activated by specific environmental inputs. The schemas activated in a specific situation directly determine how the person affectively responds to the circumstance. For example, if a person is concerned over whether or not he is competent and adequate, he may be assuming the validity of the schema, "Unless I do everything perfectly, I'm a failure." In this case, he will be construing situations in terms of the question of adequacy even when the question is *not* related to the situation. For instance, while swimming at the beach (an apparently fun activity *not* related to personal competence), this person may be thinking, "Is my swimming good enough? do I look as good as the others?," and so forth.

Thus, the depressed patient's conceptualizations of specific situations are distorted to fit the schemas. The orderly matching of stimulus and appropriate schema is upset by the intrusion of overly active idiosyncratic schemas which displace more appropriate ones. As these idiosyncratic schemas become more active, they are evoked by a wider range of stimuli which are less logically related to them. The patient loses control of his thinking processes and is unable to invoke other more appropriate schemas.

In milder depressions the patient is able to view his negative thoughts with some objectivity. As the depression worsens, his thinking is increasingly dominated by negative ideas, although there may be no logical connection between actual situations and negative interpretations. The patient is less able to entertain the notion that his negative interpretations are erroneous, possibly because the stronger idiosyncratic schemas interfere with reality testing and reasoning. These hypervalent schemas lead to distortions of reality and consequently to systematic errors in the depressed person's thinking.

**Cognitive Errors**

These systematic errors in the logic of the depressed person's thinking include arbitrary inference, selective abstraction, overgeneralization, magnification or minimization and personalization.

1. *Arbitrary inference* refers to the process of drawing a conclusion in the absence of evidence to support the conclusion or when the evidence is contrary to the conclusion.

2. *Selective abstraction* consists of focusing on a detail taken out of context, ignoring other more salient features of the situation, and conceptualizing the whole experience on the basis of this element.

3. *Overgeneralization* refers to the pattern of drawing a general conclusion on the basis of a single incident.

4. *Magnification and minimization* is reflected in errors in evaluation that are so gross as to constitute a distortion.

5. *Personalization* refers to the patient's proclivity to relate external events to himself when there is no basis for making such a connection.

The cognitive theory offers a hypothesis about forming a predisposition to depression. Briefly, the notion is that early experiences constitute a basis for forming a negative view about one's self, the future, and the world around. These negative concepts are formulated in terms of schemas. Schemas may be latent but they can be activated by specific circumstances which are analogous to experiences initially responsible for embedding the negative attitude.

For example, disruption of a marital situation may activate the concept of irreversible loss associated with death of a parent in childhood. Alternatively, depression may be triggered by a physical abnormality or disease that activates the notion he is destined for a life of suffering. While these and other events might be painful to most people, they wouldn't necessarily produce a depression unless the person is particularly sensitive to the situation because of previous experience and consequent predepressive cognitive organization.

In response to such traumas the average person will still maintain interest in and realistically appraise other non-traumatic aspects of his life. However, the thinking of the depression-prone person becomes markedly constricted and negative ideas develop about every aspect of his life.

There is substantial empirical support for the cognitive theory of depression. Naturalistic studies, clinical observations and experimental studies have recently been reviewed (2). Studies have documented the presence and intercorrelation of the constituents of the "cognitive triad" in association with depression. Several studies document the presence of specific cognitive deficits (e.g., impaired abstract reasoning, selective attention) in depressed or suicidal persons (3). The presence of dysfunctional attitude or schemas has recently been found with depressed patients (4). However, more experimental support is needed. This theory has led to a specific psychotherapy for depressed, suicidal patients.

## OVERVIEW OF THE TECHNIQUES
## OF COGNITIVE THERAPY

The cognitive theory forms the basis for "cognitive therapy." This therapy consists of a number of specific techniques for treating depressed patients. These techniques have been compiled in a Treatment Manual (4). This section will review a few of these techniques to provide a flavor for how this treatment is conducted. Then an illustrative case example follows.

Cognitive therapy is a short-term, time-limited psychotherapy usually involving a maximum of twenty sessions over ten to twelve weeks. The therapist actively directs the discussion to focus on selected problem areas presented by the patient. Questioning is frequently used to elicit specific thoughts, images, definitions, and meanings. For example, the therapist might say, "What was it about the telephone call which made you most upset?" "What did the phone call mean to you?," or "What were you thinking just as you hung up the telephone?" In addition, questioning is used to expose inner contradictions, inconsistencies, and flaws in logic of the patient's thinking or conclusions. Skill and tact are required, however, to assure that this questioning is not construed as an interrogation or cross-examination, which might lead the depressed person to conclude that his reasoning powers are defective.

The therapist and patient collaborate to use an empirical methodology to focus on specific problem areas. The therapist must clearly understand the patient's conceptualizations of himself and the world around him. In essence, he must be able to see the world "through the patient's eyes." If the patient's conceptualizations differ from the therapist's views of reality, the collaborators tend to reconcile the differences with a logical empirical approach.

In essence, the patient's thoughts are treated as if they were hypotheses requiring validation. During this validation process (often conducted as homework), the patient needs to clearly understand what beliefs or ideas (hypotheses) are being tested and, therefore, must understand the purpose of each homework assignment. Technically, cognitive therapy may be compared to a scientific investigation: (a) collecting data that are as reliable and valid as possible; (b) formulating hypotheses based on the data; and (c) testing and, if indicated, revising hypotheses based on new information.

The data consist of the patient's "automatic thoughts," feelings, and wishes (5). These automatic thoughts or cognitions are collected as oral or written reports from the patient.

The therapist accepts these cognitions as truthful (although not necessarily *accurate*) representations of reality, since the basic premise of the cognitive theory is that the depressed person negatively misconstrues his experiences.

First, the therapist tries to elicit automatic thoughts surrounding each upsetting event. He tries to obtain specific evidence for or against the patient's potentially distorted or dysfunctional thinking by questioning the patient about the total circumstances of a particular event.

Secondly, the cognitive therapy helps the patient to identify or infer the assumptions or themes in the recurrent negative automatic thoughts. For example, such a theme might be "expecting to fail" or "reading rejection into personal situations." The therapist helps the patient to see that such a belief may not necessarily reflect reality. For example, the therapist would use logic, persuasion, and evidence from the patient's current and past functioning to get the patient to view a belief (e.g., "I am unable to learn") as an idea or hypothesis requiring validation rather than as a belief.

Thirdly, the cognitive therapist teaches the patient to identify specific errors of logic in his thinking (e.g., arbitrary inference, overgeneralization, etc.). Learning to recognize and correct these errors helps the patient to repeatedly assess the degree to which his thinking mirrors reality.

The patient and therapist collaborate to identify basic attitudes, beliefs, and assumptions, which (according to the model) shape moment-to-moment thinking. Sometimes, an attitude may be so dominant or pervasive that despite changes in environmental events, the conclusion never varies (e.g., "I can't be happy unless I'm loved"). By articulating these attitudes, the therapist helps the patient not only to develop a basis for empirical validation, but also to recognize subsequent cognitions based on these attitudes.

Cognitive therapy techniques are designed to facilitate changes in specific target symptoms found in depression (e.g., inactivity, self-criticism, lack of gratification, suicidal wishes). The specific techniques are described in detail elsewhere (4). Here we will describe just a few of these techniques to illustrate the nature of the treatment.

In general, a therapy session begins with a discussion of the formerly assigned homework. This homework generally focuses on the patient's thinking. The latter part of each session is spent developing and planning the subsequent homework assignment.

In the initial sessions, therapy tends to emphasize increased activity and environmental interaction (i.e., behavioral changes). In the course of such changes, the patient learns to monitor and recognize his thinking in regard to his behavior or activity. This early emphasis on behavioral objectives is based on our recognition that the severely depressed patient is often unable to engage in cognitive tasks because of difficulty in abstract reasoning.

As the depression lessens, concentration improves and the intensity of the affect decreases. The patient is taught to collect, examine, and test his automatic thoughts (e.g., Triple Column Technique below). In subsequent sessions, the assumptions supporting these cognitions are identified and subjected to empirical validation through homework assignments. These cognitive-change techniques require a greater ability to abstract and use logic. Therefore, they are employed after the depression lessens in severity. However, the therapist may employ these cognitive-change techniques from the outset if the patient is only moderately depressed.

We will describe a technique with a primary behavioral objective (the Graded Task Assignment) and one with a primary cognitive objective (the Triple Column Technique). However, a task designed to alter mainly behavior, will also influence the patient's thinking. Similarly, a cognitive change may result in a behavioral change as well.

### Graded Task Assignment

The Graded Task Assignment is based on the assumption that the depressed patient has difficulty completing tasks which had been relatively simple, prior to the depression. Although the patient has the skill and information necessary to perform the task, he experiences difficulty with it because he thinks "I can't do anything" or "It's useless to try." The end result of such thinking is decreased activity and further negative self-evaluation. This reaction is a logical result of an overgeneralized belief that "because an activity is no longer simple, therefore, it is impossible." The cognitive therapist approaches this problem from an empirical viewpoint ("Would you be willing to test your belief?") rather than trying to take an opposing stand ("Yes, you can do it if you try.") since this latter strategy may alienate the patient. The Graded Task Assignment consists of subdividing the major task into mini-tasks which are within the patient's capability. Thus, this technique not only increases activity by inducing the patient to undertake more tasks but it also helps the patient recognize and correct unrealistically negative cognitions which maintain inactivity.

Other techniques designed to change behavior include *Activity Scheduling* (the patient and therapist collaborate to schedule hourly assignments); the *Mastery and Pleasure Technique* (scheduled activities are rated according to the amount of mastery or pleasure obtained with each); and *Cognitive Rehearsal* (the patient imagines each step in the sequence leading to completion of the assignment). Each of these techniques is used to help the patient reevaluate his initial negative beliefs in hopes of making an appropriate cognitive change (e.g., "I *thought* that I couldn't do anything but the evidence is that the tasks are hard to do but not impossible."). In using these techniques the therapist emphasizes the immediate goal of relieving the patient's self-debasement.

## Triple Column Technique

A number of specific techniques are designed to help the patient identify and reevaluate his thinking. For example, the Triple Column Technique is often used to help the patient to identify and reality test upsetting cognitions. The patient records the events associated with unpleasant affect as well as the actual cognitions or automatic thoughts associated with the dysphoria. Next, the patient attempts to answer these cognitions using concrete evidence ("facts") to test the validity and reasonableness of each cognition. The evidence for and against each specific thought (e.g., "I'm a complete failure," or "Everyone is disgusted with me.") is examined. In this way, the patient learns to see his cognitions as psychological events or responses rather than as an accurate reflection of reality. The therapist helps the patient categorize his cognitions under relevant themes such as self-blame, inferiority, or deprivation. The patient learns that of the many ways to interpret life experiences he tends to persevere in a few stereotyped, self-defeating patterns.

As the patient distances himself from his automatic thinking and as he learns to answer his distorted negative thoughts with concrete evidence, he begins to reconceptualize problems and to develop alternative methods of problem solving. This problem solving involves a search for alternative interpretations and solutions to problematic events. Therapy is not simply thinking positively but rather thinking realistically and logically.

The latter stages of cognitive therapy involve identification of chronic attitudes and assumptions by which the patient constructs and orders his experiential world. The content of these attitudes is inferred from the recurrent themes present in the patient's cognitive response to specific situations. Some of the attitudes found to be associated with depression include notions such as: "I must be successful in whatever I undertake"; "My value as a person depends on what others think of me"; and "I can't live without love." The patient learns to examine and assess the reasonableness of these basic attitudes by considering the evidence for and against each belief. He is often asked to undertake homework to test out the validity or the general applicability of a specific attitude.

The following case example serves to illustrate a number of the specific ingredients in cognitive therapy. The case history is presented to exemplify practical issues in differential diagnosis and treatment planning. In applying cognitive therapy to a specific patient, the therapist judiciously selects techniques from a variety of possibilities. The basic guidelines for the selection of the most pertinent techniques are detailed elsewhere (6). This case example illustrates the use of a few of the many techniques of cognitive therapy.

## Case Report

Mr. L., a 52-year-old, married father of two, retired naval officer, was self-referred. He sought treatment stating "Maybe I am a manic-depressive and need lithium." He complained of guilt, difficulty concentrating, suicidal ideation, early-morning and sleep-onset insomnia, anorexia, a fifteen-pound weight loss, social withdrawal, decreased libido, intermittent impotency, lack of interest in formerly enjoyable activities, and mild psychomotor retardation. Although he had no history of alcohol addiction, he had been given to excessive drinking since the onset of the depression.

His depression had been triggered three years previously when he discovered his wife's extramarital affair with a fellow officer. His wife terminated the affair when Mr. L. found out. A year later he had resigned from the service as a consequence of his depression.

He believed he had forced his wife to stay with him by his discovery, although there was no evidence, even after several interviews with her that this was a valid belief. She stated she chose to stay with him because she loved him. She saw the affair as a symptom of difficulties in the relationship. He spent most of his waking moments thinking about the affair, which he interpreted in terms of personal failure and inadequacy.

He had two other episodes of the depressive syndrome in the past. Each episode lasted one year, each remitted without formal treatment, and each was associated with the failure to get promoted on time. Each of these events was construed by the patient as testimony to his incompetence.

There was also suggestive evidence of hypomanic episodes with increased activity, euphoria, energy and feelings of creativity, but these episodes failed to meet criteria for hypomania (6). the patient presented evidence by history and mental status of obsessive-compulsive personality. He showed significant concern over issues of respect, control, and time.

Treatment consisted of both chemotherapy and cognitive therapy administered simultaneously. Hourly sessions of cognitive therapy were conducted once weekly for a total of 16 sessions. Chemotherapy consisted of amitriptyline maintained at 100–150 mg/day until the 16th week of treatment when it was discontinued. The therapy sessions initially included only the patient but subsequently included his spouse as well. The patient's response to this combination approach, according to the Beck Depression Inventory (BDI), is shown in Table 17-1.

TABLE 17-1

| Week No. | Initial | 2 | 5 | 6 | 8 | 10 | 12 | 16 | 24 |
|---|---|---|---|---|---|---|---|---|---|
| BDI | 19 | 10 | 7 | 4 | 5 | 1 | 0 | 2 | 7 |

Chemotherapy was used in hopes of providing rapid symptomatic relief as the patient appeared very suicidal and hopeless at the beginning of treatment. Hospitalization appeared imminent if symptomatic relief coud not be provided rapidly. We also hoped, by responding to the patient's expectation for, and indeed, near insistence on drug treatment, to create a milieu in which psychological treatment might be accepted at least as a adjunct treatment.

Cognitive therapy was designed to help the patient: (a) identify and record his negative automatic thinking; (b) identify stimuli which triggered these negative thoughts; (c) provide methods to control these thoughts; (d) provide methods for the patient to refuse and correct these thoughts; and (e) identify and correct the silent assumptions or themes which ran throughout and supported his negative thinking.

*Step 1:* The patient recorded his negative thoughts and associated environmental events in his notebook. He reported a profusion of negative automatic thoughts or cognitions. These cognitions were repetitious, upsetting, distorted, and generally reflected a very negative view of himself. The content consisted of statements such as, "I am a failure in my occupation. My wife has shown me I'm a failure in marriage. I can't get a job in civilian life. No one respects me. I've never succeeded at anything. Why bother to apply for a job, they'll never hire someone as old as I am. I can't even play tennis anymore," and so forth.

*Step 2:* By recording the environmental events associated with negative thinking, the patient identified stimuli for this thinking. Exacerbating stimuli included playing tennis, having dinner with his wife, and looking at old Navy pictures. Drinking alcohol or walking in the woods alone decreased the frequency of the thoughts. The patient's concentration was severely impaired because of this recurrent stream of self-critical thinking.

*Step 3:* The patient used a wrist counter to monitor the frequency of these thoughts and the stimuli associated with them. On the average, these thoughts occurred about 60 times per hour during most of the day.

The patient was instructed to record and graph the exact number of negative thoughts per minute for four days for every waking minute using a stopwatch and counter. With this technique he reduced the thoughts to as few as 3 to 7 per hour. He gained some control over his thoughts with this technique. In addition, he began to look at his thinking more objectively (i.e., to regard these thoughts as upsetting yet repetitious psychological events, rather than accurate reflections of reality).

*Step 4:* After he learned to control and to become more objective about his negative thoughts, he was able to begin to correct, validate, and/or refute each thought. When asked for evidence that these thoughts were true, he repeated the previous experiences of delayed promotion, failure to make Admiral, and his current difficulty with sexual performance. He felt his wife was too ashamed of her affair to seek a divorce. This inference explained why she was still living with him when he believed she still loved her former paramour. Furthermore, the paramour had been of a higher rank than the patient. This fact was seen by the patient as evidence that he wasn't good enough for her. He saw his wife as a bright, attractive, talented, artistic, and much admired and respected woman. In comparison, he saw himself as an occupational, marital, sexual, and social failure. He attributed his many military honors to "the system," while he attributed occupational failures to himself. In reviewing these thoughts he learned to identify and correct the cognitive distortions of overgeneralization, arbitrary inference, and magnification.

He learned to identify specific themes which were inferred from the negative automatic thoughts he recorded. He learned to evaluate these themes with logic and, at times, with experimental testing. Examples of these themes are "Unless I do everything perfectly, I'm a failure. If I am not rewarded and respected, I'm a failure. If I make a mistake, it means I'm defective. Because my wife had an affair, she no longer loves or respects me. I can't enjoy anything if I'm not the best."

Initially, the patient enumerated a plethora of specific events from his past, each of which he construed as supporting these themes. Often his evidence went back five to twenty-five years prior to treatment. By reviewing the evidence point by point and suggesting alternative interpretations of the events reported, enough doubt developed in the patient's thinking that he would consider running an experiment to test the assumption or theme under consideration. For example, he was directed to intentionally lose at several sets of tennis with a mediocre player, while trying to identify what else he might be enjoying while playing. He reported enjoying the exercise, conversation, weather, and other players at the club, thereby disentangling the issues of achievement and enjoyment.

He learned to see his wife's affair more as a reflection of her view of herself and the marriage rather than conclusive proof of some permanent defect in himself. By learning how he had inadvertently blocked communication (at least from his wife's viewpoint), he could take corrective action to discuss and solve problems rather than concluding that he was a total failure by overgeneralizing from a few complaints from his wife.

At six-month follow-up, the patient's Beck Depression Inventory was six. He was taking no medication. He was employed full time, still married and not drinking excessively. He and his wife reported a dramatic improvement in marital satisfaction.

This case illustrates the use of combined chemotherapy and cognitive therapy. The combination treatment may have certain advantages. Chemotherapy may provide rapid symptomatic relief (e.g., for insomnia) and it may sufficiently match the patient's expectations, so that cognitive and behavioral change techniques can be applied. Cognitive therapy may have resulted in sufficient correction of how this patient chronically gives distorted negative meanings to events both past and present, to provide prophylaxis against future depressions.

Furthermore, this case illustrates how a cognitive or behavioral approach can involve the couple or family system. Often the spouse can provide information to correct cognitive distortions (7). Furthermore, as the spouse becomes aware of the patient's negative thinking, he or she can resort to verbal and nonverbal behaviors to consistently "dis"confirm the patient's negative automatic thinking.

## OUTCOME STUDIES OF COGNITIVE THERAPY

We have briefly presented the cognitive model of depression. This model has been a basis for developing a specific cognitive therapy for depression. The rationale for the cognitive therapy of depression is derived from this formulation: if the source of the depression is a hypervalent set of negative concepts, then the correction and damping down of these schemas may be expected to alleviate the depressive symptomatology. In cognitive therapy, the therapist and patient work together to identify distorted cognitions, derived from his dysfunctional beliefs. These distorted negative cognitions and dysfunctional beliefs are subjected to logical analysis and empirical testing. Moreover, through the assignment of behavioral tasks, the patient learns to master problems and life situations which he previously considered insuperable, and consequently, he learns to realign his thinking with reality.

Studies of the efficacy of cognitive therapy have implications for the cognitive model. If techniques to correct cognitions offer no specific advantage over no treatment or nonspecific treatment controls, we might conclude that negative cognitions, although present in association with a depressed mood, may simply be a secondary effect of the mood itself, an epiphenomenon, rather than having a causal relationship to the disorder. Secondly, if dysfunctional attitudes contribute to a predisposition to depression and if these attitudes are corrected with cognitive therapy, then patients treated with cognitive therapy may be afforded some prophylaxis against relapse compared to no treatment or perhaps to other treatments.

A number of outcome studies comparing the efficacy of cognitive therapy with other treatments for depression are now available. To date three controlled outcome studies with depressed students have been conducted, two of which used a group-treatment format. Cognitive therapy exceeded the results obtained in waiting-list, supportive-treatment, or positive-experience control groups.

Shipley and Fazio (8) treated twenty-four subjects with an individual approach which provided functional problem-solving alternatives. Twenty-five depressed controls received a nonspecific interest-support treatment. The experimental treatment resulted in significantly greater improvement than the control treatment. In addition, these effects were independent of the subjects' initial expectancies.

Taylor and Marshall (9) conducted a controlled-treatment comparison among groups which received cognitive modification, behavior modification, cognitive *and* behavior modification, as well as a waiting list group. They found that patients in all active treatment groups showed significant improvement in depression compared to the waiting-list control subjects. The combination treatment was superior to the cognitive and the behavioral treatments alone.

Gioe (10) compared a modified cognitive-modification treatment in combination with a "positive group experience," a cognitive-modification treatment, a treatment consisting of a "positive group experience" alone and a waiting-list control. Using a group-therapy modality with ten depressed students in each group, he reported that the combination treatment package was clearly superior in alleviating depressive symptomatology.

Turning to studies of cognitive therapy in depressed psychiatic patients, we find a total of four controlled outcome studies and three case reports. Cognitive therapy has exceeded the results of waiting-list group, insight therapy, behavior therapy, nondirective therapy, and pharmacotherapy.

Shaw (11) treated depressed patients referred from a University Health Service. Psychometric ratings, self-reports, and independent clinical evaluations were used. A group-therapy format was employed with one therapist treating eight subjects in each group. All active treatments produced significantly better results than a waiting-list control. Cognitive therapy was found to be more efficacious than behavior therapy (interpersonal skills training), nondirective therapy, and a waiting-list control.

Rush and coworkers (7) reported on cognitive therapy of three patients with chronic relapsing depression. The main behavioral modality consisted of the use of activity schedules. The cognitive approach was directed at exposing and correcting the patient's negative misevaluations of his activities. These patients, although not previously helped by drug therapy, showed prompt and sustained improvement with therapy according to clinical and self-report measures.

Morris (12) compared a "didactic cognitive behavioral program," an "insight-oriented therapy" (an experiential and unstructured program which focused on self-understanding), and a waiting-list control group with depressed female outpatients. Twenty-two subjects were treated in the cognitive-behavioral group, seventeen in the insight group and twelve served as controls. The cognitive-behavioral program was superior. Furthermore, the cognitive-behavioral treatment was as effective in a three-week period as in a six-week period when the number of sessions (4) remained constant. This latter finding emphasizes a notable feature of the cognitive approach (i.e., significant change can occur during a brief time period).

Using a single-subject design, Schmickley (13), reported significant improvement in eleven clinical outpatients as a direct result of four one-hour sessions of cognitive-behavioral treatment intervention. At termination, improvement was found with eleven of twelve psychometric and behavioral measures.

We recently undertook an intensive pilot study at the University of Pennsylvania (14). We compared the relative efficacy of cognitive therapy with a tricyclic antidepressant drug (imipramine hydrochloride) in the treatment of forty-one depressed outpatients. Cognitive therapy was found to be more effective than imipramine.

We have recently extended our study to forty-four depressed outpatients, and follow-up data are now available. All patients were self-referred psychiatric outpatients who satisfied research diagnostic criteria for the depressive syndrome (6). All had a diagnosis of depressive neurosis according to the Diagnostic Statistical Manual-II (15). As a group they were generally white, partially college educated, and in their mid-thirties.

Their past histories and Minnesota Multiphasic Personality Inventories indicated a substantial degree of psychopathology. In general, the patients had been intermittently or chronically depressed almost nine years, and one-fourth of these patients had been hospitalized for depression in the past. The average patient had seen over two therapists prior to the study. On the average, the current episode of depression had been present for just less than twelve months at the time of entering the study. At the start of treatment, all patients were moderate-severely depressed by self-report (Beck Depression Inventory) (16), observer evaluation (Hamilton Rating Scale) (7), and therapist rating (Raskin Scale) (18). Seventy-five percent of these patients reported significant suicidal ideation at the start of treatment. In essence, our unipolar depressed patients generally had a substantial degree of psychopathology *and* a history of *poor* response to other psychotherapies.

Patients were randomly assigned to either individual cognitive therapy or pharmacotherapy (imipramine hydrochloride) for twelve weeks of treatment. Prescribed psychotherapy consisted of twice weekly hour-long cognitive therapy sessions for a maximum of twenty visits. Pharmacotherapy consisted of not less than 100 mg/day, but not more than 250 mg/day of imipramine prescribed in twenty-minute, once weekly visits for a maximum of twelve weeks.

Therapists consisted mainly of psychiatric residents who had treated only two "practice" cases with supervision prior to treating research cases. The methodology of cognitive therapy was specified in a treatment manual (4). The therapists were systematically supervised on a weekly basis by three experienced clinicians. All sessions were audiorecorded and spot checked for adherence to protocol.

Both treatment groups were equivalent with respect to demographic characteristics, histories of illness, treatment and mean severity of depression at the start of treatment. Of nineteen patients assigned to cognitive therapy, eighteen completed treatment over a mean period of eleven weeks. Of twenty-five patients assigned to pharmacotherapy, seventeen completed treatment over the same mean period of time.

By the end of active treatment, both treatment groups showed statistically significant decreases ($p < 0.001$) in depressive symptomatology according to self-reports, observer evaluations, and therapist ratings. By the end of treatment, cognitive therapy resulted in significantly greater improvement than did pharmacotherapy on self-reports and observer-based clinical ratings of depression ($< 0.01$). The response rates to both pharmacotherapy and cognitive therapy exceeded the usually reported degree of response to placebo in depressed outpatients (19). In addition, both treatments resulted in substantial decreases in subjective reports and interviewer-based ratings of anxiety.

Interestingly, the dropout rate during active treatment was

significantly greater with pharmacotherapy than with cognitive therapy (p < 0.05). However, even when these dropouts were eliminated from the data analysis, cognitive therapy patients showed a significantly greater improvement in depressive symptomatology than the pharmacotherapy patients (p < 0.05).

Follow-up data at three and six months after termination of treatment for those who completed cognitive therapy and pharmacotherapy are shown in Figure 17-1. Treatment gains were maintained for both groups. A greater number of the drug-treatment group returned to treatment during this period compared to cognitive-therapy patients. The cognitive-therapy patients showed significantly lower levels of depression at three months (p < 0.05) and a trend toward lower levels at six months (p < 0.10).

Also those patients who had dropped out of both cognitive

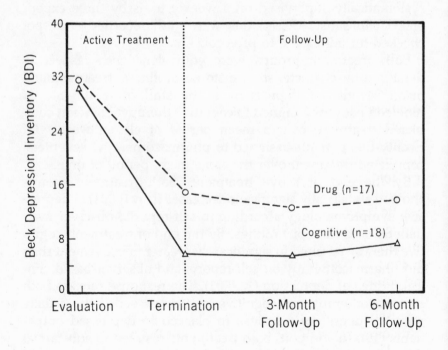

Figure 17-1 *Severity of depression during treatment and six-month follow-up for patients completing treatment*

therapy and pharmacotherapy were followed up at three and six months after they would have completed treatment. When both those who completed and those who dropped out of therapy are combined in a comparison of cognitive therapy and pharmacotherapy groups, cognitive therapy resulted in statistically significant lower levels of depression at both three months ($p < 0.05$) and six months of follow-up ($p < 0.05$).

This is the first study to show that any psychotherapy was equivalent to or exceeded the efficacy of pharmacotherapy in the relief of the acute symptoms of the depressive syndrome. Of course, our results await confirmation. In addition, our follow-up data indicated that treatment gains are maintained over time. Our preliminary data suggest that cognitive therapy may exceed pharmacotherapy in preventing relapse or need for further treatment, once both treatments are discontinued since a greater number of pharmacotherapy patients returned to treatment during follow-up compared to the cognitive therapy cases.

Several other studies (20, 22) have compared different psychotherapies directly or indirectly with antidepressant pharmacotherapy in the treatment of depressed outpatients. The psychotherapies studied included interpersonal therapy (20), marital therapy (21), and supportive-expressive group treatments (22). These psychotherapies did not compare with the efficacy of antidepressant medication in the relief of the acute symptoms of the depressive syndrome. These studies also indicate that the increased amount of therapist contact time for patients in cognitive therapy in itself is insufficient to account for the greater efficacy of cognitive therapy in symptomatic relief.

In general, psychotherapy outcome studies of both depressed students and psychiatric outpatient populations have shown that cognitive therapy is more effective than waiting-list and other active-treatment controls, including pharmacotherapy (the most effective treatment known to date for the depressive syndrome). Secondly, the potential prophylactic value of cognitive therapy is implied by preliminary follow-up data. These findings are consistent with the notion that cognitions and schemas play a major role in the induction or maintenance of depression. Additional studies are needed to identify the predictors of response to this treatment and to determine the applicability of this psychotherapy to other populations.

## SUMMARY

The cognitive theory of depression offers a testable set of hypotheses to explain the symptomatology and the predisposition of relapse in patients with the depressive syndrome. The cognitive triad (negative views of self, future, and world), specific thinking errors deficient in logic, and the existence of hypervalent schemas form the cornerstones of this model.

This cognitive theory is the basis for a specific psychotherapy for depression—cognitive therapy. This treatment consists of a number of techniques, a few of which are described and illustrated above. Seven controlled outcome studies in depressed students or psychiatric outpatients show cognitive therapy to exceed the efficacy of waiting-list, nondirective, supportive and behavioral-therapy controls. Our recent study in moderate-severely depressed outpatients show that cognitive therapy was more effective than imipramine hydrochloride in providing acute symptomatic relief and in decreasing premature dropouts from treatment. Additional studies of the actue and prophylactic effects of this psychotherapy are indicated.

## ACKNOWLEDGEMENTS

The authors wish to express sincere appreciation to Ms. Josephine Rahn for her assistance in typing the manuscript, and Ms. Charlotte Hardy, M.S.W. for her editorial assistance.

This work was supported in part by U.S. Public Health Service grants MH-28459-02 (A.J.R.) and MH-19989-06 (A.T.B.).

## REFERENCES

1. Beck, A. T. *Depression: Clinical, Experimental, and Theoretical Aspects.* Harper & Row, New York, 1967. Republished as *Depression: Causes and Treatment.* University of Pennsylvania Press, Philadelphia, 1972.

2. _____ . *Cognitive Therapy and the Emotional Disorders*. International Universities Press, New York, 1976.

3. Neuringer, C. Dichotomous Evaluations in Suicidal Individuals. *J. Consult. Psychol.* 25:445, 1961.

4. Beck, A. T., Rush, A. J., and Shaw, B. F. *Cognitive Therapy of Depression — A Treatment Manual*, mimeograph, University of Pennsylvania, 1977. (Available from Mood Clinic, Rm. 519, 133 S. 36 St. Philadelphia, Pa. 19104)

5. Beck, A. T. Thinking and Depression: I. Idiosyncratic Content and Cognitive Distortions. *Arch. Gen. Psychiatry* 9:324, 1963.

6. Feighner, J. P. *et al.* Diagnostic Criteria for Use in Psychiatric Research. *Arch. Gen. Psychiatry* 26:57, 1972.

7. Rush, A. J., Khatami, M., and Beck, A. T. Cognitive and Behavioral Therapy in Chronic Depression. *Behav. Ther.* 6:398, 1975.

8. Shipley, C. R. and Fazio, A. F. Pilot Study of a Treatment for Psychological Depression. *J. Abnorm. Psychol.* 83:372, 1973.

9. Taylor, F. G. and Marshall, W. L. A Cognitive-Behavioral Therapy for Depression, *Cognitive Therapy and Research* 1:59, 1977.

10. Gioe, V. J. Cognitive Modification and Positive Group Experience as a Treatment for Depression. (Doctoral dissertation, Temple University, 1975.) *Dissertation Abstracts International*, 36:3039B, 1975. (University Microfilms No. 75–28, 219).

11. Shaw, B. F. A Comparison of Cognitive Therapy and Behavior Therapy in the Treatment of Depression. *J. Clin. Consult. Psychol.* 45:543, 1977.

12. Morris, N. E. A Group Self-Instruction Method for the Treatment of Depressed Outpatients. (Doctoral dissertation, University of Toronto, 1975).

13. Schmickley, V. G. The Effects of Cognitive-Behavior Modification upon Depressed Outpatients. (Doctoral dissertation, Michigan State University, 1976). *Dissertation Abstracts International*, 37:987B, 1976. (University Microfilms No. 76–18, 675).

14. Rush, A. J., Beck, A. T., Kovacs, M., and Hollon, S. Comparative Efficacy of Cognitive Therapy and Pharmacotherapy in the Treatment of Depressed Outpatients. *Cognitive Therapy and Research* 1:17, 1977.

15. American Psychiatric Association. *Diagnostic and Statistical Manual of Mental Disorders-II*. Washington, D.C., 1968.

16. Beck, A. T., Ward, C. H., Mendelson, M., Mock, J. E., and Erbaugh, J. K. An Inventory for Measuring Depression. *Arch. Gen. Psychiatry* 4:561, 1961.

17. Hamilton, A. A Rating Scale for Depression. *J. Neurol. Neurosurg. Psychiatry* 23:56, 1960.

18. Raskin, A. *et al.* Differential Response to Chlorpromazine, Imipramine,

and Placebo: A Study of Subgroups of Hospitalized Depressed Patients. *Arch. Gen. Psychiatry* 23:164, 1970.

19. Morris, J. B. and Beck, A. T. The Efficacy of Antidepressant Drugs: A Review of Research (1958–1978). *Arch. Gen. Psychiatry* 30:667, 1974.

20. Klerman, G. *et al.* Treatment of Depression by Drugs and Psychotherapy. *Am. J. Psychiatry* 131:186, 1974.

21. Friedman, A. S. Interaction of Drug Therapy with Marital Therapy in Depressive Patients. *Arch. Gen. Psychiatry* 32:619, 1975.

22. Govi, L. *et al.* Drugs and Group Psychotherapy in Neurotic Depression. *Am. J. Psychiatry* 131:191, 1974.

# 18 Suicide Precipitated by Psychotherapy

Alan A. Stone, M.D.

This paper is meant to be a clinical contribution only. It is based on data derived from psychotherapy supervision and clinical observation during a period of time that Kahne has called "an epidemic" of suicide (1).

During the course of that "epidemic" it became painfully apparent that many psychiatrists possess no systematic or comprehensive approach for dealing with suicidal patients. Under the pressure of that experience my colleague, Dr. Shein, and I developed a detailed clinical approach based on a theoretical model which attempts to combine the social perspective of Durkheim and the psychodynamic perspective of ego psychology (2–4). This clinical approach applied by a psychotherapist is aimed at "monitoring suicidal intent" by focusing on certain kinds of interpersonal communication and interaction. I shall not here review our strategy; it has been published elsewhere, but for purposes of the current discussion it should be clear that we placed great emphasis on the psychotherapist's active involvement and interaction with the patient as a diagnostic and therapeutic tool.

Based on that work and our subsequent efforts to educate psychiatrists and students in its application, we have been repeatedly confronted by a series of axioms which apparently are part of the folklore which surrounds suicide. The major function of these axioms would seem to be to insulate psychotherapists from the kind of intense involvement we recommend and to relieve them of their responsibility. These axioms continue in usage though clearly incorrect in view of the results of published research and in terms of our own clinical experience.

If patients talk about it, they won't do it.

If the therapist talks about it too much, he may suggest it to the patient.

If a patient really wants to kill himself, you cannot stop him.

All of these axioms minimize what has been the predominant emphasis of much of the recent suicide literature—the importance of enhancing the capacity of the psychotherapist to predict and prevent suicide (5–7). But there is an area where there are no axioms and which has thus far been virtually taboo; it goes beyond raising questions about competence to predict and prevent. Put starkly, the question is, can psychotherapy precipitate or contribute to a suicide? A review of the *Psychological Abstracts* over the past ten years reveals hundreds of scientific articles on suicide, but not one deals specifically with this question (8, 9). There are a number of possible explanations for this, for example, anxiety over malpractice suits, reluctance to wash professional linen in public, and finally, the difficulty of attributing any result to psychotherapy, good or bad.

I shall comment only on the last of these. The demonstration of causal links in the area of behavioral science is an enterprise beset with philosophical and scientific hazards. Attempts to assert that psychotherapy causes anything, seem particularly fraught with such hazards. Therefore, I can only offer my own clinical impression that psychotherapy, whether it cures or not, often has a powerful impact which can be either benign or malignant. I propose to present three types of malignant psychotherapy, each of them illustrated by a case example. I do not suggest that these are the only ways in whch psychotherapy can lead to suicide; there may be others, but each of these, although there is considerable overlap in dynamics, has sufficiently distinctive characteristics so as to be considered a separate constellation. All of these constellations were drawn from my experience in a setting where an attempt was made to treat the most seriously mentallly ill with psychotherapy. The last type which I shall describe is, I believe, by far the most common and is apt to occur outside the hospital and in a variety of professional relationships.

## EXTERNALIZING THE SUPEREGO

The first and most unusual configuration resulted from a resident psychiatrist's utilization of a radical psychotherapeutic technique which had been devised by a very senior person with extensive experience. Briefly, this technique attempted to externalize the superego of the psychotic patient. Thus, to use Freud's (10) colorful terminology, the "self-reproaches and self-revilings," "the delusional belittling," the "distressing self-abasement" with which the patient attacks himself are all taken up by the therapist, who then reiterates them to the patient in a kind of confrontation with himself. The theoretical assumptions which underlie this approach cannot be spelled out here; however, I am convinced that they are mistaken and incorrect and that the technique fails to recognize that in the very sick patient there has been a fusion between the self-destructive component of the id and the punitive superego. Thus the technique which attempts to externalize the superego introjects in fact externalizes the id. This clearly is an extremely dangerous approach which undermines whatever defensive containment of self-destructive impulses existed. An example will illustrate this. It is based on a tape recording of an interview with the resident, with the resident speaking in the first person.

This patient was approximately twenty-two years old at the time of admission and had apparently suffered from chronic schizophrenia for several years. He had led an increasingly isolated life, had no significant object relations, and his sole tangible interests were in trees and bird watching. He could develop some affect and intensity when he talked about these subjects, but otherwise was bland and withdrawn. The working assumption of therapy was that this man lives in his own world, a world of trees and birds, otherwise profound emptiness, and it was my task to somehow find a way into his world. As my supervisor said, if you're in Greece, it's important to speak Greek. So the first stage was a kind of joining in, joining in the craziness. I would sit there and look out the window; there was not much possibility of meaningful contact except at the most superficial level, and I would look at the trees and I would free associate. The patient would look out the window and look back at me with a strange look on his face. True enough, it did seem to enhance our relationship.

The patient began to develop a kind of relationship to me on that level, and at some point along the line referred to his own life as being like a blighted tree, and he could see himself going to the chronic hall on the grounds to which at that time all the blighted people eventually went. The supervisor felt his point was, well, this is the punishment; now what is the crime? The supervisor has his own particular technique; it is somewhat like that of a surgeon who does a brilliant operation; the patient does well in his hands; as to whether some other surgeon can do the operation with a similar deft technique is another story.

So I attempted to use my supervisor's technique which he was teaching me and which was based a lot on his sense of humor and his way of placing emphasis; such as, a patient says she's no good, she's terrible, she's rotten, she should die. He says, "So already you should die; so you're rotten and terrible." You know he can do it with—I think it has something to do with the kind of old Jewish sense of humor that he has. But I, as an unanalyzed psychiatrist, a resident, coming from a somewhat inhibited Yankee family—I had a hard enough time with a sense of humor anyway. Although I liked his sense of humor and appreciated it, I couldn't quite graft on that inflection. So if I said, "You should die," it came out like that—"You should die." But as my supervisor said it—"You should die already," it was somewhat different. I still can't quite do it to this day. He could get the patients to laugh at themselves and then look at themselves.

So in my efforts to get to the crime, knowing the punishment, I began putting it that way to the patient. He was a blighted tree; now, what had he done to deserve this kind of treatment? The man became more and more agitated; it was a fierce agitation, terrible depression; before, in psychotherapy, there was a bland nothing affect and he became just terribly agitated and depressed, and said that the crime was that he had been born, which left me somewhat aghast and stunned. I had a sudden feeling of overwhelming helplessness which I'm sure the patient himself must have felt. I got a very good sense of what he was going through, but at that particular time I didn't know what the hell I was going to do with it, except I knew the man was suicidal and he should be on special nursing.

This all took place in a very short time; from his admission to his death was 62 days. It was a matter of two months, and a chronic schizophrenic patient develops what seems to be symptomatically an agitated depression with massive suicidal potential. It seemed in a way like a good prognostic sign, the fact that the prognosis was previously described as ten years and he might just be able to get out of the hospital. So we were prepared to go the whole route, and in a way I had a good feeling about the therapy; it was moving. The last time I saw him I had this awful feeling of helplessness in regard to this stunning affect-filled statement of his that the crime was that he was ever born. Since then, in thinking about it, it has made a lot more sense to me. But unfortunately what happened then was we were going to ride this out, we were going to continue on this course. The patient got to know another young patient with a sociopathic personality, who said to the patient (this is as I got it later) that he would help him commit suicide if he wanted to. He would raise a ruckus which would call all the staff off, including the special nurse who was guarding him so that he would get the chance to put this plastic bag, which he had on a record jacket over his head. This was the first case of a plastic bag suicide at the hospital, and led to all plastic bags being removed from record wrappers. Anyway, the sociopathic patient, himself probably quite depressed and at times suicidal, was dealing in a way with his own problems in a projective way, and he created a riot kind of situation in which everyone came running, including my patient's special. The patient then put the plastic bag over his head, lay down on his bed, and went to sleep.

This particular constellation can be characterized as follows: The psychotherapist utilized a technique which established communication with a patient who has previously been walled off in his autism. Having achieved contact, the psychotherapist mobilizes an agitated depression by confronting the patient with a self-destructive introject. The patient accepts this as a reality and not as an introject to be analyzed as his therapist has hoped. Forced to contemplate his profound loneliness based on this introject and the hopelessness of altering it, he commits suicide.

## INTERRUPTING THE AUTISTIC DEFENSE

The second constellation is in my experience somewhat more common. It occurs most frequently when particularly good psychotherapists attempt to work with very chronic schizophrenic patients who have settled into hebephrenic desuetude and who have reached that stage described by Modell where their delusional system often is more gratifying than persecutory, and in which they have in effect established a new equilibrium (11). Those who have seen "The Man of La Mancha" will remember the dramatic confrontation between Quixote and his doctor-duelist, the Knight of the Mirrors, who forces Quixote to confront the discrepancy between his dream and reality. The talented psychotherapists, however, whom I have in mind are not so cruel or so insensitive, and the process I have in mind is quite different. Rather, it consists of a much less conscious and much more supposedly kind strategy.

The therapist, typically a young resident, takes on the difficult hebephrenic patient whose life has in fact passed him by, whose family has long since extruded him, and who has no meaningful interpersonal situations available outside the hospital, even if the patient were willing to participate in them. Into this psychosocial context comes the psychotherapist who focuses solely on the psychic states of the patient. He explores with care and sympathy the various primary process fantasies, symbolic distortions, and in effect sets up communication. This process slowly wins the trust of the patient who gradually begins to give up the primary process, the hallucinations and delusions diminish, and the resident reports to his supervisor with great satisfaction that his patient is now "talking straight."

It is at this point that the hebephrenic desuetude is transformed into a schizophrenic depression, and although there are important intrapsychic considerations which related to the loss of the delusional system as transitional object, it is also imperative to realize that the patient now confronts a reality which would doubtless be unbearable to many human beings, particularly when contrasted with the grandiosity of the previous wish-fulfilling fantasy. An example will illustrate:

> One resident whom I supervised spent a year and a half working to establish a relationship with a regressed hebephrenic woman who lived largely in a hallucinatory world of self-fulfilling fantasies in which she was a socially active dubutante. Gradually she gave up these delusions as her ingenious therapist made headway. When after 18 months of painstaking work she surfaced in the world of reality, she discovered she was fat, forty, and friendless, and made a drastic suicide attempt.

These and similar cases exemplify the schizophrenic depression which often occurs in the successful psychotherapy of schizophrenics. But they demonstrate that there are enormous hazards in depriving a patient of autistic defenses when there are no gratifying object relations or sublimations to replace them.

## THE SYMBIOTIC TRANSFERENCE

The third constellation is in my experience by far the most typical. What one finds here is the rather rapid development of what might be called a symbiotic psychotic transference in which the patient very quickly comes to hope and believe that all possible gratification now comes from the therapist. This fantasy is sometimes, but not always communicated to the therapist. It has repeatedly been my experience as a consultant that as one explored the psychotherapeutic history of border-line patients who go sour and require hospitalization, the transference is often of a symbiotic psychotic nature, but for a variety of reasons had not been acknowledged in therapy. I would like to give particular emphasis to this point because it has been so striking in problem cases where the therapist has seemed to have no awareness of the quality of the psychotic transference fantasies or their intensity.

Essentially what happens is that the patient gradually gives up the overt symptomatology, there is a general sense of satisfaction on the part of the therapist, the family, and others who know about the case, and the patient enters the honeymoon phase; and this I mean literally. There is the expectation that there will be endless comfort and gratification derived from the psychotherapist. What typically happens is that the attachment becomes so intense—whether this is consciously or unconsciously observed by the therapist—that there is a backing off on the psychotherapist's part, and what the patient experiences then is the loss of an anaclitic object relationship. It is as though from the patient's point of view he had finally been united with the good mother only to be once more rejected. Again let me emphasize that I believe this situation is far more common than most therapists realize since they seldom, in my experience, are able to acknowledge the intensity of the transference.

The case that follows was written up with the assistance of the resident who treated the patient.

This eighteen-year-old girl was first admitted to a mental hospital following a suicidal gesture. During the ten months prior to this, the patient had demonstrated many symptoms indicative of a serious emotional disorder. These symptoms had included intermittent and transient paralyses, aphonia, blindness, episodes of syncope, severe psychogenic pain, uncontrollable laughing and crying spells, and hearing loss. There was marked hypochondriacal concern and preoccupation. A central and dominant symptom during this period of time was severe, unremitting diffuse abdominal pain which began after the patient had left home to attend college. The patient's past history revealed that she was the third of three children. She was always considered a "problem child" and all developmental phases were stormy. The patient was an aloof, distrustful, and frightened child with many temper tantrums, nightmares, bowel complaints, sleeping problems, and severe nail-biting.

There is no evidence for overt mental illness in the patient's family. The patient's mother has psychophysiologic abdominal pain and bowel complaints and is also somewhat phobic. The patient's father is an extremely hard-driving and successful business man who has no significant complaints of an emotional nature, but has been somewhat distant from his family. Her relationship with her parents has been and remains hostile, dependent, and symbiotic. The working diagnosis was border-line schizophrenia.

*Course of Psychotherapy.*   This patient had been in intensive psychotherapy for approximately 16 months at the time of her suicidal attempt. During the first eight months of this time she had been a hospital inpatient, but improved sufficiently to be discharged and continue as an outpatient. Within three weeks of initiating treatment with a resident, the patient's somatic symptoms disappeared. The transference relationship, even during the initial stages of psychotherapy, was positive, eroticized, and intense. A desire to displace all of the therapist's other patients was freely expressed.

During the first several months the patient displayed a wide variety of antisocial symptoms, but gradually it became apparent that she genuinely wanted to be "good" in order to gain the love the therapist. In time she decided that being "good" included having a steady job, not acting out with sex or drugs, and only being "appropriately rebellious." When a job had been secured and suitable living accommodations arranged, the patient was discharged from the hospital. During the ensuing eight months the patient looked "as if" she were any other young adult female secretary in a metropolitan office. The transference relationship continued on an intense, positive, and deeply dependent basis. Gradually it became symbiotic as illustrated graphically by the following fantasy: The patient wished to be physically attached to the therapist, perhaps with epoxy cement and carried around with him forever.

In retrospect it became apparent at this point that because of the therapist's own narcissistic involvement, he was unable to deal with this transference issue in an objective fashion. In part, the therapist's own fantasies of omnipotence were coming true. This very sick primitive patient had made a startling recovery and no overt psychotic thinking or behavior could be observed outside the transference. The therapist elected to deal with "issues" at this point in a "realistic" manner. It was obvious to him that the patient's object relationships were impoverished both in quality and quantity. A prime example was the lack of age-appropriate dating behavior. This realistic approach occurred to the therapist during a period of time when he was becoming aware of the intensity of the transference-countertransference relationship and the deep dependency needs involved. During one hour he spontaneously suggested to the patient that she begin dating. The therapist even implied that he would be willing to discuss with the patient some of the social skills necessary for dating and that he indeed would even help the patient meet nice young men either by encouraging her friends or her family to fix her up with appropriate people.

Although the patient responded positively to this suggestion, in the next interview she was overtly and severely depressed. The depression continued and worsened. The patient became circumstantial, tangential, and rambling. Her affect became labile and unpredictable and finally within a week she made a very serious suicidal gesture. She was readmitted and at this time was grossly psychotic. Most of the symptoms noted earlier in her illness reappeared and she was clearly in a decompensated state. The patient subsequently made it quite clear that she felt the therapist's discussion about dating was an attempt to get rid of her. She now demanded open physical affection from the therapist (to hug her) and when this was not forthcoming, made another suicide attempt in her therapist's office.

This patient in some sense had agreed to "stay well" and "behave" as long as the therapist did not challenge the wishes or fantasies that surrounded a "yearned for" dependent symbiotic life with him.

It is my impression that a somewhat similar constellation can occur whenever a transference of an anaclitic dependent nature develops and is then broken off by the therapist who does not appreciate its impact on the patient. Recently, a student lawyer working in the neighborhood law office submitted a personal experience report as required for my course in Human Relations. In that report he described a situation which I believe may in many respects parallel the constellation I have just described.

This student lawyer became involved in a messy and disputed divorce case in which he was representing the wife. He approached his task with the zeal one might expect of a student working in poverty law. Within a very short time, however, he found himself involved in every facet of his client's life. A deeply dependent woman, she was embroiled in a sado-masochistic way not only with her husband and children, but with numerous social agencies. The student became the inter-mediary with all of the agencies and her husband, and, as to the children, he became her confidante and advisor. His single client soon left him almost no time for any other activity. After several months of deep involvement, and in the face of ever-increasing demands and nightly telephone calls, he withdrew from the case. Within days his client made a desperate suicidal attempt which led to her commitment at a state mental institu-tion which, incidentally, resulted in the collapse of all of the legal and social work the student had done.

The common element in these cases is the development of a symbiotic relationship in which all possibility of gratification becomes focused on the therapist—he becomes the only one. This in my experience is an extremely hazardous situation; typically it occurs between a male therapist and a female patient.

Both these cases, I believe illustrate transferences of the most primitive dependency type. The therapist is pressured by his sense of power and his wish to give on the one hand, but eventually becomes uncomfortable with the intensity of the relationship. He then breaks off or attempts to dilute the relationship and the patient perceives this as a threat to the finally achieved or reachieved symbiosis with the mother. Thus in the first case the patient saw the offer to help her date as a rejection, a loss of symbiotic fusion. Up until that point the patient had been willing to enjoy her inner life with its fantasy of symbiotic union with the therapist and dispense with her other symptoms. The therapeutic situation was in its dyadic nature inherently never contradictory to this inner fantasy life—she never had to share. Reality never presented a confron-tation to the patient's sense of being loved or to the therapist's sense of having cured. When the therapist tried to introduce the third figure seen by him as helping and as a further instance of his willingness and power to give, the patient experienced it instead as the symbiotic figure attempting to break up the dyadically sensed gratifying symbiosis. This was felt as abandonment, and the sense of gratification derived from the fantasy was undermined by this act of the therapist. This loss of fantasy gratification produces enormous depression, suicidal ideation, and in this case, and others not reported here, it also produced serious suicidal attempts.

## SUMMARY

I have presented clinical case material which I think demonstrates that psychotherapy can precipitate suicidal or serious suicidal attempts. Although I have suggested three separate constellations, they each lead to the same psychic state for the patient. He is more or less forcibly induced to see his reality situation as empty of any possible gratification. Furthermore, the context of this malignant insight is such that he feels helpless and hopeless of altering it. Thus the therapist unwittingly leads the patient into a situation which is analogous or rather identical with that which characterizes the seriously suicidal patient. It is done by confronting him with an intolerable introject that cannot be managed by stripping away wish-fulfilling fantasies when there is nothing to replace them, and finally by offering the possibility of symbiotic gratification and then withdrawing it.

It may be hoped that these clinical examples will alert psychotherapists to the possibility of malignant intervention.

## REFERENCES

1. Kahne, M. Suicide Among Patients in Mental Hospitals. *Psychiatry* 31:32, 1968.

2. Stone, A. A. and Shein, H. M. Psychotherapy of the Hospitalized Suicidal Patient. *Am. J. Psychother.* 22:15, 1968.

3. Stone, A. A. Treatment of the Hospitalized Suicidal Patient. *Current Psychiatric Therapies*, Vol. IX, Grune & Stratton, New York, 1969, pp. 209–217.

4. Shein, H. M. and Stone, A. A. Monitoring and Treatment of Suicidal Potential Within the Context of Psychotherapy. *Compr. Psychiat.* 10:59, 1969.

5. Schneidman, E. S. and Farberow, N. L., Eds. *Clues to Suicide*. McGraw-Hill, New York, 1957.

6. Farberow, N. J. and Schneidman, E. S. *The Cry for Help*. McGraw-Hill, New York, 1961.

7. Robins, E., Gassner, S., Kayes, J., Wilkinson, R. H., and Murphy, G. E. The Communication of Suicidal Intent: A Study of 134 Consecutive Cases of Successful Suicide. *Am. J. Psychiat.* 115:724, 1959.

8. Bloom, V. An Analysis of Suicide at a Training Center. *Am. J. Psychiat.* 123:918, 1967.

9. Tabachnick, N. Countertransference Crisis in Suicidal Attempts. *Arch. Gen. Psychiat.* 4:572, 1961.

10. Freud, S. Mourning and Melancholia (1917). In *Standard Edition*, Vol. 14, Hogarth Press, London, 1957, pp. 237–259.

11. Modell, A. H. Some Recent Psychoanalytic Theories of Schizophrenia. *Psychoanal. Rev.* 4:181, 1956.

# PART III

# Children and Adolescents

# 19 Depression and Suicide in Children

## James M. Toolan, M.D.

*The author notes that childhood depression has become an accepted diagnostic entity, an affective disorder related to unipolar and bipolar illnesses. He indicates the importance of trying to distinguish between depression as a symptom and depression as a syndrome. Clinicians treating depressed children need to keep abreast of contemporary research on the role of metabolic dysfunctions in depression.*

This paper presents an overview of depression and suicide in children. When I first published my paper on depression in children and adolescents (1) in 1962 the subject was very controversial. Not only were there supposed to be no depressive children, but some of the foremost analysts in the country said there could be no depression in children because depression is a superego phenomenon, and children do not have sufficiently well-developed superegos (2). This was somewhat circular reasoning but very popular at the time; if the facts did not fit the theory, throw the facts out.

European investigators have paid more attention to this subject; for example, Spitz (3), a European working in Mexico, came up with what was called anaclitic depression as early as 1948. Americans, however, were late to investigate depression in children, and when they did tremendous controversy arose which lasted throughout the sixties and well into the seventies (4). We are now beginning to see an acceptance of this diagnostic entity; a listing of depressive disorders in childhood and adolescence is included in the recently published *Diagnostic and Statistical Manual III* (5)—interestingly, in the same category as adult depression—whereas *DSM I* and *II* did not even mention the subject. One should remember that a diagnosis of schizophrenia in children, now so readily accepted, was met with skepticism for many years, too.

**Age-related Symptoms**

It is my thesis that children evidence depression, schizophrenia, and other illnesses with different symptomatology at different developmental levels. You would not expect an infant of twelve months to have feelings of guilt such as you might find in a fifty-year-old depressive or psychotic. My theory is developmental and posits, like Lewis's (6), that the clinical picture differs depending on the age of the child, on the developmental level of the ego structure and the superego structure of the child, and on the ability of the child to tolerate pain when the trauma, either psychological or biological, sets off the depression. Children of twelve months evidence depression in one way, at five years in another, at ten and fifteen years in still other ways. By age twenty the clinical picture will resemble adult depression, except that we do not usually see, even at that age, some of the delusional symptoms of impotence, worthlessness, and wretchedness that we so frequently see in adult depressives.

Engel (7), working with an infant with a gastric fistula, was one of the first to show how a physical insult could set off a depressive reaction. Bowlby (8) studied the effect of institutionalization and separation on infants; he never used the word depression in describing the clinical picture but used the words protest, despair, and detachment, all of which I consider to fall within the spectrum of depression. Despert (9), a Manhattan child psychiatrist described depression in children as early as 1952. Agras (10) spoke of the relationship between depression and separation anxiety. I think that is an interesting concept which is receiving increasing attention. For example, we are now beginning to realize that some of the tricyclic antidepressive medications work very well with phobic reactions, which in turn seem to be related to depression and separation anxiety. Campbell (11), in 1955, related depression in children to manic depression; that theory was, however, not accepted. Anthony and Scott (12), in a very scholarly paper, could find only about a dozen cases of childhood manic depression in the entire body of literature on the subject. Now in *DSM–III* we see childhood depression listed as an affective disorder, related to what we now call unipolar and bipolar depressive illnesses. This is a very interesting classification, and one that is being discussed at great length.

**Depression—Symptom or Syndrome?**

One of the important issues is the problem of distinguishing sufficiently between depression as a symptom and depression as a syndrome or illness. I do not think anyone questions now that children have depressive symptoms which manifest themselves in various ways. For example, in my 1962 paper (1) I mentioned the work of Spitz and Wolf (3) on anaclitic depression in infants under one year of age. I described the behavioral disorders of children five and ten years of age who manifested depression. Gould (13) describes the specific acting out of adolescents, based on his observation of many hundreds of cases a generation or so ago in Bellevue. Lesse (14) points to the occurrence of masked depression, which is now an accepted diagnostic entity found in *DSM–III* and applicable to any age group.

Melita Sperling (15) coined the term "depressive equivalents" back in the fifties, a phrase which I have found very useful. Various behavioral manifestations in youngsters such as eating and sleeping problems are depressive equivalents. I do not mean by this, however, that every eating and sleeping problem is a depression, nor is Lesse maintaining that every problem that is masked is necessarily related to depression. I do believe that we may be dealing with two basic entities: one, anxiety, and the other, depression, and that perhaps the interrelating of these states and how the individual reacts to them may produce what we see as the final clinical picture. It is very difficult at times for the clinician to know whether the patient is suffering primarily from anxiety or from depression. Sometimes I start with a patient who is primarily clinically depressed, and six months later is more clinically anxious, and vice versa, depending on the level to which therapy has progressed. I see these two, anxiety and depression, as basic mechanisms.

Cytryn and McKnew, et al. (16–18), working at the National Institute of Mental Health in Washington, have made an earnest attempt to distinguish between depression as a symptom and depression as a clinical entity. They stated that a major depression can either be recurrent or singular, which is almost word for word the way it is listed in *DSM-III*. They identify minor depression, which is listed as dysthymic disorder in *DSM-III*—a somewhat awkward term. The third category to which they refer is masked depression. These categories are very much like the classifications in *DSM-III*, which shows the strong influence of the work of Cytryn and McKnew on the members of the task force who prepared the manual.

## Clinical Studies

Currently we have many fine clinical reports, among them Christ's (19) study based on 10,412 patients—a very large number. We still urgently need, however, follow-up studies— what happens to a depressed child a year or more after the initial diagnosis. I have been able to follow some youngsters and note their behavior as adults. It is interesting and unfortunate that many of them do remain depressed throughout most of their lives.

We need to refine our clinical testing of depression—a refinement that is being done in the case of schizophrenia. For example, according to *DSM-III* we cannot diagnose schizophrenia until the patient has been psychotic for six months. Certainly this is an improvement over previous hasty designations. Schizophrenia has probably been overdiagnosed in this country, particularly when we compare our statistics with those of England, Europe, and Canada. Thus we need to remember when we examine depression that we may be referring to any of ten different types. To use a medical analogy, take a diagnosis of liver disorder—when I went to medical school that label covered all aspects of liver disease. Now we can say it is acute hepatitis, or hepatoma, or cirrhosis, or a reaction to drugs—we can be very specific about the diagnostic entity involving the liver. Regrettably, this refinement in our field is still many years away.

**Depression and Metabolism**

Puig-Antich (2), has been conducting studies on the subject of metabolic dysfunctions which may give rise to depression. Certainly this is another area of which we must be aware. The question is: Does the psyche set off the physiology? Does the physiology set off the psyche? I think the answer is yes and no to both. We are really just now beginning to get some leads; there is the serotonin system, the norepinephrine system, the MHPG system, the catecholamine system, the tryptamine system, and the monamine oxidase system. Significant research into this problem is being conducted at several hospital centers, as well as at the National Institute of Mental Health. During the next five years we can expect some really significant information on the subject of metabolic disorders and their connection with mental illness.

**Medication**

Those engaged in research on the effectiveness of medication on depression in children and adolescents are facing the same dilemma as the clinicians: they are presented with a clinically diagnosed depression but the results of their work do not always agree, and they have to ask if they are dealing with the same or different illnesses. Clinical work is vitally important to research.

We need to explore the efficacy of antidepressant drugs. When prescribing medication we should be aware that some depressions are time-limited and some may respond to the magic of the prescribing physician, and that either possibility may influence the effectiveness of the medication. We really need double-blind studies (presently only Puig-Antich and a few others are undertaking them), even though these are very difficult, time-consuming, and expensive. Several years ago I felt that the use of antidepressant medication for children and adolescents was not effective, but I now must say that I made a serious error in that regard. The efficacy of antidepressant medication in treating masked depression or the acting-out behavior of youngsters remains to be proven. Only those youngsters who are really severely depressed seem to respond to antidepressants, primarily the tricyclics, in much the same way as adults do. Use of this medication entails, of course, considerable risk. We sometimes have to go to frighteningly high levels of dosage in treating depressed children, and there is always the possibility of cardiac arrhythmias. As one can kill oneself much more easily with an antidepressant than with any tranquilizer on the market, exceptional care in their use is mandatory. In this country we are just beginning to return to the employment of the monomine oxidase inhibitors, which were seldom used here for many years. It is interesting that enuresis has been seen to respond to antidepressants; many people think this response is the anticholinergic effect, and it may well be. Dr. Huessey in Burlington, Vermont, has advanced the theory that the hyperkinetic child responds to this type of medication. This leads one to wonder about the relationship between the hyperkinetic child and the depressive child. All of this data are pieces that hopefully will fit into the puzzle before too long.

**Scales and Tests**

Another important tool which has been used for years to try to delineate the different types of depression is a battery of various scales, indices, and diagnostic tests. Carlson and Cantwell (21) have recently reported using the Short Children's Depression Inventory (SCDI) in a study of 210 children. These scales showed 50 percent of the children to be at least moderately depressed. Twenty-eight percent were diagnosed as having an affective disorder. They found the SCDI a very effective screening instrument for childhood depression. Diagnostic scales which are administered to both parents and children may give divergent results. Frequently the children describe themselves as being significantly more depressed than the parents admit. It has been my impression that the parent often underestimates depression in the child, while the child is much more open about it when he feels free to do so.

## Hereditary Influence

Connors, et al. (22), working in Washington, are trying to discover the effect that unipolar or bipolar illness in a parent has on a child. They have come up with a tentative but interesting theory that the unipolar depression of a parent affects children only when the illness adversely affects the child's environment, whereas the bipolar illness seems to be more of a genetic reaction, presenting somewhat later in life. This is theoretical, but interesting and important. In my experience it is rare to see a real bipolar illness before age 18. I believe we see many more unipolar illnesses in children. The question of whether unipolar and bipolar illnesses are two separate entities is very significant; some of the pieces of the puzzle are beginning to fall into place.

## Development of Depression

I would like to describe the developmental theory that I have evolved concerning depressive illnesses in children and adolescents. Many people have theorized that depression is the result of the loss of some significant object. Abraham's (23) and Freud's (24) early theory of aggression turned inward producing depression certainly is valid, but I do not think it is as important as the loss of some significant object. The separation from or the loss of a central figure in the life of a child will frequently lead to depressive illness; however, many children react very strongly if the mother simply goes to the hospital to have an operation. The loss of the mother, or the loss of the mother's attention, has similar significance in the development of illness of a depressive nature. This has been further delineated by Sandler and Joffe (25), working in London; they have done some very intriguing work. It is not only the loss of an object that can affect the child, but the loss of a feeling of well-being previously experienced by the child can cause him to react with depression. This is somewhat similar to Freud's theory that fantasy has as much effect on psychic functioning as reality.

From these thoughts has evolved my theory that loss, affecting the individual at different developmental levels, produces different effects. I take into account not only the loss, but the age and the degree of ego integration of the individual. This phenomenon is not peculiar to children, however; if several adults suffered a severe loss today, such as relatives and friends of victims in a plane crash might do, each would react differently, for example: with repression and not even feeling the loss; denial; reversal of affect and becoming manic; somatic symptoms such as headaches as a defense; feelings of emptiness and isolation; acting out with alcohol, drugs, or sex. Such unique, idiosyncratic reactions in children, however, are further influenced by the developmental level which they have attained at the time they experience such a loss.

It is the parent who often finds it difficult to acknowledge that there is something wrong with the child. "Oh, it's growing pains, isn't it, Doctor?" Since I have never known what growing pains are, this is an impossible question for me to answer. I strongly believe that depression in children and young people should not be taken lightly. Here I am not referring to every transient emotional state of mind. All of us are human and I am sure have been depressed at some times in our lives—in fact I would say that if people are not sometimes depressed and unhappy there might be something the matter with them. I am concerned with depressions that are not transient and that are not within the ability of someone to acknowledge and still function. This type of depression is situational, and we can find it in children as well as adults. Here the depression affects the daily functioning of the child.

I am always interested when children do not function well in school, especially when they do not concentrate. Over and over again the parental reaction is, "Johnny just doesn't want to work," or "Johnny's lazy." Possibly—or is he having trouble concentrating, which is a typical symptom of depression in adults. The same thing is true of the somatic and masked-type of depression, and of acting out. Parents and others in contact with acting-out children may hear the statement: "They're just bad—they're no good—lock them up." But it is incumbent on us to ask, "what is making them behave the way they do?"

**Therapeutic Plan**

I want to give a brief overview of the therapeutic program for the depressed child. In treating depression, whether we handle it in essentially a psychotherapeutic fashion, whether we use environmental manipulation with acting-out youngsters (which we may have to do), or whether we use medication with or without psychotherapy, we must be aware of the child as a growing organism—in short, that depression may not only be interfering with his functioning at the moment of consultation but it may also distort his whole future. For example, if a child cannot concentrate in the sixth grade and drops out of school by the eighth or ninth grade, then that child's whole future life has been adversely affected. For these reasons we should not treat depression lightly or ignore them.

I know that the idea that depression in children is a serious illness is not a uniformly accepted thesis, but I think more and more people are beginning to hold this opinion. Masterson (26) in his work on the adolescent borderline disorder, which is now a new diagnostic entity, advances the theory that the borderline adolescent is reacting to an inner core of overwhelming depression. Until one can get into that core—a difficult and time-consuming task—there will be no significant therapeutic changes.

I should like to reiterate that all depressions in children should be taken seriously until proven otherwise. This requires, as does every clinical case, a good history from the parents, often from a teacher and a physician, and especially from the child himself. Children, I believe, are amazingly honest and frank if they can trust the therapist. One thing I have noticed is that children feel they are not allowed to tell some facts to the therapist because their parents have said, "You can tell the doctor everything except the fact that your father is a bookie," or "your father beats me," or "your father is an alcoholic." Children are often caught in a real bind in therapy, so that it takes a while for a child to really feel comfortable in it.

### Effect of Patient's Depression on Therapist

Therapists have to ask themselves how they feel when treating depressions, and how many depressed patients they can handle in any one day before they become affected. In a sense depression is contagious; if I am with depressed people all day, at the end of the day I can almost feel depression entering into my body. Often depressed patients, even adolescents, tend to make the therapist feel bored, as they can become monotonous in their subject matter. They may make the therapist impatient and wish to do something quickly. He may become frightened; many adolescents attempt suicide, as do children (27). Most therapists are considerably troubled when patients are suicidal, and some may solve that problem by putting the patient in the hospital, possibly therapeutically valuable, but not always necessary. The therapist is working with a degree of anxiety present at all times. Perhaps not everyone should treat depressed children or adolescents; I do not think everyone should treat schizophrenia, either. The depressed child in therapy is in my opinion a very difficult patient because he will basically test, and test, and test. The child finds it very hard to trust, and I think it is very important that we realize this.

Depressives almost always present with low self-esteem and feelings of worthlessness, and consider that the only reason any therapist is interested in them is the fee he will receive, an impression we have to overcome before a fruitful therapeutic relationship can be established. Another problem in working with depressives is termination. When there is an improvement should one ask: is this the time to end therapy or are we just getting down to the painful area? I think quite often the therapist does not want to face such painful affects any more than the patient, and therefore both of them will often run away from it. It is imperative in working with depressive children to work with their parents. I find that my most difficult job is not convincing the patient that he or she needs help, but quite often convincing the parents. I will never forget one college student who entered therapy with a severe depression and after the fourth or fifth session said, "Well, I've got a dilemma, Doc." When I asked, "What is it?" he replied, "My father said he wanted to get me a Mercedes sports car, but he couldn't afford one if I stayed in therapy." Nice choice. Obviously, the father would rather take the chance that his son would kill himself on the highway than admit to himself that his son needed psychotherapy.

## Suicide

In my opinion most cases of depression in children and adolescents require intensive therapy. This may be modified in cases that react favorably to antidepressant medication or perhaps even lithium. One of the controversial areas in adult medicine today is how to treat unipolar and bipolar depressions. Should we essentially be medically oriented—give the patients antidepressant medication and/or lithium—or should we try to get into the psychological problems that underlie their depression? This is a value judgment. I am not prepared to offer any final conclusions. As Pfeffer (27, 28) and others have shown there is a very high percentage of suicidal ideation and suicidal behavior in children.

Similar observations were the basis of my interest in the subject of suicide and depression in children and adolescents about 20-odd years ago at Bellevue. In one year, approximately half of the admissions to our inpatient adolescent unit were for suicidal threats and suicidal gestures. Even for an inpatient unit such as Bellevue, this was a fantastically high percentage. I began to think, "Why are these kids threatening to kill themselves—why are they running away from home?" And I concluded that they must be depressed, but all the literature at the time said they could not be depressed. Obviously, they were!

Suicide is one of the most common causes of death in older

adolescents and college-age students—unfortunately in some of the most capable and brilliant. If anything, the suicidal level appears to be increasing rather than decreasing, particularly in the young, and the present statistics on suicidal attempts are absolutely meaningless. Even completed suicides are suspect, because so many are disguised as accidents. Where was the proof that it was suicide? I have known cases where the youngster has actually hanged himself, which is not an infrequent method of suicide, where the authorities have said, "Well, how do we really know the verdict? Let's call it accidental, because perhaps he was just playing around." The fact that he was naked, the fact that he had been unhappy, the fact that this happened when there was no one around, is overlooked. So even statistics on actual suicides, as opposed to suicidal attempts, are grossly underreported.

The other statistic to be kept in mind is the number of accidents reported. Accidents occur much more frequently than suicidal attempts, and probably many or even most accidents are semi-intentional. I question whether there are many genuine accidents in life. I am extremely skeptical about one-car automobile accidents. When you work with depressed people you can sometimes have an uncanny notion of who is going to attempt or commit suicide in the disguised fashion of an accident.

Another attitude concerning suicide that we must always question is the one expressed by the comment, "Oh well, it was just a gesture—an attempt to gain attention." The "Friday night special" in the emergency room presents the typical young female who is upset because her boyfriend or husband has gone off with another woman. Band-Aids are put on her wrists or her stomach washed out, and she is sent home and told not to come back. But why would anyone make a suicidal gesture unless he or she were desperate? Her boyfriend did run out on her—she has a right to be depressed—but does she have to use this method of calling attention to her plight? People who resort to this extreme are in my opinion really desperate. They urgently need help and should be seen as soon as possible after the attempt. As an example, a patient was admitted at midnight who definitely attempted to kill herself. The nurse notes at 5 A.M. "unhappy because she did not succeed," the psychiatrist comes in at 10 A.M., the patient has her makeup on and is looking fine, saying, "I want to go home—it was all a mistake. I just lost count of the pills." Denial, by that time, has altered the clinical picture. We have to be very skeptical about such a sudden change of mood folllowing a suicidal attempt, and I think a period of observation is needed in order to truly evaluate such patients. Suicidal patients are often very difficult because they so frequently deny the seriousness of their attempts. All of us who work with youngsters should keep this in mind.

It has been my experience that it is not unusual for parents of suicidal youngsters to say: "How could he do this to us?" They are affected by the child's behavior and will react in their own way to the child's depression and suicidal behavior. I use it as an axiom never to treat a child or an adolescent living at home without having the parents involved in some form of therapy. When I have occasionally ignored this rule, I have done so to my grief. In large clinics the parents of depressed and/or suicidal children or adolescents are not seen or are seen by another therapist who seldom consults with the child's therapist. Such a therapeutic approach will rarely prove efficacious.

**Conclusion**

Childhood depression is now recognized as a valid clinical entity and has been formally baptized by *DSM-III.* I believe that now the major work must be: trying to understand the difference between and really delineate the clinical symptoms and syndromes. A great deal of research is being done on the neuroendocrinological and other metabolic dysfunctions that give rise to depression, and this is probably going to be one of the most exciting fields over the next several years. Clinicians—like it or not—are going to have to keep abreast of the findings. They also will have to keep up with the new work being done on the diagnostic indices of depression, as well as on antidepressant medication. Even non-physicians are going to have to know at least some of the physiological factors behind depression; they are going to have to know how to work with people on medication, whether in a clinic or in an individual setting.

## SUMMARY

Childhood depression is now recognized as a valid clinical entity which is listed in the *Diagnostic and Statistical Manual III* as an affective disorder related to unipolar and bipolar illnesses. The author's therapeutic approach to childhood depression is based upon the psychoanalytic theory of personality development. He theorizes that the child's level of ego development will produce varying clinical pictures necessitating different technical approaches. He notes that one of the important issues is the problem of distinguishing between depression as a symptom and depression as a syndrome. There is a need to refine the diagnosis of depression and to delineate the various types of depression. Clinicians treating depressed children need to keep abreast of contemporary research on the role of metabolic dysfunctions in depression, as well as the new work being done on the diagnostic indices and the use of antidepressant medication.

## REFERENCES

1. Toolan, J. M. Depression in Children and Adolescents. *Am. J. Orthopsychiatry* 32:404, 1962.

2. Rochlin, G. The Loss Complex. *J. Am. Psychoanal. Assoc.* 7:299, 1959.

3. Spitz, R. and Wolf, K. M. Anaclitic Depression: An Inquiry into the Genesis of Psychiatric Conditions in Early Childhood. *Psychoanal. Study Child* 2:313, 1946.

4. Rie, H. E. Depression in Childhood: A Survey of Some Pertinent Contributions. *J. Am. Acad. Child Psychiatry* 5:653, 1967.

5. *Diagnostic and Statistical Manual of Mental Diseases*, 3rd. ed., Am. Psychiatric Assoc., Washington, 1980.

6. Lewis, M. and Lewis D. O. Depression in Childhood: A Biopsychosocial Perspective. *Am. J. Psychother.* 35:323, 1981.

7. Engel, G. L. and Reichsman, F. Spontaneous and Experimentally Induced Depressions in an Infant with a Gastric Fistula. *J. Am. Psychoanal. Assoc.* 4:428, 1956.

8. Bowlby, J. Childhood Mourning and Its Implications for Psychiatry. *Am. J. Psychiatry* 118:481, 1960.

9. Despert, J. L. Suicide and Depression in Children. *Nerv. Child,* 9:378, 1952.

10. Agras, S. The Relationship of School Phobia to Childhood Depression. *Am. J. Psychiatry* 116:533, 1959.

11. Campbell, J. D. Manic-Depressive Disease in Children. *J. Am. Med. Assoc.* 158:154, 1955.

12. Anthony, J. and Scott, P. Manic-Depressive Psychosis in Childhood. *J. Child Psychology and Psychiatry* 1:53, 1960.

13. Gould, R. E. Suicide Problems in Children and Adolescents. *Am. J. Psychother.* 19:288, 1965.

14. Lesse, S. Hypochondriacal and Psychosomatic Disorders Masking Depression in Adolescents. *Am. J. Psychother.* 35:356, 1981.

15. Sperling, M. Equivalents of Depression in Children. *J. Hillside Hospital,* 8:138, 1959.

16. Cytryn, L. and McKnew, D. H. Proposed Classification of Childhood Depression. *Am. J. Psychiatry* 129:149, 1972.

17. _____ . Factors Influencing the Changing Clinical Expression of the Depressive Process in Children. *Am. J. Psychiatry* 131:879, 1974.

18. Cytryn, L., McKnew, D. H., and Bunney, W. E. Diagnosis of Depression in Children: a Reassessment. *Am. J. Psychiatry* 137:22, 1980.

19. Christ, A. E. Depression: Symptoms vs. Diagnosis in 10,412 Hospitalized Children and Adolescents. *Am. J. Psychother.* 35:400, 1981.

20. Puig-Antich, J., Blau, S., Marx, N., et al. Prepubertal Major Depressive Disorder: A Pilot Study. *J. Am. Acad. Child Psychiatry* 17:695, 1978.

21. Carlson, G. and Cantwell, D. A Survey of Depressive Symptoms In a Child and Adolescent Psychiatric Population. *J. Am. Acad. Child Psychiatry* 18:587, 1979.

22. Connors, K. et al. Children of Parents with Affective Illness. *J. Am. Acad. Child Psychiatry* 18:600, 1979.

23. Abraham, K. Notes on the Psychoanalytic Investigation and Treatment of Manic-Depressive Insanity and Allied Conditions. In *Selected Papers,* Hogarth, London, 1927.

24. Freud, S. *Mourning and Melancholia* (1917). In *Standard Ed.,* Vol. 14, Hogarth, London, 1949.

25. Sandler, J. and Joffe, W. G. Notes on Childhood Depression. *Int. J. Psychoanal.* 46:88, 1965.

26. Masterson, J. F. *Treatment of the Borderline Adolescent: A Developmental Approach.* John Wiley & Sons, Inc., New York, 1972.

27. Pfeffer, C. R., Conte, H. R., Plutchik, R., et al. Suicidal Behavior in Latency-Aged Children: An Empirical Study. *J. Am. Acad. Child Psychiatry* 18:679, 1979.

28. Pfeffer, C. R. The Family System of Suicidal Children. *Am. J. Psychother.* 35:342, 1981.

# 20 Adolescent Suicide

Howard S. Sudak, M.D.
Amasa B. Ford, M.D.
Norman B. Rushforth, Ph.D.

*The authors review studies related to the cause, diagnosis, and treatment of suicide in adolescents and young adults. The two- to three-fold increase in suicide rates for these groups over the past 25 years is examined from epidemiological, individual, and biopsychosocial perspectives. The results of an epidemiological study carried out by the authors in Cuyahoga County, Ohio, are summarized.*

Although, in general, suicide rates have remained remarkably stable over the past 25–30 years, there has been a definite and alarming increase in completed-suicide rates among adolescents and young adults. Not only do the adolescent and young-adult suicide rates differ from the rates in children and adults by virtue of their steep increase but there are other discrepancies as well. Traditional suicide data, using profile analyses, over the past 50 years, have shown that whites are approximately three times more likely to complete suicide than blacks (1), males are roughly three times as likely to complete suicide as females, and females three times as likely as males to attempt suicide (2). Also, in general, there is an increased rate of completed suicide with increasing age—particularly for white males. Most of these disparities are ill-understood. The male-female disparity is generally explained along cultural and gender-role-assignment lines, namely, since women are allowed more latitude for expression of affect, they are apt to select readily available means when they make rather labile suicidal moves. Such available agents (e.g., Librium ®) are likely to be of low lethality. This contrasts with males, on whom our society places a higher premium for emotional control and who, therefore, are more likely to brood for considerable periods of time before giving in to suicidal feelings. Thus, they have sufficient time to gain access to suicidal methods of higher lethality (e.g., guns). Since women also tend to pick methods that are less painful or less cosmetically disfiguring, they are more apt to eschew guns and select methods such as pills, which are less quickly lethal than the methods that men favor.

The black/white disparities are equally perplexing. Why are black rates lower than white rates and why do black rates peak, for black males at age 25–30, in which age range their rates are not only higher than for comparable aged white males but also higher than for older black males? Hendin (3) suggests that blacks "age quickly" and by age 20 have already begun to lose hope. By contrast, the future may hold more hope for discontented depressed young white males, so that they tend to put off suicide until they are older and more hopeless. Perhaps ghetto black males reaching age 35 have already done more compromising with their aspirations. Other theories regarding the lower rate in black males have to do with the possibility of more family support; better status integration in blacks (less being out of phase with one's equally disadvantaged peers because of poorer job opportunities and, in general, less chance for upward socioeconomic change). The "vicissitudes of aggression" theory has long been felt to account for the disparity between blacks and whites, namely, groups that internalize their aggression will have high suicide and low homicide rates, while groups that externalize their aggression will have high homicide and low suicide rates. This view, promulgated by Henry and Short (4) was felt by Hendin (3) to have been somewhat disproved by Wolfgang's (5) studies of murder/suicide victims. Also, young black males in Harlem were shown to have both high suicide and high homicide rates (6).

Although there has not been a marked increase in suicides in prepubertal children, they too show some remarkable variations from the general pattern. In particular, prepubertal boys make more *attempts* than prepubertal girls (in contrast to all older children and adults). Otto (7) feels that boys who attempt suicide have more serious psychiatric diagnoses than girls. We speculate that males, for some reason, are generally more prone to suicide than females. Why children generally have such low rates is not clear. Many authorities feel that either psychological or biological factors related to hormonal changes at puberity are what protect the prepubertal child (8), while other theories posit that children have more supportive families which help prevent suicide; children have a certain cognitive immaturity which precludes their becoming hopeless enough to suicide; or their concepts of death are immature and make suicide not wished for. Certainly children are less able to implement a highly lethal plan than young adults or adolescents, and it is also known that the incidence of major depressive disorders is lower in children, so there is a lower prevalence of depression (resulting in suicide) in prepubertal children.

Turning to adolescents we find, comparing U.S. 1950 with 1975 rates, a 300 percent increase for white males, age 15 to 19, and a 200 percent increase in white females, age 15–19 (3.7/100,000 in 1950 to 13/100,000 in 1975 for males; and 2.0 to 3.0/100,000 for females); for 20 to 24-year-olds, rates have gone from 9.4 to 27/100,000 for white males and 3.5 to 7/100,000 for white females). For black males, ages 15 to 19, the rate was 7/100,000 in 1975 and other figures are comparable to whites. These figures need to be contrasted with data for "all-age" white males for whom the rates went from 19/100,000 in 1950 to 20/100,000 in 1975 and "all age" white females (5/100,000 to 7/100,000); for "all-age" black males, the rates went from 7 to 11/100,000 and from 2 to 3.3/100,000 for "all-age" black females in 1950 compared to 1975 (9).

## ETIOLOGICAL THEORIES OF ADOLESCENT SUICIDE

What models are most useful in understanding suicide in the young: psychological, sociological, or disease model? (10) What is the validity of studying attempters—i.e., are they a similar population to completers? Clearly, these represent two subpopulations with some overlap. Shall we study patients already in therapy who commit suicide (who would be few in number)? The psychological autopsy-type of study is the approach favored by Shaffer and Fisher as was exemplified by Shaffer's study of 30 children, 15 years of age or less, who suicided in England (10). It is noteworthy that two-thirds of these children were "anti-social" and one-third were in some sort of disciplinary crisis at the time of the suicide completion.

## Epidemiological Approaches

"Profile analyses" using a given year and studying people of various ages in that year have been the traditional way to view suicide data. Profile rates were stable until the 1950s, when increases began to be noted in the adolescent groups. Solomon and Hellon (11) in Canada and later Murphy (12) in the United States began to study suicide rates using cohort methods. In cohort studies one follows a subpopulation across time, and thereby, one can study a given group and see what happens to it as it ages (rather than looking at different groups at different ages). Then, for example, a cohort of 15- to 19-year-olds born during 1936–1940 can be compared with a cohort of 15- to 19-year-olds born during 1941 to 1945, etc. From such studies it was seen, from 1950 on, approximately, that each successive five-year cohort has appeared to have higher rates than the preceding one, not only as subjects age within the cohort but across subsequent cohorts as well. Should this alarming trend continue, it predicts increases in suicide rates across all ages. Note that rates remain higher even after adolescence with each successive cohort.

Since suicide is only one form of increasing violent deaths in the young, another approach is provided by Holinger and Offer (13) who study proportions of subpopulations (by age) to the entire population and correlate these with various violent death rates in that subpopulation. They found positive correlations between the proportions of adolescents and young adults, age 15 to 24, to the general population, for suicide, homicide and nonmotor-vehicle accidents, and found a significant negative correlation for motor-vehicle accidents. Thus, one might predict future rates based on expected future proportions. The postwar baby-boom individuals have now passed through adolescence and are young adults—thus the proportions of adolescents to the rest of the population has begun to decline in recent years. National suicide figures appear to support Holinger and Offer's hypothesis, since suicide rates for adolescents have begun to show a slight decline also. Conversely, Holinger and Offer found that, as the proportion of older people in our society increases (relative to the rest of society) their suicide rates have decreased. They feel this may be due to improved social programs for this larger number of elderly (i.e., that Medicare or other health benefits improve morale or the quality of life in the older range enough to affect the suicide rates favorably). In the 1950s, white males, age 50 to 55, had a rate of 37/100,000; by 1975 this had dropped to 30/100,000. In 55- to 59-year-olds, the rates went from 43 to 32/100,000; and for 60-year-olds and older, the rates dropped from 53 to 37/100,000. This was less true, however, for black males and white and black females.

Why should an increased population of adolescents result in more violent deaths? Holinger and Offer postulate, along the lines of Brenner (14), who showed that increased suicide and homicide rates correlate with increased unemployment, that there is more adolescent unemployment when there is a surplus of adolescents, thus more competition for jobs; they also concur with Easterlin (15) who showed that the increased population results in worse economic conditions for that subpopulation. They speculate, regarding the negative correlation for motor vehicles, that in good economic times more adolescents drive cars (and consequently die) but in bad times the adults are the ones who are driving. Their interpretation for the positive correlation is that increased competition, less self-esteem, and a greater failure rate create a vicious cycle with increased isolation and high homicide, suicide and nonmotor-vehicle death rates.

Using data on suicides from 1958 to 1982 in Cuyahoga County, the authors attempted to test Jeffrey Boyd's (16) hypothesis that the increase in adolescent and young adult suicide rate was due primarily to the increased availability of handguns. Boyd found that the age-adjusted rates of suicide by guns had increased between 1953 and 1978, whereas the rates by other means had not. We also attempted to replicate the United States/Canadian/Australian cohort studies (17) using the smaller but more reliable data-set generated by a single metropolitan county.

In studying only persons who were younger than 40, we found particularly large cohort increases for males of both races. In general, male rates were higher than female and city higher than suburban. Suicide rates increased in parallel for both firearm and nonfirearm deaths (for adolescents, young adults, city, and suburbs). For city nonwhite males, age 20 to 24, however, the increases by firearms were much higher than by nonfirearms.

We found increased proportions of young adults in the Cuyahoga County population from 1960 to 1970, and 1970 to 1980. For adolescents and young adults we found that increased proportions did correlate positively with increased suicide rates in 1970 as compared with 1960. For 1970 to 1980, however, there was no positive correlation. Thus, our data from 1960 to 1970 did fit the population hypothesis but the data from 1970 to 1980 did not at all. Perhaps the data are valid natioinally, but some cities will deviate, particularly those cities with large geographic population shifts.

Regarding handguns, it is too simplistic to blame them alone for the increase in suicide rates. Rates are high and increasing in countries with low gun use. There are conflicting data in the United States regarding projected rates once better gun control is established. When one means is less available (e.g., coal gas in great Britain [18]) rates initially decrease although they may rise again by other means. Clearly, however, gun control should have some beneficial effect on homicide rates. Also, even if suicidal patients were to turn to other means, they probably would be less quickly lethal so that there should be some reduction of completed-suicide rates because of the greater chance of intervention by others.

During the last 25 years, changes in several factors may be associated with the rising rates of adolescent suicide both nationally and in large urban communities. Some of these factors have been implicated in previous studies of suicide, factors such as increased population density giving rise to greater competition, failure, and decreased income, alienation due to social disorganization, increased migration and social mobility, deteriorating neighborhoods, rapidly expanding suburbs, increased criminal victimization, and unemployment; family and personal disorganization with increased divorce rates, illegitimate pregnancies, diminished religious and moral values, increased child abuse, exposure to violence in multiple ways; and increased use of alcohol and drugs. Many of these social changes could lead to lowered self-esteem, reduced coping skills and loss of hope.

**Individual Studies**

Puig-Antich (19), Carlson and Cantwell (20), and others, have all deviated from the analytic view that held that prepubertal children could not have adult-type depressions. Puig-Antich found 80 percent of seriously suicidal children fitted the *DSM–III* criteria for major depressive episode. He validated this with evidence from family histories, finding more concordance in monozygotic than dizygotic twins, and more depressive-spectrum diseases in first-degree relatives of depressed children, etc. The age of onset appears significantly negatively correlated with genetic loading. Biological markers also appear to validate the entity although there are some problems to be expected because of endocrine immaturity. Nonetheless, he found a growth hormone hyporesponse to insulin-produced hypoglycemia, cortisol hypersecretion, positive dexamethasone suppression test, and increased growth hormone levels during sleep in depressed children. Fewer REM sleep changes were found than in adults with major depressive disorder, however.

Puig-Antich (19) employs the Kiddie-SADS-P in which parent and child are both interviewed. The Kiddie-SADS will emphasize symptoms more than regular, open-ended interviews—the latter are better for ascertaining psychodynamics. He feels that the parent/child interviews complement one another since the child can tell of the internal aspects and subjecive feelings while the parent relates objective findings (such as weight loss).

**Psychological Theories**

Furman (21) has raised uncertainties stemming from relying on the descriptive diagnosis of depression. She points out that similar symptoms can have vastly different psychodynamics across different developmental stages and, conversely, similar psychodynamics can cause very different symptoms at different developmental stages. She questions the validity of the concept of depression per se in such children and feels that children's suicidal behavior relates more to personality disturbances than to depression. Sadomasochistic fixations and early deficiences in bodily self-love contribute to the tendency to suffer and lead to personality problems rather than depression. Depressive symptoms may represent a defense against feeling real sadness. Treatment with chemicals may preclude working through the depression to the underlying sadness, so one may mistakenly feel the problem has been solved. She also describes how vulnerable adolescents may encounter life events that engender heterosexual or homosexual feelings in them, which in turn causes them to regress to earlier sadomasochistic levels. Often they will re-enact much of their sadomasochism with their therapists.

Novick (22) describes the "suicide sequence." He and his colleagues (Moses Laufer, Mary Hurry, et al.) studied seven adolescents who made suicide attempts while in psychoanalytic therapy. They concluded that suicide is the end point of a pathological regression rather than an impulsive act. The attempt occurs within the context of a severe long-standing disturbance. Failure occurs related to the struggle surrounding an attempt to separate from the mother. Sexual impulses are viewed as a hostile separation threat and a sadistic oedipal triumph. This is followed by a regressive intensification of a sadomasochistic tie with the mother (which gets displaced to another person). Since it is no longer directed at the mother, there is less guilt present to prevent the suicide. There is also a denial of the reality of death. The dynamics of the attempts are often not understood until *years* after the attempt. For instance, a 19-year-old college student whose attempt was precipitated by college rejection, revealed only years later in analysis, that he had applied to college after the deadline! Also a young woman who, after three years of analysis, casually mentioned that it was her mother's car that she had demolished in her very serious suicide attempt—a car that her mother "just loved." Novick et al. feel that the "sequence" is precipitated by external events which impose upon the adolescents responsibility for taking steps leading to a decreased tie to the mother. Their failure to take the step makes them conscious of their dependency upon the mother. This leads to a regression to infantile sadomasochistic dependence. The adolescent, terrified of being abandoned, submits to the mother and creates situations where he or she is repeatedly forced to submit. In this dependent state, all sexual and aggressive feelings may bring about anxiety. The adolescent may be aware of the incestuous nature of some of his or her sexual feelings and this creates panic that the suicide may be an attempt to resolve. Such adolescents provoke rejection, and blame outside persons; suicide reasserts that control over external events; they make others sorry, with the result that they will not have sexual or aggressive impulses to contend with any longer. Novick feels that many such adolescents have altered ego states at the time of the attempts—may perhaps even be psychotic.

Theories of the effects of contagion go back at least as far as Goethe's *The Suffering of Young Werther* (23). It is claimed that a spate of suicides followed the publication of this romanticized story of suicide. Motto (24, 25) published two studies of suicide rates following newspaper blackouts to ascertain the effect of diminished publicity. One study revealed no effect and the other found a positive one. Regarding temporal factors, Phillips (26) showed that adolescent suicides were not sensitive to effects such as the day of the week, in contrast to adult deaths where there is a strong tendency toward this. Phillips has also demonstrated significant contagion effects in suicidal behavior (27).

Effects of the economy have already been alluded to as well as effects of divorce, less adherence to religion, breakdown in family stability, increased gun availability, the role of television, our frontier mentality, the role of violence in general, and the fear of war, particularly nuclear destruction. Mack has written of some existential concerns and anxieties of school children regarding nuclear destruction (28). It is unclear whether such global factors have a causal relationship to suicide. Although such a hypothesis may be attractive, its validation appear very difficult.

## DIAGNOSIS

Gammon, John, and Weissman used the Kiddie-SADS-E and compared data derived from (a) the mother, (b) the patient to (c) chart information and (d) all chart diagnoses in order to form (e) a best diagnostic estimate. They found that (a) and (b) correlated very well with (e) and each other but that the (c) to (e) and the (d) to (e) correlations were poor (29). They also noted that their approach downplays Axis II diagnoses. We suspect this is because such diagnoses are largely made intuitively rather than based on more "objective" diagnostic material. In 6 of their 12 cases they made a diagnosis of Bipolar Disorder on the Kiddie-SADS, yet no such diagnosis was made on the charts. Also, only two of the four past suicide attempts which they learned of via the Kiddie-SADS were noted on the patients' charts.

Friedman, et al. (30–33) found a remarkable association between borderline personality disorder and affective disorder in adolescent inpatients: over 50 percent of their 76 patients had affective disorders and one-third of these affective-disorder patients had an Axis II diagnosis (in all cases but one this was a borderline personality disorder). In the group with no Axis II diagnosis, males equaled females. In the group with an Axis II diagnosis (BPD) there were far more females than males. Over half of the affective-disorder patients, but only a third of the nonaffective-disorder patients had made suicide attempts. If there was coexistent borderline personality disorder, the attempts were both more frequent and severe. Also a history of dysthymia indicated a worse prognosis. The irony, therefore, is that the population one is most likely to consider low risk, namely, adolescent girls with personality disorders, is the one which, if there is a coexistent affective disorder, is at the highest risk!

A similar concern about the prognostic import of dysthymia was made by Kovacs at the 1983 APA meeting (34). She studied 65 children, age 8 to 13, with three diagnoses: major depressive disorder, dysthymia, and adjustment disorder with depressed mood. An earlier onset was found in the dysthymics than in the major depressive disorders (with adjustment disorders falling in the middle). Recovery was slowest in the dysthymics (three years); intermediate in the major depressive disorders (8½ months) and fastest in the adjustment disorders (6 months). She also found a greater likelihood of recurrence of the major depressive disorder (MDD) if the diagnosis of the dysthymic disorder preceded the first diagnosis of major depressive disorder. This suggests that dysthymic disorder in children marks an early and severe episode of a major depressive disorder. Note that 73 percent of children initially diagnosed as dysthymic received the diagnosis of major depressive disorder within 5 years.

## TREATMENT

### Group Approaches

Ross and Motto (35) employed group therapy as an adjunct to individual therapy in 17 suicidal adolescents and found no suicide attempts or completions in their two-year follow-up. The anxieties which would be engendered in therapists, were group therapy the only modality offered to acutely suicidal adolescents, probably precludes the usefulness of this method as a sole therapy.

### Family Therapy

Richman (36, 37) has noted the close association between "separation" and "death" in the families he has studied. He described the invariable isolation of the suicidal adolescent within the family, while at the same time outside intimacies are being prohibited for him or her. He found that the family establishes special (covert) rules regarding the expression of aggression (and may give covert messages regarding suicide—cf., Sabbath's "Expendable Child" [38]). Therapists need to be exquisitely sensitive to separation issues with suicidal patients. Since the suicide threat or act generates a crisis, Richman feels that crisis techniques may be useful.

## Individual Psychotherapy

Toolan (39) much prefers long-term therapies to crisis techniques. The latter, he feels, really are band-aid treatment. He involves the adolescent's family, preferring to see the family himself (even though he is also seeing the child), since the advantages are claimed to outweigh the confidentiality-issue disadvantages. He explicates some of the difficult transference and countertransference problems which often occur in the treatment of suicidal adolescents.

## Cognitive Therapy

Beck, Bedrosian, and Epstein (40, 41) write of the depressive triad, namely, negative views of the self, the world, and the future. Cognitive theory holds that depressed patients have idiosyncratic interpretations and assumptions which cause them to have negative affects; furthermore, they process data in selective ways to validate their depressogenic assumptions. Thus, therapy is via cognitive assessments which are achieved through "collaborative empiricism." They advocate the use of instruments such as the Beck-Kovacs-Weissman Scale of suicide ideation (42) and stress that therapists must discuss the adolescent's suicidal ideation in depth. The directness of cognitive therapy may hold an extra appeal for adolescents, they assert, although some adolescents and younger patients may find one-to-one therapy difficult so that therapists may have to employ tape recordings or diaries of the adolescents or perform activities with the adolescents to help move therapy along.

Cognitive therapists believe that if one thinks depressed one feels depressed, whereas more traditional therapists are apt to believe that one who feels depressed will think depressed. Everyone agrees that depressed patients end up scanning negatively, however, and that their thinking patterns should be addressed. It is a cause-and-effect dilemma, although traditional schools may focus more on questions such as what were the losses; where is the anger (is it internalized); with whom is the patient identifying; what is in it for the patient to be depressed; and what biological or genetic factors may be involved?

## Pharmacotherapy

According to Puig-Antich (43) for children, and perhaps, but not necessarily, for adolescents, if they have a major depressive disorder, according to *DSM-III* criteria, and if there are no cardiac problems, the primary treatment is through imipramine, 1.5 mg/k/day. Every three days this can be raised to 3,4,5 mg/k/day. It should not be increased if the resting heart-rate is more than 130 or if the P–R interval is more than 0.21 sec., or if the QRS widens to more than 130 percent of the base line, or if the systolic blood pressure is more than 145 or the diastolic blood pressure is more than 95mm/Hg. If one treats for five weeks and there is no change, plasma levels should be rechecked and the dose increased if needed, etc. If the child or adolescent responds, then one treats for three months before discontinuing medication. It is of interest that there is some tentative evidence that children may be more responsive than adolescents to tricyclic antidepressants.

## Efficacy Issues

Outcome studies of psychotherapy for suicidal adolescents are no different from other psychotherapy outcome studies. Adherents of each discipline claim superiority for their own method. It would appear that psychotherapy is helpful, but it is not clear what kind, duration, or frequency of psychotherapy is most helpful (44).

In *Suicide in America* (3) and elsewhere (45), Hendin makes some cogent points regarding therapy. He warns that being "the rescuer" may not be helpful. Since the patient often invites rescue, one may inadvertently be supporting such a pattern.

Also, appeals to patients to live for his or her parents' sake or some other's sake fail to emphasize that one should want to live for one's own sake. Suicidal patients can be so manipulative themselves that we should not end up manipulating or coercing them, nor should we allow them to control us through their suicidal threats. Of course, there are times we are forced into being rescuers, but it is crucial to analyze what has happened in such interactions with the patient as soon as possible.

### Prevention, Postvention

Hill (46) has reported on his experiences in high schools in Cuyahoga County following suicide incidents. In his work with students he divided the initial reactions to the suicide of a fellow student into four phases. (a) Retreat to a safe place through flight. Generally, this was to the home of a close friend of the decedent. Considerable crying, silence, and withdrawal are seen in this initial reaction. (b) Preoccupation with the issues of "why" the suicide occurred. (c) The need to blame oneself or others. Not surprisingly, the closer the individual was to the decedent the more likely he or she was to blame himself or herself for the suicide. (d) The tendency to overfocus or to overgeneralize. The individual would look for simple, single causes (e.g., "his father was so mean") or would tend to blame everything on a more impersonal, global structure (such as the school administration or our national government, etc.).

Hill found that the faculty and students go through similar phases, need the same kind of reassurance and support, and the primary difference was that the faculty members were often less open in their concerns than were the students. Since schools provide captive audiences, they constitute an ideal plan in which to attempt preventive, interventive, and postventive efforts with students and faculty. Hill found it useful to encourage students and faculty to call him at the local Suicide Prevention Center should the need arise after his school visits.

Ross espouses "Peer Counseling" for the problem of suicide in the schools (47). Since close friends are the ones most likely to know of an imminent suicide, she feels that they are in a particularly good position to insure that their friends receive help. She stresses the need to educate students regarding the signs and symptoms of depression and suicidal behavior. Students are disabused of the concept of being "disloyal" to their friends if they breach confidences revealed to them by instilling in them the contrary concept, namely that it is disloyal to a friendship not to break confidence in order to help someone who is depressed or to thwart a suicide attempt. Ross is well aware of the danger that such educational programs can be very stimulating and carefully tries to make sure that, rather than exciting students or unduly alarming them, she follows a middle path—one which engenders neither contagion nor panic, but alerts students and faculty to what is needed.

## CONCLUSION

Since each school of psychotherapy makes similar claims regarding the efficacy of its own idiosyncratic brand, critics often wonder if the parochial differences which separate us are less important than the factors which are common to most psychotherapies, namely, the establishment of an unusual dyad between patient and therapist in which the patient is able to talk about difficult, painful topics with someone remarkably nonjudgmental, which tends to provide support and enhance self-esteem. Granted this much, most of us are convinced that there is more to our psychotherapeutic efforts than simply the relationship.

In summary, it is clear that insular, intradisciplinary approaches to the problem of suicide are limited. To approach the problem of suicide solely from a psychological, sociological, biological, or epidemiological vantage point is probably too narrow a focus to give us much new insight. Multidisciplinary approaches appear to be much more promising and new computer-assisted statistical techniques may make possible future multifactorial approaches to this distressing problem.

## SUMMARY

Etiological theories of suicide are reviewed from epidemiological, individual (both biological and psychological), and psychosocial perspectives. Cohort and population-model approaches as explanations for the two- to three-fold increase in completed suicide rates observed in adolescents and young adults over the past 25 years are presented. The results of the authors' study of suicides in adolescents and young adults in Cuyahoga County, Ohio, to test these hypotheses are summarized. This study revealed marked cohort differences in suicide rates and provided partial support for the "population-model" approach.

Differences between suicide rates in adolescents and other age groups are discussed, as are data from some minority groups. The role of depression in adolescents and various studies of diagnostic approaches (e.g., structured diagnostic assessments, biological markers, clues during intensive psychotherapy or psychoanalysis, studies of high-risk diagnostic groups) are reviewed. Lastly, treatment employing individual, family, and group approaches to classical psychoanalytic or cognitive psychotherapy as well as the role of pharmacological treatments are considered.

## REFERENCES

1. Frederick, C. J. Current Trends in Suicidal Behavior in the United States. *Am. J. Psychother.* 32:172–200, 1978.

2. Hankoff, L. D. and Einsidler, B. Eds. *Suicide: Theory and Clinical Aspects.* P.S.G. Publishing Co., Littleton, Mass. 1979.

3. Hendin, H. *Suicide in America.* W. W. Norton, New York, 1982.

4. Henry, A. and Short, J. *Suicide and Homicide: Some Economic, Sociological, and Psychological Aspects of Aggression.* Free Press, Glencoe, Ill., 1954.

5. Wolfgang, M. *The Subculture of Violence: Towards an Integrated Theory in Criminology.* Tavistock Publications, London, 1967.

6. Hendin, H. *Black Suicide.* Harper & Row, New York, 1969.

7. Otto, U. Suicidal Acts by Children and Adolescents. *Acta Psychiatr. Scand. (Suppl)* 233:7–123, 1972.

8. Shaffer, D. Suicide in Childhood and Early Adolescence. *J. Child Psychol. Psychiatry* 5:275–291, 1974.

9. Solomon, M. I. and Murphy, G. Cohort Studies of Suicide. In *Suicide in the Young,* Sudak, H. S., Ford, A. B. and Rushforth, N. B., Eds. Wright PSG, Littleton, Mass. 1984.

10. Fisher, P. and Shaffer, D. Methods for Investigating Suicide in Children and Adolescents: An Overview. In *Suicide in the Young*.

11. Solomon, M. I. and Hellon, C. P. Suicide and Age in Alberta, Canada 1951–1977: A Cohort Analysis. *Arch. Gen. Psychiatry* 37:511–513, 1980.

12. Murphy, G. E. and Wetzel, R. D. Suicide Risk by Birth Cohort in the United States, 1949–1974. *Arch. Gen. Psychiatry* 37:519–523, 1980.

13. Holinger, P. C. and Offer, D. Toward the Prediction of Violent Deaths among the Young. In *Suicide in the Young*.

14. Brenner, M. H. Mortality and the National Economy: A Review of the Experience of England and Wales, 1936–1976. *Lancet* 2:568–573, 1979.

15. Easterlin, R. A. *Birth and Fortune*. Basic Books, New York, 1980.

16. Boyd, J. H. The Increasing Rate of Suicide by Firearms. *N. Engl. J. Med.* 308:872–874, 1983.

17. Rushforth, N. B., Ford, A. B., Sudak, H. S., et al. Increasing Suicide Rates in Adolescents and Young Adults in an Urban Community (1958–1982): Tests of Hypotheses from National data. In *Suicide in the Young*.

18. Kreitman, N. The Coal Gas Story: United Kingdom Suicide Rates 1960–1970. *Br. J. Prev. Soc. Med.* 30:86–93, 1976.

19. Puig-Antich, J., Blau, S., Marx, N., et al. Prepubertal Major Depressive Disorder: A Pilot Study. *J. Am. Acad. Child Psychiatry* 17:695–707, 1978.

20. Carlson, G. A. and Cantwell, D. P. Suicidal Behavior and Depression in Children and Adolescents. *J. Am. Acad. Child Psychiatry* 21:361–368, 1982.

21. Furman, E. Some Difficulties in Assessing Depression and Suicide in Children. In *Suicide in the Young*.

22. Novick, J. Attempted Suicide in Adolescents: The Suicide Sequence. In *Suicide in the Young*, op. cit.

23. Goethe, W. *The Suffering of Young Werther* (1774). Bantam Books, New York, 1962.

24. Motto, J. A. Suicide and Suggestibility: The Role of the Press. *Am. J. Psychiatry* 124:252–256, 1967.

25. Motto, J. A. Newspaper Influence on Suicide: A Controlled Study. *Arch. Gen. Psychiatry* 23:143–148, 1970.

26. Phillips, D. P. Teenage and Adult Temporal Fluctuations in Suicide and Auto Fatalities. In *Suicide in the Young*.

27. Phillips, D. P. Motor Vehicle Fatalities Increase just after Publicized Suicide Stories. *Science* 196:1464–1465, 1977.

28. Mack, J. E. and Hickler, J. *Vivienne: The Life and Suicide of an Adolescent Girl*. Little Brown, Boston, 1981.

29. Gammon, G. D., John, K., and Weissman, M. Structured Assessment of Psychiatric Diagnosis and of Psychosocial Function and Supports in

Adolescents: A Role in the Secondary Prevention of Suicide. In *Suicide in the Young*.

30. Friedman, R. C., Corn, R, Aronoff, M. S., et al. The Seriously Suicidal Adolescent: Affective and Character Pathology. In *Suicide in the Young*.

31. Friedman, R. C., Clarkin, J. F., Corn, R., et al. DSM–III and Affective Pathology in Hospitalized Adolescents. *J. Nerv. Ment. Dis.* 170:511–521, 1982.

32. Clarkin, J. F., Friedman, R. C., Hurt, S. W., et al. Affective and Character Pathology of Suicidal Adolescents and Young Adult Inpatients. Paper presented at the American Association of Suicidology, 15th Annual Meeting, New York, New York, April 17, 1982.

33. Friedman, R. C., Aronoff, M. S., Clarkin, J. F., et al. Suicidal Behavior in Depressed Borderline Patients. *Am. J. Psychiatry*, in press.

34. Kovacs, M. Longitudinal Course of Childhood Depression. *Arch. Gen. Psychiatry* (forthcoming).

35. Ross, C. P. and Motto, J. A. Group Counseling for Suicidal Adolescents. In *Suicide in the Young*.

36. Richman, J. Family Therapy of Attempted Suicide. *Family Process* 18:131–142, 1979.

37. Richman, J. Family Determinants of Suicide Potential. In *Identifying Suicidal Potential*. Anderson, D. and McClain, L. J., Eds. Behavioral Publications, New York, pp. 33–54, 1971.

38. Sabbath, J. C. The Suicidal Adolescent–the Expendable Child. *J. Am. Acad. Child Psychiatry* 8:272–289, 1969.

39. Toolan, J. M. Suicide and Suicidal Attempts in Children and Adolescents. *Am. J. Psychiatry* 118:719–724, 1962.

40. Bedrosian, R. C. and Beck, A. T. Cognitive Aspects of Suicidal Behavior. *Suicide Life Threat. Behav.* 9:87–96, 1979.

41. Beck, A. T. and Epstein, N. Cognitions, Attitudes, and Personality Dimensions in Depression. Paper presented at the Annual Meeting of The Society for Psychotherapy Research, Smuggler's Notch, Vermont, June, 1982.

42. Beck, A. T., Kovacs, M., and Weissman, A. Assessment of Suicidal Intention: The Scale for Suicide Ideation. *J. Consult. Clin. Psychol.* 47:343–352, 1979.

43. Puig-Antich, J., Perel, J. M., Lupatkin, W., et al. Plasma Levels of Imipramine and Desmethylimipramine and Clinical Response to Prepubertal Major Depressive Disorder. *J. Am. Acad. Child Psychiatry* 18:616–627, 1979.

44. Parloff, M. B. Psychotherapy Research Evidence and Reimbursement Decisions: Bambi Meets Godzilla. *Am. J. Psychiatry* 139:718–727, 1982.

45. Hendin, H. Psychotherapy and suicide. *Am. J. Psychother.* 35:469–480, 1982.

46. Hill, W. H. Intervention and Postvention in Schools. In *Suicide in the Young.*

47. Ross, C. P. Mobilizing Schools for Suicide Prevention. *Suicide Life Threat. Behav.* 10:239–243, 1980.

# 21 Modalities of Treatment for Suicidal Children

Cynthia R. Pfeffer, M.D.

*Childhood suicidal behavior requires a multimodal treatment approach that involves individual, family, environmental, and psychopharmacological interventions. The best therapeutic outcome evolves when these modalities are used in combination. Personal characteristics of the therapist influence the therapeutic efficacy. Systematic research to evaluate the most effective treatments for suicidal children is needed.*

There is a paucity of literature on clinical practice and research of the treatment of suicidal children and adults. Lesse notes that "despite the veritable renaissance of interest in suicidal patients, there has been a most pathetic and dangerous void in the development of pragmatic guidelines and techniques in management of patients who have suicidal ideas or drives" (1) (p. 308). He believes that "the greatest scotomatized therapeutic void in management of suicidal patients exists among psychotherapists. Psychotherapists frequently fail to evaluate the intensity of the depression. They are particularly lax in their evaluation of the intensity of the patient's suicidal preoccupations and drives" (p. 309). This problem is even more serious in regard to treatment of suicidal children where less is known about the naturalistic course of childhood suicidal behavior than adult suicidal behavior. In fact, it has been only relatively recent that suicidal behavior in young children has been recognized and the characteristics of this phenomenon studied. The present paper utilizes a literature review to outline the types of treatments that have been described for suicidal children. It is hoped that this review might stimulate interest in systematically investigating treatment modalities for suicidal children.

## ACUTE MEDICAL MANAGEMENT OF SUICIDAL CHILDREN

Family physicians and pediatric emergency room staff are the most frequent initial contacts for suicidal children (2). However, severe childhood depression is often underrecognized; and, as a result, many children who do not manifest overt suicidal actions are not referred by primary physicians to mental health professionals (2). This may be due to the great variation in pediatricians' and other physicians' attitudes toward depressed and suicidal children. Pediatricians, in general, have limited experience in evaluating and treating childhood suicidal behavior (3). Many pediatricians admit that they ask patients about suicide only if there are overt indications of such behavior while other pediatricians say this issue never arises in their practice (3). Pediatricians generally believe that psychotherapy of the child and family is the treatment of choice for childhood depression; yet, if suicidal behavior occurs, they often recommend inpatient treatment (4). Pediatricians are insufficiently aware of the multiple modalities of treatment required for suicidal children.

Corder and Haizlip (2) developed a screening checklist that can be used to aid family physicians and pediatricians in the evaluation of suicidal risk in children. Among the questions to be addressed to the child and family are those relating to such issues in the child as physical complaints, accidents, environmental changes, losses, school problems, death preoccupations, changes in behavior or mood, suicidal ideas or acts, and depression. Corder and Haizlip recommended that children, who demonstrate a predominance of positive response patterns on this checklist, should be referred for comprehensive psychiatric evaluation. Such a structured format has a beneficial effect on eliciting information that may oridinarily be overlooked by the physician or minimized by the family.

With regard to the actual treatment, Lewis and Solnit (5) strongly advise that collaborative efforts are essential between pediatricians, child psychiatrists, nurses, and social workers. Admission to a hospital should be the first treatment step to provide life-supporting medical emergency care. The usefulness of the hospital is its ability to protect the child from harm while physical and psychological care are offered and the diagnosis is confirmed. When acute hospital medical care is no longer necessary, a definitive plan for sustained treatment should be made that would include psychiatric inpatient or outpatient care. The report of the British Working Party in Child and Adolescent Psychiatry (6) adds to Lewis and Solnit's recommendations by advocating that both involvement of the parents and follow-up care are essential. These two suggestions are often overlooked in the treatment plan; and, as a result, recurrence of suicidal behavior is more likely.

## PSYCHIATRIC INTERVENTIONS

### Therapist Characteristics

Psychiatric intervention is the most crucial factor in alleviating childhood suicidal tendencies. Among the key elements of enhancing the effects of psychiatric treatment are the characteristics of the therapist.

The therapist must be available to his suicidal patient willingly, without delay, and at all hours (7, 8). One of the most important aspects of treatment of suicidal children is to strengthen and intensify supportive empathic personal relationships. Schechter states that "not only is there a need to make a quick and firm relationship with the therapist, who must be most giving, but also, as soon as possible to give interpretation so that the child can understand his motivation" (9) (p. 140). Thus, the therapist must be very active in working with the child in connection with his worries, sadness, and behavior. This is crucial since many suicidal children tend to be withdrawn and unable to readily express their feelings and responses. Ackerly states that therapy should help modify "the projection-introjection systems so that the child can introject a good object: when he then projects onto the world, there will be better and more hopeful image and ego ideal" (10) (p. 258). The therapist must be able to be honest with his suicidal patient, be consistent in his actions and statements, and be able to provide an atmosphere of trust so that the child is aware that the therapist has his best interest in mind. The therapist must have a sense of caring, respect, and concern for his young suicidal patient. Above all, the therapist must realize that he cannot rescue all patients and that the responsibility for living is shared by the patient, the family, and the therapist. Therefore, the therapist's role is to facilitate the life-preserving desires but not to omnipotently rescue the patient.

Toolan (11) believes that only highly experienced and adequately trained therapists should work with suicidal and depressed children. In fact, because of the complex nature of childhood suicidal behavior and the variety of medical and psychosocial interventions required, child psychiatrists should be the only professionals responsible for the initial stages of psychiatric management. Once the degree of suicidal risk is adequately determined and a treatment plan organized, other medical health professionals may be included in the primary care of the child. Toolan, remarking about the process of treatment, notes that the therapist who works with suicidal children may become either overly frightened by the child's suicidal propensities or may "believe that he can omnipotently handle any problem and thus not protect the youngster adequately" (11) (p. 593). These are two of the main issues in the therapist's countertransference and conscious responses that may interfere with an effective intervention approach.

Finally, Lesse states that "the therapist must have a positive feeling with regard to the value of life. There should be no confusion between the act of saving the person's life and the long-term psychotherapeutic re-education of the severely depressed patient. The therapist must have the capacity to phychically transfuse the severely depressed patient during the initial phases of treatment" (1) (p. 311). This principle is of paramount importance for suicidal children for whom it is essential that the therapist be extremely active in fostering an empathic and intense therapeutic relationship.

**Initial Steps**

One of the initial decisions of intervention involves whether to psychiatrically hospitalize a suicidal child in order to protect the child from harm. Eisenberg (12) proposes that the decision to hospitalize the suicidal youngster is based on a risk-rescue ratio and the psychosocial resources of the patient's family. He believes that if the risk-rescue ratio is balanced toward the rescue side and if the parents are concerned and understand the child's problem, outpatient treatment is feasible. However, if these parameters are not met, psychiatric hospitalization is indicated. Another specific indication for psychiatric hospitalization is a child's major affective disorder with concomitant suicidal behavior. Such a child may be at greatest risk for suicidal action. Other parameters indicating the need for psychiatric hospitalization include the child's degree of assaultive behavior, the intensity of depression, anxiety and antisocial behavior, and family turmoil that includes separations and severe parental psychopathology (13). These factors raise the level of unpredictability for the child and parents to form a sufficient therapeutic alliance with the therapist on an outpatient basis.

One of the most important aspects of the initial psychiatric intervention is to interview the parents to assess their degree of insight and ability to make sufficient changes in the family dynamics. The quality of the family members' communication about the child and their psychiatric status regarding their affective states and judgment are important variables to be evaluated. The risk of suicidal behavior will be higher if the family atmosphere is rejecting and humiliating (8). Sabbath (14) proposed that one important factor to promote suicidal behavior is the degree of parental conscious or unconscious wishes that the child interprets as the parents' desire to be rid of him.

The expendable child is one who believes he is no longer tolerated or needed by the family. Therefore, if there is a feeling in the family that the child must die, the risk of suicidal behavior may be too great for the child to safely remain in the home. In such a case, psychiatric hospitalization is warranted.

## PRINCIPLES OF PSYCHOTHERAPY

During psychiatric treatment, it is essential to be aware of certain consistently observable intrapsychic features of suicidal youngsters. Ackerly (10) advocates that psychiatric treatment should focus on helping the child (a) alter his expectation of abandonment and punishment, (b) decrease emphasis on an ideal self, (c) develop healthier identifications, and (d) modify aggressive responses to frustrations and disappointments. This can be accomplished by understanding the therapeutic transference which centers on reliving previous experiences and use of adaptive mechanisms to cope with stress.

During psychiatric treatment the focus must be on depression and its components of low self-esteem, helplessness, hopelessness, and response to loss. Toolan (15) hypothesizes that depression is the reaction to either loss of an object or loss of a state of well-being. Such perception of loss leads to diminished self-esteem and helplessness. Children use a variety of defense mechanisms such as regression, denial, projection, and somatization to ward off these painful feelings. Treatment should be geared to helping the child develop adequate coping mechanisms against stress and painful affects. The therapeutic work with suicidal children includes gratifying wishes, attaining goals that would enhance self-esteem, and diminishing helplessness and hopelessness by strengthening the child's positive relationships to the therapist and other supportive individuals.

Glaser (16) emphasizes that the psychodynamics of children with mild depression are similar to the dynamics of children with severe depression. The essential factor in the dynamics are the child's responses to loss. Therefore, it is essential to address within the treatment setting the psychodynamics of depression but also to assess constantly the descriptive signs and symptoms of the severity of the depression. These include withdrawal, sadness, vegetative signs, and changes in academic and behavior responses. The risk of suicidal behavior is parallel to the degree of depression. Therefore, the therapist must always be aware that the interpretation of the psychodynamics of depression is not the only element that decreases suicidal tendencies. Intervention that may include noninterpretative methods such as use of medication must be involved in the management of severe childhood depression.

Some suicidal children exhibit overt depression while others display extreme rage episodes and ego deficits. These aggressive suicidal children often use suicidal behavior as a device to alter their frustrating environmental conditions. Glaser (16) believes that different therapeutic techniques are needed with these types of suicidal children than with overly depressed suicidal children. He warns that if a therapist does not respond immediately and firmly to such patients, these children will feel uncared for and rejected. He advocates responding to these children's behaviors as if they were inappropriate. Glaser believes that these youngsters often require psychiatric hospitalization to provide a highly structured environment that insures better controls for the patient.

## PSYCHIATRIC OUTPATIENT TREATMENT

Although there are relatively few published reports of outpatient treatment of suicidal children, all reports illustrate some common trends in the treatment process. First, psychiatric treatment is a long-term process lasting more than one year. Second, an intense patient-therapist relationship is needed to resolve the child's conflicts that produced the suicidal behavior. Third, expression of aggression is a central problem for suicidal children. Finally, suicidal behavior is a symptom with multiple conscious and unconscious meanings. Case reports have provided insights into the dynamics and process of psychiatric treatment of suicidal youngsters. The following three examples are of the treatment of a preschool child, an elementary school child, and a teenager. They illustrate the trends just outlined.

## Case Vignettes

Milner (17) describes the psychoanalysis of a three-year-old girl whose refusal of food was her suicidal symptom. Not eating symbolized the child's wish to destroy her mother who the child believed withheld love from her. The analyst interpreted that the child's angry and greedy feelings were worrying her. The child's suicidal ideas represented the child's identification with the bad image of her mother and the child's attempts to destroy her own bad feelings. The child experienced her wishes in oral terms. Food refusal represented the child's defense against her urges to destroy her mother, whom she viewed as wishing to retaliate against her. By means of the transference to the therapist the child relinquished her suicidal symptoms, her sense of self-esteem rose, and her angry wishes were brought under better control. This case illustrated the effects of an early mother-child relationship that fostered a basic sense of badness in the child.

Aleksandrowicz (18) provides a synopsis of the psychotherapy of a seven-and-a-half-year-old girl who jumped from her third-floor apartment window. The child had very poor self-esteem. She blamed her mother for her troubles. She was afraid that her angry wishes could kill other people and felt guilty about her angry feelings toward her mother. This example illustrates the effects of a highly conflictual mother-child relationship that decreased the child's self-esteem and aggravated the child's frustrated, angry, and greedy feelings. Self-punishment was a means of decreasing the child's emotional pain. The intense relationship with the therapist was the main factor in overcoming the child's symptoms by means of working through the effects of the child's fantasies on her coping style.

Kernberg (19) observes that many suicidal dynamics can be found in a single patient. She describes the psychoanalysis of a 15½-year-old girl and shows that various layers of suicidal tendencies can be explored at different stages of the regression within the transference. The suicidal threats gratified multiple needs in the transference. They expressed greediness by trying to make the therapist provide unlimited gratification. They signed omnipotence and control over the therapist by attempting to protect against depreciation. They portrayed the struggles of the patient in regard to her identity as a woman. The transference allowed these issues to be explored and understood.

Each of these clinical reports illustrates the most important features of outpatient psychotherapy. These features include the intensity of the patient-therapist relationship, themes that focused on self-esteem, expression of intense sadness and aggression, and parent-child relationships which were portrayed in the transference with the therapist. Throughout these treatments, risk of suicidal behavior was present and a change in the treamtent plan with the possibility of psychiatric hospitalization needed to be considered frequently.

## PSYCHIATRIC HOSPITAL TREATMENT

Acute psychiatric hospital care of suicidal children focuses on protecting the child while evaluation of appropriate long-term treatment is in process (20). Psychiatric hospital care has greater flexibility than psychiatric outpatient treatment. It utilizes a variety of treatment modalities and incorporates more systematic observations of the child.

The principles of hospital psychotherapy are similar to that of outpatient psychiatric treatment (21). In contrast to outpatient psychotherapy, psychiatric hospital care provides a constant structured environment. In addition, it includes therapists who are available at all times to provide auxiliary ego support to the child in order to maintain a balance of the child's affect expression, impulse regulation, and reality assessment. All hospital staff are therapists who work intensely with every child. Most of the children who are admitted to an acute psychiatric hospital require long-term residential care after acute psychiatric hospitalization.

## ENVIRONMENTAL SUPPORT

Supportive people within the child's environment must be available to interact with the suicidal child in every sphere of his activities. This is easily accomplished in a psychiatric setting. However, during psychiatric outpatient treatment, a therapeutic team must be created to include school personnel, family members, peers, and other emotionally important people who are trained to recognized signs of impending suicidal behavior. These supportive people must have a system of direct communication to the child's therapist who can advise the best means of intervention. Such a therapeutic approach makes childhood suicidal behavior an important concern for a large group of people.

Therapeutic work with parents should be aimed at guiding the parents so that they can provide better parenting for their child. Treatment must help the parents recognize and respond to the seriousness of their child's distress. Another goal is to define and separate spouse conflicts from the parents' conflicts with their child. The parents must develop an objective appreciation of the needs of their child and learn to respond in a manner that will alleviate stress on the child.

Other supports for the child can be provided within the school setting. Educational programs to inform children about signs of suicidal behavior may be helpful in preventing suicides. Educating children to inform teachers, guidance counselors, principals, or school psychologists about suicidal tendencies in themselves or their peers may help diffuse a child's suicidal crisis. Furthermore, it is important to educate school professionals about how to recognize and work with suicidal children. The support system that includes school professionals must be encouraged to form active relationships with mental health professionals who can consult with school personnel on the evaluation and treatment of suicidal children.

## PSYCHOPHARMACOLOGICAL INTERVENTIONS

A variety of medications may be indicated for suicidal children. The choice of medication depends upon the severity of symptoms and type of psychiatric diagnosis of the child. For example, a suicidal child with a severe attention-deficit disorder may require a stimulant drug; an actively psychotic suicidal schizophrenic child may need a major tranquilizer; and a suicidal child with a major depressive disorder may require an antidepressant. Medication utilized in conjunction with appropriate psychotherapy has the greatest beneficial effects for the treatment of suicidal children.

## SUMMARY

Childhood suicidal behavior is a complex symptom that requires a carefully planned treatment program that includes multiple modalities of care. These modalities combine individual, family, environmental, and psychopharmacological interventions. The therapist's personal conscious and unconscious characteristics may have a great influence on treatment outcome. A supportive patient-therapist relationship is one of the most important elements in diminishing the child's suicidal proclivities.

Treatment requires a long-term approach that constantly reassesses potential for serious suicidal risk. Psychiatric hospitalization may be required to protect the child from self-inflicted harm and to allow evaluation and appropriate intervention. Psychotherapy used in conjunction with medication, when indicated, may permit the best therapeutic outcome. Finally, planning systematic studies of psychiatric treatment efficacy for suicidal children remains one of the most challenging aspects of improving prevention measures against suicidal tendencies in youngsters.

## REFERENCES

1. Lesse, S. The Range of Therapies in the Treatment of Severely Depressed Suicidal Patients. *Am. J. Psychother.* 29:308–326, 1975.

2. Corder, B. F. and Haizlip, T. M. Recognizing Suicidal Behavior in Children. *Medical Times,* September Issue, pp. 25S–30S, 1982.

3. Hodgman, C. H. and Roberts, F. N. Adolescent Suicide and the Pediatrician. *J. Pediatr.* 101:113–123, 1982.

4. Cohen-Sandler, R. and Berman, A. L. Diagnosis and Treatment of

Childhood Depression and Self-destructive Behavior. *J. Fam. Pract.* 11:51–58, 1980.

5. Lewis, M. and Solnit, A. J. The Adolescent in a Suicidal Crisis: Collaborative Care in a Pediatric Ward. In *Modern Perspectives in Child Development,* Solnit, A. and Provence, S. Eds. New York International Press, New York, 1963.

6. British Working Party in Child and Adolescent Psychiatry. The Management of Parasuicide in Young People under Sixteen. *Bri. J. Psychiatry* 7:182–185, 1982.

7. Glaser, K. Suicidal Children—Management. *Am. J. Psychother.* 25:27–36, 1971.

8. Stone, M. The Suicidal Patient: Points Concerning Diagnosis and Intensive Treatment. *Psychiatr. Q.* 52:52–70, 1980.

9. Schechter, M. D. The Recognition and Treatment of Suicide in Children. In *Clues to Suicide,* Schneidman, E. and Farberow, N., Eds. McGraw-Hill Book Company, New York, 1957.

10. Ackerly, W. C. Latency-age Children Who Threaten or Attempt to Kill Themselves. *J. Am. Acad. Child Psychiatry* 6:242–261, 1967.

11. Toolan, J. M. Depression and Suicidal Behavior. In *Treatment of Emotional Disorders in Children and Adolescents,* Sholevar, P., Ed. Spectrum Publications, New York, 1980.

12. Eisenberg, L. Adolescent Suicide: on Taking Arms against a Sea of Trouble. *Pediatrics* 31:315–320, 1980.

13. Pfeffer, C. R. and Plutchik, R. Psychopathology of Latency-age Children: Relation to Treatment Planning. *J. Nerv. Ment. Dis.* 17:193–197, 1982.

14. Sabbath, J. C. The Suicidal Adolescent—the Expendable Child. *J. Am. Acad. Child Psychiatry* 8:272–289, 1969.

15. Toolan, J. M. Therapy of Depressed and Suicidal Children. *Am. J. Psychother.* 32:243–251, 1978.

16. Glaser, K. Psychopathic Patterns in Depressed Adolescents. *Am. J. Psychother.* 35:368–382, 1981.

17. Milner, M. A Suicidal Symptom in a Child of Three. *Int. J. Psychoanal.* 25:53–61, 1974.

18. Aleksandrowicz, M. K. The Biological Strangers: an Attempted Suicide of a 7½-year-old Girl. *Bull. Menniger Clin.* 39:163–176.

19. Kernberg, P. F. The Analysis of a 15½-year-old Girl with Suicidal Tendencies. In *The Analyst and the Adolescent at Work,* Harley, M., Ed. Quadrangle, New York Times Book Company, New York, 1974.

20. Pfeffer, C. R. Psychiatric Hospital Treatment of Suicidal Children. *Suicide Life Threat. Behav.* 8:150–160, 1977.

21. Pfeffer, C. R. A Model for Acute Psychiatric Inpatient Treatment of Latency-age Children. *Hosp. Community Psychiatry* 30:547–551, 1979.

# 22 Depressed Hospitalized Preschoolers

**Perihan A. Rosenthal, M.D.**
**Stuart Rosenthal, M.D.**
**Mairin B. Doherty, M.D.**
**Donna Santora, M.D.**

*The authors explored the depressive symptomatology in 9 hospitalized preschool children with suicidal thoughts and behaviors and compared them with 16 suicidal and 16 behavior-disordered outpatient preschoolers. Results indicate that suicidal preschool-age inpatients show significantly more morbid ideas, depressed mood, weepiness, and parental psychopathology than the suicidal and behavior-disordered preschool outpatients. Two of the children did not suppress cortisol post-dexamethasone.*

Studies of suicidal thoughts and behaviors in psychiatrically hospitalized children are scanty. Rosenthal and Rosenthal previously studied 16 preschoolers (1–2), however, they were all outpatients. Bender (3) reported a 13- to 17-year follow-up study of children observed between 1936 and 1938 on the children's ward of the Psychiatric Division of Bellevue Hospital who had fantasied, threatened, and attempted suicide (4). Her follow-up report was complete only concerning the 18 children under the age of 13, but 17 suicidal adolescents had also been identified from the approximately 2000 children admitted to the children's service during those years. Her youngest patient was a 6-year-old boy. In the course of 14 years during which all of these children reached adulthood, none committed suicide.

Bender (1) commented that

They tended either to direct their aggression against the environment in a social delinquent behavior, or they submitted to the intolerable situation, suffering emotional and intellectual flattening and, in many instances, accepting refuge in institutions.

Mattson, Seese and Hawkins (5) studied 170 children, aged 7 to 17.9 years, who were evaluated as psychiatric emergencies during a 2-year-period at the University Hospital, Cleveland. In this population, 75 children were referred because of suicidal attempts or serious threats; of these 33 required inpatient admission and 17 remained inpatient for over 2 months.

Paulson, Stone, and Sposto (6) identified 39 children aged 12 and under from 662 inpatients and/or outpatients of the Child Psychiatry Division of the UCLA Neuropsychiatric Institute from July, 1970 through June, 1974. Cases included in the study showed severe depression, suicidal attempts, suicidal behaviors/suicidal threats, suicidal ideation, death wishes, self-abuse, and/or danger to self and others. Five cases under 4 years of age were subsequently excluded because their behavior did not appear to have the intention of terminating life. Of the 34 remaining children, two were 4 years and three were 5 years of age. It is unclear which children in their sample were inpatients. The length of follow-up for the 13 children located was from 3 to 7 years, with a mean of 4.4 years. None had committed suicide.

Pfeffer and co-workers (7) identified some degree of suicidal risk in 72 percent of 58 children between ages 6 to 12 years, consecutively admitted to a psychiatric hospital from December 1976 to June 1978. This sample was predominately of lower socioeconomic status and a replication and cross-validation of this earlier work (8) studied 65 children, ages 6 to 12 years, from predominantly middle-socioeconomic-status families, who were admitted between March 1979 and June 1981. In this population, 78.5 percent showed suicidal ideas, threats or attempts.

Tishler (9) reported 4 children with self-destructive behavior who were seen in a children's hospital emergency room. The two younger children (4 and 5 years, respectively) tried to harm themselves, one by ingestion and the other by hanging.

To our knowledge, this study of suicidal thoughts and behaviors in psychiatrically hospitalized preschoolers is the first to be reported.

## POPULATION

Nine patients with a history of suicidal behaviors were identified from a total of 23 preschoolers admitted between April 1, 1981, and July 1, 1983, to the Child Mental Health Unit at the University of Massachusetts Medical Center. Children were referred by their pediatricians, mental health professional, Head-Start personnel or Massachusetts Department of Social Service. The 1 girl and 8 boys were white, and ranged in age from 3.5 to 5.5 years with a median age of 4 years. Two children were from middle-class backgrounds and others from lower socioeconomic status. One family was intact, 7 divorced (4 remarried) and there was 1 single parent. Three children were referred because of suspected suicidal behaviors (jumping from roofs, self-stabbing, and overdose), 3 because of nonsuicidal self-injury, 2 because of serious aggression to others, and 1 for fire setting. In those cases where suicidal ideation was not appreciated by parents at the time of admission, they subsequently recalled incidents of life-endangering behavior which they had failed to identify as potentially suicidal, i.e., running in front of a car, cutting self with a razor blade, fire setting with a potential for self-immolation, and forceful self-injury at a time of emotional upset, e.g., banging head on a stone hearth or slamming whole body against a wall.

## ASSESSMENT

Following a preadmission psychiatric interview with the child, parent(s), and referring agent, the decision to hospitalize was made. Thereafter, diagnostic information was gathered by an interdisciplinary team to compile a bio-psycho-social data base, which included a developmental history, mental status evaluation, and a pediatric, neurological and neurodevelopmental examination. Eight of 9 children had a dexamethasone suppression test.

The mean length of stay was 26 days and during that time, suicidal ideas, threats, and gestures were carefully observed by nursing and ward milieu staff involved in direct patient care. They reported morbid thoughts, verbal expression of death wishes, accident proneness, impulsivity, disregard for personal safety, and self-injurious behavior. An individual diagnostic play assessment by an expressive arts therapist (DS) explored the children's thoughts and feelings as projected onto toys in their symbolic play and this helped to clarify the psychodynamic ramifications of the suicidal ideation and the intentionality of their behavior. Parents were subsequently invited to view these play sessions and frequently expressed amazement at how perceptive, vulnerable, and hopeless their child felt in the face of the stresses that had impinged on them.

The children were diagnosed by their attending psychiatrist (MBD) who pooled information from a number of sources and ascribed the diagnoses according to *DSM–III* criteria.

Finally, all children were assessed by a research psychiatrist (PAR) using the Preschool Depression Scale (PDS). She was blind to patient past history, reason for admission, and hospital diagnoses. The Preschool Depression Scale is an objective observational scale, which records information on 36 items in 4 major areas (cognitive/developmental maturity; temperamental/ interactional pattern; affective/behavioral presentation; and vegetative/psychophysiological symptoms). Patients scoring under 65 are estimated to have a diagnosis other than depression, 65 to 100, mild to moderate depression, and 100 or over, severe depressive symptomatology.

The 9 suicidal inpatient preschoolers were assessed for type of death-seeking behavior, depressive symptomatology, behavioral difficulties, parent-child interactive factors, and were compared with 16 suicidal and 16 behavior-disordered outpatient preschoolers previously reported.

TABLE 22-1
Type of Death-Seeking Behavior[a]

|  | Inpatients (N = 9) | Outpatients (N = 16) |
|---|---|---|
| Purposely setting self afire | 1 | 1 |
| Drug ingestion | 2 | 4 |
| Jumping from high places | 2 | 5 |
| Cutting/stabbing | 3 | 1 |
| Running into fast traffic | 1 | 5 |
| Putting rope around neck | 1 | 0 |

[a]These are initial behaviors obtained by history.

## RESULTS

Table 22-1 shows the types of death-seeking behaviors found in the inpatient and outpatient populations. Although differences did not reach statistical significance, inpatients showed more episodes of cutting or stabbing and outpatients greater incidence of running into fast traffic.

Comparing suicidal inpatients and outpatients in Table 22-2, the 2 groups had similar occurrences: sleep disturbances (88 percent and 75 percent), eating disturbances (11 percent and 12 percent), and loss of interest (33 percent and 38 percent).

TABLE 22-2
Depressive Symptomatology[a]

|  | Suicidal Inpatients (N = 9) | | Suicidal Outpatients (N = 16) | | Behavior-Disordered Outpatients (N = 16) | |
|---|---|---|---|---|---|---|
|  | N | % | N | % | N | % |
| Depressed mood | 9 | 99 | 8 | 50 | 4 | 25 |
| Weepiness | 7 | 77 | 4 | 25 | 4 | 25 |
| Loss of interest | 3 | 33 | 6 | 38 | 0 | — |
| Hyperactivity | 8 | 88 | 9 | 56 | 15 | 94 |
| Hypoactivity | 1 | 11 | 7 | 42 | 0 | — |
| Sleep disturbances | 8 | 88 | 12 | 75 | 9 | 56 |
| Eating disturbances | 1 | 11 | 2 | 12 | 2 | 12 |
| Morbid ideas | 9 | 100 | 8 | 50 | 0 | — |

[a]All symptoms but weepiness significantly differentiated suicidal from behavior-disorder outpatients.

However 100 percent of inpatients vs 50 percent of outpatients showed depressed mood and morbid ideas (p < 0.05). Inpatients also showed a significantly greater incidence of weepiness (p < 0.05) and hyperactivity (p < 0.05). Hypoactivity was the only symptom which was more prevalent in the suicidal outpatient group.

The suicidal inpatients and outpatients were more clearly differentiated from behavior-disordered outpatients by morbid ideas, depressed mood, and weepiness. Although hyperactivity characterized the majority of the behavior-disordered outpatients and the suicidal inpatients both hyperactivity and hypoactivity was present in the suicidal outpatient. The 3 groups were comparable with regard to other depressive symptoms including irritability, feelings of helplessness, somatic complaints, separation anxiety, and nightmares (Table 22-2).

Table 22-3 reviews other behaviors which distinguished the groups. Suicidal inpatients and outpatients showed a high incidence of nonsuicidal self-aggression and failure to show pain or cry after injury. The behavior-disordered outpatients showed significantly less aggression to self and all showed the pain and crying response to injury. The suicidal outpatients showed a significantly higher incidence of running away from home than did either the inpatient population or the outpatient behavior-disordered group.

Table 22-4 reviews parent-child interactive factors. The earlier

TABLE 22-3
Other Distinguishing Behaviors

| | Suicidal Inpatients (N = 9) | | Suicidal Outpatients (N = 16) | | Behavior-Disordered Outpatients (N = 16) | |
|---|---|---|---|---|---|---|
| | N | % | N | % | N | % |
| Aggression to self (nonsuicidal) | 8 | 88 | 13 | 81 | 5 | 31 |
| No pain, crying after injury | 8 | 88 | 12 | 75 | 0 | 0 |
| Running away from home for few hours | 2 | 22 | 11 | 66 | 2 | 12 |

TABLE 22-4
Parental Behaviors

|  | Suicidal Inpatients (N = 9) | | Suicidal Outpatients (N = 16) | | Behavior-Disordered Outpatients (N = 16) | |
|---|---|---|---|---|---|---|
|  | N | % | N | % | N | % |
| Child unwanted | 6 | 66 | 13 | 81 | 4 | 25 |
| Child abused or neglected | 7 | 77 | 13 | 81 | 4 | 25 |
| Intense anger displayed toward child | 5 | 55 | 4 | 25 | 11 | 69 |

study had shown a greater frequency of unwanted children and child abuse/neglect in the suicidal outpatients compared to the behavior-disordered outpatients, however, anger was more frequently displayed onto the child in the behavior-disordered group. These items did not differentiate between suicidal inpatients and suicidal outpatients, and this was also the situation with other parent/child interactive factors, such as inconsistent handling of the child, projective identification with the child, and vicarious gratification from the child's behavior.

Suicidal inpatients and outpatients did not differ significantly in the frequency and type of parental psychopathology in their families, however, family psychiatric history did differentiate the suicidal inpatients group from the behavior-disordered patients. Forty percent of the inpatient families had one or multiple family members who attempted suicide and 55 percent of the mothers had diagnoses within the depressive spectrum complicated by substance abuse, compared with none of the mothers of the behavior-disordered outpatients.

Table 22-5 shows dexamethasone suppression test (DST) findings, preschool depression scale (PDS) scores, and *DSM-III* diagnosis. PDS ratings identified profound depressive symptomatology (scored over 100) in 3 children (#3, 7, 9), mild and moderate symptomatology (scored between 65–100) in 4 children (#1, 2, 4, 8) and absence of depressive symptomatology in the remaining two children (#5, 6). Accord-

TABLE 22-5
Diagnosis and DST Findings

| Child | Age | Dexamethasone Suppression Test (DST) | Preschool Depression Scale (PDS) | DSM-III Diagnosis |
|---|---|---|---|---|
| 1 | 4 | not given | 90 | Dysthymic disorder |
| 2 | 5 | suppressed | 80 | Atypical depressive disorder w/complicated bereavement |
| 3 | 3 | suppressed | 111 | Posttraumatic stress disorder |
| 4 | 3.3 | suppressed | 70 | Posttraumatic stress disorder |
| 5 | 3.1 | suppressed | 58 | Oppositional disorder w/depressed mood |
| 6 | 3 | did not suppress | 45 | Adjustment disorder w/depressed mood |
| 7 | 5 | did not suppress | 105 | Bipolar disorder (mixed) |
| 8 | 4.5 | suppressed | 75 | Dysthymic disorder |
| 9 | 5 | suppressed | 110 | Major depressive disorder |

ing to *DSM-III*, 3 children met criteria for major affective disorder (#2, 7, 9) and this was substantiated by high scores on PDS. However, only one of the children (#7) with Major Depressive Disorder (Bipolar Disorder mixed) failed to suppress his plasma cortisol below 5μg/per dL post 1 mg dexamethasone.

Patients with moderate scores on the Preschool Depression Scale were those who showed symptoms of behavioral disturbances with dysthymic disorder (#1, 8) and posttraumatic stress disorder (#4). Two other children, who had a low score on the PDS, were diagnosed as having oppositional disorder with depressed mood (#5), and adjustment disorder with depressed mood (#6). Patient #6 failed to suppress DST and his symptomatology prior to admission suggested a major depression which rapidly improved with the environmental change. This patient's mother was medicated for clinical depression during the child's hospitalization. Child #3, who scored high in PDS as profoundly depressed, was diagnosed by *DSM-III* as having posttraumatic stress syndrome prior to and during his first few days in the hospital. This patient had vegetative symptoms, which profoundly depressed moods, psychomotor retardation, and suicidal behavior. However, his symptoms disappeared with the environmental changes.

## ANALYSIS OF SUICIDAL THOUGHTS AND BEHAVIORS

A review of the psychodynamics of the suicidal thoughts and behaviors in the hospitalized preschoolers revealed motivations similar to those that characterized the suicidal outpatients reported previously. These included self-punishment (6 boys); reunion with a central nurturant figure (1 boy); escape and rectification of an unbearable life situation (1 girl); self-punishment and reunion (1 boy).

### Self-Punishment

Reality testing for the self-punishment group became dominated by a harsh and punitive superego, which in turn reflected a harsh and punitive family environment. All children in this group had been physically abused by their parents and came to regard themselves with the same hostility and criticism that others had expressed towards them. Children who were blamed for shortcomings in their parents or inadequacies in their environment readily assumed that they deserved punishment, and their low self-esteem and self-denigration became the nucleus for self-destructive behavior. This group of children did not view death as reversible.

### Case Vignette 1

Billy, a 5-year-old boy, was hospitalized with both homicidal and suicidal thoughts and behaviors. At home he responded to minor upsets with rage and retaliation, throwing things around the house. He sat on his infant sister's face, twisted her arm, and occasionally engaged in self-harming behaviors such as punching his head and picking at his fingers until they bled. Billy's mother reported childhood abuse and placement in an orphanage during her adolescent years. The family history was positive for substance abuse, with alcoholism in biological father and drug abuse in biological mother both pre- and postnatally. Mother was hospitalized several times for attempted suicide and she had a family history of major depression and depressive spectrum disorder, including substance abuse. Billy's birth and delivery were normal. During his first year of life his mother separated from his father, and then relocated many times due to threats of violence in the family. When Billy was placed in day care at age 2, his caretakers described his behavior as "driven" and he was eventually excluded from the program due to his violent behavior towards other children.

When Billy was 3 years old, his mother remarried and he became increasingly agitated, irritable and oppositional, with reports of recurrent nightmares. Billy was at times physically abused by his mother and stepfather who resorted to whipping when enraged by his behavior. Prior to hospitalization, Benadryl, Ritalin, and Mellaril were prescribed to control Billy's behavior without any positive outcome.

During the course of hospitalization, Billy showed marked fluctuations in mood with pressure of speech, labile affect, grandiosity, and depression. In play he exhibited themes of sibling abuse in which he choked or smothered babies and also expressed suicidal ideation, stating frequently, "I am bad" and symbolically stabbing himself in the forehead, or poking his eyes and hitting his penis with a rubber hose. The interactive pattern between Billy and his mother indicated an enmeshed symbiotic relationship in which mother tended to project her thoughts and feelings from her childhood experiences and her failed marriage onto Billy in a variety of situations. The diagnostic impression was that of a bipolar disorder, mixed, and Billy, in fact, showed failure of cortisol suppression following dexamethasone with a 4 p.m. reading of 6.4 $\mu$g/dl.

The initial hospitalization sought to stabilize Billy's mental status, whch was achieved with low dose Mellaril and to address issue of anxious attachment, separation, and anger in the mother-child relationship. However, with a shift in family dynamics, mother decompensated when Billy was discharged from the hospital, she made several suicidal attempts by ingestion and required hospitalization for herself for several months. When mother was again discharged from the hospital, Billy's aggressive and suicidal behavior escalated. He set fire to himself, tried to stab himself with a kitchen knife, and was found roaming around the neighborhood in the middle of the night. During his second hospitalization, Billy disclosed that he had been sexually abused by stepfather. Billy was eventually placed in a residential treatment setting and was making a reasonable adjustment when last reviewed.

## Reunion

Suicidal behaviors motivated by reunion fantasies are dictated by the child's wish to rejoin a loved one. This group of children viewed death as reversible.

*Case Vignette 2*

John, a 5-year-old youngster, was reportedly "blocking everything out" since his grandfather's death, had become aggressive and assaultive toward his sister and other children. He had begun waking at 4:30 A.M. to engage in disruptive behavior around the house, e.g., removing food from the refrigerator and making a mess with it in the kitchen. Mother also reported that he had on one occasion cut his wrist with a razor blade. John's parents were divorced and mother had remarried but continued to be closely involved with and dependent on her own father who was the grandparent who died. Mother's family history was positive for depressive spectrum disorder, substance abuse, and suicidal attempts in a number of family members. John had two foster placements due to tensions in the family and his mother's inability to cope and was reportedly physically abused during one such foster placement. During John's hospitalization, he showed himself to be particularly sensitive to his grandfather's death and his mother's reaction to it. In play therapy he reenacted his grandfather's death and demonstrated how the coffin had remained over ground because of a snow storm. He portrayed his mother as sad, crying, and unavailable to him. In play he developed the theme of his grandfather breaking out of his tomb to reunite the family. He also talked about babies who take pills to kill themselves so they can go to heaven to be with grandpa.

John's diagnosis was felt to be in the depressive spectrum with a complicated bereavement and it was felt that his experience of loss had been intensified due to his earlier deprivation and the central role of the grandfather as a nurturant attachment figure at times of mother's unavailability. Upon discharge, mother and John were referred to individual and family therapy around completion of the mourning process and attachment issues in the mother-child relationship. However, mother subsequently sought, once more, a voluntary foster placement for John because of her inability to cope with the demands of parenthood.

## Rectification

This group-motivated suicidal behaviors seem dictated by instinctual forces that determine the relevant fantasy (wish fulfillment).

### Case Vignette 3

Prior to her referral for psychiatric hospitalization, Beatrice, a 4-year-old girl, had been hospitalized on three occasions following repeated overdoses with her antiseizure medications. All three pill-taking incidents allegedly took place when mother was in the house in close proximity to the child but not actually supervising her behavior. Mother, a single parent with serious personality problems, was living in adequate housing in an unsafe community where the child was left outside without supervision. Mother, who had a history of alcohol and drug abuse, was seen as the black sheep of her middle-class professional family and her daughter was not accepted by her grandparents. Beatrice was a mildly neurologically handicapped youngster, with an abnormal EEG and delayed speech, but otherwise her pediatric examination was within normal limits. In her play therapy during hospitalization, she fed pills to the baby doll and then put the doll in an ambulance saying "baby is sick and needs to go to the hospital. She will die and she will come back and be with mommy." Mother was narcissitically connected to Beatrice and looked to the child for gratification of all of her wishes and needs. Due to the chronic nature of mother's personality problems, child was placed in foster care and eventually released for adoption.

## Escape

Suicidal behavior in this review category is an act of desperation by a young child who can think of no other solution for dealing with an intolerable life situation and desires to be rescued.

We did not have a patient who had an escape fantasy in the inpatient group. However, we had several in the outpatient group.

*Case Vignette 4*

R., age 5, was residing at group home for abused and neglected children. Any time he was questioned whether he wished to return to his mother or stepfather, he threatened with jumping from the third story window or run in front of a fast-moving car. He was so terrified of his mother that he would rather kill himself than live in the same household with her.

## DISCUSSION

The 39 percent frequency of suicidal behavior in the preschool-age patients admitted to a child psychiatric setting is similar to the 44 percent rate of suicidal behavior reported by Mattson and coworkers in latency-age children and adolescents seen as emergency referrals. Pfeffer and coworkers report 72 percent and 78.5 percent frequency of suicidal risk in the latency-age children admitted to their psychiatric inpatient unit, indicating that the behavior may be less prevalent in hospitalized preschoolers or that a hospitalized preschool population is biased by the referral pattern for this age group. In fact, the 23 preschoolers in our patient population were referred for the following reasons: suicidal behaviors (5), aggression to self or others (13), developmental concerns (13), abuse (9), fire setting (2).

All of the suicidal inpatients showed impulsivity and hyper-activity as part of their mental status presentation. However, impulsivity did not characterize the suicidal behavior, as all of the children demonstrated long-standing suicidal thoughts and repeated self-injurious behavior, associated with angry dysphoric feelings. However, there were also differences in the types of death-seeking behaviors in the inpatient and outpatient populations. The inpatient preschoolers tended to have more alerting presentations, e.g. purposely setting self on fire, cutting and stabbing, and putting a rope around neck, whereas the outpatient group tended to have behaviors that might be considered accidental if they resulted in death, e.g. drug ingestion, jumping from a high place, and running into traffic. All of the suicidal inpatients were markedly aggressive towards others and 89 percent showed aggression to self with behaviors such as biting, punching, scratching, purposely falling down, and bumping into furniture. Depressive states were also common in this population and appeared to occur in the context of disturbed attachment behavior with primary caretakers, depressive symptomatology ranged from major affective disorders to dysthymic disorder and adjustment disorder with depressed mood. The high incidence of depressive spectrum disorder and substance abuse in the parents of these inpatients suggested a depressive diathesis in the children.

The suicidal inpatients groups were similar to the behavior-disordered outpatients in their manifestation of impulsivity and hyperactivity. However, hyperactivity and impulsivity in the suicidal inpatients were more in the nature of psychomotor agitation.

## SUMMARY

In this study, careful evaluation of life-threatening as well as seemingly accidental behaviors in preschool-age children revealed a high incidence of depressed affect, morbid preoccupation with death, and thoughts of self-injury in the suicidal group. The psychodynamic ramification of these behaviors is frequently found in the transactional matrix of the family where the child has been exposed to a depriving and punitive environment and fails to modulate aggressive impulses to self and others. Rejecting caretakers communicate their disinterest in the physical integrity of the child's body, leading in turn to a disinvestment in it by the child.

# REFERENCES

1. Rosenthal, P. A. and Rosenthal, S. Fact or Fallacy of Preschool Age Children. *Children Today* 12:21–25, 1983.

2. Rosenthal, P. A. and Rosenthal, S. Death-Seeking Behavior by Preschool Children. *Am. J. Psychiatry* 141:520–525, 1984.

3. Bender, L. Children Preoccupied with Suicide: In *Aggression, Hostility, and Anxiety in Children*, Bender L. Ed. Charles C. Thomas, Springfield, Ill., 1953.

4. Bender, L. and Schilder, P. Suicidal Preoccupations and Attempts in Children. *Am. J. Orthopsychiatry* 7:225–234, 1937.

5. Matson, A., Sesse, L. R., et al. Suicidal Behavior as a Child Psychiatric Emergency. *Arch. Gen. Psychiatry* 20:100–109, 1969.

6. Paulson, J. M., et al. Suicidal Potential and Behavior in Children Ages 4–12. *Suicide Life Threat. Behav.* 8:225–242, 1978.

7. Pfeffer, C. R., et al. Suicidal Behavior in Latency-Age Children: An Empirical Study. *J. Am. Child Psychiatry* 18:679–693, 1973.

8. Pfeffer, C. R., et al. Suicidal Behavior in Latency-Age Psychiatric Inpatients: A Replication and Cross Validation. *J. Am. Acad. Child Psychiatry* 21:564–570, 1982.

9. Tishler, C. L. Intentional Self-Destructive Behavior in Children Under Age Ten. *Clin. Pediatr.* 19:451–454, 1980.

10. Rosenthal, P. A. and Doherty, M. Differentiating Primary Affective Disorders from Situational Depression and Other Behavior Problems in Preschool Children by "Preschool Depression Scale." Presented at the Annual Meeting of American Academy of Child Psychiatry, San Francisco, CA. Oct. 1983 (mimeo).

11. Hendrick, I. Suicide as a Wish Fulfillment. *Psychiatr. Q.* 14:30–42, 1940.

12. Klein, M. *Notes on Some Schizoid Mechanism: Development in Psychoanalysis,* Hogarth, London, 1952.

13. Carlson, G. A. and Cantwell, D. P. Suicidal Behavior and Depression in Children and Adolescents. *Am. J. Child Psychiatry* 2:361–368, 1982.

# 23 Outpatient Management of the Suicidal Child

## Lillian H. Robinson, M.D.

*Suicidal children often can be managed without hospitalization. Work with parents is necessary to alter precipitating environmental conditions. Psychotherapy is indicated for the suicidal children who need help in altering aggressive responses to frustration. Drug therapy may prove a useful adjunct. Two illustrative cases are presented.*

The title, "Outpatient Management of the Suicidal Child," may seem like an incongruity; however, therapists who treat children do manage suicidal children as outpatients, sometimes by choice, and perhaps sometimes without realizing that the children are suicidal. It is only recently that it has been acknowledged that depression occurs in childhood (1-3). There is still reluctance to recognize the suicidal child despite the fact that suicidal behavior is a major cause of emergency referrals to child psychiatry clinics and inpatient facilities (4-5). Another difficulty is that "suicidal" is not an exact designation. A continuum exists, with, at one end, the discouraged normal child who occasionally feels it might be nice to be dead, and at the other end, the despairing child who sees suicide as the only possible solution to his dilemma. Hopelessness and helplessness regarding a real or fantasied stressful situation are seen in suicidal patients of all ages, including children. However, the overt expression of this feeling may vary considerably, so that the suicidal wish or intention may not be obvious.

## ISSUES IN DIAGNOSIS

Seriously depressed children may present with quite different symptoms from those usually seen in depressed adults. They may appear "bad" rather than sad and often are brought for evaluation only because of disruptive behavior, school difficulties, or a psychosomatic problem. It is, therefore, important in evaluating all children, and particularly those who are suffering from depression, to assess carefully the suicide risk (6–8). Diagnosis of childhood depression and assessment of suicide risk is easier when the evaluator is aware of ways by which children defend themselves against depressive affect. Careful attention should be paid to fantasy material obtained from dreams, spontaneous play, or projective techniques. A clue to depression is the child's preoccupation with certain themes including thwarting, blame or criticism, loss and abandonment, personal injury, death, and suicide. One should also look for overt verbal expression of depression and suicidal ideation including talk of hopelessness, helplessness, guilt, being unattractive, worthless, unloved, or intrigued with death. The child's mood and behavior should also be noted, including psychomotor retardation, sadness, crying, disturbance in appetite and sleep, and certain defenses against depression including hyperactivity, aggressiveness, and various maneuvers which serve to distract the young patient from sadness and other painful feelings related to a perceived loss.

Cytryn and McKnew (9) have presented data which suggest that depressive fantasy is almost always present in depressed children. They found that depressive verbal expression occurs less frequently and that depressive mood and behavior is the least frequent in these children. Other authors have stressed anhedonia. Children will often complain of being bored or say that activities which they used to enjoy are not fun anymore. Loss of the capacity to enjoy play is an important indication of severe depression in childhood. Despair and hopelessness are less common than a sense of helplessness. Cytryn and McKnew (9) have suggested that "the child's maturation and growth promote a sense of optimism and exuberance and hope, all of which help to ward off any sense of despair or hopelessness." Also, in infancy the maturational push and the ability to substitute love objects counteracts the depressive process and may explain why depression in infants are short-lived except when substitute objects are not available. These authors suggest that in early childhood and latency the increasingly rich fantasy life, coupled with immature reality testing and an incompletely developed conscience, can combine to contain the depressive process on the fantasy level. Conversely, the child's immature concept of death as a temporary state and later on as permanent, but not something which will happen to him, may make suicide seem a safe way to punish parents (10–12).

In explaining the difference between the clinical picture of the depressed child and the adult, Anthony (13) attributed it to the inability of the child to talk about his feelings, incomplete superego development, and the absence of a consistent self-representation. He listed the following symptoms of prepubertal depression: bouts of crying, some flatness of affect, fear of death of self or parents, irritability, psychosomatic complaints, loss of appetite and energy, school problems, and alternate clinging to the parents and hostile rejection of them. Glaser (14) contributed to the understanding of the so-called "masked depression" in children in which the depressive affect is not obvious, and instead, one sees various defenses against depression. "Acting-out" behavior is the most common mask of depression in children, according to Lesse (15).

A number of authors including Ackerly (16), Anthony (13), and Pfeffer (17) have stressed that a parent is often severely depressed, and may behave toward the child in a disparaging, reproachful, and deflating manner, particularly when the child's depression is defended against with troublesome behavior. Very frequently the family and school regard such a child as mean, lazy, or uncooperative, and are unaware of the child's depression.

Children with impaired judgment due to organic brain

syndrome or schizophrenia may be dangerous to themselves; however, for the purpose of this discussion the term "suicidal children" will be restricted to those whose self-destructive impulses and behaviors are due to depression, either overt or masked.

## RELEVANCE OF ETIOLOGY FOR THERAPY

Whenever possible, therapy should counteract etiological factors in an illness. Unfortunately, the etiology of depression is not completely understood. It is clear, however, that an interplay of social, psychological, and genetic and biological factors can precipitate depression and suicide in children.

### I. Social Factors

1. Loss or separation from parents or other caretakers with whom the children have a close relationship.
2. Physical abuse, sexual abuse, neglect, denigration or rejection by parents.
3. Excessive demands from parents for conformity and dedication to duty.
4. Family disorganization, economic stress, overcrowding, violent parental quarrels, and psychopathology in parents, particularly depression and drug abuse.

### II. Psychological Factors

1. Difficulties in relating to others because of fears, conflicts or faulty learning.
2. Inadequate ego-defenses to cope with the feelings engendered by loss, including sadness, anger, guilt, anxiety, lowered self-esteem, and helplessness.
3. Inadequate separation-individuation, resulting in problems with dependency and ambivalence toward the mother.

### III. Genetic and Biological Factors

1. Serious, shy temperaments.
2. Metabolic factors which are, as yet, poorly understood.
3. Organic brain damage.

When managing a suicidal child, one should try to reverse the predisposing conditions when possible, and encourage discussion of, and adaptation to those conditions which cannot be changed and must be endured. The therapist's aim should be to deal with the psychological factors, helping the child alter aggressive responses to frustration and disappointment, and learn to enjoy life in spite of these disappointments. The following discussion of work with parents and psychotherapy of children who become suicidal is organized in reference to the social factors mentioned above.

## CHILDREN WHO EXPERIENCE LOSS OF CARETAKERS

The normal reaction to loss is grief and mourning; however, if the ego is unable to cope with the loss feelings, pathological depression is seen instead. Children's response to loss depends upon their developmental level. The work of Spitz (18) made it possible to understand the frequently fatal anaclitic depression in infants deprived of their primary caretaker. The treatment for this devastating illness is to restore the loss, or quickly provide a good substitute.

According to Mahler (19), a basic depressive affect emerges during separation-individuation. This process involves a psychological loss which can be difficult for a toddler to cope with, particularly if there has been some early deprivation. Loss at this time increases the normal ambivalence for the mother whom the child alternately rejects and clings to. Anthony (13) has emphasized the difficulty depressed mothers have in letting their children go, thereby increasing their vulnerability to separations.

Bowlby (20) described a predictable sequence of behavior in toddlers separated from their mothers: first the child angrily protests and demands his mother back; later, he becomes quieter and apparently less hopeful that she will return. This is referred to as the stage of despair. Eventually, the child becomes detached, appears to forget his mother and may fail to recognize her when she returns. After the mother and child are reunited, the child who has reached the stage of detachment continues to be unresponsive for a time and then becomes clingy with the mother, as well as anxious and rageful. If the separation is prolonged or repeated, there is danger that he may remain detached and never recover a close, meaningful, affectionate tie to the parent. Although this sequence is characterisic of all forms of mourning, there are certain differences in the process in young children because they have a different appreciation of time than older individuals. Detachment may develop prematurely in order to protect these young children from overwhelming sadness and anger. Bowlby (2) asserts that anger is an invariable reaction to loss and that its expression is necessary in order to complete the process of mourning. He likens the young child's reaction to pathological mourning in adults which is characterized by the inability to express the angry urges to recover the lost love object. The child who has lost his mother continues to be very attached to her, but this attachment, and his urges to recover and reproach her, have to be quickly repressed. An ego-split sometimes occurs in children in which one part of the personality denies that the love object is really lost.

I see many examples of this defense at Milne Boys Home in New Orleans. Children at this municipal home for disadvantaged boys frequently have had little contact with their fathers through the years due to early dissolution of their parents' relationships. A striking number of these youngsters deny the loss and insist that they frequently see their fathers. When pressed for details of the last encounter, they often tell of thinking they recognized him at a distance on the street sometime during the past year. They feel that he is near and potentially available to them.

The loss of the parent may be relative rather than absolute. Children feel they have lost their mother's love if she becomes depressed or if she is busy with a new baby, of if there are repeated separations because of her work, or because illness of the child or parent necessitates hospitalization. The loss may seem insignificant to individuals who are not aware of the young child's need for constancy of outer providers. Parental divorce or separation usually constitutes a double loss for a child. One parent leaves and the remaining parent is often so preoccupied with adjusting to changes that he or she is emotionally unavailable to the child. When the parent is lost through death, the child may wish to die because this seems a good way to be reunited with the parent.

These losses of the care-taking loved person precipitate mourning or depression at the time of the loss and also sensitize the child to depression later on, when a new loss can stir up old feelings of grief and despair that were overwhelming to the child when the original loss occurred and had to be repressed. Abraham (21) was the first to suggest that oedipal disappointments, arriving on top of unresolved earlier conflicts, may cause the child to feel the parent has been lost and produce severe depressive responses which recur throughout life in response to subsequent disappointments.

Jacobson (22) stressed the child's disappointment in both parents early in the oedipal period, when the discovery is made that the parents are not omnipotent. She postulated that the ego is sometimes weakened by this discovery with the result that the child becomes too intimidated by the superego, feels excessively guilty and is thus more vulnerable to depression. Anthony (13) speaks also of the "disillusionment syndrome" which is sometimes the result of disappointment in parents who fail to gratify the child's wishes to be admired and praised early in the oedipal phase. These children become pessimistic and avoid competing because they do not expect to be successful.

Suicidal children are able to benefit from outpatient therapy, provided the parents can be appropriately supportive and protective. If the parents are able to provide a suitable environment, outpatient treatment of children is often possible or even preferable. It is possible because children are much more readily supervised than is the case with adolescents or adults, and preferable because, to these children, hospitalization can seem like still another desertion or rejection by the parents. Thus, it is perceived as a new loss which can add to the difficulties.

Toolan (23) has called attention to an important issue in therapy of depressed and suicidal children. Therapists who are not well trained in child development and psychodynamics often misdiagnose these severe disorders as situational grief reactions and provide only crisis-oriented, short-term psychotherapy for children who need more intensive psychotherapy in order to resolve inner conflicts about their worthiness and to alter their basic depressive feelings. This mistake is more likely to be made if the therapist considers only the recent precipitating event, such as parental divorce, and ignores early losses, particularly those that occurred in the first three years of life, rendering the child vulnerable to depression.

The goals for therapy of the suicidal latency-age child have been formulated by Ackerly (16). He states that the child must be helped to: internalize a good object, develop a more attainable ego-ideal, modify the superego if it is too harsh, diminish the attachment to an ideal, self, form healthier identifications, modify narcissistic expectations, and later aggressive responses to frustration and disappointment. At the very least, the therapist must form a good relationship with the child and help the child give up the notion that love and acceptance are contingent on perfection.

## ABUSED AND NEGLECTED CHILDREN

Blumberg's studies indicate that although isolated, nonviolent sexual activity with adults may not be invariably traumatic for children, frequent sexual acts, even without actual coitus, are likely to have serious emotional consequences (24). Feeding, sleeping, and activity disturbances are common in sexually abused infants, and chronic depression is common for sexually abused toddlers and school-age children. Threats and bribes for collusion and secrecy add to the child's confusion. When sexually abused youngsters become suicidal, it is usually after their efforts to communicate concerns about such sexual activity have failed to bring relief.

Anger and fear are the predominant emotions experienced when one is physically attacked, and it is well known that anger and fear tend to eliminate objectivity and rationality. All available energy may be used to defend against painful feelings. Children who are frequently slapped or spanked often feel rejected and unloved and are sometimes overwhelmed and unable to cope with their feelings. Physical attack produces lowering of self-esteem when the victim is helpless and overpowered. Low self-esteem can lead to withdrawal and despair. Many studies of suicide in children reveal that physical abuse and sexual molestations are the most common immediate precipitating factors (16, 24–26). This is not at all surprising in view of the fact that anger which cannot be expressed outwardly is often turned inward upon the self.

Parents who were spanked as children sometimes feel disloyal to their parents if they do not spank. They assume that they developed their sterling characters because their parents used physical punishment, and rarely consider that perhaps it was despite this fact. Parents who have identified strongly with punitive parents, as well as those who impulsively act upon angry feelings for their children, may need a good deal of assistance in resolving conflicts centered around disciplinary measures. Some parents suppress negative feelings for their children and are only aware of their loving feelings. Often the negative feelings are obvious to the child and to others because they are expressed in hostile, punitive interactions with the child and then rationalized as appropriate, loving, disciplinary actions. Often it is possible to help parents become aware of ambivalent feelings for their children and to accept these as natural feelings which can be controlled, rather than acted upon.

Another important consideration in working with many parents who physically attack their children is the parents' depressive outlook on life. The child is often a scapegoat upon whom parents vent their anger for each other and for their own parents, whom they perceive as disapproving and ungiving. A parent's depressive affect can induce more depression in a child who is already struggling with depression resulting from physical abuse.

Therapy for abusing parents is of crucial importance in the management of the abused, suicidal child. They must be helped to understand that the child's provocative behavior is a defense against the painful feelings of depression and that punitive responses to this behavior would probably deepen the depression. If parents persist in abusing or physically punishing these children, placement in a foster home or hospitalization is indicated.

Green (25, 27) has emphasized that stopping the abuse and providing a safe environment for abused children does not alleviate their inner suffering and turmoil. He states:

> The damage to the child's object relations, ego functions, cognitive performance, and self-esteem requires direct psychotherapeutic and psychoeducational intervention. [Without this] the child will . . . project the internalized destructive characteristics of his abusing parents onto future caretakers . . . [His] fear and distrust of [them] . . . leads to provocative behavior which might elicit further punishment. . . . Psychotherapeutic intervention . . . [can] . . . modify these . . . pathological internalized objects and identifications so that the children can eventually accommodate to an average expectable environment and attain the capacity to love themselves and others. Counseling . . . for those entrusted with the . . . care of abused children should complement their individual treatment.

## CHILDREN WHOSE PARENTS MAKE EXCESSIVE DEMANDS

Malmquist (3) has called attention to families in which the child is pressured to be exceptionally good, diligent, and conforming. The parental expectations often are felt by the child to be a tremendous burden. If the excessively high goals of the parents cannot be attained, the child, who identifies with the parents and accepts these goals as his own, experiences feelings of inadequacy and worthlessness. The ability to achieve is further compromised, and a downward spiral is established.

Pfeffer and coworkers (17) discussed defense mechanisms of suicidal children who feel extremely helpless because family dynamics have reached an overwhelmingly stressful state. She suggested that the parents' lack of appropriate empathy, and inability to lend support, lead to an intense fear of abandonment which some children deal with by denial of their hostile feelings for the parents. They use idealization in order to preserve a positive nurturing image of them.

Therapeutic work with the parents is crucial when their excessively demanding, hypercritical attitudes and behavior produce depression in their children. If the parents are rigid and unable to gain insight concerning their effect on the child, hospitalization may be necessary to safeguard the child from self-destructive urges until the parents become able to modify their expectations and provide support. Objective hospital staff members have work shifts of limited hours and are more likely to be alert and effective than frustrated parents who perceive their children to be lazy and uncooperative rather than depressed. It is not unusual, however, to find that parents who seemed, at the time of the evaluation, to be quite rigid and resistant to change, work diligently with the therapist and develop empathy and understanding of the child when relieved temporarily of the child's care.

Simmons and coworkers (28) reported that 53 percent of their group of parents of hospitalized children improved significantly in their ability to maintain a suitable home environment for their children. Parent ratings indicated that the decision to hospitalize the children was due primarily to the determination that the children needed to be removed from a home in which the parents were incapable of cooperating with the therapist to alter the home environment quickly. Children in their survey who had been referred for outpatient treatment were those whose parents had been judged to have good capacity for change, and, thus, good potential for being able to create a supportive home environment.

## Case Illustration 1

Rose was ten years of age when she was referred because she had threatened to stab herself with a kitchen knife after an argument with her mother, who had insisted on helping rose with a school assignment, despite the child's wish to do it on her own. When Rose responded rudely to some of her mother's suggestions, she lost her temper and slapped Rose in the face. There had been a great deal of chronic conflict between this child and her mother. On the previous evening Rose had demanded to know what was being prepared for dinner and had then stated that she was not going to eat what her mother was preparing. She had asked permission to make a sandwich instead, but was sent to bed without any supper.

Rose is the second of four children born to upper-middle-class parents. Her birth had been complicated because of a breech presentation and she had become jaundiced on the second day of life. An exchange transfusion was performed the following day because of a rising bilirubin level, and she had remained in the hospital two days longer than her mother. She was a colicky baby who often refused her bottle. This was very frustrating to her mother who liked to keep to schedules. Talking was slightly delayed and toilet training was difficult. Her mother regarded her as stubborn and willfully dirty and often punished Rose for her accidents. A sibling was born when she was three and Rose seemed to regress and become more clinging for a time. The next sibling arrived when she was five and her mother was disappointed because Rose did not appear to be very interested in the baby.

School had always been a struggle for Rose. On psychological testing in first grade her I.Q. was in the average range of intellectual functioning but the Bender-Gestalt showed evidence of visual-motor-perceptual problems. She had a good deal of difficulty with reading, and despite tutoring and remedial help she still tested two years below grade level. She was in a special education program for children with learning disabilities.

During the diagnostic interviews, Rose always appeared sad and somewhat angry. She had a very pessimistic viewpoint and she regarded herself as "stupid" and "bad." She was having difficulty sleeping and her appetite was poor, although her parents had not been aware of this. Her mother tended instead to perceive Rose as unappreciative and a troublemaker on the many occasions when she refused to eat her dinner.

Toward the end of the evaluation, I discovered that Rose had previously attempted suicide by taking a bottle of Darvon tablets which had been prescribed for her mother. Fortunately, she had become nauseated and vomited. The parents had not taken this very seriously and were surprised that I regarded it as quite serious.

A diagnosis of major depressive disorder was made. Psychotherapy was recommended for Rose and counseling for her parents, who reluctantly agreed to stop the physical punishment and to allow Rose to have a sandwich or a bowl of cereal when she declined to eat dinner with the rest of the family. They also agreed to discontinue monitoring her school work and, instead, to leave this up to her tutor. As they acquired a fuller understanding of Rose, they became less demanding, gave her more praise, and allowed her more play time with friends. During an eighteen-month course of psychotherapy, Rose developed a much better self-image and more realistic expectations for herself. She had never really understood what a learning disability was, and her secret fear was that she was retarded. As she became more aware of her own talents, she began to deal much better with envious feelings for her sisters, who were excellent students, and she became more friendly and less sensitive about not being able to excel at academics.

## CHILDREN WITH DISTURBED, DISORGANIZED FAMILIES

Many studies have shown that psychiatric illness and drug abuse of parents, paternal unemployment, economic stress, poor living conditions, especially overcrowding, and family disorganization are quite common in the background of suicidal children (24, 29). The misery to which children are subjected is very real when their homes are chaotic and their parents are unable to manage their own lives and are even less capable of nurturing their children. Suicidal children will often need to be removed from these homes; however, some depressed, seemingly inadequate parents are able to respond to supportive intervention so that the children can be managed at home.

### Case Illustration 2

Ralph was a handsome, ten-year-old, black youngster, who was brought to a mental health center for psychiatric evaluation after he attempted to hang himself at school. He had been scolded by his teacher for not doing his work and he had been having sad thoughts about his paternal grandmother, who had died suddenly two years previously. Ralph had dreamed recently of going to heaven and being reunited with the grandmother. His teacher found him with a rope around his neck about to jump from a second-floor window.

Ralph was conceived when his mother was only 15 years of age. She was hypertensive during the pregnancy and had to drop out of school in the 10th grade.

His birth was normal with a birth weight of 8 lbs 9 oz. He became jaundiced and had to remain in the hospital for a week. His mother felt that this, and her own mother's attitude, made it hard for her to feel as close to Ralph as she would have liked. Her mother had been angry about the pregnancy; however, she was kind to Ralph. His early development was precocious and he had been a good student until the present year.

There had been many moves; when Ralph was about one year of age he and his mother moved into a home with his father. After two little sisters were born, the family moved to the home of the paternal grandparents. The grandmother assisted with the children's care while Ralph's mother returned to school. The parents separated when he was six and the mother moved with her children into a Federal housing project. Two years later she remarried and they moved to the stepfather's home. He was a heavy drinker who often accused her of being unfaithful and sometimes abused her. Six months before the suicide attempt, Ralph's mother moved back to the project with her children.

Ralph had been quite worried about his mother, who appeared very depressed herself. During the previous summer she had been hospitalized twice with gall bladder disease and had undergone a cholecystectomy. During her absence from home, he was cared for by his aunt. He missed his mother very much and became terrified and overwhelmed with grief when his maternal grandfather told him that his mother had died, and then laughed and said he was only joking. The aunt and her four children were still living with Ralph's family and this had resulted in a terribly crowded and chaotic home. Ralph was sharing a bed with his two younger sisters, both of whom were enuretic and he felt persecuted by his aunt's thirteen-year-old son who picked on him. He misbehaved at school and had trouble doing his work.

He was able to discuss his sad feelings concerning his parents' fights and their separation as well as his grandmother's death and his resentment of his cousin. His mood was predominantly sad but occasionally he smiled and joked. When he told of being forced to do an errand against his will and of hitting his head against a brick wall, he stated, "It is a good thing I have a hard head." He had been sleeping poorly and had not had much appetite for several weeks.

A diagnosis of major depressive disorder was made and the suicide risk was considered to be high. Both he and his mother were frightened by his self-destructive urges and willing for him to be hospitalized; however, the only facility with an available bed was an hour's drive from the city. Upon learning of this, Ralph's mother insisted that he be treated as an outpatient. She was afraid she would be unable to make trips to the hospital and she was sure that Ralph would feel deserted.

Arrangements were made for Ralph to have a bed of his own and he was seen for therapy three times during the next week. His sleep and appetite improved promptly and he reported enjoyable play with friends in the neighborhood. It was decided to continue twice-weekly sessions with Ralph and weekly parent counseling of the mother, who was also referred for psychiatric evaluation and treatment because of her depression. When their treatment terminated, Ralph was doing well in school and his mother was functioning well. She had helped her sister to get her own apartment and she was working part time at a job she enjoyed.

## DRUG THERAPY

The use of drugs for severely depressed and suicidal children has been studied for only a few years. Researchers stress the need for solid double-blind studies of depressed children treated with tricyclic antidepressants, MAO inhibitors, and lithium (30, 31). Cantwell and Carlson (31) stated in 1979 that although a number of open studies indicate that some children respond to these drugs, published work offers no conclusive evidence that drugs are useful for children with major depressive disorders. In the same year, Puig-Antich (30) an coworkers reported that imipramine and desmethylimipramine produce a response in children with major depressive disorder which is similar to that obtained with depressed adults, provided the plasma level is at least 146 ng/ml.

Weller, Weller, and Preskorn (32) recently reported the effect of imipramine on twenty children, ages 7–12, who met *DSM–III* criteria for major depressive disorder. They found that 75 percent improved over a period of six weeks and that improvement was associated with a plasma level of 125–225 ng./ml. Geller and associates (33) reported the use of nortriptyline in ten depressed children aged 6–11 and concluded that the drug is safe and effective in major depressive disorder in children. They reported that some children had optimum responses only after four to six weeks instead of the two-to-four-week period which is usual for adults.

Werry (34), in a 1982 review of psychopharmacology in children, stated that "the principal use of the antidepressant at present is for temporary suppression of enuresis . . . and as a second string in the management of attention deficit disorder." He quoted Puig-Antich who predicted that "a possible role for antidepressants in the management of childhood depression will soon become clear."

Puig-Antich (35) reported the finding that one-third of 43 prepubertal boys who had been accepted for treatment of major depression also fit *DSM–III* criteria for conduct disorder and both the mood disorder and the conduct disorder responded favorably to imipramine. In view of the fact that antisocial behavior and enuresis can both be seen as depressive equivalents or defenses against depression, it does not seem surprising that they would respond to antidepressants in the same way that depression does.

In 1983 Petti and Conners (36) reported favorable results of an open clinical trial of imipramine treatment of children meeting research criteria for depression. They stated that "no large study to date, has employed research criteria in selecting a group of depressed children combined with double-blind, controlled conditions to study their treatment with the tricyclic antidepressants or other therapeutic agents/interventions."

Until more conclusive evidence is available regarding the efficacy and safety of drug therapy for severely depressed and suicidal children, clinicians should proceed cautiously with the use of drugs. If drugs do become accepted as safe and effective, they should be regarded only as symptomatic treatment. Social and psychological factors needing attention should not be neglected.

## SUMMARY

Susceptible children may become depressed and suicidal in response to stressful social factors including loss or separation from parents, parental abuse, neglect, rejection, pressure, or a chaotic, disorganized family environment. Psychological factors that predispose children to suicidal behavior include inadequate ego-defenses to cope with feelings engendered by the adverse environmental circumstances. Often these children relate poorly to others and are excessively dependent.

Outpatient management is possible if the parents are able to be appropriately supportive and protective. Intensive psychotherapy is often necessary to modify a basic depressive outlook on life and to resolve inner conflict about self-worth.

The suicidal child must be helped to give up perfectionistic attitudes and to alter aggressive responses to loss and disappointment. Work with parents is important, particularly when the child's suicidal state is reactive to inappropriate parental behavior. Antidepressant drugs may prove to be a useful adjunct.

## REFERENCES

1. Schechter, M. D. The Recognition and Treatment of Suicide in Children. In *Clues to Suicide*, Shneidman, E. S. and Farberow, N. L., Eds. McGraw-Hill, New York, 1957, pp. 131–142.

2. Poznanski, E. and Zrull, J. P. Childhood Depression. *Arch. Gen. Psychiatry* 23:8, 1970.

3. Malmquist, C. P. Depressions in Childhood and Adolescence. Part II *N. Engl. J. Med.* 284:955, 1971.

4. Mattsson, A., Sesse, L. R., Hawkins, J. W., et al. Suicidal Behavior as a Child Psychiatric Emergency. *Arch. Gen. Psychiatry* 20:100, 1969.

5. Cohen-Sandler, R., Berman, A. L., and King, R. A. Life Stress and Symptomatology: Determinants of Suicidal Behavior in Children. *J. Am. Acad. Child Psychiatry* 21:178, 1982.

6. Pfeffer, C. R., Conte, H. R., Plutchik, R., and Jarrett, M. A. Suicidal Behavior in Latency Age Children: an Empirical Study: an Out-patient Population. *J. Am. Acad. Child Psychiatry* 19:703, 1980.

7. Cytryn, L. and McKnew, D. H. Proposed Classification of Childhood Depression. *Am. J. of Psychiatry* 129:149, 1972.

8. Pfeffer, C. R., Solomon, G., Plutchik, R., et al. Suicidal Behavior in Latency-age Psychiatric Inpatients: A Replication and Cross Validation. *J. Am. Acad. Child Psychiatry* 21:564, 1982.

9. Cytryn, L. and McKnew, D. H. Factors Influencing the Changing Clinical Expression of the Depressive Process in Children. *Am. J. of Psychiatry* 131:879, 1974.

10. Nagy, M. The Child's View of Death. In *The Meaning of Death*, Feifel, H., Ed. McGraw-Hill, New York, 1959.

11. Piaget, J. *The Child's Conception of the World*. Humanities Press, New York, 1960.

12. Maurer, A. Maturation of Concepts of Death. *Br. J. Med. Psychol.* 39:35, 1966.

13. Anthony, E. J. Childhood Depression. In *Depression and Human Existence*, Anthony, E. J. and Benedek, T., Eds. Little, Brown and Company, Boston, 1975, pp. 231–277.

14. Glaser, K. Masked Depression in Children and Adolescents. *Am. J. Psychother.* 21:565, 1967.

15. Lesse, S. Hypochrondriacal and Psychosomatic Disorders Masking Depression in Adolescents. *Am. J. Psychother.* 35:356, 1981.

16. Ackerly, W. C. Latency-age Children Who Threaten or Attempt to Kill Themselves. *J. Am. Acad. Child Psychiatry* 6:242, 1967.

17. Pfeffer, C. R. The Family System of Suicidal Children. *Am. J. Psychother.* 35:330, 1981.

18. Spitz, R. and Wolf, K. Anaclitic Depression. *Psychoanal. Study Child* 2:312, 1946.

19. Mahler, M. On Sadness and Grief in Infancy and Childhood; Loss and Restoration of the Symbiotic Love Object. *Psychoanal. Study Child* 16:332, 1961.

20. Bowlby, J. Childhood Mourning and Its Implication for Psychiatry. *Am. J. Psychiatry* 118:481, 1961.

21. Abraham, K. Notes on the Psychoanalytic Investigation and Treatment of Manic-depressive Insanity and Allied Conditions. In *Selected Papers of Karl Abraham, M.D.*, Hogarth Press, London, 1948.

22. Jacobson, E. The Effect of Disappointment on Ego and Superego Formation in Normal and Depressive Development. *Psychoanal. Rev.* 33:129, 1946.

23. Toolan, J. M. Therapy of Depressed and Suicidal Children. *Am. J. Psychother.* 29:339, 1975.

24. Blumberg, M. L. Depression in Abused and Neglected Children. *Am. J. Psychother.* 35:342, 1981.

25. Green, A. H. Self-Destructive Behavior in Battered Children. *Am. J. Psychiatry* 135:579, 1978.

26. Rosenfeld, A. A., Nadelson, C. C., Krieger, M., and Backman, J. H. Incest and Sexual Abuse of Children. *J. Am. Acad. Child Psychiatry* 16:327, 1977.

27. Green, A. H. Psychiatric Treatment of Abused Children. *J. Am. Acad. Child Psychiatry* 17:356, 1978.

28. Simmons, J. E., Ten Eyck, R. L., McNabb, R. C., et al. Parent Treatability: What Is It? *J. Am. Acad. Child Psychiatry* 20:792, 1981.

29. Garfinkel, B. D., Froese, A., and Hood, J. Suicide Attempts in Children and Adolescents. *Am. J. Psychiatry* 139:1257, 1981.

30. Puig-Antich, J., Perel, U. M., Lupartkin, W., et al. Plasma Levels of Imipramine and Desmethylimipramine and Clinical Response in Prepubertal Major Depressive Disorder. *J. Am. Acad. Child Psychiatry* 18:616, 1979.

31. Cantwell, D. P. and Carlson, G. A. Problems and Prospects in the Study of Childhood Depression. *J. Nerv. Ment. Dis.* 167:522, 1979.

32. Weller, Weller, and Preskorn. Depression in Children: Relationship between Plasma Levels of Imipramine and Response. Presented at the American Academy of Child Psychiatry, Washington, D.C., 1982.

33. Geller, B., Perel, J., Knitter, E. F., et al. Pilot Study of Nortriptyline in Major Depressive Illness in Children. Presented at the American Academy of Child Psychiatry, Washington, D.C., 1982.

34. Werry, J. An Overview of Pediatric Psychopharmacology. *J. Am. Acad. Child Psychiatry* 21:3, 1982.

35. Puig-Antich, J. Major Depression and Conduct Disorders. *J. Am. Acad. Child Psychiatry* 21:2, 1982.

36. Petti, T. A. and Conners, C. K. Changes in Behavioral Ratings of Depressed Children Treated with Imipramine. *J. Am. Acad. Child Psychiatry* 22:355, 1983.

# 24 The Family System of Suicidal Children

## Cynthia R. Pfeffer, M.D.

*The organizational characteristics of the family system of psychiatrically hospitalized suicidal latency-age children include lack of generational boundaries, severely conflicted spouse relationships, parental feelings projected onto the child, symbiotic parent-child relations, and an inflexible family system. Five cases illustrate a spectrum of family psychopathology and resultant childhood suicidal tendencies.*

Morrison and Collier (1) claimed that suicidal behavior of children is "a symptom of not only individual upheaval but of underlying family disruption" (p. 140). This statement has not been adequately documented with respect to latency-age children, because some studies have combined suicidal latency-age children with adolescents (1, 2), others have been based only on individual case reports (3, 4), or on cursory descriptions of the family (5). Only a few studies have more or less systematically compared families of suicidal and nonsuicidal latency-age children (6, 7).

In view of these considerations, this paper presents a formulation of the organizational characteristics of the family system of psychiatrically hospitalized suicidal latency-age children. The hypotheses are based upon my many years of treating and studying suicidal and nonsuicidal latency-age children. The description of this type of family functioning may provide a basis for additional systematic study and data useful for building a model to account for childhood suicidal behavior.

## THE FAMILY ORGANIZATION OF SUICIDAL CHILDREN

I believe that families of suicidal children are good examples of what Erikson noted as failure of generativity and what Bowen noted as lack of self-differentiation. Erikson (8) proposed that in the "psychosocial developmental phase of generativity" the primary concern of an adult is establishing and guiding the next generation. "Generativity is itself a driving power in human organization" (p. 139). Erikson emphasized that an adequately functioning family unit requires that the adults have achieved an appropriate sense of their generative potential. A compatible concept is one proposed by Bowen (9), who emphasized the importance of differentiation of self as an essential aspect of family functioning. His definition was that "the differentiated person is always aware of others and the relationship system around him" (p. 370). I have observed that parents of suicidal children are unable to develop an appropriate capacity for care because of faulty identifications with their own parents. Furthermore, these parents seem to exhibit regressive states in which they indulge themselves as if they were children.

With these more general comments in mind, I will outline hypotheses that define features of the suicidal child's family system. Many of these features may be evident in other families, although it is the degree of intensity and the fixed, long duration of these features that are very marked in families of suicidal children. The main features—appearing in combination—are:

1. *Lack of Generational Boundaries:* There is an insufficient individuation of the parents from their families of origin due to conflicts derived from unresolved childhood traumas. Because of intense ambivalence of the child's parents toward their parents or siblings, there exist problems of strongly felt and

expressed hostility, feelings of deprivation, low self-esteem, and magnified attachment to the parents' families of origin.

This hypothesis may be illustrated by Mr. A., who was so influenced by his feelings that his mother was a domineering, intrusive person that he found it very difficult to accept suggestions from his wife. Another example is Mr. B., who before his marriage had to care for his younger epileptic brother. When his own son developed epilepsy, Mr. B. conflicted by his hostility and ambivalence toward his brother, deprecated and withdrew from his son. The son eventually felt so worthless that he attempted suicide by ingesting his anticonvulsant medication.

2. *Severely Conflicted Spouse Relationships:* Fantasies and perceptions of people in the parents' family of origin are overdetermining influences on the choice of spouse and feelings toward a spouse. Interactions between the spouses are markedly ambivalent and intense anger is openly and indirectly expressed. The parental relationship centers around dependency conflicts in which one spouse is either threatened with being hurt or is capable of hurting his mate. The threat of separation is always present and one parent is often depressed or suicidal. Often these suicidal tendencies of a parent may not be immediately evident until there is a significant shift in the dynamics and equilibrium of the entire family system.

3. *Parental Feelings Projected onto the Child:* The parents display strong libidinal and aggressive feelings toward the child instead of toward each other. In addition, the parents' unconscious perceptions of others are projected onto the child.

4. *Symbiotic Parent–child Relationship:* The child may have an especially close or symbiotic attachment to a parent, usually the mother. Because of this intense and rigid interaction with the parent, the child may not be able to successfully develop autonomous functioning.

5. *Inflexible Family System:* The family relates in such an unyielding way that any change is felt as a threat to the survival of the family. Common ego defenses of the family members include denial, secretiveness, and lack of open communication. Family changes produce intense anxiety and associated regression to infantile fixations. I have observed that in these families

there is marked ambivalence, extreme hostile reactions with seemingly little expression of empathy or support to other family members. At the same time, rejection is often not felt as absolutely final and there is often a remarkable sense of hope. However, any achievement of personal goal or individuation becomes equated with separation, desertion, or untimely death. As a result, family preoccupations with these issues, especially with death are prominent. Stresses in generational boundaries, spouse interactions, and parent-child relationships may reach intolerable proportions. Eventually, suicide becomes both a means of escape and a means of effecting a family reorganization which permits the family to remain together in a more tolerable family constellation.

To summarize these concepts, the suicidal family organization can be characterized as functioning with intense ambivalence, rigid patterns of interaction, poor identity as a family unit due to lack of differentiation of generational boundaries, regressions to states of collective primitive ego functioning, levels of helplessness, low self-esteem and depression, and threats by any attempt for family differentiation or member individuation. The suicidal child has a special role of providing gratification to a parent, of being an omnipotent protector for the distressed parent, and of accepting the displaced parental hostility derived from parental unresolved infantile conflicts. Progress in individuation of the child either may threaten the emotional stability or provoke depression in the symbiotic parent.

## CASE ILLUSTRATIONS

Five cases are presented to show a spectrum of pathology ranging from relatively more subtle types of family dysfunction to overt family chaos and acting out. Each case will illustrate to a greater degree one of the mechanisms postulated for the system of family organization. However, in each case example, all of the hypothetical family mechanisms are operative. In addition, these cases will illustrate the effects of the entire family system upon the child's suicidal tendencies.

## Case 1: Lack of Generational Boundaries

Michael, age ten years, attempted to kill himself by setting the cuffs of his pants on fire after an argument with his mother. He admitted that this was his way of testing his parents to see if they loved him. He could not explain why he needed to test his parents, although his behavior coincided with the anniversary of his father's heart attack one year before and Michael's tenth birthday. The parents denied and kept secret the chronic difficulties they had with Michael's behavior which included fire setting and running away.

The father's heart attack was terrifying for the family. In fact, Michael's father put everything aside, including interactions within the family, so that he might recuperate. Because of this, Michael's mother took charge of the children and all household responsibilities but she strongly resented it and was angry at her husband. Fear of losing him awakened her previous ambivalent feelings stemming from conflicts during her childhood. She had been troubled by her parents' relationship and her father who had been a chronic hypochrondriac who complained of a bad heart. Because of his condition, her father incurred multiple medical bills which became a source of friction between Michael's maternal grandparents.

Michael's mother was aware of many parallels between her own family experience and Michael's. She considered herself and Michael to be "spoiled and a discipline problem." In addition, it appeared that her perceptions of her husband and her father were identical. She described them as "selfish and unable to share feelings." She and Michael had an especially close relationship in which they shared an exquisite anxiety whenever they were separated. She felt she was "smothering and overprotective" and believed that she and Michael were alike. Furthermore, her son, she felt, was similar to her husband; "they are both short tempered."

This example illustrates the long-standing overwhelmingly close relationship between a child and his mother. This type of relationship was intensified by the mother's unresolved childhood conflicts and struggles with her husband. The mother's hostile perceptions and angry memories of people from her past were projected onto her husband and son. The mother-child relationship reached intolerably intense proportions at the time of Michael's birthday and the anniversary of his father's heart attack. The reawakened threat of loss of his father and the stresses of his ambivalent relationship with his mother became a source of Michael's renewed conflicts about separating from and merging with his mother. Michael's fear of engulfment by his hostilely perceived mother increased his anxiety. His suicidal action was a desperate method of gaining relief.

## Case 2: Severely Conflicted Spouse Relationships

Paul, eleven years old, had a three-year history of fighting and difficulty controlling his temper. He threatened to jump out the second-story apartment window one year before his hospitalization because he hated himself and wanted to die. Although previously he had been an honor student, his school grades dropped and he was in jeopardy of not being promoted. The week before hospitalization, when his father was away on a business trip, Paul attempted to hang himself with an electrical cord.

Paul was the oldest of four children and, as a result, Paul's father wanted Paul to be very mature. If Paul did not conform to his father's expectations, Paul was beaten with a belt. The father stated that "Paul and I have identical personalities. We are both explosive."

Paul's father was the oldest of three sons. His parents divorced when he was seven years old. Paul's grandfather was physically abusive to Paul's father in contrast to the grandmother who was passive and depressed. Paul's father ran away from home when he was an adolescent but was eventually placed in a series of foster homes and a reformatory because of unmanageable behavior problems. As an adult, Paul's father had a long history of job instability.

Paul's mother was one of six children. Her parents' divorce, when she was a young adolescent, was one of the most traumatic events of her life. She helped her mother care for the younger children and hoped her father would come home.

Paul's mother was a quiet woman who was extremely involved in raising her children. However, she overly depended on Paul for help and advice especially when her husband was away. Paul resented this but felt guilty about resisting his mother.

Paul's parents never planned a legal separation although there were many separations because Paul's father stayed away from the family ostensibly on business trips. Paul covered his ears when his parents talked about separating. He stated to them that "you will be sorry if you separate." Not only was the marriage marked by intense disagreements but there had been frequent episodes of violence between the couple, which, however, seemed to diminish after Paul was born.

In this family, threats of parental separation and violence were intertwined. The parents' childhoods were enormously traumatic and their conflicts were repeated in Paul's family. Paul was a special child for each parent. He was invested with qualities of pseudomaturity, omnipotence, and heroism. Another of his special roles in the family was to maintain stability. In fact, his birth was planned as a means of reuniting the separated parents and decreasing their marital conflicts. Paul was supersensitive to his relationship with his parents. He identified with the depression and dependency of his mother and the violence of his father. His suicidal behavior was a response to his sense of helplessness that he shared with his parents.

## Case 3: Parental Feelings Projected onto the Child

Brian, nine years old, was hospitalized because of serious suicidal episodes. "I am trying to kill myself. One more accident and that ought to do it," he openly stated. In the three months before hospitalization, Brian sustained many injuries. He hit his head twice and required stitches for the lacerations. On other occasions, he broke both arms, hit his head with a shovel, acquired a laceration on the nose, and singed his hair while playing near the stove. Finally, he put a belt around his neck in an attempt to kill himself.

The history of Brian's life was unusually traumatic. His father courted his mother when she was pregnant. A girl was born and given up for adoption. "Out of pity for her sadness from the loss of the girl, I decided to marry her," said Brian's father. When Brian's mother was pregnant with Brian, she was unstable, an alcoholic, and attempted an abortion and suicide. She divorced Brian's father after Brian's birth and later surrendered Brian to his father when Brian was 4 months old. Brian never saw his mother after his second birthday.

Brian had numerous caretakers and because of this as an infant and toddler, he was withdrawn, listless and nonreactive. When Brian was 2½ years old, his father married a woman who was very ambivalent about caring for Brian. Nevertheless, during this period, Brian had more stability. At the age of five years, when a stepsister was born, Brian developed behavior difficulties. Unfortunately for Brian, his sister was favored by the parents. When a stepbrother was born, Brian was seven and one half years old. At that time, Brian had to be psychiatrically hospitalized because of uncontrollable behavior, enuresis, and encopresis. After the hospitalization, Brian was placed in a long-term residential treatment center. However, after 1½ years, the professional staff at the residential facility decided that Brian was not benefiting from the program. As a result, his parents were left with a dilemma of deciding to take Brian home or placing him for adoption. However, his parents definitely did not want him home but they were indecisive about whether to put him up for adoption. It was at this time that Brian became acutely suicidal.

Brian's catastrophies reflected the childhood conflicts of his parents. Brian's father was the youngest of three children. His father had been raised in an institution because "my grandparents were too poor to support a third child during the Depression." This event had a major impact on Brian's father who felt very guilty that Brian was in institutional care. Brian's father remembered that his parents had an unempathic, cold marriage and that they were divorced when Brian's father was seventeen years old. He described his mother as distant, hostile, and very disapproving of his girlfriends. In fact, she was argumentative with Brian's stepmother about how to care for Brian.

Brian's stepmother, much younger than Brian's father, married Brian's father against her family's wishes. Her parents had divorced when she was five years old because her father was an alcoholic. Brian's stepmother wished that her father would return home while at the same time hating his unpredictability. She felt very guilty about not committing herself to Brian's care. She liked Brian but resented that her husband had been married previously to an alcoholic.

In this example, the child's suicidal behavior resulted from his intense feelings of worthlessness. The child was an important repository of multiple unresolved parental conflicts. He was unwanted by his natural mother, rescued by his father, and ambivalently nurtured by his stepmother. He stood for every aspect of his parents' ambivalent fantasies that included a preponderance of badness, worthlessness, and rejection. Brian reminded his stepmother of her alocholic, abandoning but idealized father. His father, in turn, saw his cold, uncaring mother and hopeless, institutionalized father in Brian.

Brian's extrusion from the family and simultaneously important involvement helped to maintain that family's specific type of unstable equilibrium. Brian was considered the reason that his parents related ambivalently to each other. Brian's father hopelessly longed for a kind, nurturing mother whom he never had and hoped that his wife would fulfill this role. However, by her rejection of Brian, the stepmother disappointed her husband. Furthermore, Brian's stepmother married an older man who was like her longed-for father. Her ambivalence and hostility toward her father was acted out in her relationship with her husband and the rejection of her husband's son.

Brian's uncontrollable behavior may be understood as a "protest" against all of the unfair rejections. Although a residential placement was a tolerable alternative for him, the parents' consideration of giving him up for adoption dashed his hopes of ever establishing a more acceptable role in the family.

## Case 4: Symbiotic Parent–Child Relationship

Carol, eleven years old, was hospitalized after ingesting many of her mother's tranquilizers. She was angry about being reprimanded by her teacher and saddened by her father's drinking. Carol knew a girl who had overdosed and an aunt who was psychiatrically hospitalized after ingesting pills.

In the months preceding Carol's hospitalization, she responded to her mother's crying spells with identical outbursts of crying and statements of wanting to die. Carol's mother talked of leaving the children and threatened to kill herself and her older daughter. The mother worried that her children were growing up and would abandon her. She was distraught over her husband's violence but did not comprehend the effects that her suicidal threats had upon her children. Carol's mother had been depressed for over a year and was in outpatient psychiatric treatment.

Of the five children, Carol was unusually close to her mother and was very sensitive to her mother's mood. Carol's mother said that Carol "wants to feel the same things that I do."

Carol often clung to her mother and felt duty bound to protect her mother from her father.

Carol's mother was the second of five children, all born to different fathers. Her father left the family when she was born and she had not seen him since she was seven years old. As an adult, she met Carol's father and immediately became pregnant. However, Carol's father left the mother when she was 6 months pregnant because he intended to marry another woman, although he continued intermittent contact with Carol's mother. His visits were a major problem for the family especially because he arrived drunk and ill-tempered. Carol's mother had an intense need to be mistreated by Carol's father and did not attempt to prevent his visits. Carol regretted that the police did not incarcerate her father stating "I took the pills to get away from him."

This case is striking in the overt expression of maternal suicidal and parental homicidal tendencies. The constellation of maternal depression, helplessness, and sadistic threats to kill or leave the children were central forces in the family dynamics. Carol's mother's intense needs to be nurtured far outweighed her capacity to be a predictable, adequate mother. The mother's inability to set limits and protect herself from her violent husband was a revival of her guilt about her angry feelings toward her unpredictable, rejecting father.

Carol maintained an unyieldingly close relationship with her mother in which she strongly identified with her mother's depression and suicidal tendencies. Although Carol would display hatred toward her father, the multiple threats of losing her mother interfered with Carol's expression of anger towards her mother. Instead, Carol's aggressive impulses were directed at harming herself.

## Case 5: Inflexible Family System

Melissa, eleven years old, was hospitalized because of repeated statements that she would kill herself. As an infant she was demanding, prone to aggressive behavior and excessive clinging. She was the second of four siblings who lived in a chronically chaotic family.

Two years before her hospitalization, Melissa's mother separated from her husband who remained in the same apartment building. Marital fighting had been extreme and separations were frequent because of the father's extramarital affairs. Melissa's mother eventually decided to take charge of her life, pursue a career, provide better organization in the family, and decrease her chronic depressive state.

History showed that the paternal family was plagued bymultiple health problems which included diabetes, heart disease, and kidney ailments. Melissa's father was born with kidney and bladder dysfunction. The paternal grandfather died of a heart attack when Melissa's father was sixteen years old. As a result, Melissa's father became very close to his mother. Melissa's mother, an identical twin, always felt inferior to her twin. She remembered fighting with her father who was very authoritarian and being rejected by her mother, who favored her twin.

Shortly before her engagement to Melissa's father, Melissa's mother became pregnant. Unfortunately, the pregnancy was terminated after six months and the infant boy died within one day. For many years, Melissa's mother was depressed about this loss. Often, she went to the cemetery with Melissa and Melissa's older sister. Marital problems developed after the death of this first infant. Although Melissa's father accepted the birth of Melissa's older sister, he was very disappointed in having a second daughter one year later. When Melissa was three years old, her mother had another miscarriage. Once again, her mother became overtly depressed. Melissa responded to her mother's sadness and withdrawal with increased clinging, temper tantrums, and sleep difficulties.

This family may be characterized not only by actual separations and experiences with death but also by states of longstanding family rigidity manifest by chronic depression and repeated impulsive acting out. Many of the parental fantasies were projected onto Melissa. Melissa's mother considered herself less important and less capable than her twin. Furthermore, because of the closeness in age between Melissa and her sister, the mother referred to the girls as "being like twins." Identifying Melissa with herself, the mother said that "Melissa is the less competent sister." Melissa's father, burdened by a background of multiple health problems in his family, shared his wife's depression after the two infant deaths. He was disappointed by not having a son and projected his frustrations and sense of failure onto Melissa. His sense of damage and depression were defended against by his Don Juan affairs which helped him prove his manhood and competency. Melissa's suicidal thoughts increased not only after the drastic change in the family system with the loosening of family ties when her parents separated but also by her mother's withdrawal when she sought a career.

## INTRAPSYCHIC DETERMINANTS OF CHILDHOOD SUICIDAL BEHAVIOR

My observations point out that the child's vulnerability to suicidal behavior strongly depends upon the interactive effects within the family system. The families described in this paper have very rigid and inflexible qualities with prominent features of projections of conflictual and primitive fantasies and wishes onto other family members. This pattern of family functioning may produce pathological identifications in the child and deficiencies in the child's personal differentiation. It may be postulated that important factors that enhance a child's vulnerability to suicidal behavior are the lack of sufficient differentiation of self from parental influences as well as insufficient establishment of the child's stable and separate identity.

When the family dynamics reach an overwhelmingly stressful state, the child may experience a state of extreme helplessness. I have noted that denial, projection, introjection, and repression were among the common defenses utilized by psychiatrically hospitalized suicidal and nonsuicidal children (6). These defense mechanisms may be activated to counteract and cope with the child's desperate state. In addition, the child's dependency upon the parents for external support may be heightened. This dependency may enhance any tendency for a parent-child symbiotic relationship and its inherent aspects of poor self-differentiation of the child. Such a heightened parent-child relationship may be associated with an intense fear of parental abandonment especially since the child may perceive the parents' frequent lack of appropriate empathy and ability to adequately lend support to the child as parental rejection.

Significant defenses against fear of parental loss may be evident as the child's denial of hostile feelings toward the parent and the child's apparent idealization of the parent. It may be hypothesized that idealization may protect and preserve the child's positive kind nurturing image of the parent and as a result help to repress or remove from consciousness the child's wishes to retaliate against the frustrating hated aspects of a parent. Furthermore, it may be proposed that as a result of the enhanced symbiosis between a parent and child, mechanisms of identification with the parent and child may become more marked. Therefore, the child's hostile perceptions of the parent may be introjected and felt as the child's hatred of himself and sense that he is a bad, worthless, undesirable person. The intense pain evoked by these self-perceptions may become unbearable and the child may further attempt to deny these feelings by means of total isolation of positive hopeful wishes and fantasies from the worthless and undesirable feelings about himself. Therefore, it may be hypothesized that the suicidal behavior of the child may be an acted-out last resort mechanism to remove from consciousness the child's negative self-perceptions.

## CONCLUSION

Figure 24-1 summarizes the influences of the family system of the suicidal child. A model of the family system of suicidal latency-age children was postulated to include lack of generational boundaries, severe conflicts between the spouses, parental projection of feelings onto the child, symbiotic parent-child relationships and inflexibility in the entire family unit. In such families, progress in the child's psychological individuation and autonomy is hampered. This network of family functioning produces pathological identifications in the child in which the child's negative fantasies of the parents are internalized as intense self-perceptions of badness, worthlessness, and undesirableness. Suicidal tendencies are the mechanisms to remove from consciousness the child's negative self-images.

Finally, clinical experience has shown that the treatment of

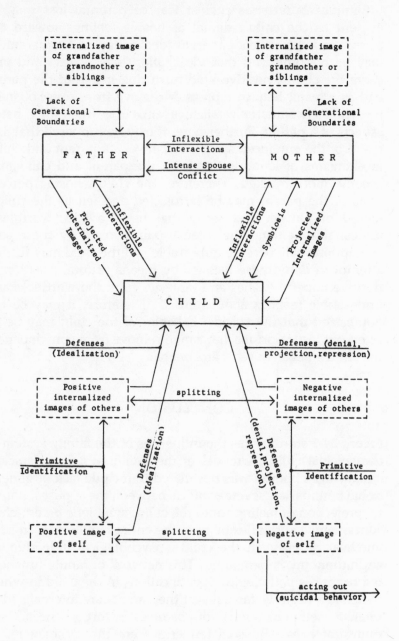

**Figure 24-1** *The Family System of the Suicide Child*

suicidal children must be intensive and of long duration (10, 11). The family model proposed in this paper has important implications for enlarging the scope of treatment of potentially suicidal children. Three aspects of intervention that are based upon a family orientation may be considered when working with suicidal children. A therapist must (a) define and offer treatment for the parental conflicts as separate issues from the conflicts of the child; (b) provide guidance to the parents so that they may respond with better parenting for the child; (c) treat the child with a variety of psychiatric inpatient and outpatient interventions.

## SUMMARY

The family system of psychiatrically hospitalized suicidal latency-age children can be characterized as functioning with intense ambivalence, rigid patterns of interaction, poor identity as a family unit due to lack of differentiation of generational boundaries, regressions to states of collective primitive ego functioning, levels of helplessness, low self-esteem and depression, and threats by any attempt for family differentiation or member individuation. The suicidal child has a special role of providing gratification to a parent, of being an omnipotent protector for the distressed parent, and of accepting the displaced parental hostility derived from parental unresolved infantile conflicts. Progress in individuation of the child either may threaten the emotional stability or provoke depression in the symbiotic parent.

In such families, progress in the child's psychological individuation and autonomy is hampered. This network of family functioning produces pathological identifications in the child in which the child's negative fantasies of the parents are internalized as intense self-perceptions of badness, worthlessness, and undesirableness. It may be hypothesized that the suicidal behavior of the child may be an acted-out last-resort mechanism to remove from consciousness the child's negative self-perceptions.

Five cases illustrate a spectrum of family psychopathology,

the mechanisms postulated for the system of family organization, and the effects of the family system upon the child's suicidal tendencies.

## REFERENCES

1. Morrison, G. C. and Collier, J. G. Family Treatment Approaches to Suicidal Children and Adolescents. *J. Am. Acad. Child Psychiatry* 8:140, 1969.

2. Sabbath, J. C. The Suicidal Adolescent—the Expendable Child. *J. Am. Acad. Child Psychiatry* 5:272, 1966.

3. Aleksandrowicz, M. K. The Biological Strangers: an Attempted Suicide of a 7½-year-old Girl. *Bull. Menninger Clin.* 39:163, 1975.

4. French, A. P. and Steward, M. S. Family Dynamics, Childhood Depression, and Attempted Suicide in a 7-year-old boy. *Suicide Life Threat. Behav.* 5:29, 1975.

5. Bender, L. and Schilder, P. Suicidal Preoccupations and Attempts in Childhood. *Am. J. Orthopsychiatry* 7:225, 1937.

6. Pfeffer, C. R., Conte, H. R., Plutchik, R., and Jerrett, I. Suicidal Behavior in Latency-age Children: an Empirical Study. *J. Am. Acad. Child Psychiatry* 18:679, 1979.

7. _____ . Suicidal Behavior in Latency-age Children: an Outpatient Population. *J. Am. Acad. Child Psychiatry* 19(4):703, 1980.

8. Erikson, E. H. *Identity, Youth and Crisis.* Norton and Co., New York, 1968.

9. Bowen, M. *Family Therapy in Clinical Practice.* Aronson, New York, 1978.

10. Mattson, A., Sesse, L. R., and Hawkins, J. W. Suicidal Behavior as a Child Psychiatric Emergency. *Arch. Gen. Psychiatry* 20:100, 1969.

11. Pfeffer, C. R. Psychiatric Hospital Treatment of Suicidal Children. *Suicide Life Threat. Behav.* 8:150, 1978. more

# 25 The "Insolvable Problem" in the Dynamics of Suicidal Behavior in Children

Israel Orbach, Ph.D.

*This paper attempts to define the characteristics of the "insolvable problem" in the dynamics of suicidal children. It posits that part of the underlying dynamics of suicidal children is being pressured to solve a problem, in the family milieu, which is beyond the child's—and often anybody else's—ability to resolve. Moreover, the paper outlines the possible relation between the insolvable problem and various determinants involved in suicidal behavior such as depression, helplessness, hopelessness, rigidity, etc. This discussion will be accompanied by case demonstrations.*

Several directions have been chosen for the investigation of the dynamics of suicidal behavior in young children. For example, Peck (1) delineates various dynamic processes in childhood suicide. Kosky (2) emphasizes the role of the loss of a parent at any early age. Green (3) investigates the impact of childhood abuse. Toolan (4), Carlson and Cantwell (5), and Kazdin et al. (6) have clarified some aspects of the relationship between depression and suicide in children. Pfeffer, Plutchik, and Mizruchi (7) focus on the dynamics of depression and aggression in different personality types of suicidal children. Orbach et al. (8) investigated children's attitudes toward life and death which characterize suicidal children. These are only a few examples of the present trends in the study of childhood suicide.

A number of investigators have repeatedly mentioned that one causal aspect in childhood is the confrontation with an intolerable life situation and insolvable problem that the suicidal child faces (9–14). However, the term insolvable problem has never been characterized or defined. Thus, it is not clear what is meant by an insolvable problem and how it is related to suicide in children.

The insolvable problem can be characterized as a phenomenological state of mind which reflects the child's experience of being trapped and incapacitated. However, it has definite situational correlates that can be defined and operationalized. Some of the situations and aspects of the insolvable problem are reminiscent of more familiar concepts and family dynamics, such as the double bind and the scapegoating process. Other aspects to be described in the paper are less known.

The main purpose of the present paper is to clarify such dynamics in relation to suicidal behavior, not necessarily to point out completely new dynamics. Further, some aspects of the insolvable problem can be reclassified into other dynamic categories regarding suicidal behavior. Yet I find that conceptualizing some of the known dynamics in terms of an insolvable problem is most useful in understanding how some situations produce suicidal tendencies and interfere with formulating clear guidelines for therapeutic intervention. Merely stating that there is a relationship between parental conflicts and suicidal behavior of the child is too generalized to foster an understanding of this relationship, whereas investigating whether the parental conflict creates an insolvable problem for the child is more conducive to understanding the phenomenon and offering a useful therapeutic plan.

Thus, the focus of this paper is to delineate some characteristics of the insolvable problem for the purpose of theoretical clarification and a more precise definition of this term. In the following sections the characteristics of an insolvable problem and its nature will be presented and their relations to suicidal behavior will be discussed.

## THE CHARACTERISTICS OF THE
## INSOLVABLE PROBLEM

### A Problem beyond the Child's Ability to Resolve

One of the characteristics of a problem which is beyond the young child's ability to resolve is its psychological complexity. Such a problem is deeply rooted in the life of the entire family as a unit, it is multidetermined and longstanding. Its resolution requires a radical change in the entire family. Complex issues appear, therefore, in decompensating families who try to stay together, in families where prolonged anger and hostility between parents are suppressed through scapegoating a child or in families which choose one child to portray an idealized image to compensate for failure, disappointments, and lack of satisfaction of the parents.

*Vignette 1*

Some of these processes are demonstrated in a family whose youngest child, a ten-year-old boy, attempted suicide several times and continued to threaten suicide. He could give no reason for his wish to die. Interesting his sister had shown the same suicidal behavior a year earlier. The suicidal behavior of the boy ceased only when a secret crisis between the parents surfaced in therapy.

For several years the father had threatened that he would seek a divorce. The mother seemingly remained untouched by these threats, but as it was learned later, she was in panic. The father did not carry out his threats, first, because of his daughter's suicidal behavior and later, because of his son's suicidal behavior. Neither the girl nor the boy was aware of the father's plans or the parents' conflicts. It seems that the two children echoed their mother's fear: If you will leave, death will occur in the family. The mother encouraged and unconsciously maintained her children's sense of dissatisfaction. In the first phase of therapy, when the boy spoke about wanting to die, she felt that she could not find a convincing reason to prevent him from doing so and would encourage him to turn to the father for a response.

The mother used her children unconsciously to prevent a catastrophic outcome—divorce—for her family. The children, who were not aware of the depth of the conflict between their parents, were driven to take an extreme position by threatening suicide and unknowingly keeping the family intact.

Two years later the mother died of cancer. The course of the illness was short. The bereaved family experienced the full mourning process, partly with therapeutic help. But the suicidal behavior did not repeat itself. It seems to me that in this case, as in many others, the destructive impact of the unresolvable problem was more powerful in the dynamics of suicide than the loss of a loved one.

*Vignette 2*

A second characteristic of this dilemma is that it is insolvable by its very nature. One example of such a problem was cited by me (15). It pertained to a girl whose mother admitted that she wished her daughter had been born a boy and that she never accepted her as a girl. The 7-year-old girl adopted a boyish manner of behavior, but this, too, was strongly criticized by both her mother and father. She desperately sought ways to satisfy her parents, but, instead, created a constant conflict between herself and her parents. There was nothing that this girl could do to resolve her mother's conflicts. For this girl, her mother's rejection was an insolvable problem.

Similar situations are created when a child with an average IQ is expected to excel in school and be the best student in his/her class, or when a child is punished for being afraid to stay alone at home at night. The common denominator in these problems is the paradoxical demand that the child should master an inner or outer reality which is beyond his control.

Sometimes the dilemma that the child is faced with can be realistically resolved, but it is simply too demanding for a young child.

*Vignette 3*

In one family a ten-year-old was burdened with household responsibilities and caring for his two younger brothers, while his parents were away for frequent hospitalization with the oldest son who was chronically ill. These demanding responsibilities were endless and not an occasional request for help. They became a routine of the family life. When the child complained about these endless duties he was severely punished.

## Limitation of the Alternatives

Under certain circumstances the insolvable problem is intensified not by the nature of the problem itself, but by the way the parents structure the alternatives for action. This structuring can take on two forms. One is simply limiting the alternatives to one possibility only, usually undesirable to the child. Narrowing down the choices of behavior can be enforced by threats, physical punishment, withdrawal of love, and other drastic means.

*Vignette 4*

The following sequence demonstrates this process in the case of a 12-year-old boy who shot himself in the chest with his father's rifle, barely missing his heart. In therapy, it was revealed that the boy, who was a brilliant student, had skipped a grade just a few months prior to the suicidal attempt, and was placed in the same classroom as his older sister. The boy felt very uncomfortable in this new arrangement and asked to return to the previous class or be transferred to a different school. His parents refused categorically and forbade him to talk about that matter again. A few days prior to the suicidal attempt the boy tried to raise that issue again. "As he started to talk," the father disclosed, "I slapped him on his face. 'But father,'" the father quoted his son, "and I gave him another one, he started to cry and then I gave him a third slap and yelled at him to stop crying like a baby. He (the boy) tried again and said 'but why . . .,' then I slapped him a fourth time across his face. At this point he stopped and went quickly to the other room."

The boy had no choice and no outlet in this situation. This incident, told by a tearful and remorseful father, demonstrated not necessarily the crucial problem in this boy's life, but the process of how a problem with no alternatives to choose from is manufactured and, subsequently, how an insolvable problem is formed. In another therapy session with the parents, this boy shared some of the events from the dramatic scene of the suicidal attempt. "I took the rifle and placed the magazine in it; I leaned over the rifle and squeezed the trigger, but it did not go off. I realized that the switch was on the safe position. This was a sign for me that I should not kill myself. I tried to get the magazine out, but it would not come out. I thought of what would happen to me if my father would discover that I had played with the rifle. I knew he would not believe me that I had tried to commit suicide. I then decided to go ahead and kill myself."

This dramatic phenomenological sequence is a mirror reflection of the father's rigid, punitive, and coercing attitude presented earlier. It demonstrates the continuity between the family interactional patterns and the internalization of these patterns in the form of rigid attitudes toward the self in the form of limitation of freedom of action.

## Vignette 5

The same process, although under less drastic circumstances, is demonstrated in the case of another child who threatened suicide. This nine-year-old boy's father temporarily lived abroad due to business affairs. This separation caused a hardship for the mother and the rest of the family, but they could not confront the father directly on this matter. Instead, the mother was constantly concerned with the fact that her son was not excelling in school (he had a B + average) because he missed his father.

She became obsessed with this issue and could talk only about school grades and homework. She would call home from work four to five times every afternoon to find out whether her son was doing his homework. Upon her arrival at home she would immediately check the homework, make corrections, give instructions, call up friends to verify that the boy wrote down all his assignments, and did not allow him to go to friends or play. This continued until the boy started to threaten suicide.

The mother would harshly block any outspoken feelings about the absence of the father, insisting that they are grown children and should not be childish. Obviously, this reflected her own need for massive denial. Here, again, one can see the process of forcefully narrowing down alternatives of coping, pushing the child into one spot, one pathway, to the point where the boy felt almost as if he was being suffocated.

A second way of limiting alternatives and channeling the experience into an insolvable problem is the double bind. In this situation the child is encouraged to take a certain course of action and then this action is blocked. New encouragement and new blocking alternate time after time.

*Vignette 6*

A 13-year-old boy who tried to electrocute himself was subject to this confusing experience by his parents and it was demonstrated time and again during the family sessions. The parents used to maneuver themselves into a bitter confrontation and the mother would turn to the boy for help, pressuring him to support her against the father. As soon as the boy complied she hastily quieted him down, accusing him of disrespectful behavior toward his father. The same maneuver was repeated by his father, leaving the boy confused, overwhelmed, and helpless.

**Every Resolution Creates a New Problem**

There are certain familial circumstances that create a series of endless problems. Any attempt to resolve one problem immediately creates a new problem. Sometimes the very resolution of the old problem constitutes a new problem. The suicidal child is constantly confronted with a problem, a conflict, a dilemma, driving him to a state of restlessness that may be followed by passivity and withdrawal.

*Vignette 7*

This process of unwittingly forging a chain of problems characterized the family of an 11-year-old boy Joe, his mother, his stepfather, his younger half-brother David, and a baby half-sister. Joe's biological father had died during the war when the boy was two years old. The stepfather had been a close friend of the biological father and his subordinate in command in the same combat unit.

The basic problem of this family was the inability to form an integrated family unit. Each of the family members suffered an inner split, which blocked them from getting close to each other. The mother, still trying to work through the mourning process after nine years, felt guilty over marrying her husband's good friend too soon. In her mind her son Joe still belonged only to the late husband. She thought that the stepfather should not be too involved with the boy's upbringing.

The stepfather felt guilty over taking his friend's wife and she did not really belong to him. Joe yearned for a warm relationship with his stepfather, but felt a commitment to carry the memory of his deceased father. David, who, together with the little girl, symbolized the unity of the new family, claimed that his mother's deceased first husband was his real father.

This multifaceted conflict was channeled toward Joe and put enormous pressure on him. There were constant complaints about his behavior, schooling, manners, loyalty, obedience, etc. He was flooded with double and contradicting messages. Any movement towards the stepfather was stopped by the mother; yet, when he clung to his mother he was accused of being spoiled and childish.

When, in the therapy process, an atmosphere of closeness was established between Joe and the parents, David protested that he felt left out and not belonging, not sharing the same common past of the other three members. This complaint triggered a new attack on Joe by the parents. Any attempt by a family member to resolve the situation created a new problem. The only outlet they adopted to cope with the vicious cycle of conflicts was to scapegoat the boy. He, in return, found refuge in suicidal behavior.

## A Family Problem which Is Disguised

Many problems that motivate a family to seek psychological help take on a disguised form or are at least not fully clear to the family. This is especially true when dealing with suicidal children since too often suicidal tendencies by the young are mistakingly labeled as an attention-seeking manipulation.

While gaining attention may be one facet of suicidal behavior, it is by no means major dynamics. This behavior is always motivated by more serious and complicated familial circumstances. However, the full range of the problems involved is disguised or well hidden. The difficulty in discovering the deeper roots of the problems or conflicts is one of the reasons for labeling the suicidal behavior as an attention-seeking manipulation. At the same time the inexplicable nature of the problem contributes to the formation of the insolvable problem involved in the dynamics of suicidal behavior.

When a crucial dilemma is kept invisible but is accompanied by constant pressure to do something, a perplexing feeling of fighting against an invisible powerful enemy emerges, driving the child to fight as if he were blindfolded. An extreme example of this process was reported elsewhere (15), but these dynamics can be identified even in the less extreme cases like the following one.

*Vignette 8*

A family of five was seeking consultation following a suicide attempt which had been threatened by the eight-year-old son, who had written a note saying: "I am doing this to my family because of school." There was an older girl, aged 11, and a six-month-old baby girl. The complaint of both the boy and his parents was what they defined as poor school achievement, lack of adjustment in school, poor peer relationships, and behavior problems.

A few sessions later a different and more fundamental problem was unfolded. The parents had a longstanding conflict over the baby who was an unplanned child. The father had put heavy pressures on the mother to abort the fetus, but the mother had refused. The father punished his wife with late working hours, constant blame, and various other tactics. The mother retaliated by refusing sexual relations, not preparing meals, and so on.

Once the baby was born, the parents never discussed the problem openly, but the mutual retaliatory actions continued. The suicidal child soon became the focus of conflict between the parents. The mother blamed her husband for lack of involvement with the boy's schooling, while the father held her accountable for the lack of attention and warmth for the boy. At the same time they took turns or joined together in angry attacks on the boy until he attempted suicide. The boy became the scapegoat for the anger toward the baby and for the longstanding mutual dissatisfaction of the parents when not meeting each other's needs (cold wife, uninvolved husband).

This interpretation gains substantial validity by the fact that there was a visible improvement in the child's behavior and the suicidal behavior disappeared when the problem between the parents was dealt with intensively in therapy.

## THE NATURE OF THE INSOLVABLE PROBLEM

The various examples cited in the preceding sections focus on some other attributes of the nature of the problem behind suicidal behavior in children.

First, the problem is one that concerns the entire family as a system. It is not a problem between the child and the family, the child and one of the parents, a specific behavior problem, a specific projection of one of the parents or dissatisfaction or a single need. The specific unresolvable problem or pressure which the family puts on the child is at times only the tip of the iceberg of a more threatening and complicated problem. Thus, a constant pressure to excel beyond the child's capability may resolve a problem of mutual parental dissatisfaction. The mother who is obsessed with her son's homework is using this device as a way of coping with the father's absence from home due to his frequent business trips. The father who rejects his daughter because she was born the wrong sex may just express a hidden anger towards his wife, inhibiting its direct expression because it may cause an unwanted separation.

These maladjustive mechanisms are not unique to families of suicidal children, but further contribute to the formation of insolvable problems and, in turn, may drive the child to suicidal acting out.

Another facet of the conflict with which the suicidal child struggles is the threat to his ego. Often the child is faced with an anxiety-provoking demand that threatens his basic identity or psychological security. This is most evident in a problem where the child's sexual identity is rejected by one of the parents. A message of this type, as subtle as it may be, is overwhelmingly threatening. The inner catastrophe is further intensified when no other alternative such as homosexual adjustment is allowed. The inner trauma may evoke the need to escape, flee, digress from this intolerable situation. A similar reaction is called for by a less drastic, but not less threatening dilemma of a boy who is being punished for showing signs of fear or lack of courage or lack of assertiveness when playing with other children.

Finally, the suicidal child has no outlet, no support system, and no refuge when coping with demands and pressures by his family. There is no one in his vicinity to whom he can turn for support and comfort or to whom he can voice his complaints.

When meeting with suicidal children it is evident, time after time, how lonely these children are. Usually they are isolated in their own families, outcast by their parents and other siblings. There is no visible support from grandparents or other more distant family members. The existence or lack of existence of a support system can often serve as an indicator of the severity of the suicidal behavior exhibited by the child. The absence of an outlet and/or comforter drives the child into estrangement in his family circle, amplifying his inner pressures created by the outer demands and leaving him in limbo.

## THE RELATIONSHIP BETWEEN THE INSOLVABLE PROBLEM AND THE TENDENCY FOR SUICIDAL BEHAVIOR

Suicide at a very young age is not a frequent phenomenon. Yet it is believed that the roots of suicidal behavior in adolescence and adulthood may be formed during childhood. In this respect it should be kept in mind that some of the causal factors for suicide in adults have also been identified as motives in childhood suicidal behavior (13). The concept of the insolvable problem can at least sketch some of the ways in which causal factors for suicide are developed.

Some of the causes given for suicide are depression, help-lessness, hopelessness, guilt feelings, feelings of failure, de-spair, rigidity, and idealization of death. It seems almost trivial to spell out how the dynamics of the insolvable problem can bring about the crystallization of such feelings.

Being confronted with a problem that cannot be resolved, on the one hand, and constant pressures to resolve it accompanied by various sanctions, on the other, can easily lead to the formation of a depressive attitude. Such an attitude carries not only a dysphoric mood, but also lays down the basis for a sense of diffused guilt. The depressive attitude can be further inten-sified by the sense of intangible responsibility for the welfare of others and by the frustrating inability to satisfy the most significant other in the child's life.

The lack of support systems and the isolation within the family circle can induce several self-destructive processes. Self-esteem is damaged and deteriorating since the parents do not act as a protective shield against frustrations and other menacing experiences in the environment. Furthermore, in the absence of an outlet for inner tensions through being listened to and sharing, the child turns his anger and other tensions against himself in a destructive way. Finally, the growing feeling of incompatibility between the child and his environ-ment will gradually give way to a dominant feeling of being different and lead to escapism.

The accumulation of failures to satisfy parents and the emergence of endless new problems leave the child with the scars of inner frustration, worthlessness, helplessness, and hopelessness. He may become dominated by a self-image of a failure—an incapable, unsuccessful individual. When the cop-ing patterns of the family persist and turn into vicious cycles, the child may grow more helpless and hopeless, being driven to feel that only a drastic action of escape may bring relief.

The coercive, limiting approach of the parents which drives the child to execute the one alternative, unpleasant to him, may be internalized in time into a narrow outlook of the world, a rigid approach in coping with problems in the future, inhibiting the more creative flexible patterns of coping. Eventually when such a single alternative repeatedly fails to achieve the desired outcome, the child may choose suicide as the only available alternative.

Further, unsatisfying life patterns described in this paper may gradually produce a basic negative attitude toward life and other people, an expectation for failure and dissatisfaction, and eventually an idealization of death. Once such a magical attitude towards death takes hold, it facilitates the suicidal behavior and the suicidal act.

The dynamics of the insolvable problem are not the only causal determinant of suicidal behavior, but I believe that it has an explanatory value in distinguishing between similar life events which lead to different behaviors: suicidal versus other maladjustive reactions. For example, when loss of a parent or rejection of a child, two frequently mentioned causes in child depression and suicide, is accompanied by the dynamics of the insolvable problem, the degree of resultant depression may be of the magnitude to lead to suicidal behavior. Similarly, severe parental conflicts may result in the child's anxiety reaction or acting-out behavior, but when such conflicts also involve an insolvable problem for the child, the risk of suicidal behavior is increased. However, even if the dynamics of the insolvable problem are shared by other pathologies, it is still important to identify them in suicidal behavior. The validation of the above hypothesis has to await a more rigorous methodologic research and systematic measurements of the present theoretic formulation of the phenomenon of the insolvable problem.

## SUMMARY

The characteristics of the "insolvable problem" in the dynamics of suicidal children are defined. The author posits that part of the underlying dynamics of suicidal children is the pressure to solve within the family setting a problem for which there is no solution. The characteristics of such a problem are as follows: (a) a situation or set of circumstances that is beyond the child's ability to resolve; (b) limitation of alternatives; (c) every resolution creates a new problem; (d) a family problem which is disguised. Other characteristics of the problem pertain to the threat it poses to the child's ego., the lack of available support systems, and the role of the entire family in the insolvable problem. The paper also points to the possible relation between the insolvable problem and various determinants involved in suicidal behavior, such as depression, helplessness, hopelessness, rigidity, etc. This discussion is accompanied by case vignettes.

## REFERENCES

1. Peck, M. Youth Suicide. *Death Educ.* 6:29–47, 1982.

2. Kosky, R. Childhood Suicidal Behavior. *J. Child Psychol. Psychiatry* 24:457–468, 1983.

3. Green, A. H. Self-destructive Behavior in Battered Children. *J. Am. Psychiatry* 135:579–582, 1978.

4. Toolan, J. M. Depression and Suicide in Children: an Overview. *Am. J. Psychother.* 35:311–321, 1981.

5. Carlson, G. A. and Cantwell, D. P. Suicidal Behavior and Symptom Depression in Children and Adolescents. *J. Am. Acad. Child Psychiatry* 21:361–370, 1982.

6. Kazdin, A. E., French, N. H., Unis, A. S., et al. Helplessness, Depression, and Suicidal Intent among Psychiatrically Disturbed Inpatient Children. *J. Consult. Clin. Psychol.* 51:504–510, 1983.

7. Pfeffer, C. R., Plutchik, R., and Mizruchi, M. S. Suicidal and Assaultive Behavior in Childhood: Classification, Measurement and Interrelations. *Am. J. Psychiatry* 140:154–157, 1983.

8. Orbach, I., Feshbach, S., Carlson, G., et al. Attraction and Repulsion by Life and Death in Suicidal and in Normal Children. *J. Consult. Clin. Psychol.* 51:661–670, 1983.

9. Jacobs, J. *Adolescent Suicide.* Wiley International, New York, 1971.

10. Glaser, K. Suicidal Children: Management. *Am. J. Psychother.* 25:27–36, 1971.

11. McIntire, M. S. and Angle, C. R. Psychological Biopsy in Self-poisoning of Children. *Am. J. Disease Children* 126:42–46, 1973.

12. Garfinkel, B. D. and Golombek, H. Suicide and Depression in Childhood and Adolescence. *Can. Med. Assoc. J.* 110:1278–1281, 1974.

13. Orbach, I. Personality Characteristics, Life Circumstances and Dynamics of Suicidal Children. *Death Educ.* October, 1986.

14. Orbach, I., Gross, Y., and Glaubman, H. Some Common Characteristics of Latency-age Suicidal Children: a Tentative Model Based on Case Study Analysis. *Suicide Life Threat. Behav.* 11:180–190, 1981.

15. Orbach, I. Assessment of Suicidal Behavior in Young Children: Case Demonstration. In *Suicidal Behavior Among the Young*, Diekstra RFW., Ed. Swets & Zeitlinger, Lisse, Holland, 1985.

# 26 Student Suicide

## Herbert Hendin, M.D.

*This chapter discusses the psychodynamic significance of suicide in the young, the family constellations that produce such suicides, the psychosocial forces contributing to the dramatic rise in the suicide rate of young people, and the special problems in the treatment of the severely suicidal young person.*

More and more young people in this culture believe feeling itself is a danger and life's best achievement is the fastest, highest possible flight from emotion. Many yong people escape into sensation—into casual sex, drugs, or the acquisition of a variety of experiences without emotional involvement. But an increasing number of young people look elsewhere for relief. When Vonnegut wrote "how nice—to feel nothing, and still get full credit for being alive—" he expressed as a wry joke what many college students are doing as a tragic actuality. The trend is toward a diminished involvement in life, an attempt to find in numbness, and limited, controlled experience some escape from the anger and turmoil without and within. There is a rising tide of college students who try to blot out their pain, anger, and frustration with the ultimate numbness.

Suicide among young people and among college students in particular has been steadily and alarmingly rising during the past 20 years. Over 4,000 of the 25,000 persons who commit suicide in the country each year are now in the fifteen to twenty-four age group. The suicide rate for this group has increased over 250 per cent in this period going from 4.2 in 1954 to 10.6 in 1973.[1] Among these staggering figures the most dramatic is the increase in the suicide rate of young men fifteen to twenty-four which has gone from 6.7 in 1954 to 17 in 1973. As these figures show, the suicide trend was evident through the "quiet fifties," persisted through the political activism of the sixties, through the many shifts in the drug culture, and continues on campus today. Underlying these shifts are the more profound changes that have occurred in people over the past 20 years and have transformed the young. Why do increasing numbers of college students want to end their lives? What does their depression say about what is changing in American life?

For the past six years I have been studying and treating young people who have made suicide attempts as part of a study of culture, character, and crisis among college students.[2] Psychoanalytic interviewing techniques emphasizing free associations, dreams, and fantasies enabled me to obtain an access to the inner life, the inner significance for these students of both living and dying. What was revealed in the lives of young people who had made suicide attempts were the ways in which death, depression, and misery had been part of their lives since childhood, and had been built into their relationship to their parents.

It is no accident that death as a motivating force in human behavior is now a major preoccupation. As parents become less able to accept or enjoy children, as young men and women find their contacts with each other full of anger, we become preoccupied with the small and large forms of destructiveness. For a nation that has been described as death denying we are becoming one that is death obsessed. For Freud there was a fairly even balance between the forces of death and life (1). But for contemporary writers as brilliant as Ernest Becker (2), the

---

[1] Rates are calculated by the National Center for Health Statistics per 100,000 of the age group.

[2] This study was supported by a grant from the National Institute of Mental Health (MH 20818-02).

struggle with death is seen as the ultimate cause of all human behavior. For an increasing number of people human behavior is death. Many American families are so filled with tension and rage, so unable to happily adjust to children, that to survive in them at all, parents and children deaden themselves.

For many young people life is a grueling war of attrition in which depression is the best available accomplice, the only way to ward off the impact of their daily lives. Such students experience death daily in their attempts to bury their anger, rage, and pain deep within themselves. As the lives of students who are severely depressed and make suicide attempts suggest, the fascination with death is often the climax of having been emotionally dead for a lifetime.

The students I saw were drawn to death as a way of life. The most seriously suicidal were those whose absorption and preoccupation with their own extinction are an integral ongoing part of their daily experience. These students see their relationship with their parents as dependent on their emotional if not physical death and become tied to their parents in a kind of death knot. Coming to college, graduating, becoming seriously involved with another person, and enjoying an independent existence have the power to free them. In fact, the meaning of suicide and depression lies in their encounter with the forces that might unleash their own possibilities for freedom.

The question is often asked if the psychology of suicide can be determined from those who made attempts and survived. My own answer is emphatically, yes. Among those who attempt suicide are the majority of those who eventually commit suicide in addition to many whose involvement with suicide will not be fatal. Some of the students I saw died from the consequences of injuries sustained in their attempts. Some, such as a student who survived a seven-story jump, survived by accident. This young woman had, and indeed a majority of actual suicides of all ages have, a history of prior attempts. Distinguishing the seriously suicidal from those whose attempts will not culminate in an actual suicide is not that difficult for any experienced clinician.

It is often said that suicidal students have been destroyed by the strain of competition and work and by parental pressure toward success. But far from being harmed by their work, many students use it as a barricade. "Work," as one student put it, was his "main defensive army." Nor were the parents of these students more achievement oriented than most. Their own problems had led them to need their children to be quiet drones. They often opposed work their children found fascinating because they were so unable to cope with pleasure and excitement. Dull, demanding mental labor was often the nexus of the suicidal students' existence. It did not have to lead to success or any pleasurable sense of achievement, but rather functioned as another link in the chain of emotional deadness that bound them to their parents.

It has been thought that the literal death or physical loss of a parent was crucial in producing suicidal people. Zilboorg (3), as far back as 1936, applied to the study of suicide Freud's observations on the importance of "ambivalent identification" with a "lost loved object" in causing depression (4). He called attention to the frequency of the actual death of a parent before or during the adolescence of suicidal patients. In my own work I found a significantly high proportion of seriously suicidal students had lost a parent. But what even these students made clear is that more than ambivalent identification with a dead parent is involved. What is crucial is the quality of feeling that flows between the student and his parents. The bond of emotional death was as powerful in suicidal students who had not experienced the actual death of a parent as it was in those who had. Both groups were pulled toward their own death primarily by the bond that had defined their relationship with their parents while their parents lived, and continued to control their lives even if their parents died.

*Vignette 1*

Leon had lost neither of his parents, although he could be said never to have had them either. He had gotten along with them by burying himself alone in his room studying, listening to music, and having suicidal thoughts. At eighteen he had already been thinking of suicide for years and in high school had compiled a list of reasons why he should not kill himself. He enumerated them to me in the mechanical manner he usually adopted: First: things were so bad that they could only get better. Second: you had no right to take your life. Third: his parents had made a great investment in his education and it would cost a lot to bury him. Fourth: his parents would blame themselves. Fifth: they would be devastated and would miss him. Since he has been at college he has had a sixth reason—his friends would feel very bad if he did it.

Leon had been able to resist his suicidal preoccupations during his lonely high school years, but after a few months at college in which he had grown close to his roommates, his need to kill himself became overwhelming. The challenge to his past isolation and deadness from his new friendships was finally pushing Leon toward suicide.

Leon wanted to hold onto his depression far more than he realized. He sees himself as always having been on "the losing side of the law of averages." He gave his dissatisfaction with his own average at college after studying hard all term as cause of his depression and sign of his bad luck. After a college mixer at which he met no one, he rode the subways and stood for a long time at one station in Harlem in a challenge to fate to see if he would be mugged. He considers it a bad omen that two of his favorite professional football teams lost on the day after he was admitted to the hospital. During the time I saw him, after his favorite team won its crucial game, he dreamed that in the last minute they lost.

Leon saw defeat as preferable to victory, but for the most part he sought an impregnability that prevented both. He had a recurring fantasy in which he was a medieval citadel under attack. He drew a map to illustrate the deployment of his protective armies. Areas were indicated in different colors to mark his social, academic, spiritual, and emotional defenses. Most of his forces were concentrated in the academic realm. Leon's map is a powerful symbol of his emotional state. He feels that he will survive only as long as his defenses hold.

Leon sees life as war and himself as the ultimate weapon. It is easier for him to see danger as an outside attack than to see his own destructiveness. After an incident in which his roommates had disappointed him, he dreamed that he was an executioner who had to decide whether people should live or die. He condemns them to death and "some kind of angel came and killed them all." Leon clearly sees himself as the Angel of Death. His suicidal preoccupations and his depression mask an image he has of himself as sitting on a time bomb that is "getting ready to explode." When I questioned him about the anger and destructiveness suggested in this image, he is quick to tell me that the most that would happen is that he would "quietly and nonviolently" kill himself.

Leon's need to hide his anger was bound up with his need not to blame his parents for his problems. He insisted that he had had little relationship to them, liked them from afar but was always irritated with them when at home. All the incidents he related of his childhood cast his mother in the role of a dampener of his or his father's pleasure or excitement. His father handled the situation by being away much of the time, leaving his mother to rule the house. Leon felt he and his parents had never been able to talk about anything, but expressed no anger or bitterness over this. His suicide note conveys the quality of his family life.

Addressing his letter to both his parents, Leon wrote that by the time they read it he would be dead and that they were not responsible for his act. (In suicide notes, such statements specifically freeing particular people of any blame or responsibility are usually to be read psychologically as meaning the opposite.) He added that he was depressed and could see nothing coming out of his life. He went on to dispose of his possessions, leaving his tapes and tape recording equipment to his mother and requesting that his favorite tape be buried with him. From beginning to end, Leon's note is about communication from beyond life. He tells his parents that it is too late to reach him but goes on to leave them equipment which permits him to speak to them, like the Angel of Death he dreams he is, as a voice from beyond the grave. In asking to be buried with the tape of melancholy songs he played again and again as accompaniment to his suicidal thoughts Leon is almost literally asking to be cemented for all eternity in his unhappy, isolated relation to his mother.

Although preoccupied with suicide for a long time, the next student only became overtly suicidal after the death of his mother. His story makes clear that his tie to her when she was alive required his own emotional death. When he says with a flat, depressed intensity, "I don't think life should be lived if it isn't worth living for its own sake. No one should stay alive for anyone else's sake," it is clear that he feels he has lived or not lived for her sake, not his own.

*Vignette 2*

Larry was a twenty-six-year-old graduate student referred for evaluation following a serious suicide attempt which he barely survived. He had been preoccupied with suicide since his sophomore year in college and had made three previous attempts. Neatly groomed and casually dressed, he seemed alternately fearful and lifeless. He says he tried to have the least possible contact with people, has only the few friends he made in high school, and spends most of his time studying in his room. While he shares an apartment with two other students, they merely live together and do not "socialize." He protected himself against letting me know or reach him by attempting to stop any observation or interpretation of his behavior by quickly saying "it is possible." Insisting on the futility of our talking and on the futility of his life, he said he could stand back and listen to our conversation and that it was like a grade Z movie. Standing back, listening while grading himself and others were characteristic ways in which he defended himself against involvement. He kept insisting that nothing can change his life to a degree that suggested a determination to see to it that nothing did.

Larry's one close relationship with a woman was shaped by his need to retain his deadness and estrangement. He lived with a woman named Jill for six months, which he describes as the liveliest, happiest, and most spontaneous time of his life. Nevertheless when the time came for Jill to leave for Europe where she had planned to live, he made no attempt to persuade her to stay and did not seriously consider going with her.

When Larry met Jill his mother was dying of cancer. When I asked him if the fact that his mother was dying made him more willing to get involved with Jill he said he had wondered many times if that were the case. During the six months after his mother died and Jill had left, Larry made several suicide attempts. While he felt they had more to do with Jill than his mother, he insisted that he was not bothered by missing Jill, but by his lack of control over the situation. The need to deny her importance to him and the pain of losing her were further expressions of Larry's general deadness.

Larry attributed the origins of his lifeless, isolated existence to being the only child of an "overbearing" mother and to having a father who was "removed and out of things." One of his earliest memories vividly dramatizes his family situation.

When he was about seven his father was away for a day and his mother was going to a shower. He does not recall what he was doing, but feels he must have "been playing in a way my mother didn't like." His mother screamed at him that she would not go to the shower because of him. Now he thinks she was looking for an excuse not to go. But the situation conveys not only her use of the role of martyr, but her message to Larry that if he is playful, mischievous or alive, she will not live or enjoy anything.

Larry saw his mother as refusing to let him grow up. Until he moved into the dorms when a college sophomore, she refused to let him have a door on his room and insisted on her right to open his mail. She seemed to have been particularly fearful of his involvement with girls. Larry felt his mother tried to live her life through him. As he spoke it was clear he felt he had performed at school and lived for his mother and not for himself. Yet he had felt lost and out of control in the unstructured life in the dorms and felt depressed and cut off without his mother while he attempted to bury himself in his studies. It was in this period that he first became preoccupied with thoughts of suicide.

Nothing outside of his family has much deep, living reality for Larry. In all his dreams he was back where he grew up with his parents. After our first session he dreamed of Jerry, a lively, outgoing boy he knew as a child and whom he associates with fun. He saw himself as rarely capable of having fun and enjoys himself only when he has had a couple of drinks or smoked pot. It is also clear that he associates fun with separating from hs mother, which he is clearly afraid to do. He says, "What's the use of talking about it? She's dead and I'm alive." Psychologically speaking, the reverse seemed truer.

Larry dreamed he had a heart attack. In actuality, not he but his father had had a heart attack a few months earlier. His father had remarried a year before that and seems much happier than when Larry's mother was alive. Larry has been afraid, since the attack, that his father would die and leave him alone. In dreaming that he and not his father had the attack, Larry feels he is saying "better me than you."

Larry feels that one life can be sacrificed to keep another alive and that his "death" had been a way of keeping his mother alive. He acknowledged at times he had wished she would die, thinking her death might liberate him. He became tearful in talking of how her death had liberated his father. When I pointed out that he seemed unable to bury her, he replied he would not know how to take the first step with the shovel. His numbness minimizes the distinction between living and dying and creates a middle state in which he figuratively does keep his mother alive through his own emotional death. Suicide is but the final dramatization of this process.

Larry's suicide attempt is not simply a journey toward reunion with a lost love object. His whole life has been a death tie to an object both needed and hated. In not living he keeps his mother alive, atones for his rage toward her, and preserves their past relationship. What overwhelmed Larry is not simply her loss but the fact that her loss constituted an invitation to live — an invitation his father could accept but that he could not.

Leon and Larry were typical of suicidal students whose intense concentration on academic work was the means they used to deal with existence and served to conceal their sense that they had no right to live. They were typical of suicidal students who had come from families in which the relationship between their parents and family life as a whole were essentially dead. Their sense of family life was rooted in this deadness and fixed in their perception of their parents as requiring their lifelessness. While they often appeared to be concerned over failure in school, they turned out to be more concerned with being working drones and not becoming too successful or finding too much pleasure in what they were doing. Like Leon who saw his academic efforts as a defensive army, these students used the continued deployment of uninteresting and methodical work in the service of a withdrawal from either satisfaction or rage. Their withdrawal signified for them a holding on to the past and strengthened the tie of numbness they had forged in their relations with their family.

When a parent had actually died — as had Larry's mother — many suicidal students felt they had no right to continue to live or tried to keep the parent alive and preserve the relationship through their own death. But living independent lives was a stimulus to death whether or not a parent had actually died. Suicidal students were generally lifeless and outwardly compliant in manner. What lay beneath this compliant surface was an enormous fury. They dreamed of themselves as forces that can and do murder the people who let them down, or as people held in the grip of a rage beyond their own control. Suicide and suicidal preoccupation was for them a way of extinguishing their anger.

Many students continued in college to use contact with their parents to control their own enthusiasm and insure their lifelessness. Elated by a new relationship, excited by school, they would call their parents when they were feeling best, knowing that their parents' lack of response would kill their mood. When happiest, one student described having the impulse to "throw herself in front of a train" or call her mother, equating the death-dealing power of both with a wry seriousness. Being happy for these students meant giving up the past; giving up sadness meant relinquishing the securest part of themselves.

What overwhelms these students is not simply grief over separating from or losing a parent, but the fact that the separation or loss constitutes an invitation to freedom. These students perceive inhibition of their power to live as the price of existing at all. The long-observed phenomenon of depressed patients becoming more suicidal as they overcome their depression takes on new significance in this light. It is said that depression operates to paralyze action and that a lessening depression makes possible an overt, actual suicide attempt. But this is an inadequate explanation for what takes place with these students.

Depression is actually a form of protective deadness which can shield the individual and may even make suicide unnecessary for some. Larry and Leon became acutely suicidal when life beckoned most and challenged their familiar depression. They broke down under the stress of probable pleasure, success, and independence. Suicide and suicidal longings are means of recapturing the depression that seems to be slipping away, the means these students used to cling to the deadness they see not merely as their best defense but as the basic human bond.

Suicide is a way of life for the many students I saw who continually killed their enthusiasm, their hope, their freedom, and finally attempted to kill themselves. It is the climax of the ongoing drama they play out with parents in which emotional death is seen as the price of domestic peace.

The method many students chose was not only their last message to their parents, but the climactic gesture that also expressed how they had lived and how they hope to resolve the conflicts that plagued them in life. One student who spent the night on the roof of his dorm thinking of jumping, spoke of it in terms of the tragic fame suicide had given Marilyn Monroe. He had the fantasy that he would call to tell his parents he was going to jump and while they got upset he would leave the receiver hanging and go up on the roof. They would call someone at school but it would be too late. The fantasy reflects the blocked communication that had always existed in his family and his wish to make his parents experience the frustration he had always endured in trying to reach them. He clenched his fists and wrung his hands as he spoke of how much he wanted to strike back.

Perhaps most important is the meaning of his preoccupation with Marilyn Monroe's suicide—the grotesque, grim wish to make a splash by jumping to a notorious death. The student who had unaccountably survived a seven-story jump had wanted the attention a spectacular death would bring. But the need such students have for a dramatic, newsworthy attempt derives from the intense experience of having been passed over by their parents. "Do I have to die before you'll notice me!" "Do you have to read it in the news before you know I'm dead?" is the cry such students are making. And they are all too willing to die to be noticed.

Physical agony was a last resort for students whose parents never cared about their emotional problems, but might respond to them if they were literally hurt. Sandra, who severed an artery in a dramatic wrist-cutting suicide attempt, told of less severe wrist cutting in high school which had gone unnoticed by her parents. (Several students had similar experiences in which they never told their parents what they had done, but seemed disappointed their parents had not noticed their scars.) After her recent suicide attempt, Sandra dreamed that she had on dungarees streaming with blood and her mother watched her without saying a word. In discussing the dream she bitterly said her mother would never acknowledge that Sandra felt pain and was hurt. The vivid childhood memory of another suicidal student is of being unjustly punished by her mother and sent to her room. She spent an hour working loose a tooth that was not quite ready to come out so as to have an excuse to leave her room and be forgiven by her mother.

Suicide for love, the wish to die when love and need are not requited are traditionally causes of suicide attempts in the young. Moreover, suicide in response to rejection suggests a strong desire for love, life, and involvement and unbearable disappointment over the frustration of such needs. It would seem to be quite different from the deathly tie to parents and the resistance to involvement that has been described.

Yet relationships that lead to disappointment and suicide often have death, disappointment, and depression built into them. The "I won't live without you" message to an unwilling partner is a restatement of earlier disappointments relived with and through a lover who remains aloof. The suicidal often make conditions for life: if I don't succeed, I'll kill myself; if you don't want me, I won't live. Such conditions are not only self-fulfilling, they are meant to be. Just as conditions for love set by one individual on another are designed to kill affection, so are conditions for living designed to kill life, not to sustain it. Such conditions are for the suicidal invariably admissions reducible to the message "I can't love you or live with you, but through my death there can be an enduring bond between us."

Suicidal patients bring death into the therapeutic relationship often by forming a death bond with the therapist. Many therapists are uncomfortable in dealing with the way in which patients incorporate them into their suicidal acts and fantasies. But recognizing and being able to deal with the patient's need to tie such a death knot is crucial to the eventual outcome of treatment of the suicidal. [Editor's note: This type of bond is illustrated in Chapter 16, case 2, case 3, and case 8.]

Suicidal students destroy any possibility for pleasure, often believing they are searching for affection at the moment when they are killing it. Their inability to tolerate or find positive experiences reflects the extreme emotional hardships they have gone through in childhood. But the more severe conflicts of the families of suicidal students only dramatize the problems shared by the families of many students today. Pleasure and enjoyment are casualties in the modern war of the family. Too many children are growing up feeling that their mothers and fathers did not regard them as sources of pleasure. Young people today with diminished capacity for enjoyment, or diminished sense of their own ability to give pleasure have for the most part grown up feeling they gave little to their parents. Even in cases where the parents did the right thing, the sense of joyless duty was often communicated.

We tend to regard the capacity for pleasure as a biologic fact in which experience determines only the particular sources of pleasure for the individual. But it is not. Children who see they are not a source of pleasure to their parents become unable to be a source of pleasure to themselves, and have few expectations of happiness with others. The unrelieved numbness of the depressed and suicidal students dramatizes how profoundly the lack of parental desire for an alive child can produce people who feel that emotional lifelessness is the price of any relationship with their parents and of survival itself. Unfortunately, we are gearing more and more people for numbness.

Society is fomenting depression in the trend toward the devaluation of children and the family. The increasing emphasis on solitary gratification and immediate, tangible gain from all relationships only encourages an unwillingness in parents to give of themselves or tolerate the demands of small children. It is not surprising that the family emerges through the eyes of many students as a jail in which everyone is in solitary confinement, trapped within their own particular suffering. The frequent absence of intimacy, affection, warmth, or shared concern, the prevalence of families in which no one had gotten what he needed or wanted has had a profound impact on this generation.

Out of the most tragic disaffection has come a rising number of young people who are drawn to numbness because it has been their only security for a lifetime. Whenever the newness of coming to college, of graduating, or finding a person or a pursuit interferes with that security and threatens to break the bond of deadness that held them to their parents, these students are overwhelmed by suicidal longings. Certainly in their attempts at suicide these young people were moving toward becoming finally and forever what they felt they were meant to be.

## SUMMARY

College students who had made serious suicide attempts were studied in detail. Short-term therapy was administered in most cases and long-term therapy in some.

The study indicates the ways in which death has become a way of life for these students—an integral, ongoing part of their adaptation. It traces the origin of this adaptation in a family relationship that the students perceived as requiring their emotional extinction. These students are tied to their parents in a kind of death knot and have become overtly suicidal when life—coming to college, graduating, becoming seriously involved with another person—threatens to unravel this knot.

The study also explores some of the psychological changes contributing to the increasing number of young suicides. It deals with the special problems involved in the treatment of the severely suicidal young person.

## REFERENCES

1. Freud, S. *Civilization and Its Discontents.* Translated and edited by James Strachey. W. W. Norton, New York, 1962.

2. Becker, E. *The Denial of Death.* Free Press, New York, 1973.

3. Freud, S. Mourning and Melancholia (1916). In *Collected Papers*, Vol. IV, Hogarth Press, London, 1949, pp. 152–170.

4. Zilboorg, G. Differential Diagnostic Types of Suicide. *Arch. Gen. Psychiat.* 35:270, 1936.

# INDEX

# TECHNICAL MATHEMATICS